PROGRAMMING FOR HEALTH AND WELLBEING IN ARCHITECTURE

Programming for Health and Wellbeing in Architecture presents a new approach to architectural programming that includes sustainability, neuroscience and human factors. This volume of contributions from noted architects and academics makes the case for rethinking the practices of programming and planning to incorporate evidence-based design, systems thinking and a deeper understanding of our evolutionary nature.

These 18 original essays highlight how human and environmental health are closely related and should be incorporated as mutually reinforcing goals in every design project. Together, these chapters describe the framework for a new paradigm of building performance and design of the human experience.

Programming—the stage at which research is conducted and goals established—provides an opportunity to examine potential impacts and to craft strategies for wellbeing in new buildings and renovations using the latest scientific methods. This book expands the scope of the programming process and provides essential guidance for sustainable practice and the advancement of wellbeing in the built environment for architecture and interiors students, practitioners, instructors and academics.

Keely Menezes, MPH uses public health frameworks to emphasize design as a tool for population wellness. She is a writer, artist, and interior designer based on Martha's Vineyard, Massachusetts.

Pamela de Oliveira-Smith is a Boston-based writer, editor and creative director.

A. Vernon Woodworth FAIA is Life Safety & Code Consulting Service Leader at Fitzemeyer & Tocci Associates, Inc., in Woburn, MA and a member of the Faculty at the Boston Architectural College. He serves as Secretary to the Human Architecture and Planning Institute, Inc. (theHAPi.org), a non-profit devoted to improving the user experience in the built environment.

PROGRAMMING FOR HEALTH AND WELLBEING IN ARCHITECTURE

Edited by
Keely Menezes MPH, Pamela de Oliveira Smith,
and A. Vernon Woodworth FAIA

First published 2022
by Routledge
605 Third Avenue, New York, NY 10158

and by Routledge
2 Park Square, Milton Park, Abingdon, Oxon, OX14 4RN

Routledge is an imprint of the Taylor & Francis Group, an informa business

© 2022 selection and editorial matter, Keely Menezes, Pamela de Oliveira Smith, and A. Vernon Woodworth; individual chapters, the contributors

The right of Keely Menezes, Pamela de Oliveira Smith, and A. Vernon Woodworth to be identified as the authors of the editorial material, and of the authors for their individual chapters, has been asserted in accordance with sections 77 and 78 of the Copyright, Designs and Patents Act 1988.

All rights reserved. No part of this book may be reprinted or reproduced or utilised in any form or by any electronic, mechanical, or other means, now known or hereafter invented, including photocopying and recording, or in any information storage or retrieval system, without permission in writing from the publishers.

Trademark notice: Product or corporate names may be trademarks or registered trademarks, and are used only for identification and explanation without intent to infringe.

Library of Congress Cataloging-in-Publication Data
Names: Menezes, Keely, editor. | De Oliveira-Smith, Pamela Jean, editor. | Woodworth, A. Vernon, editor.
Title: Programming for health and wellbeing in architecture / edited by Keely Menezes MPH, Pamela de Oliveira Smith, and A. Vernon Woodworth FAIA.
Description: New York : Routledge, 2022. | Includes bibliographical references and index. |
Subjects: LCSH: Architecture—Human factors. | Design--Human factors. | Well-being.
Classification: LCC NA2542.4 .P765 2022 (print) | LCC NA2542.4 (ebook) | DDC 720.87—dc23
LC record available at https://lccn.loc.gov/2021020284
LC ebook record available at https://lccn.loc.gov/2021020285

ISBN: 9780367758844 (hbk)
ISBN: 9780367758868 (pbk)
ISBN: 9781003164418 (ebk)

DOI: 10.4324/9781003164418

Typeset in Bembo
by codeMantra

Dedicated to John P. Eberhard
Whose insights paved the way

CONTENTS

Contributor Biographies   *xi*

    Introduction   1
    A. Vernon Woodworth, FAIA

PART 1
Human Factors   **7**

  1 Programming Interior Environments: Human Experience,
     Health and Wellbeing   9
     J. Davis Harte, PhD, WELL AP and Laura Regrut, IIDA, ASID

  2 Biophilia and Human Health   25
     A. Vernon Woodworth FAIA

  3 Beauty Is…   31
     Donald H. Ruggles AIA, NCARB, ICAA, ANFA

  4 Stress   39
     J. Davis Harte, PhD, WELL AP with A. Vernon Woodworth FAIA

PART 2
Buildings   **53**

  5 Programming for People   55
     Keely Menezes, MPH

  6 Empathetic Programming to Foster Inclusion   65
     Robin Z. Puttock, RA, LEED AP BD+C, WELL AP

7 Programming for Effective Learning 81
Laura A. Wernick FAIA, REFP, LEED AP and Erika Eitland, MPH, ScD

8 Programming for WELL Certification on a University Campus 94
*Robin Z. Puttock, RA, LEED AP BD+C, WELL AP and
Angela Loder, PhD, WELL AP*

PART 3
Streetscapes 107

9 Placemaking: Programming Urbanism for Human Engagement 109
Robert S. Tullis AIA

10 Programming for the Subliminal Brain: Biometric Tools Reveal Architecture's Biological Impact 136
Justin B. Hollander, PhD, Gideon Spanjar, PhD, Ann Sussman AIA, Frank Suurenbroek, PhD, and Mengfei Wang

11 The Future of Codes and the Architecture Profession 150
A. Vernon Woodworth FAIA

PART 4
Region 157

12 Programming in the Bioregion 159
*Philip Norton Loheed AIA, NCARB, Assoc ASLA
with A. Vernon Woodworth FAIA*

13 Regenerative Development and Design: Nature and Healing 171
Bill Reed AIA and A. Vernon Woodworth FAIA

14 Programming for Human Health in a Challenged Climate 177
John Gravelin, Eleanor Hoyt and Jim Newman

15 The Post-Pandemic City 194
Lawrence A. Chan FAIA

PART 5
Commissioning 213

16 Programming and Commissioning: A Bookend Approach to Evidence-Based Design 215
A. Vernon Woodworth FAIA

17 Life-Enhancing Habitats: Biophilia, Patterns and Wholeness   222
    Gregory Crawford

18 Epidemiologic Methods for Evaluating Architectural Design   234
    C. Robert Horsburgh, Jr., MD, MUS

    Conclusion   242
    A. Vernon Woodworth FAIA

Acronyms   *249*
Glossary   *251*
Index   *259*

CONTRIBUTOR BIOGRAPHIES

Lawrence A. Chan FAIA has over 45 years of experience as an architect, urban designer and teacher. A co-founder of Chan Krieger & Associates, he has designed and planned projects across North America and overseas on initiatives in complex urban settings at multiple scales with emphasis on shaping the public realm where buildings and open spaces are integrated components of a larger whole. A Fellow of the American Institute of Architects, his degrees include a BA (Fine Arts) from City College of New York, an MArch from the University of California, Berkeley, and an MArch in Urban Design from Harvard University.

Gregory Crawford is co-founder and co-owner of Surplus, a permaculture design collective; co-founder and co-owner of Locus, a pattern language design and placemaking organization; member of Blueprint, an international coalition for regenerative development in the humanitarian field; and founder and owner of Elsewhere, an immersive experience design company. He has worked—designing, teaching and consulting—in over nine countries, and is currently restoring an abandoned village in Portugal in accordance with pattern language methodology and biophilia. He is the author of one novel and several scientific papers, with another experimental novel and a non-fiction book about design in the works.

Erika Eitland, MPH, ScD is the Director of the Human Experience (Hx) Lab at Perkins&Will where she is focused on K-12 schools, affordable housing and urban resilience. She received her doctorate from the Harvard T.H. Chan School of Public Health in Environmental Health where she was the lead author of *Schools for Health: Foundations for Student Success* report that examined more than 250 scientific articles on the association between building quality and student health and performance. She also holds a Master's in Public Health in Climate and Health from Columbia University.

John Gravelin is a Program Manager at The Energy Coalition, a non-profit organization based in Southern California that helps public agencies pursue energy efficiency and distributed energy resource projects. John graduated from the Boston Architectural College in 2013 with a Bachelor of Design Studies in Architectural Technology, and received graduate certificates in Sustainable Design and Sustainable Community Planning and Design.

J. Davis Harte, PhD, WELL AP is Director and Faculty of the Design for Human Health, Master of Design Studies program at the Boston Architectural College. She is a wellness design researcher, educator and translator, bridging evidence and practice through work in children's places, trauma-informed design spaces and in childbirth environments. Dr. Harte is immersed in social justice design, attention restoration theory, resilience, salutogenic and therapeutic design, symbolic interactionism, neuroscience and evidence-based design, and work centers on the margins and with those who carry trauma. She co-leads the Global Birth Environment Design Network and traumainformeddesign.org.

Justin B. Hollander, PhD is a professor of Urban and Environmental Policy and Planning at Tufts University. His research and teaching is in the areas of physical planning, Big Data, shrinking cities, and the intersection between cognitive science and the design of cities. He co-edited the book *Urban Experience and Design: Contemporary Perspectives on Improving the Public Realm* (Routledge, 2020) and is the author of seven other books on urban planning and design. He was recently inducted as a Fellow of the American Institute of Certified Planners and hosts the Apple podcast "Cognitive Urbanism."

C. Robert Horsburgh Jr., MD is Professor of Epidemiology, Biostatistics, Global Health and Medicine at Boston University. He holds an AB in Architecture and History from Princeton, a Master's in Urban Studies from Yale and an MD from Case Western Reserve University. A specialist in Infectious Diseases, his career has taken him to the Peace Corps in Iran, the Centers for Disease Control in Atlanta and to tuberculosis research sites in India, South Africa, Tanzania, Peru, Brazil and the Philippines. Among his over 250 publications, Dr. Horsburgh has written several articles on hospital design and on the use of epidemiologic techniques to analyze the built environment.

Eleanor Hoyt is a sustainability professional with expertise in GIS-based hazard analysis, embodied carbon assessments and energy modeling. She is currently a sustainability consultant with Linnean Solutions and is excited by the intersection of technology, data science and climate resilience. Eleanor holds a Master's degree in sustainable building systems from Northeastern University and a bachelor's degree in geology and math from Colby College.

Angela Loder, PhD, WELL AP is Vice President, Research at the International WELL Building Institute where she helps identify current gaps and opportunities around health and building research and activates interdisciplinary collaboration on metrics and case studies. Recent projects include the 2020 *Global Research Agenda on Health, Well-being and the Built Environment* with the international IWBI Research Advisory and management of the pre-approved survey provider program for all WELL Certified projects. Her book *Small-Scale Urban Greening: Creating Places of Health, Creativity, and Ecological Sustainability* was published with Routledge in 2020.

Philip Norton Loheed AIA, NCARB, Assoc ASLA is the Principal Architect of Design Partnership Plus since 1990; President Earthos Institute, a non-profit research organization since 2009; and a Member of the Faculty of Boston Architectural College since 1972. He is a former Partner of AIA Gold Medalist Benjamin Thompson FAIA, from 1968 to 1990. He holds both Bachelor and Master of Architecture degrees from the University of Michigan together with a minor in Cultural Evolution theory; and later studied Landscape Architecture and terrain analysis at Harvard's Graduate School of Design (GSD). His studies in cultural evolution have informed and influenced many aspects of his practice as an architect, researcher and educator. Mr. Loheed has designed and built hundreds of projects worldwide in many cultural contexts.

Jim Newman is founder and Principal at Linnean Solutions, which provides resilience analysis and planning, and energy and carbon modeling. Mr. Newman helped found the Massachusetts Chapter of the United States Green Building Council (USGBC), and is a Past Chair of the Chapter. He is also a founding board member of the Resilient Design Institute, a Board member of the Center for Living Environments and Regeneration (CLEAR) and a member of the RELi Steering Committee. RELi is a resilience rating system from USGBC. Mr. Newman holds degrees from MIT and Lehigh University.

Robin Z. Puttock, RA, LEED AP BD+C, WELL AP is a Visiting Assistant Professor and Interim Associate Dean of Undergraduate Studies at The Catholic University of America's School of Architecture and Planning. Robin is also a practicing architect with over 20 years of experience in award-winning, sustainable civic architecture which has been recognized by the U.S. Department of Education and President Barack Obama. Her teaching and research focus is on sustainability, neuroarchitecture and wellbeing, and she has presented her work at the Environmental Design Research Association, the ACSA and the National AIA. Robin has a Bachelor of Architecture and a post-professional Master of Architecture, both from Virginia Tech.

Bill Reed AIA is an internationally recognized planning consultant, design process orchestrator, author, a founding Board Member of the U.S. Green Building Council and co-founder of the LEED Green Building Rating System. He is a principal of Regenesis Group, Inc.—whose work centers on a living system design process. This work is known as Regenerative Development. The objective: to improve the overall quality of the physical, social and spiritual life of our living places and thus the planet.

Laura Regrut IIDA ASID NCIDQ is the founder of LRD/Laura Regrut Design, a multidisciplinary design and research practice. LRD employs the power of design and its psychological influence to create environments that seek to increase the health and wellness of end users. Project areas include commercial, educational and residential sectors. Laura is also an interior design educator and teaches in several Boston area interior design programs with a focus on design process, sustainability and wellness. In addition, Laura enjoys bringing collaboration with national design firms into the classroom at the forefront of the latest design thinking. She holds a BS in Interior Design from the University of Cincinnati, and an MArch from the Boston Architectural College. Laura is currently working toward WELL AP certification.

Donald H. Ruggles AIA is CEO of Ruggles Mabe Studio, a boutique residential architecture and interior design firm based in Denver, Colorado. Founded in 1970, the firm is dedicated to the idea that beauty can improve the lives of its clients. Their award-winning projects have been featured in publications worldwide. Don is the author of the book *Beauty, Neuroscience & Architecture* (2017) and Executive Producer of the full-length documentary movie *Built Beautiful* (2020).

Gideon Spanjar, PhD is project leader and senior researcher of Sensing Streetscapes (www.sensingstreetscapes.com) and of the European Union-funded Cool Towns project (www.cool-towns.eu) at the Centre of Expertise Urban Technology at the Amsterdam University of Applied Sciences (AUAS). He is a member of the chair Spatial Transformation and the chair Urban

Water at AUAS. Gideon is also professor of Innovation & Urban Green Spaces at Aeres University of Applied Sciences. His professorship conducts research on the transition toward a Biobased Economy, Rewilding Cities and Climate Change Adaptation Strategies for the promotion of human wellbeing and future-proofing cities. He is an associate fellow at the Centre for Econics and Ecosystem Management and a member of the editorial board of *Rooilijn*, a peer-reviewed Dutch journal on science and policy in the field of spatial planning. His research focuses on the redesign of the built environment to promote human health and wellbeing. Gideon holds a PhD in Landscape Architecture from the University of Essex.

Ann Sussman is passionate about understanding how buildings influence people emotionally. A registered architect, researcher and college instructor, her book, *Cognitive Architecture: Designing for How We Respond to the Built Environment* (Routledge, 2015), coauthored with Justin B. Hollander, won the Place Research Award from the Environmental Design Research Association (EDRA) in 2016. The second edition of the book, with full-color images of eye-tracked architecture, comes out in July, 2021. An instructor at the Boston Architectural College (BAC), she founded and became president of The Human Architecture and Planning Institute, Inc (theHapi.org), a non-profit dedicated to improving placemaking, in 2020.

Frank Suurenbroek, PhD is Professor of Spatial Urban Transformation at the Faculty of Technology at the Amsterdam University of Applied Sciences (AUAS). His Chair conducts multiple applied research projects around the question of how today's spatial projects can shape and actively contribute to livable and future-proof cities. His research acts on the intersect between the physical and social space and the way new technologies can improve our understanding and renew the professional skills. Sensing Streetscapes is one of these projects (sensingstreetscapes.com). Frank is Board Member of two Centers of Expertise: Urban Technology; and Urban Governance & Social Innovation. He is also part of the Executive Committee organizing the Media Architecture Biennale in Amsterdam (mab20.org) and was member of the founding council for the new Amsterdam Institute to fight inequality. Frank received his Master's degrees at the Vrije Universiteit Amsterdam and University of Amsterdam and wrote his PhD about incremental urban transformation. In 2014, Frank was appointed as Full Professor at the faculty of Technology at the AUAS. Preceding this position, he worked for nine years in the practice of urban planning and design as a senior advisor at the Architekten Cie. and Inbo Urban Design.

Robert S. Tullis AIA, a 40-year Boston architect, migrated to real estate development in 2008. His well-known placemaking projects include University Park at MIT, The Grove at Farmer's Market, Americana at Brand, BelMar and Waterline Square. As Senior VP and Director of Design, he oversees the GID Development Group's mixed-use projects. He is co-chair of the Boston Society of Architects' Placemaking Network, taught placemaking at the Boston Architectural College and lectures on the importance of an architect's awareness of the spaces between buildings and the characteristics that transform them from space to place. Robert holds an AB from Colgate University and MArch from the Harvard Graduate School of Design. He is a member of the BSA, AIA, ULI and CNU and is a LEED AP.

Mengfei Wang, MDS received a Master's degree in Design Studies from Harvard University in 2020 and a bachelor's degree in Architecture from South China University of Technology in 2017. With a deep interest in the aesthetic experience of the built environment, Mengfei has conducted a range of research and applied her skills to the emerging field of neuroarchitecture. As a research assistant, she contributed to the book *Cognitive Architecture* (2021, by Ann Sussman and Justin Hollander), second edition, and their "Sensing Streetscapes" study in Boston. She works as a user experience (UX) designer and researcher in Shanghai, China.

Laura A. Wernick FAIA, REFP, LEED AP is a Senior Principal at HMFH Architects, with over 40 years of experience in the planning and design of public schools. She pairs her planning expertise with her design skills to create environments that adapt to changing pedagogy and help students flourish. Currently, she is serving as Project Director for multiple concurrent projects at Bristol County Agricultural High School. Ms. Wernick is an AIA Fellow and member and past president of the Boston Society of Architects. In 2014, she was awarded the Boston Society of Architects Women in Design Award of Excellence.

INTRODUCTION

A. Vernon Woodworth, FAIA

Our world is in upheaval. Technology is altering our cultures and our workplaces at a previously unprecedented pace, and scientific discoveries are transforming our understanding of ourselves. Likewise our understanding of the world and our place in it is evolving. These changes are re-wiring our roles, our relationships and likely our brains as well. We are coming to understand that, for good or ill, we live in a world of our own making, and that decisions we make today will impact the quality of life for future generations. There is clearly a need to address resource availability and distribution, the impacts of climate change, and the implications of increased urbanization in our planning and design of the built environment. We have gained an understanding of the consequences of human activity on the natural world as well as the nature of ecological, social and individual health, all of which can now be integrated into our building practices. The future depends upon this.

The Role of Programming

Architectural **programming**—the framing of a project's goals for economic and functional performance—provides the basis for design, and therefore for the functioning of a building throughout its lifetime. In the chapters that follow we seek to expand the boundaries of the architectural programming process to include a broader understanding of human factors, and to make optimal environmental and social performance of a building fundamental project goals. In addition our intent is to reframe programming in terms of **systems thinking**. A program typically outlines goals in terms of productivity and financial yield. Human and environmental health and wellbeing have a frequently ignored financial aspect. The long-term life-cycle implications of our buildings influence human perception, behavior and neural responses for 50 to 100 or more years. When we program, design and construct a building today we are creating tomorrow.

Our understanding of the environmental impacts of our buildings and cities has grown by leaps and bounds in recent decades. Yet much remains to be done in putting this understanding into everyday practice. Those who practice sustainable design successfully incorporate goals and best practices into their earliest programming efforts. Yet the topic has not received more than cursory mention in texts describing the programming process. If careful decision-making

DOI: 10.4324/9781003164418-1

regarding sustainable strategies is to occur, the options and implications must be explored before design begins.

A program is the essential instrument of **evidence-based design**. Site conditions, precedents, space needs and cost considerations are the backbone from which the anatomy of the program evolves. Establishing the appropriate level of analysis, the right amount of information to include, determines a program's usefulness. A program is a contract, or at least the basis of understanding, between an owner and their architect. It is also an instruction booklet, the directions to the design team regarding the intended outcome. Sustainability goals should be straightforward and succinct: energy use in annual KBTU/SF/YR, priority spaces for day-lighting, and benchmarks often associated with the USGBC LEED rating systems such as percentage of recycled construction waste and indigenous building materials, water conservation strategies and indoor environmental quality metrics. Stating these goals in the programming stage allows for their costs to be included in preliminary pricing, increasing the likelihood of their realization. However this metric-based approach is insufficient for the realization of a future where our built environment is a vital component of the living landscapes that promote healthy **ecosystems**. Such a goal requires a transformation of our way of seeing and our way of being.

Defining Value

One dimension of sustainability in building practice that receives insufficient attention in the programming process is "**service life**," the intended useful life of a building. Many building systems, from roofs to HVAC equipment, have a standard service life of 25 years. But the bones of a building can (and should) last longer, a minimum of a century or more. When calculating energy consumption and building productivity service life is the second most significant variable.

The most significant variable in a building's productivity is the wellbeing of its occupants. With the exception of the rare structure assembled without any intent of occupancy, buildings are built to house human activity. The functioning of the building is intended to facilitate the functioning of the people in it. This is where neuroscience and environmental health enter the equation. We now understand enough about the complex interaction of the brain and central nervous system with our environment to be able to design for optimal neural responses. We have evidence of the specific dynamics by which our built environments can contribute to either the nourishment or ill-health of our minds and bodies. These are breakthroughs that have the potential to retool our entire design process, with incalculable implications for the quality of the built environment and our daily lives.

Integrating Architecture and Neurobiology

The brain was once thought to establish its neural networks in childhood and young adulthood with little subsequent modification. We now know that complex systems of neural pathways work constantly to process environmental and physiological information according to both learned and inherited cognitive patterns. We also have established that the experience of subjective states (emotions, esteem, wellbeing) depends upon environmental triggering of built-in affective potentials within the central nervous system. Establishing the neurological basis for this phenomenon opens the door to a world where **emotional engagement**, productivity and happiness are more frequently facilitated by positive environmental contexts. Learning, working, healing and communing all have been shown to be facilitated by the environments in which they take place. In the face of these findings we can no longer justify the construction of buildings that lack appropriate **neurological resonance**.

Recent design practices have not acknowledged or accommodated the several million years-old evolution of our unique human brain. While we are capable of unlimited abstract explorations and imaginings, the inherited processes of our central nervous systems and primitive brain stems retain an instinctual, autonomic basis that requires the attention and understanding of environmental designers. The autonomic nervous system functions creatively when regulated, that is, when stimuli from all sources are systematically processed and integrated into a cohesive, coherent and conscious mind/body state. When this is not the case the autonomic nervous system is thrown into **dysregulation**, allowing inherited survival strategies to dictate our responses.

(Dys)regulation

Regulation as an emotional/physiological state is initially established in the caregiver/infant bonding relationship and subsequently expanded to incorporate the family group, and then the wider community. The role of ritual and traditions, group identity and **belief systems**, in the regulation of our central nervous systems is fundamental to the evolution of human culture. As a result indigenous architecture and the historic structures that we admire and take pains to preserve communicate these values and traditions, as if regulation is among their primary functions. And this may very well be the case.

We instinctually abhor dysregulation, as it threatens our survival. And yet dysregulation is present in each of us, and increasingly in the environments that we create. Personality disorders can be shown to originate in faulty bonding with the primary caregiver in infancy. Hierarchical social systems inequitably distribute **stress** and promote disharmony. Recent technology from the automobile to the internet has disrupted fundamental and long-standing patterns of human interaction. A barrage of sensory stimuli and a paucity of meaningful communication have simultaneously overwhelmed and starved our inherent social instincts.

Interdependence

To the extent that our daily experiences are designed to promote cognitive and behavioral responses it is commercial or ideological manipulation that provides the underlying agenda. Our environments rarely support what anthropologist Victor Turner termed "**communitas**," a sense of mutual identification that promotes social wellbeing. The agora and the temple, piazza and duomo, synagogue, mosque, or sanctuary and marketplace, campo, or town square, have been supplanted by television and computer screens, or the mall and the movie theater. The value of rituals and festivities in strengthening community identity has been subsumed by corporate interests, symbols have been replaced by brands, and the everyday pedestrian experience of casual interaction with neighbors and friends has been replaced by traffic jams and long commutes. With the exception of communities bound by historical identification or common interests modern cultural values are creating a landscape of degraded social interaction. Nevertheless our biology recognizes that community is not a commodity.

Environments of human habitation that create community and communicate safety were once produced spontaneously, perhaps instinctively. It is imperative that we find our way back to an understanding of scale, detail, sociability and safety that serves our deep human need for community. When we can rediscover the joy of place, and the deep release that togetherness can offer, perhaps we will be able to let go of the hunger that drives us to consume at a rate far in excess of the earth's ability to provide for us.

Commercial interests seek to stimulate the central nervous system in order to motivate specific behaviors. Think Times Square and the Super Bowl. What I will call "communitas spaces" seek to regulate the central nervous system in order to bring the individual and the group into harmony with one another and their environments. Think Notre Dame de Paris and the Lion Court of the Alhambra.

Familiarity

We recognize therapeutic places, be they buildings, public places or landscapes, because they do "something" to us, or for us. To understand this "something" the concept of regulation is inadequate. The central nervous system (CNS), which includes the continuous monitoring activity of the second-largest brain to have evolved on the planet (elephants' brains are bigger), connects our vital organs by means of the vagus nerve. Several fundamental neural pathways in the brain rely upon information from the vagus nerve for their proper functioning. Most well known are the fight/flight and freeze/fawn responses, which trigger autonomic nervous system reactions that are designed to assure our survival. This fundamental survival mechanism is constantly monitoring environmental cues for signs of danger. Safety is provided by familiarity, especially the reassuring presence and facial expressions of friends, colleagues and family members. But familiar places can also have a reassuring impact, promoting regulation and relaxing the fight/flight response. **Eye-tracking** technology has also demonstrated that our attention is automatically directed to buildings with face-like qualities, such as bilateral symmetry and fenestration that suggests facial features. The working hypothesis for this inclination is that we possess a behavioral trigger to evaluate new visual stimuli for recognition purposes. Neuroscientists refer to this process as "appraisal." According to Daniel Siegel:

> "Appraisal involves a complex web of evaluative mechanisms, in which both external and internal factors play active roles. The specific nature of appraisal incorporates past experience of the stimulus, including emotional and representational elements of memory; present context of the internal emotional state and external social environment; elements of the stimulus, such as intensity and familiarity; and expectations for the future [1]."

All of this happens literally in the blink of an eye, and without conscious participation. The psychologist Stephen Porges calls this process "**neuroception,**" defined as "how neural circuits distinguish whether situations or people are safe, dangerous or life threatening" [2]. But appraisal informs more than the fight/flight response. Our neural wiring is also constantly evaluating our sense of our body in space ("**proprioception**"), the outside world ("**exteroception**") and the presence of pain or hunger ("**interoception**"). The efficient functioning of our cognitive and relational circuits requires that all systems are communicating "safety" signals to our **amygdalae**. If these are lacking we default to fight/flight mode.

Meaning

Alan Soufre has described the lack of a safety signal in terms of a "**discrepancy**" in the generation of emotional engagement with the environmental surround. Discrepancy occurs when the external features of a stimulus do not match internal expectations. Siegel explains that "In Soufre's terms, the emotional arousal generated in response to such a discordance is called 'tension.'" Emotion and its regulation are examined within a "**tension modulation hypothesis**":

> "Such tension is not in need of reduction, but is managed within an individual's interaction with the environment, especially with significant others in the social world.

> Emotional forms of arousal are distinguished from other forms of arousal—such as those arising from exercise or drinking caffeinated beverages—in that they reflect a subjective sense of meaning, which is evaluated in response to engaging with experience (internal or external) [3]."

The fact that emotional arousal triggers a unique internal reaction in the form of "a subjective sense of meaning" is the key to success in the design of spaces for human activity. The neural circuits that appraise for discrepancy find comfort in certain visual patterns including symmetry, **prospect**, **refuge** and familiarity [4]. While our wiring seeks such comfort in human connection, the environment can satisfy this human need. Eric Fromm identified a phenomenon he called "biophilia," which Edward Wilson has subsequently described as "the urge to affiliate with other forms of life" [5]. Biophilia has been used to explain the therapeutic effects of pets on autistic individuals and the elderly, as well as the documented expedited healing experienced by in-patients provided with views of natural scenery. Could biophilia provide an explanation for the prevalence of natural forms in architectural decoration, from column capitals and friezes to gargoyles and caryatids?

Connection

An architectural setting that incorporates natural features provides subliminal reassurance, facilitating the ability to interact in social contexts. Without the interference of fight/flight signals our **resonance circuits** are able to engage. Siegel describes these as follows:

> "A set of interconnected neural regions I have called the "resonance circuits" enables us to tune into others and align our internal states with others. This circuit involves the **orbitofrontal cortex** and **anterior cingulate**, as well as other midline structures that interact with frontal (midline vertically) cortical areas. Other portions of the resonance circuit involve "**mirror neurons**" which enable us to perceive the intentional state of another person, and then imitate the other's behavior and simulate the other's internal state. Mirror neuron properties are found in the anterior cingulate, as well as a portion of the ventrolateral region called the **anterior insula**. The **insula** has also been shown to be involved in the appraisal of internal visceral states, and plays an important role in our awareness of our own bodily selves via a process called "interoception." The resonance circuits enable us to tune into others, and even to our own internal states for self-awareness. These areas also register the state of the body and also directly affect its states of activation. Information from these areas is passed on to the **hippocampus** for "**cognitive mapping**" and, in some cases, transferred into explicit memory. The orbitofrontal cortex and other middle prefrontal regions also play a major role in coordinating these appraisal and arousal processes with the more complex representations of "higher thinking" and social cognition [6]."

Both biophilic contexts and the activation of resonance circuits support our **neuroendocrine** and immunological systems. Being alone, being lost, being in threatening or unfamiliar circumstances, creates stress and "discrepancy," a dissonance with our environment that promotes dysregulation and the activation of our fight or flight responses. Social systems pay a high price for this dissonance, in the form of mental and physical health, lost productivity, social unrest and crime. Many efforts at social reform propose job-training, early childhood education or affordable housing while ignoring the subliminal messages of our environmental context.

The findings of neuroscience support the assertion that these subliminal messages are decisive in terms of behavioral and psychological outcomes.

Narrative

There is a common thread in the fields of neuroscience and environmental design that offers a bridge between the two fields. This is the human predilection for **narrative**. It seems that our brains are constantly ordering experience in terms of an evolving internal story or stories. Our conscious minds "hear" this story more than they write it. We largely inherit a sense of ourselves from our families and our social contexts. Our parents tell us their stories and, often quite aggressively, assert their expectations and projections as the basis for our own personal narratives. But it is the central nervous system's appraisal of our environmental context that most deeply influences our evolving internal story. We find our measure in our relationship to the world that we inhabit.

When the urban planner Kevin Lynch began soliciting mental maps from city dwellers he noticed several recurring themes that suggested predetermined categories of environmental perception. The subjects of his investigation tended to repeatedly identify nodes, edges, districts, paths and landmarks in their graphic representations of the city's form. The inescapable conclusion of this observation across several cities and populations is that we carry within us the expectation of these basic patterns of urban expression. It is as if a narrative structure of the built environment is part of our DNA. Urban planners have learned from this discovery of subjective narrative predispositions to provide spatial experiences that resonate. This may be only the beginning of what we can do to intentionally create a built environment that reinforces our fundamental human expectations.

However the narrative for our future development as an urban species is now very much in question. While the scientific understanding of our environmental crisis mandates immediate adjustments, our political leaders and corporate interests pursue denial as if it were a policy option. As long as the narrative of our current status ignores the reality of our neurological make-up and environmental predicament we court extinction. The alternative is not utopia, as Buckminster Fuller suggested a half century ago, but a dynamic equilibrium of human activity with natural processes. To achieve this the normative social forces of community and regulation must become central to the narrative of our environmental contexts. The dysregulation of commercial over-consumption and environmental exploitation can no longer be sanctioned by corporate or governmental forces. For designers, architects, planners and policy makers, it is imperative that we act now to direct future growth toward health and harmony. The regulation of our central nervous systems and cognitive processes is the precondition for a sustainable habitat within the larger context of healthy environmental systems. This is our program for tomorrow.

References

1. Siegel, D. (2012). *The Developing Mind*. Guilford. 150.
2. Porges, S. W. (2004). Neuroception: A Subconscious System for Detecting Threats and Safety. *Zero to Three (J)*. 24(5):19–24.
3. Ibid. 150.
4. Browning, W. D., Ryan, C. O., Clancey, J. O., Andrews, S. L., & Kallianpurkar, N. B. (2014). Biophilic Design Patterns: Emerging Nature-based Parameters for Health and Well-being in the Built Environment. *International Journal of Architectural Research*. 8(2):62–76.
5. Wilson, O., & Kellert, S. (1993). *The Biophilia Hypothesis*. Shearwater.
6. Siegel, D. (2012). *The Developing Mind*. Guilford. 157.

PART 1
Human Factors

1

PROGRAMMING INTERIOR ENVIRONMENTS

Human Experience, Health and Wellbeing

J. Davis Harte, PhD, WELL AP and Laura Regrut, IIDA, ASID

The complexities of human/environment interaction form the basis of our sense of **place** and of ourselves. As such, our health and wellbeing are entwined with this relationship along multiple dimensions. In this chapter the authors explore the intricacies of environmental psychology and the potential of evidence-based design to inform programming that ensures the built environment frames our activities and interactions with wellbeing in mind.

Designers are more interested in "health-first" designs than at any time in recent memory. Our collective global experience with an invisible chronic environmental stressor—COVID-19—has shifted our common understanding of what makes a place healthy. It is more important than ever to deliberately program spaces to actively support health and wellbeing, on both physical and mental levels. It is also essential to design with culturally enriched approaches. There is over half a century of evidence showing that environmental psychology principles can benefit design and users. More recent neuroscientific findings now contribute additional important layers to this health-first approach. The better we understand the human response to stressors and our need for social cohesion, the better we can deliberately design spaces that benefit the health and wellbeing of the occupants.

Design Meets Science

As we emerge from the COVID-19 pandemic many of us have a heightened awareness regarding the power of connection and community. We are tired of the isolation and ready to be with friends, family and co-workers again. It is not the place of this chapter to determine how returning to the workplace and life in general will occur. This will be different for each individual, place of gathering, workplace, town, city and country. The current situation is merely a benchmark for a sea change happening which will alter the field of design forever. For instance, Gensler, an industry leader, in their Design Forecast 2021 wrote: "Human-experience design is a powerful opportunity to bring people back together safely and provide spaces that allow them to feel healthy, inclusive, and purposeful; places that support community and social connection perform better" [1].

DOI: 10.4324/9781003164418-3

Such simple words. But how does the designer put this insight into action? Where does the designer go for guidance? This book is full of information on how our biology affects our perceptions, sensations, interpretations and resultant stress and recovery levels. In this chapter, we suggest designers ground their design work in science and research by employing evidence-based design (EBD) principles from the fields of psychology, neuroscience, neuroaesthetics and **salutogenic** design to achieve health-first environments that support social connection. We aim to inspire conversation about the importance of evidence-based design, including neurobiological and environmental psychological strategies, so that designers can create interiors that promote health and wellbeing.

What Is Evidence-Based Design (EBD)?

Evidence-based design (EBD) is a deliberate process that filters high-quality scientific research to guide and create the best possible design solutions and outcomes for physical environments. Many design scholars have been working to define and describe EBD and how it can be applied in practice. Typically it has been used in healthcare settings. EBD is defined by design researchers Stichler and Hamilton as "a process for the conscientious, explicit, and judicious use of current best evidence from research and practice in making critical decisions, together with an informed client, about the design of each individual and unique project" [2].

We argue that there are actually three intersecting elements that need to be included if EBD is going to succeed in practice. The first is the actual evidence—published peer-reviewed design research. The second element to consider is individual and client preferences. The third is the designer's expertise and experience in applying the evidence and preferences in the design plan. This understanding originates in the medical profession's definition of evidence-based medicine—the root of EBD—which sees evidence-based practice as a guide, not as an absolute mandate [3].

EBD practice is flourishing in the industry, with platforms to help train and monitor the impact of EBD, such as The Center for Health Design's Evidence Based Design Accreditation and Certification (EDAC) process. There is substantial evidence that using an EBD approach for hospital-based projects significantly improves factors such as patient outcomes and staff satisfaction [4]. For instance, when a hospital is designed with EBD approaches, including biophilic design elements, patients tend to create more positive associations with the healthcare setting. These gains have been shown to lead to improved patient outcomes, which, in turn, reduce healthcare system costs [5]. With a typical *monthly* expenditure of over $40 billion for healthcare construction costs in the U.S. in 2019, an application of EBD practices for better outcomes is worth incorporating [6]. Such gains in complex hospital settings suggest that an EBD approach yielding similar or greater positive effects in other interior environments is possible. Applying EBD approaches should intersect with individual client preferences, which we will discuss in the following sections.

Environmental Psychology and Interior Design

Along with EBD practice the field of environmental psychology is our next focus as a means to better understand individual and client preferences. Environmental psychology investigates and considers the interactions between people and environments (Figure 1.1). Design scholars have investigated the environment-behavior relationship since at least the mid-1960s, with the first books about environmental psychology published in the early 1970s (see, for instance, Proshansky et al. 1976, Mehrabian & Russell, 1974 and Stokols, 1978) [7–9]. Recent work by Gifford (2014), Bechtel (2010) and Kopec (2018) further contribute to our understanding [10–12].

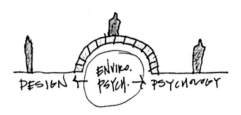

FIGURE 1.1 Environmental psychology bridges considerations between design and psychology. Image courtesy of Dax Morton, 2020.

What is environmental psychology and how is it applicable to programming? Let's first accept that our state of mind and wellbeing are influenced by both internal and external factors. You might wake up one morning and decide to feel eager for the day. That decision is an internally derived attitude. However, let's say that the external environment, your bedroom, is disorganized in such a way that you trip, step on something painful or unpleasant, become disoriented or discouraged. The original state of mind to be eager and optimistic is transformed to a negative state of mind. Our biology interacts with our environment, and vice versa. We are influenced by layers of conditioning, identity construction, cultural meaning and expectation. Our mind/brain/body has the built-in tools of sensory processing to help us make sense and meaning of our world. At times we would rather be in a more alert state, while at other times we want to be in a more relaxed state. To clarify, environmental psychology seeks to understand this interplay between people and their surroundings, and to determine how one's environment might be changed to maximize environmental quality. Understanding and applying both EBD and environmental psychological principles will help your designs be simultaneously more effective, functional and beautiful.

Learning about environmental psychology opens a door of understanding to show that multiple perspectives can all be "correct," and that the space in which a diverse group is gathered can also succeed in helping all these points of views to generate states of both alertness and relaxation. One factor that helps determine how you feel and behave is the theory of environmental load, or how much and to what degree the environment provides stimulation and how much attention we can put on the stimuli [13, 14]. For some, a tile pattern on the floor is perceived as elegant, while for others, this material might be perceived as cold and hard, or even create an optical illusion that is perceived as unsafe. These responses are individual and context dependent.

Environmental psychology for design is a large field which we cannot do full justice to in this brief chapter, however we hope this introduction provokes curiosity for the reader to explore this fascinating field more fully. Designers who leverage an environmental psychology approach are adept at understanding how stimuli affects behaviors, thoughts and the emotional states of their clients and end-users [15]. Designers can incorporate user needs assessment tools used by environmental psychology to target these emotional processes in project development.

Stages of Design: Programming for Health and Wellbeing

Next we'll discuss how EBD and environmental psychology fit within the design process, from both a research and programming framework (Figure 1.2). Dickenson and Marsden in their book *Informing Design* clarify that "research is discovery that can be generalized, while programming is information gathering pertaining to a specific project" [16].

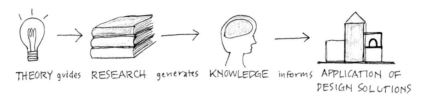

FIGURE 1.2 Overview of design programming process. Image courtesy of Laura Shue, 2020.

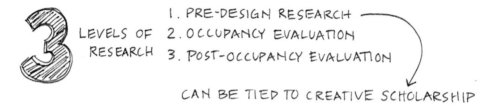

FIGURE 1.3 Levels of design research. Image courtesy of Laura Shue, 2020.

Dak Kopec, a contributor to the expansion of environmental psychology for design, outlines three *programming* phases for designers to better meet end-users' needs—Kopec calls this "research." They are pre-design research, occupancy evaluation and post-occupancy evaluation (Figure 1.3). The first step, pre-design research, is a natural activity for most designers. This is an assessment and evaluation of clients' needs prior to design, which recognizes the difference between temporary and long-standing needs, and considers creative means to bring more to the design than is readily perceived, such as scenario-planning. This may include EBD findings, creative scholarship (original and new contributions) or conducting studies, as the project allows.

The second step in design programming is occupancy evaluation. This is an evidence gathering exercise performed by conducting observations, interviews and/or surveys of end users, who are familiar with the needs and constraints of the project, to determine improvements needed, and the review of precedents and contemporaneous writing on relevant topics. The final step is post-occupancy evaluation, performed after move-in to determine if the design meets the user's needs and how it can be improved. When a design team employs these methods the outcome is more likely to match the client's ethos or company culture and to create a space that facilitates wellbeing.

Design-Related Hypotheses and Theories That Inform Programming

In design scholarship and practice it is important to have a basic understanding of theory. We define theory in the context of programming for health and wellbeing as the creation of informed explanations and predictions about how various ideas are funneled into practice. This is substantially different from the common use of the word. There are a number of influential design theories that we would like to introduce here. Multiple theories can be applied in overlapping ways in a theoretical framework to guide the process of using EBD and environmental psychological principles in design programming.

Prior to developing a theory, design researchers and social scientists first develop a hypothesis, which can be understood as a starting point to describe or explain a phenomenon. Design researchers and environmental psychologists are familiar with a large body of both hypotheses and theories, as well as conceptual models and approaches (see, for instance, Kopec, 2018). We will limit our discussion to a few of the most salient theories for programming.

The way people interact with and are influenced by space can be understood as having roots in biophilic, pleasure-arousal-dominance, and frustration-aggression hypotheses. Each of these contributes to how we make sense of our biological wiring. For instance, our early ancestors were motivated to be in a prospect-refuge location, which means that they sought to be in a protective "refuge" spot, while also having a clear sightline to the horizon to see approaching threats. There is some connection between the prospect-refuge theory [17], and biophilia, or "love of life," a hypothesis developed by E. O. Wilson [18]. The biophilic premise has captured the imagination of many designers, who work to better incorporate natural elements into their designs. There is still much to learn about the mechanisms that help make natural design features successful, but the impacts have been extensively documented as beneficial.

Prospect-refuge theory posits that humans prefer unobstructed sightlines or views to anticipate oncoming danger, with a protective buffer behind them. Expansive views with grasses and landscape are highly favored and can be translated to building interiors. This sense of prospect and refuge affords the ability to feel safe as a result of semi-enclosed surroundings, lower ceilings, and cozy lighting. It's no wonder that booth seating is so highly sought after in a dining setting. A sea of tables can be equivalent to being exposed in the middle of a field.

The second hypothesis relevant for designers, according to Kopec, is the frustration-aggression hypothesis, first proposed by Dollard et al. in 1939 [19] and later amended by Berkowitz in the 1960s and 1970s [20, 21], who added the need for behavioral cues to be present. Dollard proposed that typical behavior of aggression would ensue when stress and frustration built over the person's inability to attain a goal, such as failure to arrive at a gate on time due to crowding, poor circulation patterns and unclear wayfinding. Therefore the person may be more likely to exhibit aggressive behavior, especially if there are behavioral cues to prompt such a response. Times have changed, and moreover, our understanding of human behaviors has increased since 1939. Our current approach to this important early hypothesis is to make an effort to design interior spaces with a reduced level of possible frustrations and increased **attunement** as to how space can influence stress responses.

The third hypothesis is the pleasure-arousal hypothesis, which was first proposed with the concept "dominance" included, by environmental psychologists Mehrabian and Russell [22], and later revised and expanded by Russell [23]. They attempted to describe emotional states in terms of both environment and behavior, with emotions being a mediator, or a process connecting environment and behavior. Russell's later version, the "circumplex model of affect," created a spectrum of rankings to help generalize and score emotional states, or affective states, such as arousal, **distress** and sleepiness [24].

The most commonly used theories in design, as described by Kopec, are organized around the following four theories: integration (such as the interrelated complexities among parts of our environment that draw us in or repel us), stimulation (such as blandness, arousal, familiarity), control (such as our ability to decide where to sit or what temperature the air is) and behavior-setting (which leverages our customs and social norms, such as how to act upon entering a grocery store). These overarching theories are helpful to frame our understanding.

For example, integration theory considers the complexity around multiple design features, as individual components and as a comprehensive whole and how these design features impact the users. There is much to consider in terms of environmental triggers, attractants and aspects that are counter to their original aims. For instance, one may want to increase daylighting in a space, but then there are new problems to manage, such as glare from screens. Gifford [25] has contributed much to our understanding of integration theories.

Let's consider gestalt theory now, as design and the human experience can't be parceled into finite pieces. Gestalt is a theory and psychological approach which relates to human perception that can be summarized as, "the whole is greater than the sum of its parts." A combination of our cognition, our culture, our place in the lifespan, our situation and mood in that moment, and so forth, all influence how we perceive a space. Gestalt, an important theoretical framework developed in the late 1930s by Wertheimer and colleagues, reminds us not to divide our understanding up into smaller and smaller parts, but to appreciate the wholeness of our perceptions [26]. This is especially true in interiors, filled with numerous details, where it is the whole experience and feeling with which we connect. A client may not be able to articulate why a space doesn't work for the ethos and culture of the company, but when the gestalt is right, the space works.

Stimulation theory involves designing spaces that facilitate levels of stimulation appropriate for the activities that will occur in them. Environmental Load theory states that humans have a limited ability to handle environmental stimuli based on our attentional capacities [27]. This means that during the programming phase designers with an understanding of environmental psychology know that future users will likely have a range of abilities to screen the environment. Some will want more stimulation, while others may get easily overstimulated, resulting in negative behaviors. It is possible and desirable to create spaces that have a balance between enough and not-too-much sensory input.

Stemming from early social and personality psychology work, control theory is currently a popular trend in design research and practice. We have come to understand that spaces that offer choices will increase occupants' perceived sense of control over their environments, improving mood, wellbeing and productivity [28]. Our understanding of these aspects of human experience can be attributed to early work by Altman [29], relating to territoriality, privacy, personal space and crowding.

The last relevant theory is behavior-setting theory, a form of social learning theory. Generally, this can be understood as humans looking toward each other for positive reinforcement of behaviors. Barker and Wright as early as 1949 were exploring "person-behavior-situation variables" (p. 131) that could account for human and ecological psychology. These ideas became more formalized in the following decades and remain valid today—specifically, when we enter certain settings we know from cultural expectations how we should behave. We act one way in a school or library, and another way at a football stadium or shopping mall [30]. Designers can use these norms as guidelines or break the rules to promote a new behavior norm such as the now common "loud" spaces in libraries designed for social interaction.

Understanding design theories—of which there are many beyond those discussed here—can help us during the programming phase when designers learn about future users of the space, including both known and unknown needs and preferences. With a foundational knowledge of design theories we can more effectively tap into an empathetic understanding of the user and foster designs that support health and wellbeing in human-environment relationships. This is likely to have major positive implications when taken cumulatively, with a positive return on investment. Defensible design goals will have a theoretical basis, relevant research and outcome verification through POE. Let's delve now into more details of environmental processing, starting with the human brain from a neuroscientific perspective, followed by a look at sensation and perception through the lenses of sociology and psychology.

Neuroaesthetics and Neuroarchitecture: Brain and Environment

We move now from broad design theories to more specific neuroscientific topics. Neuroscientific knowledge is becoming more accessible each year, and more relevant for designers. There is growing interest in neuroaesthetics and neuroarchitecture among design and architecture professionals. For example, the Academy of Neuroscience for Architecture (ANFA) grew out of an AIA convention in 2002 and has become a valuable resource to the design professions. Post-graduate programs are being offered at the intersection of architecture and neuroscience [31].

Neuroscientists who also understand design study the balance between incoming stimuli and the resulting bodily process of secreting hormones and neurochemicals, and how our neural pathways respond. Our brains interpret sensations and perceptions before we are even aware that this process is happening, making the subliminal perception of our environmental contexts both powerful and invisible [32].

Recent writing by Ruggles [33] and Kopec expound on the relationship between neuroscience, human health and wellbeing as facilitated by design. Neuroscientists know that the human brain (which includes the eyes) has five primary roles: to receive, manage and interpret "sensation, perception, feelings/emotions, thoughts, actions/behavior" [34]. Thinking of these in terms of design helps us make sense of how to program a space for health and wellbeing. It isn't important to know the specific names of the brain systems, but an overarching understanding of human responses to the environment can shed light on how to program for health and wellbeing.

Design for Health and Wellbeing Framework to Understand Stimulus Response

So far we have taken a high level look at design theories and provided a brief introduction to neuroscience and design. We now offer a general understanding about how people and environments influence each other. As a point of reorientation, our goal for this and the previous sections is to provide an overview of the second component of applying EBD in practice—understanding the individual/client preferences—intersected with the evidence and your expertise.

We propose to view design, theory, evidence including neuroscience, and the other components we have introduced, through three lenses. Each is always present, but when we zoom in on one or the other, we can make better sense of the individual variables (Figure 1.4). These lenses are physical, sociological and psychological. By physical, we include both human biology and materiality of buildings and finishes. For instance, within spaces we occupy the physical can be windows, which affect solar gain and daylighting, and also the indoor air quality of a building. The other leg of "physical" is the biological processes of our bodies, such as circadian rhythm, allergies and digestion. The sociological dimension includes our cultural and societal influences, such as our school, government, region and religious systems. Finally the psychological dimension includes our emotional states, personality, preferences and cultural associations with spaces and situations.

Sensations and perception, and subsequent emotions and behaviors, as filtered through these three lenses, provide insight into how we experience design. Consider the environment to be the raw material with the potential to fulfill wants and needs, with programming being the critical opportunity in the design process to organize, listen and include these needs and wants. Using the three lenses of physical, sociological and psychological insight, the programmer knows how to leverage evidence-based design research to achieve an appropriate design intent. If the end user isn't satisfied with the design it is likely because during programming the wants and needs of the future occupants were inadequately documented.

It is essential for programmers to incorporate inclusive design as a project objective. This means that appropriate design objectives that consider the "differently-abled" are thoughtfully

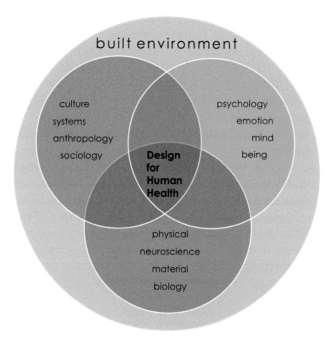

FIGURE 1.4 Design for Human Health framework. Image courtesy of J. Davis Harte.

and deliberately included. Changes to our sensory processing abilities across the lifespan are part of life. For example, babies see with different visual abilities than a teen or octogenarian.

Sensory detection abilities can change along with our brains, by means of **neuroplasticity**. Sometimes neuroplasticity is positive and the brain changes to help a person reach a goal, such as learning a new language. However, **plasticity** can also occur to compensate for a modified or injured sensory system. For instance, if a mammal loses eyesight, changes in the brain occur quite quickly to modify the input receiving abilities, by heightening the auditory processing abilities [35]. We have all adapted to specific social and environmental conditions resulting in a wide range of cognitive and behavioral proclivities. Our environments are least stressful when they support the full spectrum of human abilities [36].

With appropriate sensory input and balance in our built environments we are able to make sense of and interpret our experiences. Too much sensory input will prompt anxious states, while not enough will also put the nervous system into a dysregulated state. Therefore it is imperative that during the programming process the biological and cultural needs of the users are understood and addressed in the statement of goals and guidelines.

Given that we are an ocularcentric species—visual processing is known to involve about 50 percent of our brain [37]—it is important that we understand how visual input affects perception. As Sussman reports the visual cues from our environment subliminally direct our behaviors. If we see a streetscape devoid of interest we won't feel safe walking in that direction. We much prefer moving through a space with a certain level of visual detail and stimulation [38, 39]. Our level of attention informs our sensory processes, and the stimulation of our sensory processes informs our attention. Extensive research exists on the role of focal attention and visual perception in our ability to process and perceive environmental information [40].

An example of visual processing is how an elderly person might perceive the following floor patterns (Figure 1.5)—tile juxtaposed against wood grain with too much contrast between the

FIGURE 1.5 Disorienting design in flooring. Image courtesy of Janet Roche, MDS, 2017.

dark and light sections, might be misinterpreted as a change in elevation [41]. Flooring that is too glossy can cause glare issues or be perceived as wet and create anxiety.

Our brains can create other environmental illusions when trying to make sense of perceived stimuli. Perception is the process of understanding and organizing incoming stimuli into meaningful patterns. If there is a lack of consistency or stimuli are too extreme or outside of our understanding, inconsistent design patterns can create sensory dysregulation. Think of how you feel when you come across novel stimuli and feel attracted, as opposed to when you see the same stimuli regularly, and become habituated to it. In research on birth unit designs the nurses and midwives have stated "oh, sure, those gurneys and IV poles in the hallway—we stop seeing them. We do imagine that when families first see them they might feel upset by all the medical equipment, but it becomes invisible to us" [42]. This is a good example of environmental numbness, which can be "potentially dangerous because it can cause us to overlook problems or hazards…[H]owever, [it can] be prevented by consciously redirecting our perceptions and cognitions within environments we cannot alter, and periodically updating or refreshing our personal spaces" [43].

Vision and hearing are our most "prominent" sensory receiving modes, but it is interesting to consider how senses of touch and smell play a part in perception and interpretation of our environments. Think of arriving at a new restaurant for a meal with your friends or family. You arrive and the aroma in the air and the ambient temperature in the building inform you that the food will be delicious and the atmosphere is pleasing. The feel of the fabric on the chair or a tablecloth will also symbolically communicate to you what type of dining experience to expect. Through the modes of taste and touch, and the shared experience with your friends, the memories will become more deeply rooted than for an experience with less positive associations [44].

The next level of understanding about sensory experiences is perceptual consistency and associations between stimuli, and the learned response process. Even the way we communicate with facial expressions plays a role in how we navigate the world. This sensory processing ability of "reading" each other's expression has been explored by Malcolm Gladwell in his book *Talking to Strangers* [45]. Gladwell explores how facial expressions carry different meanings in different time periods and cultures. Voice and facial expressions are part of our inborn neurological wiring, related to our polyvagal system, and are connected with our ability to sooth and re-regulate ourselves after stress. Social concepts such as an "angry" face or a "confused" face, are not as universal as we may believe. Couple this with attitude, or the readiness of the mind and nervous system to respond to input, and it's understandable how misunderstandings can arise.

Design interpretations can have similar consequences as much of our perception, interpretation and processing happens below consciousness and is reliant on unconscious processes. We need to be intentional about how we direct scientific literacy around perception of stimuli such as colors, shapes, textures, patterns, contrast, light and darkness, as well as weight, movement and the gestalt experience. Similarly, we need to remember and acknowledge that design elements carry different meanings and weights in different cultures. Let's look at one fascinating area of design—color—in both its biological dimension and how it can be leveraged to change perceptions.

Color: Biology and Perception

As many learn in design school, color is fascinating and rich with information that can strengthen the impact of interior environments. We use color to perceive and judge space, and to understand behavioral cues—think dark moody interior, fresh white or sterile interior, color-coded signage and so on. Color also affects our emotions and can alter our mood by affecting our neurohormonal system, our chemical responses to sensory stimuli. The concept of color is a complex one. In this section, we touch on the neurobiology of color, how our bodies respond through the nervous system, when we view colors. We also explore color perception, different perceptions of similar spaces with color application. There are many other aspects to color as an important design feature that can be used with thoughtful evidence-based knowledge [46].

The biological impact of color is determined by visible light waves along the electromagnetic spectrum. Light and color are inseparable. Warm colors have longer wavelengths and cooler colors have shorter wavelengths. The perception of color is a biological function with the eyes and brain working together to interpret these wavelengths of electromagnetic energy; the eyes using light receptors to send signals to the brain which interprets sensations as color. The retina of the eye has millions of rods and cones which are light-sensitive cells and considered part of the brain. Rods help process black and white, and cones help process color.

Knowing how colors are processed by the occupants will help guide the evidence-based design decision-making process during the programming phase. For instance, the color choice of a highly specialized operating room must interact with the proper lighting choice, so the medical team is able to make accurate diagnoses that rely on skin color, or being able to quickly visualize blood [47]. Color impacts people in non-healthcare settings in a different way than in an operating room, a topic that requires further study to reveal its neurophysiological basis.

The primary perceptions that are influenced by color are size/spaciousness and temperature. There is an interesting body of research regarding human emotions based not just on color, but on each of these color dimensions individually, as well as their interactions: hue, saturation and brightness [48]. For instance, designers are familiar with the effects of light colored walls, or brightly lit rooms, appearing more spacious than dark ones [49].

Humans subconsciously create cognitive maps, or mental spatial images, to help navigate space. Interior designers who apply information about color perception, such as applying warm colors to create a sense of welcome, can aid in appropriate wayfinding plans.

There is cultural meaning associated with color. For example in the U.S., most would agree that yellow is seen as uplifting, energizing, helpful to stimulate memory and cognitive activity, and aids digestion and pain relief. However elsewhere around the world yellow can represent: "betrayal, weakness, and contradiction." In both France and Germany yellow represents jealousy [50]. Kopek observes that "many Egyptians associate (yellow) with mourning. Many Chinese associate yellow with pornography. Conversely, African cultures, including Egyptians associate yellow with money, quality, and success, while the Japanese equate the color with bravery, wealth, and refinement" [51].

A seminal study by Valdez & Mehradian [52] may be helpful for those who would like a deep dive into the science of color and emotions using the pleasure-arousal-dominance emotion model discussed in the earlier theory section. Kopec suggests these key takeaways for interior design and the application of color:

- Conceptual and symbolic: serves as a symbol to convey a message, such as in branding or meaning. For instance, green has become symbolic of nature and biophilic principles and is often used in branding for environmentally connected companies.
- Wayfinding and **placemaking**: color-coding and universal use such as red for stop.
- Association with typology: for instance, color will help create behavior-setting cues to communicate expected behavior to the users. For instance, white walls and floors mean clean and sterile and are often associated with labs and medical facilities.
- Fashion/style trends: The 2017 launch of the metallic options for the iPhone 7 in silver, gold, rose gold, (matte) black, jet black or RED had a large influence on the interior design and furniture industry, which was already morphing millennial pink into a revitalized version of 1980's Po-Mo mauve.

Salutogenic Design, Nature and Biophilia in Shaping "Health-First" Design

If you were asked to describe one example of "being healthy," the image of a child playing in nature, making sand castles at the beach, or swinging under a tree might come to mind. Health is a dynamic spectrum that is constantly adjusting and shifting as variables change. It is well known how beneficial time in nature is for children, as seen in the work of such design academics as Chawla [53]. The question is, what about the needs of our inner children? Adults also need play and nature opportunities. We reiterate that complex natural elements that create positive development in children, such as rich sensory experience, will also benefit adults, by providing opportunities for imagination-development, flow-states, social cohesion and stress-reduction. The encompassing nature of places like forests, streams and fields prompts play, creativity and experimentation.

Being separated from nature in our modern world has negative consequences, according to multiple studies [54]. We support the use of biophilic design elements, including complex stimulation for all our senses, to create soothing spaces that seek to reduce anxiety, evoke feelings of wellbeing and promote healing. This could be a functional and aesthetically pleasing combination of design elements, such as water features, nature sounds, vegetation, views, and whimsy through patterns, forms, color and light. Psychologists Stephen and Rachel Kaplan developed the **Attention Restoration Theory** (ART) with the premise that "positive distraction, soft fascination, extent and getting away" by engaging with nature can lead to mental and cognitive relief from fatigued "directed attention" [55]. More recent research supports nature as an important contributor in both disease prevention and health promotion [56]. Space affects our health, and biophilic design supports our innate need to connect with nature.

Consider design as a disease-fighting remedy, to promote wellbeing and prevent disease at the molecular level. Can design be salutogenic, or have a prophylactic impact on human health? Salutogenesis, defined as "the origins of health," is a perspective that deals with the relationships between health, stress and coping, and is a term coined by Aaron Antonovsky [57], a professor of medical sociology.

> "Salutogenic design, as I've come to define it, focuses on the positive impact of design on human health. It's a measurable aspect of design that can help a building's inhabitants operate at their peak performance. Additionally, it can help them maintain physical and mental well-being, actually helping them lead healthier and potentially longer lives. It is the ultimate investment in people, in an architectural sense [58]."

As corporations realize that caring for the health of their employees is a benefit to the bottom line and simultaneously results in healthier, happier employees, programmers are including wellness as a specific goal. This also translates to the reduction of illness and injury for staff, and a likely increase in profit in the corporate setting. A review of RAND, Employee Benefits Plan and a study out of Harvard Business School report that there is typically a 6-to-1 return on investment for wellness programs in industry [59].

The role of chief wellness officer is now beginning to emerge. Several organized pathways have been developed that aid designers in incorporating elements to achieve a "salutogenic design" such as WELL Building Certification, WELL accredited professionals (AP) and the Petals of the Living Building Challenge. Designers are tasked to incorporate solutions that focus on program elements associated with comfort, nourishment, fitness and mind, in addition to air, water and light. The use of biophilic elements produces designs that nurture our innate human connection to nature. Why do these elements make a difference in environmental design? Research supports the human need for restorative environments. Views of nature, biophilic shapes, patterns and forms, plants and vegetation, water and it's acoustic properties, natural and artificial soothing light, all

> "provide a sense of scale and a calming evolutionary memory which have been shown to reduce blood pressure and stress levels. These spaces provide a place for unconscious processing in the brain and allow a renewal of attention and focus [60]."

With wellness now an imperative in any designed environment the designer must go beyond biophilic elements and exercise, yoga and meditation rooms. We agree with WELL-certified architect Rickard-Brideau who has said "wellness and well-being are about having a positive impact on human health at the molecular level." Understanding universal environmental factors such as circadian rhythm can facilitate designing spaces where people are productive when they need to be, and can rest when it is the right time to do so. The blue spectrum of morning light tells our bodies to release cortisol and wake up while the red spectrum of evening light causes our bodies to release melatonin for sleep and physical restoration. Other environmental factors affect us on an individual level, based on genetic wiring, which activates certain genes. Hence our evolutionary memory responds to biophilic elements, like plants and natural materials.

Amazon, Apple and Microsoft are tasking designers to promote activity inside their buildings and across campus, through creative interior circulation stairs, outdoor spaces and paths, and other unusual environments providing variety, novelty and delight that humans crave. As Rickard-Brideau reminds us, enriched environments are essential for human thriving, specifically targeting spaces that prompt regular and meaningful movement to encourage "the growth of neurons in the region of the brain involved in memory formation, organization, and storage. (As we) know that physically active people score higher on memory and cognition tests."

Similar to designing spaces that encourage movement is the commonly held design principle that beautiful spaces feel better to be in. The burgeoning field of neuroaesthetics looks specifically at how the human brain perceives beauty, and how people respond. For instance, Harvard Professor Nancy Etcoff studies how beauty has many potential benefits for occupants, such as how flowers hold a powerful effect from both an emotional and evolutionary standpoint (flowers indicating fertile soil), in ways that can help patients recover and elicit positive emotions [61].

But how to explain the variety of responses people have to art and how can we enjoy a sad painting? According to Etcoff our brain activates two systems that normally operate separately when viewing art. One is focused on the piece of art or stimulus, and simultaneously the default mode network is activated which allows the mind to wander and consider ourselves, our memories and the future. This is a complex brain response using disparate parts. "It may explain why those feelings are difficult to articulate and yet are so profound" [62]. There is scientific research backing up a viewer's response to beauty. For instance, Kawabata & Zeki [63] used neuroimaging technology to view an area of the brain, the **medial orbitofrontal cortex**, and found that it activates in response to viewing something considered beautiful. Researchers study both biological and cultural, or learned, beauty. These insights support the EBD process facilitating healthier environmental design, based on a client's ethos, world-view of beauty and aesthetic preferences.

Architect Don Ruggles is similarly convinced of the importance of creating beautiful spaces. In his book *Beauty, Neuroscience and Architecture* he describes the neurological resonance of patterns of nine, **fractal** patterns and other elements of scale, pattern, color and symmetry. The root concept guiding these ideas is that humans are biologically hardwired—meaning we can't influence, but we can harness—with a nervous system that either moves us toward pleasure (approach) or away from danger (avoid). With this basic principle in mind, designers can better leverage spaces that are seen through an empathic lens to foresee how future occupants might be drawn to, or avoid, certain details, textures, materials or spaces. Mr. Ruggles provides yet another lens through which to focus the power of design for an intentional outcome [64].

In closing, programmers who use EBD, environmental psychology and neuroscientific perspectives, have access to information that can facilitate the creation of healthy and motivating environments with a layer of credibility and a measurable aspect to the design. Can design assist a building's occupants in operating at their peak performance? In order to attempt this the designer should understand the range of employee or client preferences and their individual needs for a productive, healthy and creative environment, the types of stress the occupants will be under, and the social spaces necessary for rest, relaxation, casual gathering and celebration. Can design help users maintain physical and mental wellbeing? Designers can employ elements that create restorative environments. Can design help users lead healthier and potentially longer lives? Designers can consider a salutogenic approach incorporating activity, novelty and control. Much of what designers already do is intuitively grounded in the concepts and ideas explored in this chapter. Understanding the science behind human perception and emotional connection will enhance outcomes that can be tested to prove or disprove research and theories and advance our understanding of the interaction between people and their built environment.

References

1. Design Forecast editorial team. (2020). Design forecast 2021. Reconnect: Design strategies for a post-covid world. Gensler Research Institute. https://www.gensler.com/research-insight/publications/design-forecast/reconnect
2. Stichler, J. F., & Hamilton, D. K. (2008). Evidence-based design: What is it? *Health Environments Research & Design Journal (HERD)*, 2(2), 3–4.
3. Purohit, D. (2021). Episode 205. Dr. Rangan Chatterjee, we got it wrong when it comes to weight loss, episode 205. Dhru Purohit. https://dhrupurohit.com/we-got-it-wrong-when-it-comes-to-weight-loss/#ql-video
4. Brambilla, A., & Capolongo, S. (2019). Healthy and sustainable hospital evaluation—A review of POE tools for hospital assessment in an evidence-based design framework. *Buildings*, 9(4), 76.
5. Sze, R. W., Hagerty, N. M., Sassano, C., & Kazmi, P. (2020). The business case for evidence-based design in radiology departments. *Journal of the American College of Radiology*, 17(1), 152–156.
6. Ibid.
7. Proshansky, I., & Ittelson, W., Rivlin, L. G. (eds.). (1976). *Environmental psychology: Man and his physical setting*. New York: Holt Rinehart and Winston.
8. Mehrabian, A., & Russell, J. A. (1974). *An approach to environmental psychology*. The MIT Press.
9. Stokols, D. (1978). Environmental psychology. *Annual Review of Psychology*, 29(1), 253–295.
10. Gifford, R. (2014). *Environmental psychology: Principles and practice*. (4th ed). Optimal Books.
11. Bechtel, R. B. (2010). Environmental psychology. *The Corsini encyclopedia of psychology*, 1–3. doi:10.1002/9780470479216.corpsy0311
12. Kopec, D. A. (2018). *Environmental psychology for design*. (3rd ed). Fairchild.
13. Cohen, S. (1978). Environmental load and the allocation of attention. *Advances in Environmental Psychology*, 1, 1–29.
14. Colenberg, S., & Jylhä, T. (2020). Designing for health: Strategies for enhancing employee health by workplace design. In Proceedings of the Transdisciplinary Workplace Research (TWR) Conference 2020 A. Kämpf-Dern and M. Will-Zocholl (Eds.), TWR Network. (pp. 84–95).
15. Ackerman, C. (2021). What is environmental psychology? Positive Psychology. https://positivepsychology.com/environmental-psychology/
16. Dickenson, J. I., & Marsden, J. P. (2009). *Informing design*. Fairchild.
17. Appleton, J. (1975/1996). *The experience of landscape*. (rev ed). Wiley.
18. Wilson, E. O. (1984). *Biophilia*. Harvard University Press.
19. Dollard, J., Miller, N. E., Doob, L. W., Mowrer, O. H., & Sears, R. R. (1939). *Frustration and aggression*. Yale University Press. https://doi.org/10.1037/10022-000
20. Berkowitz, L. (1965). The concept of aggressive drive: Some additional considerations. In *Advances in experimental social psychology*, 2 (pp. 301–329). Academic Press. doi:10.1016/S0065-2601(08)60109-4
21. Berkowitz, L. (1978). Whatever happened to the frustration-aggression hypothesis? *American Behavioral Scientist*, 21(5), 691–708. https://doi.org/10.1177/000276427802100505
22. Mehrabian, A., & Russell, J. A. (1974). *An approach to environmental psychology*. The MIT Press.
23. Russell, J. A. (1980). A circumplex model of affect. *Journal of Personality and Social Psychology*, 39(6), 1161–1178. https://doi.org/10.1037/h0077714
24. Ibid.
25. Gifford, R. (2014). *Environmental psychology: Principles and practice*. (4th ed). Optimal Books.
26. Behrens, R. R. (1998). Art, design and gestalt theory. *Leonardo*, 31(4), 299–303.
27. Cohen, S. (1978). Environmental load and the allocation of attention. *Advances in Environmental Psychology*, 1, 1–29.
28. Hoskins, D. (2014, Jan 16). Employees perform better when they can control their space. *Harvard Business Review*. https://hbr.org/2014/01/employees-perform-better-when-they-can-control-their-space

29. Altman, I. (1975). *The environment and social behavior: Privacy, personal space, territory, and crowding.* Brooks/Cole.
30. Barker, R. (1968). *Ecological Psychology: Concepts and methods for studying the environment of human behavior.* Stanford University Press.
31. http://www.anfarch.org/resources/education/naad/
32. Nanda, U., Pati, D., & McCurry, K. (2009). Neuroesthetics and healthcare design. *HERD: Health Environments Research & Design Journal*, 2(2), 116–133. https://doi.org/10.1177/193758670900200210
33. Ruggles, D. (2017). *Beauty, Neuroscience and Architecture: Timeless patterns and their impact on our wellbeing.* Self-published.
34. Huberman, A. (2021, Jan 4). How your nervous system works & changes. Huberman Lab Podcast. https://youtu.be/H-XfCl-HpRM
35. Wiesel, T. N., & Hubel, D. H. (1963). Single-cell responses in striate cortex of kittens deprived of vision in one eye. *Journal of Neurophysiology*, 26(6), 1003–1017.
36. Wolf, K. (n.d.). We are all disabled. Hope Heals. https://www.hopeheals.com/articles-archive/we-are-all-disabled
37. MIT News (1996, Dec 19). MIT Research – Brain processing of visual information. https://news.mit.edu/1996/visualprocessing
38. Sussman, A. (2021, Feb 20). Seeing how cars and people grab us. Genetics of Design. https://geneticsofdesign.com/2021/02/20/seeing-how-cars-people-grab-us/
39. Ellard, C. (2020). Neuroscience, wellbeing, and urban design: Our universal attraction to vitality. *Psychological Research on Urban Society*, 3(1), 6–17.
40. Kaspar, K., & König, P. (2012). Emotions and personality traits as high-level factors in visual attention: A review. *Frontiers in Human Neuroscience*, 6, 321. https://doi.org/10.3389/fnhum.2012.00321
41. Roche, J. (2017). Residential living: Flooring choices for elderly with visual acuity problems and the impact on depth perception. [Masters thesis, The Boston Architectural College].
42. Harte, J. D., Sheehan, A., Stewart, S. C., & Foureur, M. (2016). Childbirth supporters' experiences in a built hospital birth environment: Exploring inhibiting and facilitating factors in negotiating the supporter role. *HERD: Health Environments Research & Design Journal*, 9(3), 135–161. https://doi.org/10.1177/1937586715622006
43. Kopec, D. A. (2018). *Environmental psychology for design.* (3rd ed). Fairchild.
44. Malnar, J. M., & Vodvarka, F. (2004). *Sensory design.* University of Minnesota Press.
45. Gladwell, M. (2020). *Talking to strangers.* Little, Brown and Company.
46. See, for instance, the International Colour Association https://www.aic-color.org/ or the accessible book, "What is Color" by Eckstut & Eckstut, 2020.
47. Bosch, S. J., Cama, R., Edelstein, E., & Malkin, J. (2012). *The application of color in healthcare settings.* The Center for Health Design, 1–78.
48. Wilms, L., & Oberfeld, D. (2018). Color and emotion: Effects of hue, saturation, and brightness. *Psychological Research*, 82(5), 896–914. https://doi.org/10.1007/s00426-017-0880-8
49. Odabaşıoğlu, S., & Olguntürk, N. (2015). Effects of colored lighting on the perception of interior spaces. *Perceptual & Motor Skills*, 120(I). 183–201. doi:10.2466/24
50. Kopec, D. A. (2018). *Environmental psychology for design* (3rd ed). Fairchild.
51. Ibid. 152.
52. Valdez, P., & Mehrabian, A. (1994). Effects of color on emotions. *Journal of Experimental Psychology: General*, 123(4), 394–409. https://doi.org/10.1037/0096-3445.123.4.394
53. Chawla, L. (2015). Benefits of nature contact for children. *Journal of Planning Literature*, 30(4), 433–452.
54. Louv, R. (2008). *Last child in the woods: Saving our children from nature-deficit disorder.* Algonquin Books.
55. Kaplan, S. (1995). The restorative benefits of nature: Toward an integrative framework. *Journal of Environmental Psychology*, 15(3), 169–182.
56. Kuo, M. (2015). How might contact with nature promote human health? Promising mechanisms and a possible central pathway. *Frontiers in Psychology*, 6, 1093.
57. Antonovsky, A. (1996). The salutogenic model as a theory to guide health promotion. *Health Promotion International*, 11(1), 11–18.
58. Rickard-Brideau, C. (2015, Mar 31). What's the next big step in building? Salutogenic design. Metropolis. https://www.metropolismag.com/interiors/whats-the-next-big-step-in-building-salutogenic-design/#:~:text=Salutogenic%20design%2C%20as%20I%27ve, operate%20at%20their%20peak%20performance
59. Bravo. (2019, Mar 21). Do wellness programs save companies money? https://www.bravowell.com/resources/do-wellness-programs-save-companies-money#:~:text=A%20report%20by%20the%20International, on%20an%20employee%20wellness%20program.

60. Rickard-Brideau, C. (2015, Mar 31). What's the next big step in building? Salutogenic design. Metropolis. https://www.metropolismag.com/interiors/whats-the-next-big-step-in-building-salutogenic-design/#:~:text=Salutogenic%20design%2C%20as%20I%27ve, operate%20at%20their%20peak%20performance
61. Etcoff, N. (2011). *Survival of the prettiest: The science of beauty.* Anchor.
62. Pak, F. A., & Reichsman, E. B. (2017, Nov 10). Beauty and the brain: The emerging field of neuroaesthetics. The Harvard Crimson. https://www.thecrimson.com/article/2017/11/10/neuroaesthetics-cover/
63. Kawabata, H., & Zeki, S. (2004). Neural correlates of beauty. *Journal of Neurophysiology*, 91(4), 1699–1705.
64. Ruggles, D. (2017). *Beauty, Neuroscience and Architecture: Timeless patterns and their impact on our wellbeing.* Self-published.

2
BIOPHILIA AND HUMAN HEALTH

A. Vernon Woodworth FAIA

Our instinctual responses to our environmental context may be the largest single factor in determining health and wellbeing. If these responses have been inhibited or blunted by dysphoric exposure we become numb and unresponsive. Health is associated with feeling alive, and seeing life makes us feel alive. It is not an exaggeration to say that our experience of nature is healing. There is, in fact, significant evidence that this is the case. This chapter surveys some of this evidence and suggests including our propensity for biophilia in the programming process.

Our Sense of Self

Our species has co-evolved in relationship to the complex and visually stimulating fabric of nature. An ecological understanding of *Homo sapiens* would emphasize that we cannot really be understood outside the context of our environmental niche. However human culture promotes a sense of our dominance over the natural world, celebrating human accomplishments while overlooking the natural systems that sustain all life, including our own. We have reached a point in our evolution where we can no longer ignore our reliance on nature, and for this we need to respect and cultivate our biophilic instincts.

Biophilia is a felt and measurable response from the deepest layers of our being. However the culture of commerce has reduced this response to another opportunity for exploitation. In this process we have created an environment of alienation where life has been marginalized. Re-imagining our world and ourselves through the lens of biophilia is a necessity for the future health and wellbeing of the planet.

Evaluating Impacts

In the early years of modern psychology Carl Jung pioneered the word association test, noting timing and emotional content as well as verbal responses. Jung was interested in the apparent spontaneity of responses, and experimented as well with monitoring heart rate, blood pressure and galvanic skin response (GSR). This experimental approach revealed underlying "complexes" related to **trauma** and/or family patterns, and facilitated the process of psychotherapy

DOI: 10.4324/9781003164418-4

by promoting the integration of unconscious contents. The physiological responses monitored, being involuntary, originated in the autonomic nervous systems of his subjects, and were typically associated with emotional content.

In evaluating responses to environmental stimuli researchers still monitor heart rate, blood pressure and galvanic skin response, although newer technologies have expanded their repertoire. Most significantly, electroencephalography (EEG) and eye-tracking have provided insight into the autonomous responses of the central nervous system. EEG measures electrical brain activity and is a fundamental tool in psychophysiological research and cognitive neuroscience. Eye-tracking measures visual responses to stimuli in terms of areas of focus and time spent looking at any given point.

While not a biometric device, Virtual Reality (VR) technology has expanded the scope of experimental evaluation of reactions to stimuli by providing an effective means for exposure to artificial environments. In conjunction with eye-tracking VR can measure attention to specific elements in simulated environments [1], providing valuable information to designers. It has been found that physiological reactions do not significantly differ between virtual exposure and real exposure to the same environment [2]. Consequently the impact of a proposed design can be effectively evaluated prior to its construction.

Biophilia

Humans are wired to respond to living things. *The Biophilia Hypothesis* articulated by Edward O. Wilson and Stephen R. Kellert in 1993 states that "human beings' innate connection with nature is essential for their wellbeing" [3]. There is ample scientific evidence to support this claim. In a study of simulated office-space Yin et al. concluded that "physiological results indicated consistently that biophilic interventions had positive effects on reducing stress levels" and "positive effects on improving participants' creativity" [4]. In fact a "meta-analysis" summarizing the health benefits of outdoor nature showed that increased green space exposure is widely associated with significant decreases in diastolic blood pressure and heart rate [5]. Conversely, we also have ample evidence that urban environments impact people's neural social stress processing and are associated with higher rates of psychosis, anxiety disorders and depression than rural environments.

Further analysis of biophilic impact reveals that fractal patterns found in nature are directly responsible for positive stimulation of human neural activity and parasympathetic system mechanisms [6]. Rachel and Stephen Kaplan have advanced an "Attention Restoration Theory" (ART) that articulates the influence of nature on cognitive activity via a state they call "effortless attention" [7]. This theory observes that nature itself promotes a state of "soft fascination" by drawing our interest while allowing simultaneous mental processes such as reflection and imagination. ART goes beyond the dynamics of attention to establish benefits for stress management and health promotion.

Biophilic stimuli have the potential to impact our autonomic nervous system, and the role of biophilia in stress management and the promotion of wellness is clear. With this information, and the tools to evaluate the impacts of our environments virtually, a new dimension in design becomes available.

Biophilic Design

Understanding that there are direct and immediate physiological responses to specific stimuli, and that these stimuli can be intentionally introduced to facilitate specific desirable cognitive and physiological responses, is the essence of biophilic design.

The opportunities to facilitate our biophilic responses in constructed environments are plentiful and readily available. These include views to nature, natural **ventilation** and daylight, access to green plants and water features, and the use of natural materials and biomorphic forms for indoor elements [8]. The sustainability consulting firm Terrapin Bright Green has identified four distinct areas of biophilic input:

1. visual connection with nature,
2. dynamic and diffuse light,
3. bio-morphic forms and patterns, and
4. material connection with nature.

Terrapin Bright Green has also proposed 14 patterns of biophilic design which fall within the four broad areas described above. The identification of these specific patterns allows for the systematic employment of design interventions to facilitate aspects of the biophilic response. Whether attention, stress-relief, healing or creativity is sought, the design of the built environment can facilitate these outcomes. And the more we are exposed to biophilic stimuli the more pronounced are the results, from our physical health to our brain structure itself [9].

Patterns of Biophilic Design

- Nature in the Space

  1. Visual Connection with Nature
  2. Non-Visual Connection with Nature
  3. Non-Rhythmic Sensory Stimuli
  4. Thermal and Airflow Variability
  5. Presence of Water
  6. Dynamic and Diffuse Light
  7. Connection with Natural Systems

- Natural Analogs

  8. Biomorphic Forms and Patterns
  9. Material Connection with Nature
  10. Complexity and Order

- Nature of the Space

  11. Prospect
  12. Refuge
  13. Mystery
  14. Risk/Peril.

Project Planning

Armed with the knowledge that the design of our environments can result in decreased blood pressure, improved short term memory, decreased negative and increased positive emotions, lower systolic and diastolic blood pressure and skin conductance levels, reduced absenteeism, improved academic performance, increased physical activity, improved mental health and cognitive function, enhanced immune function, and increased parasympathetic and lowered sympathetic nerve activity [10], the design professions are now able and ready to introduce biophilic principles into the built environment. This must be accomplished systematically by establishing desired outcomes at the earliest project planning stage.

An architectural program will establish the use and size of required spaces, the optimum relationship of such spaces to one another and additional requirements from energy performance to branding. The biophilic aspects of a design can also be determined and described during the programming phase. A valuable tool for this exercise is the "Biophilic Interior Design Matrix" created by Stephen Kellert, consisting of six element categories and 72 related specific attributes. The elements differ somewhat from Terrapin Bright Green's patterns, with some overlap, while the specific attributes offer multiple application opportunities. Listed below are several of these opportunities in the context of their applicable elements.

Biophilic Interior Design Matrix

1. Actual Natural Features
   - Air
   - Water
   - Plants
   - Natural Materials
   - Views and Vistas
2. Natural Shapes and Forms
   - Shells and Spirals
   - Curves and Arches
   - Inside/Outside
   - Fluid Forms
   - Botanical Motifs
3. Natural Patterns and Processes
   - Sensory Richness
   - Age, Change and the Patina of Time
   - Area of Emphasis
   - Patterned Wholes
   - Patterned Spaces
4. Color and Light
   - Composition
   - Communication
   - Preference
   - Engagement
   - Pragmatics
5. Place-based Relationships
   - Geographic Connection to Place
   - Historic Connection to Place
   - Ecological Connection to Place
   - Cultural Connection to Place
   - Integration of Culture and Ecology
6. Human-nature Relationships
   - Prospect/Refuge
   - Order/Complexity
   - Curiosity/Enticement
   - Mastery/Control
   - Attraction/Attachment.

Planning for biophilia goes to the heart of the user experience and therefore to the value and effectiveness of the design. In our next section we will see how it also impacts the bottom line.

The Economics of Biophilia

In their working paper on *The Economics of Biophilia,* Terrapin Bright Green points out that productivity costs (related primarily to employees) are 112 times greater than energy costs in the workplace. Terrapin's business plan is based on the readily understandable statement that "introducing certain elements of nature into commercial buildings results in increased productivity and employee satisfaction" [11]. However productivity is not the sole benefit of biophilia. Enhanced learning comprehension and test scores have been demonstrated in multiple educational environments. Biophilic elements also can enhance social fabric, strengthening a sense of community. However the proven efficacy of biophilia in increasing healing rates may hold the greatest economic benefit of this approach.

As stated in their *Economics* report Terrapin Bright Green claims that "in the $2.5 trillion healthcare industry, simply increasing views from hospital beds to nature could yield over $93 million in annual savings nationwide as patients require less time in the hospital to recover from major surgery" [12]. Elsewhere it has been noted that

> "mental disorders have become one of the largest factors in (the) global disease burden. Approximately one in five adults in the U.S. experiences mental illness, including anxiety and depression, which are often associated with, or triggered by, a high level of stress. Better understanding of interventions that ameliorate stress and anxiety are needed given their negative consequences for human health [13]."

Along with the health benefits of biophilia the economic incentive to adopt its principles becomes considerable. In fact these benefits need not be limited to the workplace and the hospital, as all interior and exterior environments can benefit from their application.

Conclusion

Evidence-based design adopts the position that design decisions have predictable outcomes, and that such decisions should be based on the outcomes sought. With the scientific investigation of biophilia we have conclusive evidence of strategies capable of facilitating a range of desirable outcomes that can be used effectively in all conceivable environments. The early planning phases of a project provide an opportunity to establish the strategies and goals for a given project.

Biometrics and VR technology provide the means for evaluating the effectiveness of these strategies. In a similar manner the **commissioning** phase can evaluate the effectiveness of the strategies as implemented. Insights regarding the relationship of neuroscience to endocrinology make it clear that the environments that we construct impact us in ways that could not previously be imagined. The concept of biophilia bridges the gap between the unfolding explorations of neuroscience and the environmental crisis that threatens to disrupt civilization irrevocably.

Salingaros has described the benefits of biophilia as follows:

> "since biophilia is an essential part of human biology, building according to its principles…satisfies part of what is required for sustainability, in two ways. (i) The built structures are conceived as extensions of our biology and our ecosystem; (ii) we feel healthier in them, and therefore we will feel more motivated to preserve them against wear and tear and replacement [14]."

With an evolving sense of self that prioritizes natural patterns and systems as essential to well-being perhaps homeostasis can be restored, not only to our autonomic nervous systems, but also to the all-encompassing systems of our biosphere, on which all life depends.

References

1. Yin, J. & Spengler, J. D. (2019). "*Going Biophilic: Living and Working in Biophilic Buildings*". *Case Studies in Urban Health*. Ch. 40 Oxford, UK: Oxford University Press. doi:10.1093/oso/9780190915858.003.0040
2. Ibid.
3. Wilson, O. & Kellert, S. (1993). *The Biophilia Hypothesis*. Shearwater.
4. Yin, J. et al. (2019). Effects of Biophilic Interventions in Office on Stress Reactions and Cognitive Function: A Randomized Crossover Study in Virtual Reality. *Indoor Air: International Journal of Indoor Environment and Health*. 29(6). 1028–1039. doi: 10.1111/ina.12593.
5. Ibid.
6. Browning, W. D., Ryan, C. O., Clancey, J. O., Andrews, S. L. & Kallianpurkar, N. B. (2014). Biophilic Design Patterns: Emerging Nature-based Parameters for Health and Wellbeing in the Built Environment. *International Journal of Architectural Research*. 8(2). 62–76.
7. Kaplan, R. & Kaplan, S. (1989). *The Experience of Nature: A Psychological Perspective*. Cambridge University Press.
8. Yin, J. & Spengler, J. D. (2019). "*Going Biophilic: Living and Working in Biophilic Buildings*". *Case Studies in Urban Health*. Ch. 40 Oxford, UK: Oxford University Press. doi:10.1093/oso/9780190915858.003.0040
9. Preuß, M., Nieuwenhuijsen, M., Marquez, S., Cirach, M., Dadvand, P., Triguero-Mas, M., Gidlow, C., Grazuleviciene, R., Kruize, H. & Zijlema, W. (2019). Low Childhood Nature Exposure Is Associated with Worse Mental Health in Adulthood. *International Journal of Environmental Research and Public Health*. 16. 1809. doi:10.3390/ijerph16101809.
10. Yin, Jie, et al. (2018). Physiological and Cognitive Performance of Exposure to Biophilic Indoor Environment. *Building and Environment*. 132. 255–262.
11. Terrapin Bright Green. (n.d.). *The Economics of Biophilia: Why Designing with Nature in Mind Makes Financial Sense*. https://www.lbhf.gov.uk/sites/default/files/section_attachments/the_economics_of_biophilia_-_why_designing_with_nature_in_mind_makes_financial_sense.pdf
12. Ibid.
13. Yin, J. (2018). Effects of Biophilic Interventions in Office on Stress Reactions and Cognitive Function: A Randomized Crossover Study in Virtual Reality. *Wiley*.
14. Salingaros, N. A. (2019). The Biophilic Healing Index Predicts Effects of the Built Environment on our Well Being. *Journal of Biourbanism*. 1(8). 13–34.

3
BEAUTY IS...

Donald H. Ruggles AIA, NCARB, ICAA, ANFA

An experience of beauty activates our central nervous systems in a manner that galvanizes us, providing a sense of release that is healing and the essence of wellbeing. Neuroscience has provided convincing evidence that this is the case. Why then has the practice of architecture turned its back on this essential quality? Understanding the nature of beauty has always been a central preoccupation of the arts, and architecture cannot serve its purpose without this understanding. In this contribution Don Ruggles summarizes key points from his more extensive writings and insightful documentary "Built Beautiful: Beauty, Neuroscience and Architecture" in hopes that we will find our way back to this central value.

Imagine being in a room you don't want to leave. The space calms you, and even makes you feel whole, nourished and hopeful. Instead of a room, it could be a building or a piece of art that you go out of your way to engage with on a routine basis. This is beauty. This is wellbeing.

Conversely, picture a room that is unsettling and overwhelms the senses to the point of discomfort. This room makes you want to leave as quickly as possible. This is the opposite of beauty. This is stress.

In general terms, human kind is subconsciously aware of buildings we routinely approach or avoid. This is the power of architecture and art at work, and neuroscience is uncovering the mystery of designs and patterns that have such an effect on us, whether positive or negative, and why they do.

In roughly 400 BC, Plato wrote that the three ultimate values were truth, goodness and beauty. Vitruvius wrote in the 1st century BC that the three fundamental components to architecture were strength, utility and beauty. Then in the 16th century, Andrea Palladio wrote that the three essentials were firmness, commodity and delight. All were masters that worked hundreds of years apart, agreeing that there are three basic qualities of a successful building: structure (form), program (use) and aesthetics (beauty).

For over 2,500 years, mankind has been on an introspective journey to understand beauty: How it applies to our lives, how it affects us and how to create it. That journey was in earnest until roughly the early 1900s, when the modern movement theorized that form, utility and craft should be the new trilogy and that beauty was no longer the goal of architecture and art.

DOI: 10.4324/9781003164418-5

Today, as I look at our profession, I am struck by how architectural education has rendered the words "beauty" and "inspiration" irrelevant. They have become tattered, romantic notions from a forgotten time. This is a grave misstep. Beauty and inspiration have a fundamental role to play in our lives, our health and our wellbeing. Now, thanks to recent advances in neuroscience, biology and psychology, we can verify this scientifically. By placing this insight on a scientific basis we have the opportunity to recover the role that beauty can play as an essential aspect of our wellbeing.

Exciting discoveries started with the work of Anjan Chatterjee and his book *The Aesthetic Brain* [1]. In this work the author explores the Pleistocene epoch, a period beginning some 2.4 million years ago, when the evolution of modern humans took shape. Chatterjee describes how during this period humankind came to associate the image of an open savannah with something bountiful, safe and habitable. Over time, knowing their offspring would thrive in this environment, the sight of such an open space and the recognition of the patterns associated with the savannah came to trigger physical relief in early humans (Figure 3.1).

The beauty of the Savannah: We respond to a broad and dramatic view as beautiful and inspiring as a result of 2.4 million years of evolution. We feel intuitively that it is safe, bountiful and full of pleasure.

Chatterjee, based on a 1992 paper written by Gordon Orians and Judith Heerwagen [2], asserts that the visual image of an open savannah creates a physical signal that becomes associated with survival and modulates subconscious human biology accordingly. Through the millennia, this reaction to the patterns embedded in the savannah-scape became intuitive and influenced the neuronal growth of the primitive brain, effectively encoding a favorable reaction into our genetics responses to their environment. Whether positive and supportive or negative

FIGURE 3.1 The beauty of the Savannah: We respond to a broad and dramatic view as beautiful and inspiring as a result of 2.4 million years of evolution. We feel intuitively that it is safe, bountiful and full of pleasure. Image courtesy of Getty Images.

and stressful, they are always intuitive. Renowned cognitive psychologist Steven Pinkert has asserted such, noting that our senses are acutely acclimated to respond accordingly to surroundings that will impact survival.

Denis Dutton echoes this notion, writing, "There are an infinitely large number of universal dispositions and behavior patterns—particularly persistent desires, motives, capacities, and emotions—that point directly back to the Pleistocene conditions where they first arose" [3].

As an architect interested in understanding how my work impacts others this was quite a revelation. Dutton establishes clarity about the ability of visual patterns to trigger physical responses so powerful that they encode themselves in our genes. They become hereditary. I knew firsthand that visual stimuli, beautiful or otherwise, could elicit a physical response. But the idea that this response might become physically embedded and then passed on echoed with an intuitive conviction I had long held. It resonated powerfully with a sense of enduring wisdom I had drawn from traditional architecture all these years: certain repetitive patterns elicit a positive and powerful response.

In my quest to understand beauty in art and architecture, I never imagined how close the answer had been all this time, literally lying within us, in our biology.

★ ★ ★

At the most fundamental level, humankind is genetically predisposed to seek two things: survival and pleasure. Every day, our bodies process billions of actions without us even knowing it. All of them are geared toward these two goals. An amazing 95 percent of all actions processed by our brains are intuitive and subconscious, and all are geared to support our wellbeing.

To simplify a very complex situation, according to neuropsychologist Rudolph C. Hatfield, writing in "Essentials of the Brain," "Some anatomists prefer to divide the brain into three sections: the forebrain, the midbrain and the hindbrain" [4]. For this analysis, we will combine the hindbrain and the midbrain into one category, the **ancient brain**.

The ancient brain refers to the brain stem. Thought to have evolved during the Pleistocene period, it consists of the medulla, pons, thalamus and the midbrain. This is the center for our primitive and emotional responses—survival and pleasure—and is responsible for the more remedial, life-sustaining functions. It is here where the patterns of the savannah (safely spaced trees, open verdant countryside, water, food and shelter) encoded themselves to trigger a pleasure response.

Many other patterns also encoded themselves in the ancient brain through the millennia. Happen upon a large snake, for example, even for the first time, and we are intuitively alerted to danger triggering a survival response automatically.

Many biological triggers evolved from multiple visual patterns built up in our ancient brain during the Pleistocene period. But what did these triggers do? How did these triggers affect our biology with survival or pleasure in mind? Enter the modern forebrain (Figure 3.2).

The nervous system at work: Our intuitive brain recognizes unpleasant patterns and alerts us to danger before we are aware of its presence.

Surrounding the ancient brain is the modern brain or, more precisely, the cerebellum and the frontal cortex. This is the center of rational thought. Judgment, reasoning, language and analytics originate in this portion of the brain. The modern brain is believed to have evolved during the Holocene period of the past 12,000 years.

The forebrain is responsible for higher-order cognition and consists of the limbic system, the thalamus, the cerebrum and the basal ganglia. The modern brain takes the information released by the ancient brain and converts that information to feelings, thought, memory and action.

FIGURE 3.2 The nervous system at work: Our intuitive brain recognizes unpleasant patterns and alerts us to danger before we are aware of its presence. Image courtesy of Unsplash.

The constant flow of information needed to feed both the ancient brain and the modern brain comes from our nervous system.

The nervous system, simply put, collects information. There is a never-ending process of multidirectional communication going on between our brain and every cell in our body. These communication pathways are electrical and hormonal in nature, and together make up our nervous system.

Current thinking has our nervous system divided into two distinct categories: the limbic nervous system and the autonomic nervous system. The limbic system is involved in motivation, emotion, learning and memory. The autonomic nervous system is responsible for control of the bodily functions not consciously directed, such as breathing, immunity, the heartbeat and digestion.

The autonomic nervous system is bifurcated into two subcategories. There is the "sympathetic" and the "parasympathetic." The sympathetic one corresponds with survival and the parasympathetic one corresponds with pleasure.

When something triggers the sensation of imminent danger, the autonomic nervous system switches into sympathetic mode. It's sympathetic to the fact that all bodily functions and resources should temporarily be diverted to the muscle groups that will enable survival. This is the classic fight-or-flight or flight-or-freeze reaction. It is a danger signal that initiates the adrenal gland to release hormones to prepare the body, at the cellular level, for action.

Adrenaline and norepinephrine released during a sympathetic event raise the heart rate, narrow mental focus and, in effect, put a person into survival mode. Cortisol then is released to signal the body to slow down bodily functions that are not immediately essential, such as reproduction, immunity and cellular repair. This all happens instantaneously and unconsciously. It is an autonomic response mechanism that emanates from the ancient, intuitive brain.

Following this activation, a rational reaction takes place in the cortex in the modern brain. This helps determine a course of action based on how dangerous the threat is and the avoidance tactics necessary for survival.

The sympathetic response is characterized by a sense of stress and danger. In contrast, the parasympathetic mode in our autonomic nervous system equates to pleasure. It is the stress-relieving and calming mode that results in our sense of wellbeing. Hormones such as dopamine, serotonin, DHEA and oxytocin change our cellular behavior. These chemicals are responsible for our feeling happy, wonderful, beautiful and inspired.

Importantly, critical functions involved in cellular repair occur when the autonomic nervous system is in parasympathetic mode. It is in this mode when our immune system is most available for action, and that the body is able to defend and mend itself. It is not just a pleasure response. It is also a wellbeing and a longevity response.

★ ★ ★

This analysis goes deeper than the ancient brain, however; it goes straight to the heart. It turns out that "follow your heart" is an honest representation of our emotions and autonomic response. The neurological pathways through which the heart communicates with the brain are the vagus nerve, and the efferent and afferent nerves running through our spinal cord. Both pathways are a direct link to the medulla, in the ancient brain.

The heart's nervous system contains sensory neurites and local circuit neurons of various types, and these sensory neurites are distributed throughout the heart. They sense and respond to many types of biological information, including blood pressure, heart rate, hormones and neurotransmitters. With every heartbeat, a burst of neural activity is relayed to the brain, where this information is converted into neurological information. Then, this neural information is sent back to the heart to inform its performance. The heart is intricately linked with the state of our autonomic nervous system, and the differences between the sympathetic mode and the parasympathetic mode are quite significant and important to our health and wellbeing.

The heart dictates our emotional actions, which leads to the feelings one has. This is known as bottom-up emotion tempered by top-down logic.

The point of this biological diversion is to demonstrate that humans, over millions of years, have evolved sophisticated and automatic response mechanisms that tie our cellular biology to our surroundings. In recognizing that visual patterns can subconsciously activate survival (sympathetic) and pleasure (parasympathetic) responses, we are confirming that art and architecture—both schemes of visual patterns at their essence—have an important role to play in the creation of a beautiful and healthy environment.

Sympathetic and parasympathetic reactions emanate from the ancient brain. Neuroscience has isolated trust, loyalty and intuition in this portion of the brain. These are cognitive traits called emotions. Once the ancient brain is activated, it then activates the cortex or the modern brain. This is the center of rational and analytical thought, language, writing, learning and curiosity. These are cognitive traits called feelings.

"Emotions happen in the background of our consciousness. It is not until they register in the foreground as a feeling that we are aware of having an emotional experience. Feelings include fatigue, energy, excitement, wellness, sickness, tension, relaxation, surging, dragging, stability, instability, balance, imbalance, harmony, and discord. Others are aware of these feelings by changes in our facial expression, body posture, the tone of our voice, etc. When we weep, others may wonder whether we are sad or happy or just stressed out, but they can tell that we are having an emotional experience that has been translated into a feeling because we are displaying it" [5].

Rita Carter points out in the book *Mapping the Mind* [6] that our limbic neurological system goes through three stages in forming and responding to emotional experiences:

1. automatically triggering a response or an action,
2. the action itself is endowed with pleasure, and
3. afterwards there is a sense of fulfillment or contentment.

This sequence is important because humans are curious. We delve into the unknown with caution, but with unheeded thirst to understand. Why? We simply have to know. Professor Irving Biederman, with Edward Vessel, proposed in "Perceptual Pleasure and the Brain" [7] that humans have

> "an innate hunger for information: Human beings are designed to be "infovores." It is a craving that begins with a simple preference for certain types of stimuli, then proceeds to more sophisticated levels of perception and cognition that draw on associations the brain makes with previous experiences."

Reviewing the sequence above: step one is about curiosity. Step two is the pursuit of pleasure and step three is the pleasure reward (i.e., contentment). It is the feeling of curiosity and the innate hunger for information that will lead us to beauty and wellbeing.

When we view a pattern that has the promise of beauty, it activates our curiosity and we turn our gaze to take a closer look. The parasympathetic nervous system then alerts the cortex that a pattern is in our view that registers in our limbic brain as safe and pleasurable. The curiosity leads to anticipation, which is followed by a release of dopamine. The feeling of pleasure is the reward from the dopamine. The result: The proclamation, "It's beautiful."

This leads to another cycle. Curiosity is activated even more, which leads to more anticipation, which is followed by pleasure, which initiates the proclamation "absolutely beautiful." And on and on the cycle goes. The more profound the pattern, the more curiosity, and the more pleasurable the experience.

Professor Harry Francis Mallgrave, in *Architecture and Embodiment* [8] describes this as follows:

> "Beauty, like art, is a neurological activity, an urge for and feeling of pleasure emanating from the brain's lowest or most primal reaches and associated with awe or wonder. And it is more than a passing fancy. When we taste a good wine, embrace a heartwarming friendship, enjoy the view from a mountain top, or succeed in our endeavor to elaborate upon the elements of a design skillfully, we feel revitalized. We feel a sense of happiness and harmony with the things around us, together with a sense of pride in our creative achievement."

Mallgrave continues,

> "The world appears beautiful because we are experiencing a moment of flourishing or vitality, rather than mere survival. What biologists are demonstrating today is that there is indeed something substantive (electric and chemical) to the pleasure that we term "beauty," something we can take to the bank. And this is indeed an impressive beginning

because, if nothing else, a neglected artistic term has been reclaimed from somewhere in our historical past."

It appears to be so simple: Intuitive emotions generated by recurring simple physical patterns become feelings. I realize that the proclamation, "It's beautiful" is nothing more than a physical reaction—the release of dopamine—to the recognition of a pattern that starts in our ancient brain as an intuitive emotion and ends in our modern brain as a physical feeling.

The result of the dopamine release is a sense of contentment and pleasure. This is a powerful and compelling reward. I believe this explains why beauty is such a strong motivator and source of inspiration in architecture and art. It's so striking, we've given it a word: "beautiful" and it makes us feel good both emotionally and physically.

This is a nontrivial departure from the idea that "beauty is in the eye of the beholder." It turns out that beauty resonates in all of us uniformly due to our common evolutionary history originating in the Pleistocene period and is in fact "in the brain of the beholder." The primacy of our pursuit of survival and pleasure is fundamental to understanding the important role that beauty plays in our lives and wellbeing. From the first moments of birth, pleasure is one of the primary motivators in life. It links directly with the genetic development of reacting to patterns such as the savannah environment and ultimately to architecture and art.

But what of these patterns? What might be their origin? How do they apply to art and architecture? What does this all mean and why should we care? All of these are important questions.

Yet, isn't something still missing here? Linking imagery and physical patterns with subconscious action is one thing. But when we experience beauty it may start unconsciously, but it clearly ends up as something very conscious indeed. It is a visceral, physical feeling. The result is that it is often motivating. It inspires action. It draws us toward it in a bewildering, compulsive manner. This is the beauty I have known. This is the beauty I have strived to achieve in my work over the years.

Architecture is fundamentally about shelter. This is what humankind expects from architects. Closely attached to that expectation is the idea that architecture will support our health and wellbeing. Without delivering these qualities, a structure is placing the occupant into a survival /stress mode, which is not healthy. Rather, architects should be charged with designing forms and spaces that support health and wellbeing by providing environments that are free of stress inducing forms. If you design to this stress-free environment then a state of health and wellbeing will result, which is the model that will lead to a pleasure/beauty response. That, in turn, leads to the multiple health and wellbeing benefits originating from the autonomic nervous system and a parasympathetic state.

Today architecture is at a crossroads. Architects would do well to endorse and accept that neuroscience, biology and psychology have provided the profession with the information and means to improve our environment and the health and wellbeing of society in general. Additionally, architects should recognize the utilization of the pleasure of beauty as the means to rebalance current-day design equations into a proper balance. Frankly, our future health and wellbeing depend on it.

References

1. Chatterjee, A. (2014). *The Aesthetic Brain: How we evolved to desire beauty and enjoy art.* OUP USA.
2. Orians, G. H., & Heerwagen, J. H. (1992). Evolved responses to landscapes. In J. H. Barkow, L. Cosmides, & J. Tooby (Eds.), *The adapted mind: Evolutionary psychology and the generation of culture* (pp. 555–579). Oxford University Press.

3. Dutton, D. (2009). *The Art Instinct: Beauty, pleasure, and human evolution.* Bloomsbury Press.
4. Hatfield, R. C. (2013). *Essentials of the brain: An introductory guide.* Fall River Press.
5. Eberhard, J. P. (2007). *Architecture and the brain: A new knowledge base from neuroscience.* Greenway Communications. p. 72.
6. Carter, R. (1999). *Mapping the mind.* University of California Press.
7. Biederman, I., & Vessel, E. (2006). Perceptual pleasure and the brain. *Scientific American*, 94(3), 247–253.
8. Mallgrave, H. F. (2013). *Architecture and embodiment: The implications of the new sciences and humanities for design.* Routledge.

4
STRESS

J. Davis Harte, PhD, WELL AP with A. Vernon Woodworth FAIA

Our wellbeing depends upon a state of equilibrium or regulation in which the central nervous system is free from fear and the fight/flight/freeze responses which are triggered by signals of danger or discrepancy. Stress can rouse us to overcome obstacles or, when we are vulnerable or overloaded, it can interfere with our homeostasis. An understanding of the role of stress in both physical and mental health has identified it as a factor in high blood pressure, heart disease, obesity, diabetes, substance abuse, insomnia and depression. Stress originates in social relationships where there is inequity or misunderstanding, in triggers of memories that involve painful emotions, and in environments that convey uncertainty, disorientation and danger. By understanding the role of stress in human health and wellbeing designers can seek to reduce stressors and promote regulation through a lens of health equity.

Environmental Stressors

Humans rely upon our inner physiological and psychological states to respond to our circumstances in a manner that enhances our survival status. Some of us may be endowed with a natural resilience that allows us to take this ability for granted. Others may be hampered by historical or developmental deficits or traumas, or may have never experienced a supportive environment that provided us with a secure sense of identity. Regardless of our innate resilience we will all be subject to stress throughout our lives and will benefit from opportunities to reduce environmental stressors and to increase our resilience (Figure 4.1).

Programming in architecture and design is a monumental task, being the foundation for all future activities, resting solely on this finite window of the design process. Does reading this idea raise your stress response? Each of us puts out and pulls in thoughts, interactions, responses and stimuli all day, every day. Finding the balancing point of just enough in, just enough out can be challenging. This chapter seeks to increase understanding of what stress and stressors are, how stressors affect our bodies, and how designers can use this knowledge in programming. Stress is viewed through a combination of lenses, specifically those provided by neuroscience and environmental psychology. Readers will leave feeling better equipped to design

DOI: 10.4324/9781003164418-6

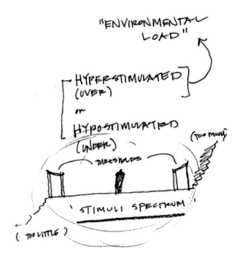

FIGURE 4.1 Environmental load. Image courtesy of Dax Morton, 2020.

"neutral"—not threatening—spaces, or, better yet, positive ones that facilitate human thriving today, and tomorrow.

One way to picture this balancing act is with the term **allostasis**, which is the assessment of our inner bodily processes and thoughts, as compared with external (physical and psychological) stressors and input. We tend to accumulate the stressors of our environments and experiences and store these in our bodies in the form of **allostatic load**, defined as "the cumulative burden of chronic stress and life events" [1]. The source of allostatic load is "environmental load," our daily experience of stress. Having excessive environmental load is likely to lead to a higher allostatic load on the body and can result in distress, anxiety and illness. Systems plagued by stressors experience similar dysregulation. However, there are many ways to release this burden and prevent allostatic load accumulation, depending on the individual's stance, time, place and environment.

The concept of environmental stress has roots in psychology. External factors cause irritations, disturbances, disharmony and dysregulation for both individuals and communities. Environmental stress relates to the concept of **environmental risk factors**, which the World Health Organization credits as a major contributor to death, disability and lack of wellbeing worldwide [2]. Some examples of environmental risk factors are traffic noise exposure, air pollution, mental stress, loneliness and lifestyle risk factors such as lack of good quality food.

Humans are constantly balancing external and internal stress sources, and simultaneously improving ways to manage each. We have limited attentional capacity, which is regulated by our "salience network" which filters relevant information. We perceive stimuli through our seven senses, and then internally process this information. I say seven senses, because in addition to the common five, it is also important to recognize the senses of proprioception, our body relative to space around us, and vestibular, our body in relation to gravity and movement [3] (Figure 4.2). According to Lazarus' theory of psychological stress [4], how a person "appraises" a situation is one component to stress management, the other component is "coping," For example, two siblings growing up in the same household, who experienced the same dysfunctional family dynamics, can appraise the situations as anywhere from traumatic to unpleasant. The

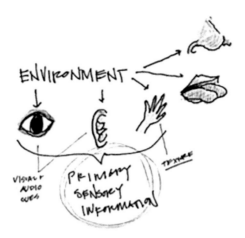

FIGURE 4.2 Five of seven senses. Image courtesy of Dax Morton, 2020.

appraisal of the situation is the first step in making sense of the situation. Later, we will discuss coping and how design may support individual and collective coping and therefore, resiliency.

With practice we have the ability to tap into our brains' neuroplasticity to improve our coping skills to handle perceived stresses. The term "perceived stress" is used here because it is not uncommon for experiences that are not inherently dangerous or risky to be perceived as such, resulting in stress. The threat may not be real, but our bodies still process this information in a way that causes harm to our physical systems, our bodies and minds. We may make a series of less optimal choices that feed into a loop of unhealthy behaviors, all originating from the perception that we are under threat.

Let's also keep in mind that there are different types of stress (experienced in our body) and stressors (external forces). In addition to the commonly experienced negative-version of stress—"distress"—stress can also be a positive factor. Healthy stress is called "**eustress**" and it can be health promoting [5]. For instance, having some internal pressure to rise in the morning occurs because of morning cortisol elevation, as well as external demands and eagerness to face the day. The cortisol and adrenaline morning surge, along with our own agenda, work together to prompt us into action. We can feel a short-term boost of focus and experience a feeling of excitement that motivates us to perform. When we skip breakfast to jump right in on an important task, we stay alert as we sit at our desk, feeling slight hunger, but also leveraging adrenaline and dopamine, the hormone that motivates us to learn and to strive for something. After we take a morning break, eat some food and return to our desk, we may feel less attentive to the task at hand, having eaten and now struggling with the "rest and digest" part of our physiological process.

Another common way to understand stress, and to provide more clarity, is to define stress as either chronic or acute. Chronic means sustained and ongoing, such as being in quarantine during a pandemic, while acute stress occurs over a shorter and more finite time period, such as a move or catching a flight.

Ideally, through design, we can foster a positive dynamic between the two types of stress—eustress and distress—positive stress and negative stress. Stimuli originating from outside the individual are subject to design interventions, and thus present us with opportunities to improve experiences and outcomes. Thoughtful design grounded in evidence can facilitate more eustressing states of mind (pleasant thoughts prompted by lovely stimuli such as songbirds at a feeder and windchimes occasionally clanging).

Design features from our built environment received through our senses (especially vision) influence our state of mind and nervous system through appraisal and neuroception before we even realize we are being influenced. This is supported by the latest neuroscience research, as "sensory events can arrive in our awareness already pre-labeled as 'potential threats' or 'neutral'" [6]. Attending to this preconscious process can make the difference in how a space is perceived, influencing the wellbeing of occupants and the quality of activity that takes place.

Internal stressors can be mediated with evidence-based design strategies that support stress-reduction. Our amygdala is the brain area which manages our emotions. Author and Psychologist Daniel Goleman coined the phrase "amygdala hijacking" for instances when the amygdala has detected a threat and reacts—often in a very inappropriate manner for our modern cultural expectations [7, 8]. When we overreact and later say, "What was I thinking?" we have likely experienced an amygdala hijacking. When designers understand the concept of "sensory load," such as the nature of stimuli in a space, combined with our emotional responses and reactions, they are empowered to facilitate a distress-neutral space. We can leverage interior design to facilitate the ongoing skill building of emotional intelligence. As a result, when a situation is seen as less of a threat by the amygdala, the emotional and thinking brain can make better choices. We will explore more design-specific stress-reduction and tolerance-increasing options later in this chapter, but first, let's take a deeper dive into stress and human functioning.

Stress and Human Functioning: Brief History, Disease and Definitions

Here is a closer look at our current understanding of stress. The term is typically used to describe human ailment. The term was originally limited to physics, to describe a "physical strain on a body," before the definition was expanded in the early 19th century. Stress, as we know it today, can be incidental (acute), prolonged, systemic or chronic. For example, a bout of the flu is incidental, or acute; a pandemic, or a chronic condition is prolonged, racism is systemic, and pollution is chronic. Stress does not live in a vacuum, though, and our ability to handle stressors is known as "resilience." Resilience is an individual, community or system's capacity to respond to stressors without loss of homeostasis. Greater resilience implies an ability to respond effectively to high levels of stress. It is possible for a person, or a system, to expand its "window of tolerance" [9]. Our window is the span between hyperarousal and hypoarousal, in which we can operate at an optimal level. If we move outside of our window, the likely response is either rigidity or chaos—and not harmonious or well-adapted. The proverbial straw that broke the camel's back.

This modern integration of neuroscience into our daily lives has helped to improve our understanding of stress, and how we experience it. The central nervous system processes sensory input in tandem with all other biological systems. Our neurophysiology evolved to protect us from regular threatening occurrences, which are no longer common, such as immediate risk-of-life dangers. Our ancestors were limited to functioning in coordination with the sun, whereas modern humans have modified this practice with electric lighting. Our ability to preserve food with refrigeration, or other means, has created a different range of caloric options than were available to early humans, who were subject to regular feast/fast cycles.

Stress as a human health concept was first advanced by Dr. Hans Selye, a medical doctor who borrowed the term from the field of physics and adapted it to describe his observations. In his patients he noticed a common response or physiological process experienced as stress [10]. Dr. Selye was one of the first to link the stress response to the hypothalamic-pituitary-adrenal

(HPA) axis. The HPA involves first the release of adrenaline and norepinephrine and then cortisol, each of which serves a role in creating optimal conditions for us to manage acute (short-term) stress. Dr. Selye developed the General Adaptation Syndrome (GAS) theory, the process of first having an "alarm reaction," followed by a stance of "resistance" and then a state of "exhaustion." He brought this theory to wider prominence based on his scientific studies, and although other academics, such as William James, had previously investigated the role of energy and exhaustion on human states, it was Selye who focused on the biochemical mediators and our ability to adapt to stress [11].

Our current understanding of the stress and adaptation cycle has evolved into both a more clear and a more complex understanding. The field of positive psychology, for instance, has expanded in both popularity and credibility over the past two decades, with a four times increase in publications centered on a perspective of factors that enable individuals and communities to thrive. Investigations of resilience and adaptation explore factors which help humans to rebound after a crisis, as well as how to develop a growth-mindset around human stress experiences.

We now know how stress activates hormones, neurotransmitters and other stress responses in a complicated system of communication to help protect us, and we know what effect both acute and chronic stresses have on our feelings of health or dis-ease.

There is ample evidence that repeated adrenaline and cortisol secretions, resulting from the alarm reaction phase as outlined in the GAS, can lead to uneven blood vessel interiors and make blockages more likely [12]. Chronic stress impairs the immune system which declines in functionality, consequently reducing energy supply for the body's stress response, affecting blood pressure, ability to focus or rest and affecting behavioral choices [13].

Trauma creates a chronically stressed condition. Trauma (and other types of chronic stress responses) occurs when stress remains unresolved and allostasis, or internal balance, is not restored. This relates back to the General Adaptation Syndrome theory, where the resistance stage is extended beyond the body's ability to resolve, and the individual adjusts to a higher baseline level of stress. This causes continued secretion of cortisol (reactive cortisol, which goes beyond the body's natural and necessary resting cortisol levels), resulting in a cascade of physical and emotional consequences. A person becomes "stuck" in the fight/flight/freeze response, believing that all sensory input is a threat.

The nervous system is organized into two main "branches," also known as the HPA axis, as mentioned previously. The two branches are the sympathetic system and the parasympathetic system. The sympathetic system corresponds to bodily functions that help prepare us for either fight or flight. Many stress researchers also support the concept that a person in a stressful situation may also adapt by responding with a freeze or fawn response—hiding and hoping not to be located (dissociation) or trying to please and soothe the one creating the stress through accommodation [14]. The second HPA branch is the parasympathetic system, which, when activated, provides calm and relaxed feelings. This is also known as the "rest and digest" or "feed and breed" mode. Para comes from the word "beside" and is seen in the nervous system as longer, slower nerves that extend around the sympathetic system, also related to the vagus nerve, which will be discussed shortly.

One way to picture the parasympathetic system is as the nerves wrapping around us, like a soothing hug, which relaxes our digestion (we salivate more), cools us off, calms us down and slows our heartbeat. If you are about to give a public talk, your mouth becomes dry, as the sympathetic system takes over and tries to "protect" you from the threat. The butterflies you feel are your digestive track shutting down, to concentrate on circulating air and blood. Only the essential life-supporting bodily functions are prioritized, to enable you to either "fight" or "flee." In this way a balanced HPA axis is essential in creating a healthy system.

People who experience "toxic stress" have a dysregulated HPA system. The sympathetic system is engaged far more than the relaxing parasympathetic system. Toxic stress is a term used to describe institutionalized stressors such as those found in abusive relationships. Living under toxic stress conditions is often associated with both physical and mental diseases. This is due to the fact that the HPA also oversees the secretion of cortisol which, when consistently elevated, is associated with changes to the immune system, increasing infection and inflammation. If this cycle continues, people are more likely to manifest Type 2 diabetes, obesity and cardiovascular disease. Additionally, sustained elevated cortisol levels tend to lead to memory and cognition issues, depression and other metabolic conditions, as well as an elevated HPA axis response cycle [15]. This is especially well documented in the seminal adverse childhood experiences (ACE) study led by Felitti et al. [16]. For more on trauma-informed design specifically, see Harte & Roche (2020) or visit traumainformeddesign.org [17].

Coping strategies vary based on age and life experiences [18]. Recent evidence indicates that mature adults use more proactive coping behaviors to deal with minor hassles in their daily lives, resolving these problems before they become stressful, than do younger adults [19]. This is the case despite the frequency of reported stressors being consistent between both age groups. Thus proactive coping is an effective adaptation to stress. How can we design our spaces, our buildings and our streetscapes to better support proactive coping, on an individual scale as well as on a systems scale?

Stress and Systems Health

It is well known that communities experience stress in a different but related way from individuals. Factors that impact individual resilience include personal agency and the quality of relationships. Factors that impact systemic resilience are these same elements, plus access to resources and energy transfer, such as a multiplicity of response options and support networks. It makes sense for us to discuss design's role in systems-wide stressors, such as the COVID-19 pandemic, as well as cultural stress, such as political uncertainty. First, let's frame this section with a definition of health equity, by the Robert Wood Johnson Foundation (RWJF): "Health equity means increasing opportunities for everyone to live the healthiest life possible, no matter who we are, where we live, or how much money we make" [20].

The Center for Disease Control (CDC) joined the American Medical Association and over 170 other organizations, in April 2021, in stating that racism is a "serious public health threat" [21].

The systemic inequities that are coded into past policies of community development are responsible for massive systemic stressors. One has only to begin understanding the principles behind redlining, for instance, to see that environmental stressors and environmental racism are in need of immediate intervention. Historic redlining involves ranking certain neighborhoods on a scale and disapproving loans to non-dominant groups for home purchases in the higher ranking neighborhoods. The consequences are devastating and on-going over many generations. Preterm birth, negative health outcomes and higher maternal death rates are all correlated with historical redlining and systemic racism [22–24].

There seems to be no limit to the systemic stress that can occur. Lead poisoning is 100 percent preventable, gravely disabling and disproportionately affects marginalized communities [25]. Black students in the U.S. experience higher levels of trauma from seeing police violence towards black people on the media, and share the burden with other Black activists, of "racial battle fatigue," than do white counterparts [26]. People who experience a natural or man-made disaster in their region also experience system-wide stress, which is moderated by positive social bonds [27].

Populations living in areas where environmental racism has been institutionalized, who experience limited access to nourishing food, healthy places to play, interesting and aesthetically pleasing places to explore, biophilic environments, meaningful work opportunities, cultural enrichment, appropriate medical facilities and quality education are not faring as well as those who have access to these things; those who do not live under the mantle of racism or anti-ism. It is evident that systemic stress, which creates higher than ideal allostatic loads for marginalized people, especially women of color, contributes to higher death rates and increased toll from

FIGURE 4.3 JUSTICEscape Privilege and Pedagogy. Image courtesy of Nina Briggs and Corey Norman.

the coronavirus, for example [28]. Food apartheid alone is sufficient to create systemic health inequities [29]. Between lax legislation, lack of sufficient testing and research, indifference and housing discrimination, these problems will persist until there is sufficient political sea change and direct action by the design and architecture community.

Many important architecture and design thought leaders are working tirelessly to express, unpack, dismantle, teach and reframe systemic stress from multiple viewpoints [30–33]. Hundreds of anti-racist de-colonizing design resources lists have been offered since the death of George Floyd in the spring of 2020 [34]. Ongoing systemic racism is creating untold health effects on our fellow citizens, and therefore on ourselves, and change is afoot.

Armed with these insights, the architect and designer must continue (or start) to create an equitable, appropriately represented, just, culturally enriched and healthy society, through the intentional, EBD, anti-racist programming and design of buildings, neighborhoods and cities. Applying design opportunities for social cohesion and stress mitigation are more important than ever, and a starting point for systems-level stress reduction (Figure 4.3).

Fundamentals of Resilience: Lowering Baseline Stress, Increasing Tolerance, Hormesis, and Community Examples

Let's shift from the systemic-level stress conversation back to the individual-level stress adaptation process. Stress reduction can be supported by spaces that offer opportunities for self- and co-regulation. The skill of re-regulation is achieved through manipulation of the vagus nerve, which is a key biological network that can be accessed by design to increase opportunities for self-soothing. The vagus, whose name is etymologically related to the word "wandering," is the longest neural system in our body, connecting all vital organs, and has been linked to the fight/flight/freeze response. Stephen Porges introduced the polyvagal perspective in 1994 to describe the autonomic nervous system (including the HPA axis) as one that can adapt and be linked to behavior [35]. If appropriate practices are implemented with consistency, a person is able to tone their vagus nerve over the course of days or weeks, thereby increasing their tolerance to stress and enhancing their resilience. The result? Using attunement and reciprocity, with our voices and facial expressions, we can achieve feelings of safety, which then leads to resilience and re-regulation of our nervous systems [36].

Social cohesion/connection has much to do with resilience, as well as the meaning-making process that precedes and follows a stressful or traumatic experience [36]. Multiple people can experience the "same" trauma while some stay "traumatized" and others rebound quickly and easily. Could our resilience be the result of healthy relationships? Many research studies indicate this is the case. Positive social support and healthy attachments create a buffer effect for human stress and wellbeing. For instance, neighborhoods with attributes that promote social cohesion and a sense of safety show a significantly higher likelihood of reporting less perceived stress [37].

Do you ever feel stressed out because you feel wired and can't sleep? Or groggy and can't focus and be attentive to an important task? Our circadian clocks have so much to do with our alertness, and design grounded in EBD can modulate this animal function. Neuroscientists have recently located a dynamic in our brains called the melanopsin pathway [38]. This pathway is associated with activating our circadian rhythm systems. Humans have a primary circadian "clock"—a central pacemaker—located in our brains (part of the hypothalamus), with related "clocks" that coordinate with this main pacemaker. These circadian clocks are located in the liver, lungs and kidneys, as well as a few other bodily locations [39]. This circadian system, when primed with appropriate and sufficiently bright daylighting first thing in the morning on a regular basis, can help us feel more awake when we want to be alert, and more restful when we want to be asleep. One reason this happens is because of the increase in dopamine that our bodies release with regular sufficient and appropriate sunlight exposure [40]. This explains why people (and animals) tend to feel happier and more energetic in the summer.

One means of designing spaces to support this daily process is to provide positive destinations to encourage people to go outside the first hour or two after they rise each morning. Also a reduction in exposure to short-wave blue-light later in the day is consistent with our circadian wiring. This can be done by limiting direct overhead lighting and reducing the time spent in front of blue-light emitting screens. Managing our light exposure each day helps diminish depression, increase feelings of wellbeing and promote more rejuvenating sleep and attentive alert states [41]. Spatial design can encourage options for exposure to sufficient daylight, ideally not through windows, which reduce the amount of light photons that enter our retinal ganglion cells [42]. An added benefit in choosing to dim bright lights later in the day is the opportunity to exert personal agency over the environment [43].

Design Applications to Promote Resilience

With a growing understanding of how our built environment and our central nervous systems interact with each other we now turn our attention to further design opportunities. Design offers specificity of sensory input, including increased stimulation with positive distractors or beautiful aesthetics, and respite spaces to allow a break from overstimulation. Design can support a person's daily self-care tools or practices, such as light/dark control to support sleep and circadian cycles, mindfulness, nutritional choices, breathing patterns and movement.

Designing spaces that create a neutral sensory exposure or positive sensory input will help foster a sense of safety, comfort and reassurance—all arriving in our systems subliminally. Other than facial recognition our state of calmness or excitation is a background frequency responding to environmental cues. Just as there are differences between individuals in preferences about color or density, so too are we different in our abilities to screen or filter our sensory environment. For instance, some people become anxious at the sound of a TV in the background, whereas having ambient soft music on at all times can be very soothing. We all screen our environments on an ongoing basis, in the process of appraisal discussed earlier (Figure 4.4).

Spaces can support better quality sleep, referred to as "sleep hygiene" [44]. Many people seek specific spaces to support a meditation, yoga or breathwork practice, time with family, or a dedicated place for play (hobbies or games) and rest (reading nooks, bird-watching). Activities such as yoga or breathwork sessions that span the entire arc of the stress experience, including self-induced increase in stress or resolution, serve the individual or community by reducing allostatic load. There is direct measurable gain in cardiovascular health with stress resolution, as well as improvement in cognitive experience, together with increases in self-confidence, **agency** and control over physiological and emotional states.

Why are spaces with a biophilic element effective? Once we have a basic understanding of how our eyes connect to our nervous system to take in and interpret visual sensory information we can better understand the intuitive design sensibility. Spaces that have a balanced level of neutral visual stimuli with captivating views have been shown to be beneficial for health outcomes [45].

The more we learn to toggle attention between focus (spotlighted attention) and restoration (alert relaxation), the more a sense of control over emotional status is experienced. When one can deliberately activate attentive focus on demand, and then activate "rest" mode when it is time to release effort, the more stress reduction is prompted [46]. This process of "task switching" is a learned skill that the designed environment can support for all occupants.

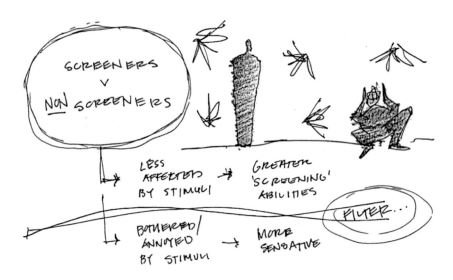

FIGURE 4.4 Screeners versus non-screeners. Image courtesy of Dax Morton, 2020.

Roger Ulrich's famous experiment (1984) with gallbladder surgery patients established the basis for evidence-based design. We can expand the conclusions from this study to infer possible additional neurological mechanisms that may be at work in this study. It has been shown that eye movement can influence one's state of mind. When one is experiencing an acute stressor, such as a challenging conversation with one's boss, the eyes will focus directly on the "danger" (focal vision), as a response to a felt sense of threat. Research in the biophilia realm has demonstrated our reactions to positions of "prospect," which encourage a soft, sweeping eye-gaze, inform our central nervous systems that "all is well here, I can see any oncoming dangers and can remain hidden from predators."

Eye movement's connection to our mental state has become an important tool in helping people recover from post-traumatic stress disorder and other acute stressors, using the EMDR approach [47]. EMDR employs an eye-movement desensitization and reprocessing approach that has been shown to have positive benefits on health and wellbeing. It makes sense, then, that design features and space plans with sitelines that encourage gentle sweeping gaze (panoramic viewing) will express to the brain that all is well, and one is safe. The healing impact of views to nature in the hospital may not be solely about seeing nature. Feeling secure from a prospect position, with softly focused, sweeping eye-gaze providing a balm for the nervous system may also be a significant factor.

Along the lines of intentionally designing to activate our biological systems, let's consider the idea of hormesis, which is an intentional increase of environmental stressors, in mild to moderate doses, so as to build resilience [48]. The easiest way to understand this is through the activity of "exercise." We slightly stress ourselves, and then we grow stronger or more flexible [49]. Understanding that this is part of the stressor/stress/health equilibrium spectrum will help us achieve design that is beneficial for all occupants. This perspective suggests the advantages of tolerating some discomfort, as self-development often begins with something that feels unpleasant (e.g., sitting down to focus on writing a chapter, getting a vaccine, or creating a new habit of waking earlier to take a morning walk).

FIGURE 4.5 Stress and the mind. Image courtesy of Dax Morton, 2020.

Stress Reduction beyond the Individual

On the scale of community or region, similar principles for stress reduction and coping skill development can be considered—namely, seeking a homeostasis of sensory stimuli and increasing opportunities for stress tolerance through positive social bonds and tapping into our internal biological systems. This can include engineering opportunities to manage noise, vibration and social isolation, as well as sensory loads. Zoning and building code policies with a social infrastructure sensitivity can encourage safe neighborhood interactions, which bring about a greater sense of community, in turn, enhancing social resilience [50]. This can take the form of multi-generational housing or third spaces, such as a cafe, to create opportunities for residents to find common interests and reduce isolation. Just as we have moved from the segregation of uses to a preference for specific mixed-use opportunities, our codes can begin to reflect the lessons of neuroscience and sociology around wellness and community-building.

Urban settings with clear wayfinding, pronounced imageability (clear mental image of object or space) and **emotional nourishment** will encourage positive behavioral changes and enhance stress reduction while promoting resilience. Because forward motion alleviates feelings of anxiety, having places to go and things to do, to connect socially or to disconnect and self-regulate, and to recover and experience restoration, all constitute **affordances** for stress reduction. As Ruggles [51] says, "beauty is a physical reaction to a pattern that conveys the emotion of pleasure." The experience of beauty infuses the central nervous system with a sense of wellbeing, reducing allostatic load and enhancing resilience. A built environment expressing social cohesion and the appreciation of beauty, including the beauty of our own biological neural wiring, not only reflects on the cultural context, it actually enhances it (Figure 4.5).

References

1. Guidi, J., Lucente, M., Sonino, N., & Fava, G. A. (2021). Allostatic load and its impact on health: A systematic review. *Psychotherapy and Psychosomatics*, 90(1), 11–27. https://doi.org/10.1159/000510696

2. Münzel, T., & Daiber, A. (2018). Environmental stressors and their impact on health and disease with focus on oxidative stress. *Antioxidants & Redox Signaling*, 28(9), 735–740. https://doi.org/10.1089/ars.2017.7488
3. Volbert, T., & Cupitt, L. (2013). What are the 7 Senses? 7 Senses Foundation. http://www.7senses.org.au/what-are-the-7-senses/
4. Lazarus, R. S. (1990). Theory-based stress measurement. *Psychological Inquiry*, 1, 3–13. https://doi.org/10.1207/s15327965pli0101_1
5. Lazarus, R. S. (1993). From psychological stress to the emotions: A history of changing outlooks. *Annual Review of Psychology*, 44(1), 1–22. https://www.annualreviews.org/doi/pdf/10.1146/annurev.ps.44.020193.000245
6. Yilmaz, M., & Huberman, A. D. (2019). Fear: It's all in your line of sight. *Current Biology*, 29(23), R1232–R1234. https://doi.org/10.1016/j.cub.2019.10.008
7. Goleman, D. (1995, 2005). *Emotional intelligence*. Bantam Books.
8. Salopek, J. J. (1998, October). Train your brain. *Training & Development*, 52(10), 26+. https://go.gale.com/ps/anonymous?id=GALE%7CA21244424&sid=googleScholar&v=2.1&it=r&linkaccess=abs&issn=10559760&p=AONE&sw=w
9. Siegel, D. J. (2010). *The mindful therapist: A clinician's guide to mindsight and neural integration* (Norton Series on Interpersonal Neurobiology). WW Norton & Company.
10. Krohne, H. W. (2002). Stress and coping theories. *International Encyclopedia of the Social Behavioral Sciences*, 22, 15163–15170. https://poliklinika-harni.hr/images/uploads/440/teorije-nastanka-stresa.pdf
11. Jackson M. (2014). Evaluating the role of Hans Selye in the modern history of stress. In D. Cantor & E. Ramsden (Eds). *Stress, shock, and adaptation in the Twentieth Century* (pp. iv–xiv). University of Rochester Press.
12. Patterson, M. (2019). The brain on stress: How trauma, depression, and chronic stress alter brain function. National Center of Continuing Education, Inc. https://www.nursece.com/courses/88-the-brain-on-stress-how-trauma-depression-and-chronic-stress-alter-brain-function
13. Ibid.
14. Walker, P. (2014). *Complex PTSD: From surviving to thriving*. Azure Coyote.
15. Dingman, M. (2014, June 4). Know your brain: HPA axis. Neuroscientifically challenged. https://www.neuroscientificallychallenged.com/blog/2014/5/31/what-is-the-hpa-axis
16. Felitti, V. J., Anda, R. F., Nordenberg, D., Williamson, D. F., Spitz, A. M., Edwards, V., Koss, M. P., & Marks, J. S. (1998). Relationship of childhood abuse and household dysfunction to many of the leading causes of death in adults: The Adverse Childhood Experiences (ACE) Study. *American Journal of Preventive Medicine*, 14(4), 245–258. https://doi.org/10.1016/S0749-3797(98)00017-8
17. Harte, J. D., & Roche, J. (2021). Form follows feeling: Trauma-informed design and the future of interior spaces. ArchDaily. https://youtu.be/PQjlBwPlW8s
18. Prenderville, J. A., Kennedy, P. J., Dinan, T. G., & Cryan, J. F. (2015). Adding fuel to the fire: The impact of stress on the ageing brain. *Trends in Neurosciences*, 38(1), 13–25. https://doi.org/10.1016/j.tins.2014.11.001
19. Neubauer, A. B., Smyth, J. M., & Sliwinski, M. J. (2019). Age differences in proactive coping with minor hassles in daily life. *The Journals of Gerontology: Series B*, 74(1), 7–16. https://doi.org/10.1093/geronb/gby061
20. Braveman, P., Arkin. E, Orleans, T., Proctor, D., & Plough, A. (2017, May 1). What is health equity? Robert Wood Johnson Foundation. https://www.rwjf.org/en/library/research/2017/05/what-is-health-equity-.html
21. Wamsley, L. (2021). CDC Director Declares Racism 'A Serious Public Health Threat'. NPR. https://www.npr.org/2021/04/08/985524494/cdc-director-declares-racism-a-serious-public-health-threat
22. Mendez, D. D., Hogan, V. K., & Culhane, J. F. (2014). Institutional racism, neighborhood factors, stress, and preterm birth. *Ethnicity & Health*, 19(5), 479–499.
23. Thomas, M. D., Michaels, E. K., Reeves, A. N., Okoye, U., Price, M. M., Hasson, R. E., Chae, D. H., & Allen, A. M. (2019). Differential associations between everyday versus institution-specific racial discrimination, self-reported health, and allostatic load among black women: Implications for clinical assessment and epidemiologic studies. *Annals of Epidemiology*, 35, 20–28.
24. Lister, R. L., Drake, W., Scott, B. H., & Graves, C. (2019). Black maternal mortality-the elephant in the room. *World Journal of Gynecology & Womens Health*, 3(1). https://doi.org/10.33552/wjgwh.2019.03.000555
25. IHCDesign. (2020). The changing reality of disability in America: 2020. https://youtu.be/lHK7wjPXHH8
26. Hotchkins, B. K., & Dancy, T. (2017). A house is not a home: Black students' responses to racism in university residential halls. *Journal of College & University Student Housing*, 43(3), 42–53.

27. McGuire, A. P., Gauthier, J. M., Anderson, L. M., Hollingsworth, D. W., Tracy, M., Galea, S., & Coffey, S. F. (2018). Social support moderates effects of natural disaster exposure on depression and posttraumatic stress disorder symptoms: Effects for displaced and nondisplaced residents. *Journal of Traumatic Stress*, 31(2), 223–233.
28. Washington, H. A. (2020). How environmental racism is fuelling the coronavirus pandemic. *Nature*, 241–241. https://www.nature.com/articles/d41586-020-01453-y
29. Reese, A. M. (2019). *Black food geographies: Race, self-reliance, and food access in Washington, DC*. University of North Carolina Press, ISBN 978-1-4696-5150-7
30. Briggs, N. M. (2020). JUSTICEscape. https://www.justicescape.com/
31. Gibson, E. (2020, Oct 12). Lesley Lokko resigns as dean of architecture at New York's City College in "profound act of self-preservation." https://www.dezeen.com/2020/10/12/lesley-lokko-resigns-black-dean-new-york-city-college/#:~:text=Scottish%2DGhanaian%20architect%20Lesley%20Lokko,of%20empathy%20for%20black%20women
32. Lorenzo, D. (2020, Aug 19). How OCAD's Dori Tunstall is rewriting the rules of design education. FastCompany. https://www.fastcompany.com/90541079/how-ocad-us-dori-tunstall-is-rewriting-the-rules-of-design-education
33. Wilkins, C. (2007). *The aesthetics of equity: Notes on race, space, architecture, and music*. University of Minnesota Press.
34. https://placesjournal.org/reading-list/resources-on-anti-racism/?cn-reloaded=1&cn-reloaded=1
35. Porges, S. W. (2017). *Norton series on interpersonal neurobiology. The pocket guide to the polyvagal theory: The transformative power of feeling safe*. W W Norton & Co.
36. Peavey, E., & Cai, H. (2020). A systems framework for understanding the environment's relation to clinical teamwork: A systematic literature review of empirical studies. *Environment and Behavior*, 52(7), 726–760. https://doi.org/10.1177/0013916518815535
37. Henderson, H., Child, S., Moore, S., Moore, J. B., & Kaczynski, A. T. (2016). The influence of neighborhood aesthetics, safety, and social cohesion on perceived stress in disadvantaged communities. *American Journal of Community Psychology*, 58(1–2), 80–88.
38. Lucas, R. J., Peirson, S. N., Berson, D. M., Brown, T. M., Cooper, H. M., Czeisler, C. A., Figueiro, M. G., Gamlin, P. D., Lockley, S. W., O'Hagan, J. B., & Price, L. L. (2014). Measuring and using light in the melanopsin age. *Trends in Neurosciences*, 37(1), 1–9. https://doi.org/10.1016/j.tins.2013.10.004
39. LeGates, T. A., Fernandez, D. C., & Hattar, S. (2014). Light as a central modulator of circadian rhythms, sleep and affect. *Nature Reviews Neuroscience*, 15(7), 443–454. https://doi.org/10.1038/nrn3743
40. Arns, M., Swanson, J. M., & Arnold, L. E. (2018). ADHD prevalence: Altitude or sunlight? Better understanding the interrelations of dopamine and the circadian system. *Journal of Attention Disorders*, 22(2), 163–166. https://doi.org/10.1177/1087054715599574
41. LeGates, T. A., Fernandez, D. C., & Hattar, S. (2014). Light as a central modulator of circadian rhythms, sleep and affect. *Nature Reviews Neuroscience*, 15(7), 443–454. https://doi.org/10.1038/nrn3743
42. Hraška, J., Hanuliak, P., Hartman, P., Zeman, M., & Stebelová, K. (2014). Comparative study of window glazing systems influence on melatonin secretion in patients in the hospital wards. In *Advanced Materials Research* (Vol. 899, pp. 288–293). Trans Tech Publications Ltd.
43. Lucas, R. J., Peirson, S. N., Berson, D. M., Brown, T. M., Cooper, H. M., Czeisler, C. A., Figueiro, M. G., Gamlin, P. D., Lockley, S. W., O'Hagan, J. B., & Price, L. L. (2014). Measuring and using light in the melanopsin age. *Trends in Neurosciences*, 37(1), 1–9. https://doi.org/10.1016/j.tins.2013.10.004
44. Walker, M. (2017). *Why we sleep: The new science of sleep and dreams*. Simon & Schuster.
45. Ulrich, R. S. (1984). View through a window may influence recovery from surgery. *Science*, 224(4647), 420–421. https://doi.org/10.1126/science.6143402
46. Huberman, A. (2021b). Using science to optimize sleep, learning & metabolism. Huberman Lab Podcast. https://youtu.be/nwSkFq4tyC0
47. Shapiro, F. (2017). *Eye movement desensitization and reprocessing (EMDR) therapy: Basic principles, protocols, and procedures*. Guilford Publications.
48. Calabrese, V., Scuto, M., & Calabrese, E. J. (2020). Hormesis, resilience and mental health: Enhancing public health and therapeutic options. In J. Sholl & S. I. Rattan (Eds). *Explaining health across the sciences. Healthy ageing and longevity* (Vol. 12, pp. 497–520). Springer. https://doi.org/10.1007/978-3-030-52663-4_28
49. Rattan, S. I., & Demirovic, D. (2010). Hormesis can and does work in humans. *Dose-Response*, 8(1), dose-response.
50. Klinenberg, E. (2018). *Palaces for the people: How social infrastructure can help fight inequality, polarization, and the decline of civic life*. Crown.
51. Ruggles, D. H. (2017). *Beauty, neuroscience & architecture*. Fibonacci. 87.

PART 2
Buildings

5
PROGRAMMING FOR PEOPLE

Keely Menezes, MPH

> As our appreciation for the importance of design in human wellbeing increases it becomes ever clearer that various populations are underserved by environmental affordances. This is a form of discrimination that creates stress, shame, and low self-esteem while limiting options to the affected groups and individuals. The author makes the case that a practice of universal design informed by careful understanding of human factors will benefit all of us through unintended consequences and greater social equity.

Lara Americo is an artist and musician. She lives in New York City, where she is the proud parent to a family of sweet potato plants. She identifies as queer and transgender, and when she is out and about, it can be stressful to find a public restroom she feels comfortable using. She shared her experience in an interview with Rolling Stone:

> "You stand outside the bathroom for maybe a minute or two to make sure no one is coming out or no one is coming in. Then you go inside and if you hear someone, you just look down and hope they don't look at your face…. You run into the stall and you lock the door as fast as you can, and then you do what you have to do. If you hear someone walk in, or you hear someone else in there, you have to wait until they leave. Once you hear that they are gone, you can run out. Washing your hands is a difficult situation because it takes time, so hopefully you brought disinfectant [1]."

She has other options, too. None of them are ideal. She could use the restroom that corresponds with the gender she was assigned at birth, at the risk of disapproving glances, hateful remarks or potentially, violence. She could see if she can find an all-gender restroom, and in the meantime, just hold it. And hold it.

It is not uncommon for trans individuals and other gender minorities to feel like public spaces do not serve them. Professor Susan Stryker, who transitioned more than 20 years ago, still finds herself looking over her shoulder when she enters public restrooms and other sex-segregated spaces. Stryker calls this added mindfulness, added stress, added risk of altercation "the tax." She says, "you get taxed for just walking around, being trans in the world" [2].

Gender minorities are not the only people who are required to pay this metaphorical tax, simply because their environment was not built to accommodate them. In bathrooms alone,

DOI: 10.4324/9781003164418-8

people in wheelchairs pay the tax of the inevitable splashback from handwashing over countertops that are not low enough for use from a seated position. People who are breastfeeding pay the tax of cramped bathroom stalls often being the only area where they are guaranteed privacy. People who wash their feet before prayer pay the tax of uncomfortably folding their bodies to do so in waist-height sinks.

This phenomenon does not begin and end with bathrooms. Our built environment as a whole was largely designed to serve a narrow slice of humanity: people who are able-bodied, healthy, average height, average weight, atheist, sober, literate. In constructing our built landscape, we cannot view the mean, median or mode of the human condition as an adequate basis for design decisions. Not when doing so costs the people our structures serve their dignity, their safety or their peace of mind.

The architectural programming process has the power to set goals for the world we move through. It has long done so in terms of functional capacity and economic outputs, but these measures can lose sight of what building projects are really meant to facilitate: the lives of people. Increased focus on capital in development projects has resulted in programming metrics with a skewed sense of value. Great design affords the ability for all people to flourish in the built world as inherently valuable, and worthy of the utmost priority.

Universal Design

A framework that may be helpful in applying this notion to practice is that of **universal design**. Interchangeable with "inclusive design" and "human-centered design," the terms refer to the "design and composition of an environment so that it can be accessed, understood, and used to the greatest extent by all people regardless of their age, size, ability or disability" [3]. Rather than seeing our built environment being suited to serve all people as a component luxury, the **principles of universal design** see this as being an integral characteristic of good design.

These principles are heavily influenced by the Americans with Disabilities Act of 1990, which is a landmark piece of civil rights legislation offering legal protections against discrimination for people with disabilities. The passage of the ADA reshaped the way the American landscape was required to accommodate and include people with disabilities and functional limitations. It massively expanded these individuals' license to occupy public space.

While the ADA marked the culmination of efforts by a watershed movement, and its positive effects continue to be felt today, universal design sees the ADA not as an end, but as a beginning. Today, more than one quarter of Americans are living with a disability [4]. As we live longer, this number continues to increase. Rather than accessibility being an addendum or an asterisk, it is an essential element in the fabric of our built environment, and the starting point for design solutions that benefit all of us.

The Seven Principles of Universal Design were put forth in 1997 by a team of designers, engineers, and architects led by Ronald Mace [5]. They are as follows, accompanied by examples and relevant guidelines:

Principle 1: Equitable Use: The design does not stigmatize or disadvantage any group of users.

- 1a. Provides the same means of use for all users: identical whenever possible; equivalent when not.
- 1b. Avoids segregating or stigmatizing any users.
- 1c. Makes provisions for privacy, security, and safety equally available to all users.
- 1d. Makes the design appealing to all users.

    For example, all people are welcome to use the same vehicles for public transportation, and entryways and seating have expanded options that facilitate this. Or, wherever staircases are offered, elevators are offered as well, and are not significantly inconvenient or challenging to locate.

Principle 2: Flexibility in Use: The design accommodates a wide range of individual preferences and abilities.

2a. Provides choice in methods of use.
2b. Accommodates right- or left-handed access and use.
2c. Facilitates the user's accuracy and precision.
2d. Provides adaptability to the user's pace.

For example, countertops and desktops are of varying heights. Seating is light, durable, and movable, and features such as height and armrest position are varied or can be adjusted. Areas of high stimulation are abutted by areas of low stimulation. Space is available off of transit corridors to allow for conversation or rest. Lighting is able to be changed to adjust brightness or glare.

Principle 3: Simple and Intuitive Use: Use of the design is easy to understand, regardless of the user's experience, knowledge, language skills or current concentration level.

3a. Eliminates unnecessary complexity.
3b. Is consistent with user expectations and intuition.
3c. Accommodates a wide range of literacy and language skills.
3d. Arranges information consistent with its importance.
3e. Provides effective prompting and feedback during and after task completion.

For example, instructions provide a combination of written language and symbols, and writing incorporates plain language principles. Multiple language options are available without diminished experience. Space organization and wayfinding cues make navigation simple and intuitive.

Principle 4: Perceptible Information: The design communicates necessary information effectively to the user, regardless of ambient conditions or the user's sensory abilities.

4a. Uses different modes (pictorial, verbal, tactile) for redundant presentation of essential information.
4b. Provides adequate contrast between essential information and its surroundings.
4c. Maximizes "legibility" of essential information.
4d. Differentiates elements in ways that can be described (i.e., make it easy to give instructions or directions).
4e. Provides compatibility with a variety of techniques or devices used by people with sensory limitations.

For example, important information is relayed through engaging multiple senses, such as crosswalk indicators using a combination of visual and aural cues, or train platforms using brightly colored tactile paving. Written communication uses large font sizes, symbols and appropriate levels of contrast. Structurally similar areas of buildings are differentiated by distinct colors or material finishes.

Principle 5: Tolerance for Error: The design minimizes hazards and the adverse consequences of accidental or unintended actions.

5a. Arranges elements to minimize hazards and errors: most used elements are most accessible; hazardous elements are eliminated, isolated or shielded.

5b. Provides warnings of hazards and errors.
5c. Provides fail safe features.
5d. Discourages unconscious action in tasks that require vigilance.
   For example, elevator doors bounce back when obstructed. Walkways are level. Doors are light and do not close quickly. Emergency response information is relayed in a variety of methods.

Principle 6: Low Physical Effort: The design can be used efficiently and comfortably and with a minimum of fatigue.

6a. Allows the user to maintain a neutral body position.
6b. Uses reasonable operating forces.
6c. Minimizes repetitive actions.
6d. Minimizes sustained physical effort.
   For example, motion-sensing doors are used at the entrance of a building. Entrances are smooth and at ground-level. Clear lines of sight are provided. Levered handles are used instead of turning knobs. Fire alarm pulls do not require two hands.

Principle 7: Size and Space for Approach and Use: Appropriate size and space is provided for approach, reach, manipulation and use regardless of the user's body size, posture or mobility.

7a. Provides a clear line of sight to important elements for any seated or standing user.
7b. Makes reach to all components comfortable for any seated or standing user.
7c. Accommodates variations in hand and grip size.
7d. Provides adequate space for the use of assistive devices or personal assistance.
   For example, seats on buses, in theaters, or in classrooms are of multiple sizes. Floor plans include open areas which individuals with wheelchairs, strollers and bicycles may occupy. Doorways are wide, and hallways and dead-ends have ample space for turning.

The Curb Cut Effect

While these guidelines are rooted in advocacy for those with disabilities, you may notice some of the examples denote benefits for other groups on the margins of design consideration. Comfortable spaces to rest along transit pathways without obtrusion: these directly benefit disabled individuals who may tire easily or require occasional decreases in environmental stimulation. But they might also benefit the traveler reading their map in an unfamiliar city, as well as the local who is late for work trying to move past them. Someone whose shoe has just come untied, someone who must respond to an urgent email. Someone who just received terrible news, someone who just received wonderful news.

This phenomenon is commonly referred to as the curb cut effect, when the design considerations for one group constitute positive externalities for groups wider than intended. It gets its name from curb cuts, the gentle concrete slopes that marry the sidewalk with the street. They began being poured by disability activists in rogue acts of **informal urbanism** during the 1970s and 1980s, then became mandated with the passage of the Americans with Disabilities Act. Originally intended to benefit wheelchair users, they immediately facilitated regular use by people pushing strollers, people pulling suitcases, people pushing carts, people on skateboards, people who are injured, the list goes on. The ADA was met with significant opposition over the costs its environmental changes would impose on taxpayers. But today we all benefit from the changes to our landscapes made by a broadened consideration of the human experience.

While the principle of the curb cut effect was inspired by environmental characteristics for the benefit of those with disabilities, it applies to all sorts of people-centered design interventions. Consider bike lanes. At the turn of the 21st century, New York City established an initiative to increase their saturation of bike lanes due to high rates of injury and fatality for cyclists riding throughout the city. Not only did they see the risk of serious injury for cyclists drop by 75 percent from 2000 to 2013, the risk of injury for pedestrians dropped by 40 percent as well [6]. Residents also reported observing safer driving behaviors on streets narrowed by bike lanes, activity levels increased in residents, and streets where these changes were made saw considerable rises in retail sales and property values. This was not only a public health victory, it was a community-level win, win, win situation.

Also consider some of the innovations made by Denise Resnik in developing First Place, an apartment complex in Phoenix intended to facilitate independent living for individuals across the autism spectrum [7]. They minimized sensory overload by using muted color palettes, heavily dampening acoustic reverberation, and offering ample low-arousal "escape" spaces. This was balanced by dedicated sensory rooms filled with color, texture, and tactile games and toys. There are common spaces where residents can gather, embellished by alcoves and window seats for anyone who may want to spend time with others but dislikes being at the center of the action. Shower controls are at the far end of the shower to reduce contact with water at too hot or too cold a temperature. Doorways to individual apartments are recessed from hallways to ease the transition between one's own space and public space. All of these elements combine to create an environment suited to serve the unique needs of many individuals with autism spectrum disorder. But does it not sound…great?

This type of thinking—seeing people-centered environmental changes as holding the potential for a cascade of positive externalities, rather than benefiting a minority at the expense of the majority—is essential in enhancing our built environment to the benefit of human wellbeing.

Redefining Disability

It is important to note that many people who qualify as having a disability do not consider themselves to be disabled. This belief is particularly salient in the Deaf community, where deafness is often viewed as a trait and a culture, not a limitation. Where deafness is a rich and varied way of experiencing the sensory environment; one that is not lesser than that of those who hear, just different.

DeafSpace is a term used to describe the minor alterations to the built environment a group of deaf people might make in order to create space for themselves. This could be re-orienting chairs to be in a circle to facilitate clear sightlines for a visual conversation. It could be drawing blinds to eliminate glare and backlighting. In 2005, architect Hansel Bauman created the DeafSpace Project (DSP) in conjunction with the Deaf Studies Department at Gallaudet University [8]. The DSP took this term to new heights, and established the *DeafSpace Guidelines*, a catalog of design elements that use the sensory experience of deafness to guide design.

The guidelines are connected by five concepts that are detailed below. Take the exploration of these concepts as an invitation to imagine a built environment that has been entirely shaped by the culture of deafness. An environment defined by the promotion of community building, visual language, personal safety and wellbeing. A world that is quieter, but no less vibrant.

Sensory Reach

Spatial orientation that allows for visual and tactile awareness. Information may be gleaned from the movement of shadows, the sensation of vibrations, or the reading of subtle cues in the expressions and positions of surrounding individuals. 360 degree spatial awareness allows for consistent personal orientation and increased ease of wayfinding. An appropriate balance of transparent materials that extend lines of sight and reflective materials that increase visual information are used throughout the space. Varying degrees of enclosure allow for an individual to feel secure from behind while absorbing the sensory environment before them.

Space & Proximity

Space that allows individuals to stand at a distance where they can see one another's facial expressions and full "signing space." This is typically a greater distance than individuals stand in spoken conversation. Space allows for conversation groups to grow in numbers without the compromise of visual connection. Seating is oriented circularly rather than linearly, and furniture is easily moved if necessary.

Mobility & Proximity

Transit spaces that allow for continued conversation. This includes wide distances for clear communication, as well as smooth, easily traversable surfaces that minimize hazards. Ramps are used in favor of stairs. Gathering space maintains wide channels so conversations may pass through without interruption.

Light & Color

Electric lighting and architectural elements that combine to provide soft, diffused light. Glare, patterned shadows, and backlighting are minimized. Lighting and window coverings can be configured throughout the day as needed. Cool colors that contrast skin tones are used to highlight visual communication cues and increase ease of wayfinding.

Acoustics

Sonic landscapes that are configured in a way that minimizes audial distraction, especially for those who use assistive hearing devices. Harsh reverberation caused by hard building materials can be distracting, and even painful. Acoustics are engineered to reduce the transfer of noise from distinct areas of the space. Noisy appliances such as HVAC systems are placed where they will cause the least disruption.

There are commonalities between these concepts and the principles of universal design. They build on one another, put forth a vision for a built environment defined by ease and comfort. The potential for rich sensory experiences and flexible use shows us that the "normal" way of doing things might be a painfully narrow way to see the world.

The way we conceptualize disability is as social as it is physiological. We see differences among us as grounds for exclusion, we establish in-groups and out-groups, we create policies and programs that segregate and stigmatize. And all the while, in the same context, we plan and construct buildings. And so, our built environment is a macrocosm of our flawed social schema.

Perhaps no individual person is disabled, rather they are met with an environment that is disabling. Perhaps the primary modalities of accommodation are a more salient reflection of power differentials between people than they are normalcy among them. What a powerful notion this would be to offer the architects of our future.

Principles in Concert

The considerations outlined thus far are numerous. Including them all may feel like a heavy lift when there are already so many boxes to tick, so many perspectives to weigh, as an architect or designer. Let the following illustrate one organization's laudable effort to incorporate ideas of universal design, mixed use and the promotion of wellbeing into the spaces they create. And it starts, perhaps you could guess, in the bathroom.

Stalled! is a cross-disciplinary research project that seeks to use bathroom design as a means to combat social inequity. The project is being conducted by MIXdesign, an inclusive design think-tank, research group and consultancy, which, in the case of Stalled! "takes current controversies about transgender access to public bathrooms as a point of departure to address the design consequences of creating safe, inclusive restrooms for everyone, irrespective of age, gender, religion, and disability" [9].

They suggest that the solution to sex-segregated public restrooms being the single-user stall, while having the potential to be a safer or less stressful option, is inherently stigmatizing. By separating the space trans individuals, gender non-conforming individuals or people with disabilities can comfortably use the bathroom, segregation continues. (One might say it adheres to the second principle of universal design, Flexibility in Use, but violates the first, Equitable use.)

As a response, Stalled! advocates for a new sort of multi-user solution. The process of retrofitting existing sex-segregated restrooms into universally accessible, safe and comfortable multi-user restrooms is detailed below (Figures 5.1–5.5):

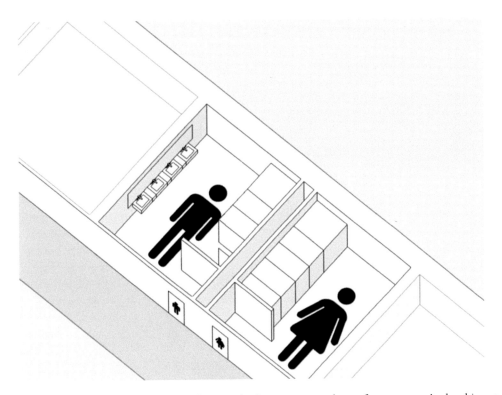

FIGURE 5.1 The process begins with a standard sex-segregated set of restrooms. A plumbing stack wall separates the restroom space into individual men's and women's rooms. A series of stalls and urinals, paralleled by a wall of sinks, is present in each room. Image courtesy of MIXdesign.

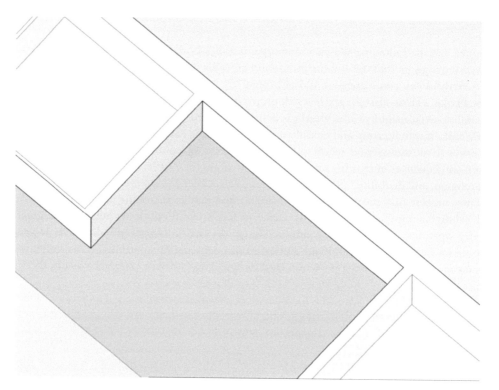

FIGURE 5.2 The plumbing stack wall is removed, and the corridor wall is removed as well. Rather than a separate, enclosed space, the restroom is now treated as "a porous extension of the hallway." Image courtesy of MIXdesign.

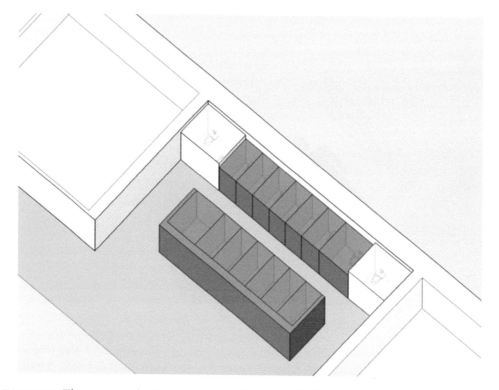

FIGURE 5.3 Three types of stalls are included (dark): standard, ambulatory and ADA. They are abutted by caregiving rooms on either side, which contain sinks and changing tables. All stall doors extend fully to the floor to maximize privacy. Image courtesy of MIXdesign.

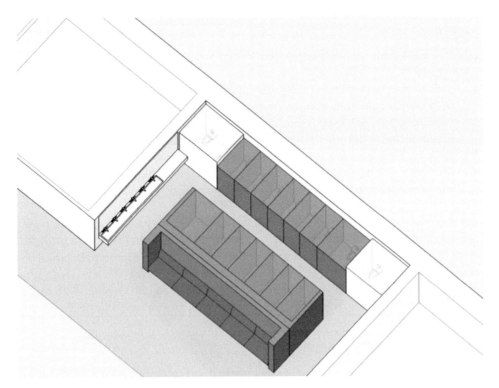

FIGURE 5.4 Sinks and counters offer a communal washing and grooming station. A lounge area occupies the space facing outward to establish a comfortable social arena and place to wait. Image courtesy of MIXdesign.

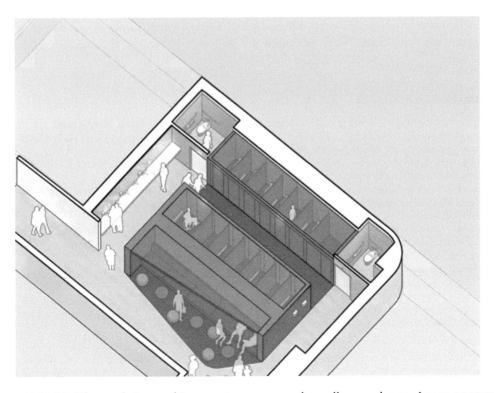

FIGURE 5.5 The result is a multi-use restroom space where all are welcome. Image courtesy of MIXdesign.

Stalled! describes this approach to restroom design as having three main advantages:

1. *Safe*: Restroom users can visually monitor the space and one another, reducing the risk of harassment, confrontation or violence.
2. *Nonbinary*: No individual is forced to choose an option that does not align with their gender identity, and other categorizations (age, race, ability) become irrelevant as well.
3. *Inclusive*: This space meets the restroom needs of trans individuals, gender minorities, differently-abled people, caregivers, parents, everyone. No individual is required to use an alternate facility.

Stalled! shows us that with intentionality, inclusive design can be simple, functional, beautiful and achievable. There are details unspecified in the open-source plans Stalled! has published—what sort of door handles are used, what sort of lighting, acoustics and materials. Just as no list of principles or concepts can be exhaustive, there are infinite instances in the design process where a choice can be made in favor of inclusion. When the inclusive option is chosen with consistency, practices change, standards change. And we all are the beneficiaries.

Implications for the Programming Phase

The considerations offered in this chapter were inspired and created by people for whom architectural obstacles are a reality. These approaches are too often beyond the scope of architectural consideration as a result of exclusion of these individuals from design disciplines.

We are all experts of our own realities. No one is a greater authority on how space can serve people with functional limitations than people with functional limitations themselves. This is true for people of all types, people inhabiting all features and facets of identity and experience. The architectural programming process must include people. Different people, people who move through the world differently and need different things to feel like their environment is serving them. People who approach problems differently. The solutions might surprise you.

References

1. Lang, N. (2016, March). What It's Like to Use a Public Bathroom While Trans. *Rolling Stone*.
2. Mars, R. (Executive Producer). (2020, September 8). Where Do We Go from Here? (412) [Audio podcast episode]. In *99 Percent Invisible*. PRX, Radiotopia.
3. National Disability Authority. (2020). *What Is Universal Design?* Centre for Excellence in Universal Design. http://universaldesign.ie/what-is-universal-design/
4. Centers for Disease Control and Prevention. (2020, September 16). *Disability Impacts All of Us*. Disability and Health Promotion. https://www.cdc.gov/ncbddd/disabilityandhealth/infographic-disability-impacts-all.html
5. National Disability Authority. (2020). *The 7 Principles*. Centre for Excellence in Universal Design. http://universaldesign.ie/what-is-universal-design/the-7-principles/the-7-principles.html
6. Blackwell, A.G. (2017). The Curb-Cut Effect. *Stanford Social Innovation Review*.
7. Anthes, E. (2020). *The Great Indoors: The Surprising Science of How Buildings Shape our Behavior, Health, and Happiness*. Macmillan.
8. Gallaudet University. (2020). Campus Design and Planning: DeafSpace https://www.gallaudet.edu/campus-design-and-planning/deafspace/
9. Stalled! (2021). MIXdesign. https://www.stalled.online/home

6
EMPATHETIC PROGRAMMING TO FOSTER INCLUSION

Robin Z. Puttock, RA, LEED AP BD+C, WELL AP

If we wish to understand and address the stressors in an environmental context we may wish to seek input from the users. The author does just this with students who have been diagnosed with Autism Spectrum Disorder, and finds that they can vividly portray their emotional reactions to specific spaces and moments in their day. In fact they can describe in clear terms how they would prefer their environments to accommodate them. Just as empathy is an essential ingredient of the therapeutic relationship, it can also inform the design process, helping us to create spaces that communicate safety and wellbeing.

Torture Starts

One morning a sketch appeared on a family's whiteboard calendar. Their 11-year-old daughter had drawn on the square for September 6th, the first day of school, a sketch of a school building with a frown face below and the words "torture starts" (Figure 6.1). This sketch could be considered a fairly commonplace metaphorical, even comical, reaction to the end of summer. However, since the sketch was made by an autistic child, it signals concerns that are deeply troubling.

The sketch highlights the intense feelings this sixth grader, Ella B., has about going to school. In particular, the sketch emphasizes a school building. This little girl could have drawn more frown faces or perhaps even a teacher with a frown face but instead she drew a building. There was a reason for that. This sketch single-handedly inspired my research and sparked a goal to spread awareness about the significant role played by environmental design in the efficacious inclusion of children with autism.

The Spectrum

Autism Spectrum Disorder (ASD) is a neurodevelopment disorder characterized by deficits in communication, social skills, flexibility and sensory integration as well as restricted, repetitive patterns of behavior, interests and activities [1]. The word "spectrum" is used because of the "heterogeneity in the presentation and severity of ASD symptoms, as well as in the skills and level of functioning of individuals who have ASD" [2]. These deficits often manifest in inappropriate affect, also known as an apparent lack of empathy [3].

DOI: 10.4324/9781003164418-9

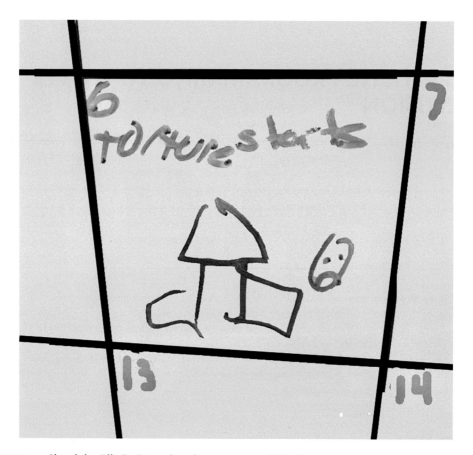

FIGURE 6.1 Sketch by Ella B. Printed with permission of Ella B's mother.

Because this essay focuses on inclusion in educational environments, it is valuable to understand that the U.S. Department of Education defines autism as

> "a developmental disability significantly affecting verbal and nonverbal communication and social interaction, generally evident before age three, that adversely affects a child's educational performance. Other characteristics often associated with autism are engaging in repetitive activities and stereotyped movements, resistance to environmental change or change in daily routines, and unusual responses to sensory experiences [4]."

The U.S. Department of Education uses the wording from the most recent version of the Individuals with Disabilities Education Improvement Act 2004 (commonly referred to as IDEA), which is federal legislation requiring special education services be available to children and youth with disabilities. These special education services provided are based on individual need per the student's Individual Education Plan (IEP). The scope of these services can be push-in support, allowing the child to remain in the mainstream classroom, pull-out support, requiring services to be delivered outside of the mainstream classroom or a combination thereof.

In addition, the 5th edition of the Diagnostic and Statistical Manual of Mental Disorders (DSM-5) identifies three specific "levels" of severity for ASD, descriptions of the amount of support required related to both social communication and restricted, repetitive behaviors. The severity levels are described as: Level 3—Requiring very substantial support, Level 2—Requiring substantial support, and Level 1—Requiring support [5]. The severity level description in the DSM-5 for Level 1 goes on to state that "without supports in place, deficits in social communication cause noticeable impairments" [6]. One might infer that conversely, with supports in place, impairments may not be noticeable. It is this possibility that invites the question, "What supports will allow for students with Level 1 ASD to be included in mainstream classroom settings?"

Square Peg, Round Hole

In his moving memoir on parenthood of an autistic child, Paul Collins writes, "Autists are the ultimate square pegs, and the problem with pounding a square peg into a round hole is not that the hammering is hard work. It's that you are destroying the peg" [7].

For the past 15 years, researchers have wrestled with the question of what environmental supports can foster inclusion for children with Level 1 ASD. The research focus has consistently been on Level 1 ASD as those are the children who are most likely to be able to access environmental supports. To discover which environmental supports are most effective for inclusion, agreement must first be reached on the definition of inclusion. Inclusion is a complex and highly controversial word, the interpretation of which in and of itself can be considered to be on a spectrum. For some, inclusion means the presence of all students in all environments, regardless of the effect on the student or their peers. For others, inclusion means that all students have equal access to the curriculum in the manner which is appropriate, even if that means a separate dedicated school that meets their specific needs. For yet others, it can mean a hybrid of the two previous interpretations, meaning that all students are included in the least restrictive environment (LRE), ideally in the same facility. This essay, the focus of which is fostering the inclusion of Level 1 ASD students in educational environments, will be using the Individuals with Disabilities Education Improvement Act (IDEA) definition for LRE:

> "to the maximum extent appropriate, children with disabilities…are educated with children who are not disabled, and special classes, separate schooling, or other removal of children with disabilities from the regular educational environment occurs only when the nature or severity of the disability of a child is such that education in regular classes with the use of supplementary aids and services cannot be achieved satisfactorily [8]."

A Day in the Life

In order to discover the environmental supports that can foster inclusion, one must first understand the environmental stressors of a typical elementary school day. The author has identified six parts of a student's day while interacting with educational environments that cause the most stress based on the ASD diagnostic criteria outlined above. These parts are the approach to the school environment, the arrival at the school environment, the content delivery within the school environment, the transitions within the school environment, the recreation experiences within the school environment and the departure from the school environment.

Research and analysis of these six most stressful parts of the school day based on the ASD diagnostic criteria yielded a list of environmental stressors, numbering in the hundreds, and as a result, these stressors have been categorized into three main types: **social stressors** (resulting from social situations), **mental stressors** (resulting from pedagogical conditions) and **sensory stressors** (resulting from the surrounding built and natural environments). Obviously, the list is too exhaustive for inclusion in this essay; however, examples of each are provided here for illustration purposes.

Consider it is lunchtime and a young student with ASD needs to find a seat in a cafeteria. The only seats available are next to other children and this young student was hoping to sit by himself today. This is a social stressor resulting from an unavoidable social situation, exacerbated for a student with ASD who has social skill deficits.

It is now content delivery time in the classroom and the fourth-grade curriculum includes team teaching of history and English together as a block. Two teachers teaching the same content; however, they often have differing opinions on tasks, their order, their due dates. This is an example of a mental stressor resulting from a pedagogical condition, exacerbated for a student with ASD who has communication and flexibility deficits.

Finally, consider transition time in a corridor in the middle of the day. There are hundreds of students chaotically jostling around in the somewhat narrow corridor, talking excitedly and squeaking their sneakers on the freshly polished vinyl floors while glaring sunlight streams through the clerestory windows. Perhaps the smell of cafeteria food is wafting through the corridors. This is an example of sensory stressors resulting from the natural and built environments, exacerbated for a student with ASD who has sensory integration deficits.

This comprehensive list of stressors, though unique, is not entirely new knowledge as several researchers in the past 15 years have also generated their own lists of stressors. Many of these researchers have also generated exhaustive lists of design guidelines as a result. These researchers include architects performing post-occupancy analyses of their own built work, such as *ga architects* [9].[1] These researchers also include architects performing literature reviews and interviews of the users of the inclusive design work of other architects such as Keith McAllister [10][2] who has focused on the work of Clare Vogel [11], and Simon Humphreys [12], Magda Mostafa [13][3] and Rachna Khare [14].[4]

The guidelines generated by these various research methodologies are certainly a starting point and have the capacity to "draw designers" attention to certain aspects which they might fail to notice otherwise, thereby assisting them in asking some important questions to future users from the very first design phase" [15]. Design guidelines can also assist people with autism to identify ways that the built environment can be better designed to reduce their stress by acting as a framework to identify and overcome the issues encountered as a result of a student with communication deficits [16]). And finally, the vast number of guidelines alone supports the need to search for a more holistic solution for inclusive design.

However, the guidelines as described above also present a fair amount of challenges. They are vast, seemingly contradictory to an untrained eye and are too complex to be effective without exhaustive study. In addition, the guidelines have significantly less value, and could potentially be detrimental, if applied to design without a sophisticated understanding of ASD. Specifically, a designer needs to understand that students with ASD have "differing severity of the autism inherent within the spectrum" [17] as well as a "varying and differing range of sensory difficulties of individual ASD sufferers to contend with" [18]. Marijke Kinnear, Stijn Baumers and Ann Heylighen describe these sensory difficulties, which can occur for each of the senses as "hypersensitivity, hyposensitivity, and internal interference. Hypersensitive individuals experience difficulties in processing even modest levels of light, colours, smells and textures… causing considerable stress, whereas hyposensitive people specifically look for these same stimuli" [19]. In simplistic terms, what is stressful to one child with ASD is a delight to another. This is perhaps one of the most challenging parts of designing inclusively for this population. The challenge is only intensified by the communication deficits common in those with ASD, which create further barriers to understanding their needs.

The Irony of Empathy

So, the question remains, how can we design to foster inclusion of high functioning autistic children when they cannot typically speak for themselves and the stressor spectrum among the population is so great? The answer to this question, in part, came to me when I revisited how my research had begun: the empathy I felt when looking at a child's sketch on her family's whiteboard calendar. I was troubled. I was angry. I was affected. I was inspired. Could the answer be empathy? Must we be able to first empathize with these children with ASD before we can design for them? If so, how do we gain empathy for a population who struggles with communication?

The origins of the word "empathy" can be traced to the ancient Greek "empatheia." "Em" meaning "in" and "pathos" meaning "feeling." In 1868, the term "Einfühlung" was coined by the German philosopher Rudolf Hermann Lotze [20]. The term gained popularity in 1873 when Robert Vischer published *On the Optical Sense of Form* [21]. In 1909, American psychologist, Edward Titchener coined the English word as a translation of the German word "Einfühlung" [22]. The Oxford English Dictionary (OED) defines empathy as "the ability to understand and share the feelings of another" [23].

The irony of this essay is that it proposes a theory using empathy to design environments for a population that exhibits a lack of empathy. And how can we as designers gain empathy for a population that has communication deficits?

The Empathy Sketchbook

The answer to this question came to me once again as I looked at Ella B's whiteboard sketch. "Torture Starts." What if I collected sketches from children with ASD? What if I asked the children about specific times during their school day so I could learn more about their stressors? What if I asked them what their "dream" school would be like so I could develop and propose spatial strategies for school buildings that serve them?

I now had a mission. Using my personal and professional networks, I spent several months speaking to parents and teachers. As a result, I collected dozens of sketches. I compiled the most insightful, often powerful sketches and paired them with descriptive quotes from the children (provided by their parents and teachers) into what I called an Empathy Sketchbook. I then showed the sketchbook to designers and administrators to see its effect. The result was universal. The Empathy Sketchbook was a powerful tool to inspire change in the design community. The reaction inspired me to continue with the work, collecting more sketches and looking for trends. I saw that the children's sketches, inspired by both the six parts of a school day and the "dream school" prompts, tended to fall into three discrete spatial strategy categories: the effectiveness of calming surroundings, the power of individual control and the enthusiasm for physical activity. Pairing the graphics with the verbal and/or written testimony, I was able to see that these three main "dream school" strategies either prevented, reduced or relieved stress in the children.

Key findings are illustrated by the selected sketches included within the pages of this essay. For the most part, these powerful sketches speak for themselves. However, there are deeper meanings to most of them that become apparent only when pairing them with the testimony of the children shared with their parents and/or teachers; trusted adults with unique relational connections with these children. Figure 6.2 features a sketch by a nine-year-old who drew his idea of a "dream" school approach. He told his mother, "the front doors should be automatic but there should be signs so people know. There should be lots of windows so you can see inside. Even the walls could be windows." He wanted plenty of signage and automation to simplify the approach. He also wanted as much glass as possible to maximize his information about the upcoming entry sequence. He did not want to be surprised. This careful sketch and associated narrative highlight several diagnostic criteria of ASD including deficits in flexibility and clearly shows us what is important to him as it relates to approach and arrival.

Figure 6.3 is a plan and elevation sketch of how a child with ASD would like to arrive at school and depart. It is very important to him that the spaces are sized generously enough to avoid unwanted sensory input. He described "the lobby should be big enough so no one has to touch each other when they walk in or out." This sketch highlights how sensory integration issues can affect the beginning and end of a school day for a child with ASD and the simple adjustments designers can make to foster inclusion.

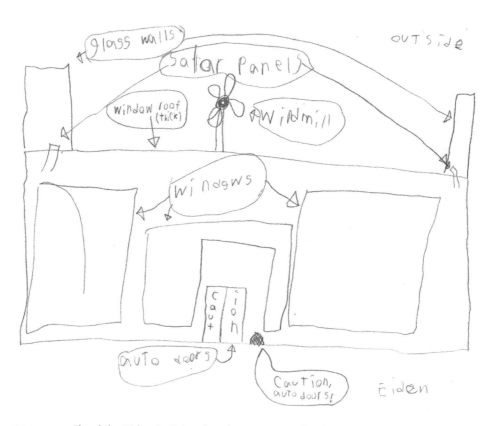

FIGURE 6.2 Sketch by Eiden A. Printed with permission of Eiden A's mother.

Empathetic Programming to Foster Inclusion 71

FIGURE 6.3 Sketch by Bobby L. Printed with permission of Bobby L's mother.

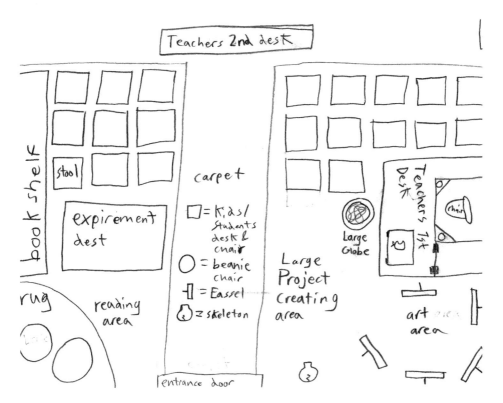

FIGURE 6.4 Sketch by Jared G. Printed with permission of Jared G's mother.

Another child focused on what was important to him when it comes to content delivery: order, rules, predictability and control (Figure 6.4), highlighting flexibility deficits associated with ASD. His mother said he reported "there should be a place for each topic. Experiments should take place at the experiment area. There should be a place to make large projects and a place for art projects. There should be an area for reading. The teacher should have two different desks, one with its own light, the other one with a lifting panel with brackets so only the teacher can sit at it. The teacher can work at one desk and put her stuff on the other desk."

The desire for options to help navigate unstructured social situations during recess time is demonstrated in Figure 6.5. This sixth grader said that "the monkey bars should have two paths so I can read sitting on top of one side of the bars while other kids can swing by on the other side. I can be near them but not with them." This testimony is particularly moving because it reflects a desire to be near people but not have to interact with them.

Another socially stressful time during a child's school day is lunchtime. In the plan sketch shown in Figure 6.6, a 5th grade girl identifies several design strategies to help her navigate during this unstructured social time, often in a highly sensory space. She reported to her father "there should be different chairs so different amounts of kids can sit at each place. If a band is playing, we don't need to talk during lunch." The strategies highlighted here are specific to seating arrangements and acoustics. However, a deeper look reveals the stress of self-selected social groupings and sensory solutions when these situations arise.

Another one of the stressful times during a school day is the act of transition: between arrival, content delivery, recreation, or departure. Figure 6.7 features an ideal design of a school corridor, in both plan and elevation. The young artist identifies solutions that can compensate for communication deficits in children with ASD who might not be able to, or comfortable with, asking about what events are in the future. A calendar in the hallway would reduce the stress resulting from this particular communication deficit. The young student describes "people should stay on their side of the hallway. I'd like to see the calendar posted and have options of things to drink while I walk."

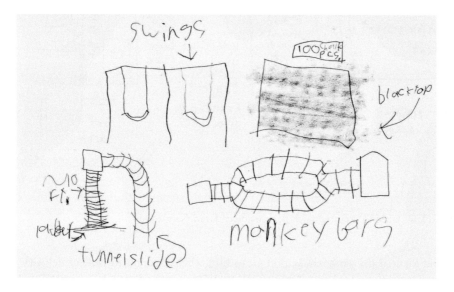

FIGURE 6.5 Sketch by Bobby L. Printed with permission of Bobby L's mother.

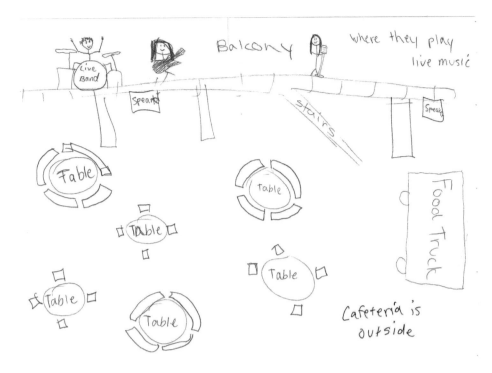

FIGURE 6.6 Sketch by Audrey P. Printed with permission of Audrey P's father.

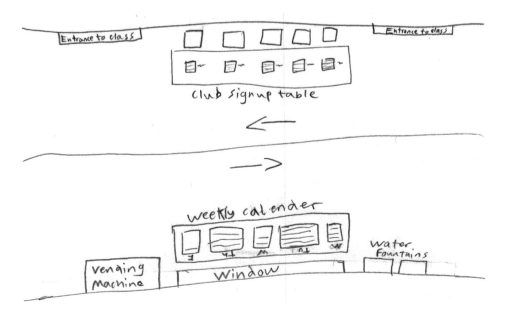

FIGURE 6.7 Sketch by Jared G. Printed with permission of Jared G's mother.

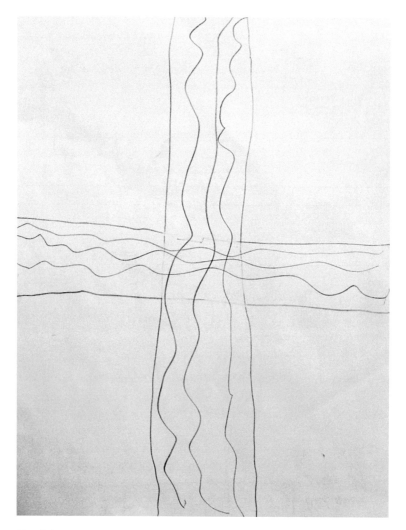

FIGURE 6.8 Sketch by Justin P. Printed with permission of Justin P's mother.

Perhaps one of the most poetic, empathetic sketches obtained to date is Figure 6.8. In this simple drawing of a school corridor, the young student shows how he would like to transition from class to class. "I would like to swim from class to class. When I am swimming, I don't hear anything. I don't talk to anyone. I love the way the water feels. And it's just fun." Of course, upon a quick review, a designer can most likely not accommodate such a request. However, the main idea of this essay and the associated research is the importance of using these sketches to teach the designers to design empathetically. If a child wants to transition between classes in a quiet environment, how can the educational environment accommodate that? How can that same environment provide non-acoustical sensory stimulation?

Reading the Sketchbook

Review of these sketches begins to give the reader an empathetic understanding of what young students with ASD consider to be stressful educational environments. However, in-depth

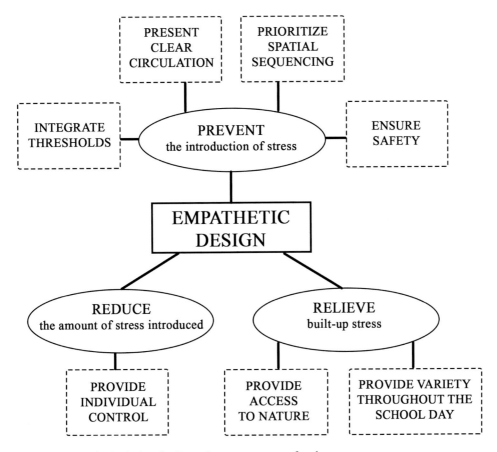

FIGURE 6.9 Empathetic design findings. Image courtesy of author.

analysis of the entire collection of sketches and associated testimony has yielded several key findings which support a new design theory called Empathetic Design, inclusive design possible only when empathy is gained for the user. These findings, described below as spatial strategies, prevent, reduce and/or relieve stress in children with ASD (Figure 6.9) and thus foster inclusion in educational environments.

Prevent the Introduction of Stress

The first group of spatial strategies that foster inclusion, based on analysis of the children's sketches, is categorized by approaches that prevent the introduction of stress. There are four key findings in this category. First, and of highest priority, is the ability of safe environments to prevent the introduction of stress. Durable materials used in finishes, furniture and equipment as well as room layouts that allow for observation, reduce occurrences of injury and property damage that can cause stress.

The second finding is that the prioritization of spatial sequencing prevents the introduction of stress. This has a variety of meanings depending on the specific artist. It can mean locating noisy areas adjacent to other noisy areas and quiet areas adjacent to other quiet areas. It can also mean providing spaces in between noisy areas and quiet areas to ease the transition between programmatic spaces. Sketches support that this finding can be applied to all of the senses as kitchen smells, for example, can be quite objectionable to children with ASD trying to concentrate in a math class.

The third finding evident in the children's sketches and associated testimony suggests the ability of integrated thresholds between all programmatic variations to prevent the introduction of stress. This can be as simple as a hand washing station at the entry of an eating area to reinforce the programmed use of the space or a coatroom between a noisy corridor and a quiet classroom to lessen the perceptible shift in acoustics.

The final finding in the category is the ability of clear circulation and wayfinding to prevent the introduction of stress. This is evident in Figure 6.8. This wayfinding, however, can be a balancing act. Long straight corridors are easy to understand and observe, however, they can also cause anxiety. In addition, wayfinding that can appear to clarify spatial relationships to a neurotypical person can be very confusing to a child with ASD. Both of these scenarios, as well as countless others, highlight the need to become very familiar with the needs of the user, to truly understand their perceptions and to work with them.

Reduce the Amount of Stress Introduced

Even though the previous category recognizes the strategies that prevent the introduction of stress, this prevention can only be applicable to certain types of stress, caused by the specific stressors as listed above. Some level of educational environmental stress is unavoidable in children. However, neurotypical children have innate coping skills that help to reduce their stress level and allow for efficacious inclusion in educational environments. Neurotypical children can reduce their stress level by commiserating with a friend, problem solving with a teacher and/or naturally integrating sensory inputs. In contrast, children with ASD have social, communication, flexibility and sensory deficits that make few, if any of these strategies available. The sketches of "ideal" educational environments drawn by children with ASD reveal a common theme: the desire to have individual choice and control in each educational environment throughout the school day. This can be seen in many manifestations throughout the sketches, focused primarily on environments that provide choice and control in social and sensory environments.

The second collection of spatial strategies evident from the analysis of the sketches is categorized by methods that reduce the amount of stress that is introduced during the school day. There is one overall key finding in this category: providing individual choice and control in each educational environment reduces the amount of stress introduced during the school day. This individual choice and control can alleviate the stressors brought on by the social, flexibility and sensory integration deficits often found in children with ASD.

As social, communication, flexibility and sensory stressors often overlap, there is also overlap between environments that provide social and sensory choice and control. Three examples of ways to incorporate individual choice and control in educational environments are included here:

- Reduce the stress resulting from insufficient sensorial environments by providing personal equipment in each environment and, likewise, provide access to a place of refuge in each environment for children seeking a reduction of sensory input. Other strategies to provide an increase or decrease in sensory input is to design spaces within environments that offer different views. These can be highly sensorial views to the exterior or calming views of a plain wall. Providing options for opposing needs in the same environment can accommodate children with ASD who have different sensory integration deficits.

- Reduce the stress resulting from social environments by providing a variety of social grouping environments in each educational environment. For example, in cafeterias, instead of one large space, provide several spaces varying in size, acoustics or brightness. In classrooms, provide window seats, tables and desks all within sight and earshot of the content delivery. In addition, for children who would like to sit by themselves or in smaller groups, provide moveable seating. Finally, taking the idea of individual control and choice even further, provide a variety of seat designs: seats that spin, seats that are built-in, soft seats, rigid seats, etc.
- Reduce the stress resulting from flexible active learner and/or active environment educational environments by providing order and predictability. One strategy to do so might involve a variety or personal storage options. Some children need all clutter to be out of sight. Other children will forget where their supplies are if they are not visible and organized. Some students get anxious when they think that another student can gain access to their possessions. Therefore, a variety of open, closed and lockable personal storage is ideal.

Relieve the Built-up Stress

The third and final category of spatial strategies that foster inclusion, based on the analysis of the children's sketches, is characterized by strategies that relieve the built-up stress during the school day that cannot otherwise be avoided. This stress might not be able to be avoided for one of two reasons: the prevention strategies are not applicable to specific stressors and/or the reduction strategies fostering inclusion through individual choice or control might not be an option at that particular moment. For example, students might be required to eat at a certain time, learn math at a certain time, or endure either a loud fire drill or the smell of the air being circulated by the HVAC system.

The two findings that relieve this built-up stress are: access to nature and access to variety throughout the school day. The first finding is to provide ample and frequent access to nature. Much has been written about this relationship and it is widely agreed upon to reduce built-up stress. This can be accomplished with views to nature from corridors, nature in the content delivery, even pathways through nature during approach, arrival and departure. It has been proven that this strategy is even more effective if the child is engaged in exercise while outdoors.

The second finding is to provide ample access to a variety of environments throughout the school day. The strategies presented in this category, variety, will appear to be similar to those of the previous category, individual choice and control, however, the strategy of variety can be used when the child does not have control over their immediate environment, but must endure the stress until it can be relieved. The thought is that the more varied the offered environments are during the day, the better the chance that a child with ASD will be able to identify with a stress relieving environment during at least one time during the day. Therefore, being exposed to different environments can be beneficial to the overall reduction of stress build-up.

There are six spatial strategies that can be used to provide variety throughout the school day. A brief summary of the strategies and examples are provided here:

- Relieve built-up stress by providing a combination of hypo and hyper sensory environments that students experience throughout the school day. This can include a big, noisy gymnasium and a quiet alcove in a library. Each child may be required to attend physical education and the library each day, but the environments are very different and thus each environment will have the ability to relieve stress in some children with ASD.

- Relieve built-up stress by providing a variety of social group settings that students encounter throughout the school day. For example, physical education classes can be quite large and pull-out special education instruction is typically small class sizes. This variety can be pedagogical, but also has environmental design aspects.
- Relieve built-up stress by providing a variety of volumetric environments that students experience throughout the school day. For example, the corridors might have high ceilings and the classrooms might have low ceilings. Or perhaps some corridors have high ceilings and others have low ceilings.
- Relieve built-up stress by providing a variety or views throughout the school day. Perhaps an art classroom can provide views to nature and a reading class can provide only clerestory views.
- Relieve built-up stress by providing a variety of storage options throughout the school day. This can translate into a variety of classroom storage options as mentioned in the category above, gym lockers concealed in a locker room and open storage in the art room.
- Relieve built-up stress by providing a variety of finish selections encountered by the child during the school day. In terms of maintenance and security, the user will have a strong opinion regarding the finishes to be used on a project. However, there is still room for variety. Analyzing the children's sketches, there is a delicate balance between neat and chaotic or between institutional and domestic. The finishes need to strike a balance between the two and again, a deep understanding of the specific user must exist in order to be successful.

Conclusion: Designing for All Learners

Empathetic Design is a theory of design that requires the designer to have empathy for the user in order to foster inclusion. The entirety of this essay focuses on a user with autism. However, it must be noted that it is the opinion of the author and many others in this field of research, including Ulrike Altenmüller-Lewis, that built environments that support children with autism "have the potential to improve the life of children…with autism, and as a by-product anyone in their environment" [24]. As an idea, this is not a novel concept; however, as a practice for inclusive design as it relates to educational environments for children with ASD, the theory is valuable.

Achieving empathy for a population known for its deficits in communication as well as its lack of empathy is a distinct challenge, especially in an inclusive environment with neurotypical children. As such, no specific guidelines have been presented here, only findings based on empathy gained from analysis of children's sketches. Each project type and program will be unique as will be the user. As the architect Christopher Beaver states,

> "the heart of the brief cannot be written down. It has to come from an understanding of the autistic mind; the things that are comforting and give a sense of security, a feeling of space where there are places for being alone and for socializing, an easily understood geography…This understanding can only come with time and patient observation" [25]

and, I would like to add, with sketches.

Notes

1 Christopher Beaver's guidelines include: acoustics—noisy spaces are to be avoided, ventilation—must be sufficient and controllable by the users, heating—invisible and silent systems are preferred, lighting—avoid fluorescent lighting due to the acoustic concerns and allow all lighting, natural and artificial to be

flexible and controllable by the user, color—user defined balance between neutral, calming and stimulating, planning—simple layout, logical spatial adjacencies based on use and acoustics and elimination of corridors as much as possible, maintenance—use friendly materials that are easy and inexpensive to replace, cleaning—durable and easily cleaned surfaces, outdoor spaces—secure, flexible outdoor space and wayfinding—curved walls and color coded.

2 McAllister defines 16 design criteria necessary in autism design that include: guidelines regarding thresholds, sightlines, glazing and acoustics. He further breaks these 16 criteria down into four category bands—control and safety, classroom character, classroom usage and classroom physical factors.

3 Mostafa compiled six architectural factors that affect behavior: acoustics, visual (colors & patterns), visual (lighting), texture, olfactory and spatial sequencing of functions.

4 Rhana Khare's dissertation, Designing Inclusive Educational Spaces for Autism, develops a theory that 18 detailed environmental design considerations enable students with autism (2009). These environmental design considerations, which Khare refers to as design parameters, are: physical structure, visual structure, visual instruction, opportunities for community participation, opportunities for parent participation, opportunities for inclusion, opportunities for future independence, space standards, withdrawal spaces, safety, comprehension, accessibility, space for assistance, durability and maintenance, sensory distraction management, opportunities for sensory integration, flexibility, and monitoring for assessment and planning. These design guidelines identify six categories: site selection, site planning, building design, classroom design, outdoor play area and landscaping and illustrate each category with suggestions regarding each of the 18 design parameters, resulting in hundreds of design guidelines.

References

1. American Psychiatric Association. (2013). *Diagnostic and Statistical Manual of Mental Disorders* (5th ed.)
2. American Psychological association. (n.d.) *Autism Spectrum Disorder.* https://www.apa.org/topics/autism-spectrum-disorder
3. Oberman, L. M. and Vilayanur, S. R. (2007). Broken Mirrors: A Theory of Autism. *Scientific American Special Editions* 17(2s). 20–29. doi:10.1038/scientificamerican0607-20sp
4. Individuals with Disabilities Education Improvement Act, §§ 300.8 (c) (1) (2004).
5. American Psychiatric Association. (2013). *Diagnostic and Statistical Manual of Mental Disorders* (5th ed.)
6. Ibid.
7. Collins, P. (2004). *Not Even Wrong: Adventures in Autism.* New York: Bloomsbury. 225.
8. Individuals with Disabilities Education Improvement Act, §§ 1412 (a) (5) (2004).
9. Beaver, C. (2006, November 1). *Designing Environments for Children and Adults with ASD* [PowerPoint presentation and transcript]. Autism Safari 2006, 2nd World Autism Congress & Exhibition.
10. McAllister, K. (2010) *The ASD Friendly Classroom: Design Complexity, Challenge and Characteristics* [Paper presentation]. Design Research Society International Conference, Montreal, Canada. 1–18.
11. Vogel, C.L. (2008, May/June). Classroom Design for Living and Learning with Autism. *Autism Asperger's Digest,* 30–39.
12. Humphreys, S. (2005, February/March). Autism and Architecture. *Autism London Bulletin,* 7–8.
13. Mostafa, M. (2014, March). Architecture for Autism: Autism ASPECTSS^{TM} in School Design. *International Journal of Architectural Research* 8(1). 143–158.
14. Khare, R. and Mullick, A. (2009). Incorporating the Behavioral Dimension in Designing Inclusive Learning Environments for Autism. *International journal of Architecture Research* 5(3). 45–64.
15. Kinnaer, M., Baumers, S. and Heylighen, A. (2015). Autism-friendly Architecture from the Outside in and the Inside Out: An Explorative Study Based on Autobiographies of Autsitic People. *Journal of Housing and the Built Environment* 31(2). 179–195.
16. Ibid.
17. McAllister, K. (2010). *The ASD Friendly Classroom: Design Complexity, Challenge and Characteristics* [Paper presentation]. Design Research Society International Conference, Montreal, Canada. 1–18.
18. Ibid.
19. Kinnaer, M., Baumers, S. and Heylighen, A. (2015). Autism-friendly Architecture from the Outside in and the Inside Out: An Explorative Study Based on Autobiographies of Autsitic People. *Journal of Housing and the Built Environment* 31(2). 179–195.
20. Lotze, R.H. (1868). *Geschichte der Aesthetik in Deutschland.* Munich, Germany: Cotta.
21. Vischer, R. (1994). On the Optical Sense of Form: A Contribution to Aesthetics. *Empathy, Form, and Space: Problems in German Aesthetics* (H.F. Mallgrave & Eleftherios Ikonomou, Trans.). Getty Center for the History of Art and the Humanities. 89–123, Manitoba, CAN.

22. Titchener, E. (1909). *Lectures on the Experimental Psychology of the Thought Process*. The MacMillan Company.
23. Oxford English Dictionary. (1989). Empathy. in *Oxford English Dictionary*. Oxford University Press.
24. Altenmüller-Lewis, U. (2107). Designing Schools for Students on the Spectrum. *The Design Journal* 20(1). S2215–S2229.
25. Beaver, C. (2006, November 1). *Designing Environments for Children and Adults with ASD* [PowerPoint presentation and transcript]. Autism Safari 2006, 2nd World Autism Congress & Exhibition.

7
PROGRAMMING FOR EFFECTIVE LEARNING

Laura A. Wernick FAIA, REFP, LEED AP and Erika Eitland, MPH, ScD

> The growing brain requires specific input according to developmental stages and individual predispositions. With increased neurological insight into the learning process and a better understanding of the nature of the maturing central nervous system we are now able to provide educational contexts that facilitate cognitive attention, social interaction, creativity and wellbeing. The authors describe how the need for safety, community engagement and nature all play a role in the wellbeing of the school community.

Schools carry great meaning in our society. They are the physical manifestation of a community's aspirations for a collective future. These spaces can support academic learning as well as our children's physical health and sense of wellbeing, both social and emotional. The buildings are a promise to the community at large, providing centers for after-school activities and civic functions—programs with ripple effects well beyond the student population. Schools, as with all major building projects, now have another promise and obligation to the future to leave the smallest possible footprint on our shared natural environment.

In many cases, schools are a community's single largest financial investment. Decisions made during the planning and design process both affect and reflect a community's priorities and values regarding its student population, its civic role, and its commitment to the greater physical environment. It is the designer's responsibility to be aware of all threads influencing a community's decision-making process and to identify and contextualize the implications of all stakeholder design decisions.

Programming initiates a two-way conversation. The programmer is able to listen and learn as much as she can about the goals and needs for that specific community while also orienting stakeholders to the magnitude of their endeavor and the potentially broad-reaching implications of their decisions. The programmer is listening, but also raising awareness.

Key Planning and Programming Elements

1. Neurological research has led to a deeper understanding of how we learn. Pedagogy and curriculum design today are heavily influenced by that research. Planning for

DOI: 10.4324/9781003164418-10

supportive spaces and spatial relationships requires a basic understanding of this research and how it is being interpreted within educational communities.

2. Children are particularly sensitive to the built environment. They spend a significant portion of their lives inside school buildings and the physical qualities of the classroom such as acoustics, light, thermal control, air movement and visual connections to the natural environment have a direct effect on their ability to learn. These physical qualities impact health, wellness and learning.

3. Students need to feel safe to learn. The physical safety of students, teachers and visitors is a key parameter when planning a school. Its basic concepts must be brought forth during programming.

4. The natural environment is integral to learning and should not be ignored during programming. Connections to nature both visually and through active play have been shown to support learning. Also, our natural environment is our children's future. Each programming effort is an opportunity to help a community understand the potential to reduce our carbon footprint and to model sustainability for the students and for the community.

5. Community engagement plays a significant role in most strong schools. It helps students feel physically and emotionally secure and models the values of good citizenship. During the programming phases of the design process, community participation sparks insights and builds momentum around a unified vision for a supportive academic environment—one that can also be welcoming and inviting for parents and other community members. A school building should be a center and resource for the entire community as well as a place for learning.

Part 1 of this chapter will look at these key elements that should be part of the planning for schools conversation. This includes neurological factors that support and impact learning, physiological and health factors that impact learning, parameters for safety, the role of the community and the role of the natural environment in creating places for effective learning.

In Part 2 we will see how communities put this knowledge to work in the planning process to create effective learning environments.

Part 1: Factors that Support Effective Learning

Neurological Research and Learning

Neurological research has brought new clarity to how the human brain grows, retains information and, ultimately, how we as humans learn effectively. This research, in turn, has inspired new teaching techniques and methods that align with the results of the research. These teaching methods tend to emphasize the importance of:

- social and emotional resilience and growth,
- collaboration and communication skills,
- complex problem solving,
- initiative and independent thinking, and
- physical engagement in the learning process including hands-on activities.

The physical orientation of space within a school building and the furniture layouts within those spaces can help support those teaching methods. The more we understand the "how and why" behind teachers' pedagogy, the better we can program for the spaces to support effective learning.

Our brains have tremendous potential for change and growth, which occurs in response to stimulus. This ability to change is a result of either neuroplasticity, change in response to stimulus, or, neurogenesis, the ability to produce new neurons and synapses. As you learn something new the synapse is changing. This capacity for change is generally termed plasticity. The degree of modification to the brain depends on the type of stimulation that takes place.

Long-term learning correlates with profound change in the brain, which, in turn, supports the ability to make more complex correlations and connections. While infants experience extraordinary growth of new synapses, plasticity occurs throughout our lives. Learning through new and different modes, such as reading, singing, memorization or hands-on projects can help support plasticity by creating new, or reinforcing existing pathways. The more pathways are reinforced through repetition, or through understanding similar material in different ways, the more effective the learning is. These approaches are more beneficial for learning because they involve a greater number of neural connections and more neurological crosstalk. For instance, learning that stimulates both visual imagery as well as verbal connections can create more robust learning than learning that is solely involving one or the other. Connecting math with spatial awareness activities can reinforce natural connections from different parts of the brain.

Project-based learning that uses hands-on activities, such as building a model of the solar system with complex problem solving, or teaching another student about the movement of Earth around the sun, is more likely to ingrain the knowledge than simply reading a book about the solar system. In figuring out how to build a model, the physical connection between the hand's activity and the brain as one puts the model together, and the thought processes necessary to explain the learning to someone, creates overlapping and robust neural connections.

Emotions can impact plasticity as well. Understanding and remembering take place in the hippocampus, which is deeply embedded in the cerebral cortex and part of the limbic system. The limbic system supports emotions, and motivation as well as learning and long-term memory. The higher-level cognitive functions, such as creating, evaluating, analyzing, and applying, also involve the cortical areas. While we often think of learning as a purely cognitive function, there is a strong interdependence on body and mind, cognitive and emotional functions, analytical and creative modes. Emotional health is essential to cognitive growth. Nurturing is crucial to the learning process. Social and emotional wellbeing promote optimal learning by stimulating neuroplasticity and neurogenesis. At a basic level it is necessary to learn how to manage one's own emotions to learn effectively but it is also important that the school environment help minimize excessive stress and support student emotional engagement and motivation to help students to learn.

Why is this type of understanding important for programming and planning a school? Administrators use this information to set educational goals and plans for their schools and their teachers. Pedagogy (how one teaches) is shaped by this information, as is the development of curriculum (what one teaches). Educators are creating activities not just to convey facts, but to engage each student on many levels, to build and reinforce skills and support academic, social and emotional growth.

Planning for a new school needs to reflect the school's goals for their students' learning, the actual pedagogy practiced within the school, and the activities that form the curriculum. The appropriate physical space can then be created to support those goals and activities.

For instance, the traditional classroom may no longer be the primary learning space if research is leading educators to different types of learning activities. Project-based learning is now being heavily utilized. Research indicates that hands-on activities connecting physical manipulation and problem solving, with research and presentation can effectively build and reinforce neural pathways. If hands-on, project-based learning is a key element in the learning experience this will have implications for spatial layouts, storage requirements, access to infrastructure such as water and power, as well as floor finishes, furniture, acoustics and perhaps ventilation.

If a school determines that more small group learning activities encourage a greater sense of emotional security and support greater student engagement in learning, this approach might lead to fewer large classrooms and more small collaborative spaces. The way spaces are configured in relationship to one another may change. More transparency between rooms may be required and different furniture might be used. Any of these approaches may also have implications for how technology is used within the classroom and across the school. All of these decisions ripple out beyond the immediate learning spaces impacting places for planning, for students with special needs and for components as simple as display of student work. Educational programmers need to be aware of pedagogy but also think about activities as varied as professional interactions among educators, parental involvement, community engagement, and maintenance and servicing.

Childhood Health and Learning

Similar to the neurological research section, environmental and child health research has elucidated the sensitive relationship children have to their school surroundings driven by their limited ability to make decisions, rapidly developing bodies and the unique spaces they occupy.

The environmental conditions they are exposed to have both short- and long-term impacts on their social and physical health and subsequently their thinking and performance. For example, a school building's untreated leaky pipe can lead to excess moisture, dampness and even mold growth. These conditions can lead to eye, nose and throat irritation or cause an asthma attack, which not only distracts a student from their classwork but may cause them to leave the classroom to seek out an inhaler from the school nurse. If this was an isolated incident, the student may have missed a single math or English class, but unfortunately environmental conditions may persist over time, resulting in many math or English classes missed by the end of a school year. Therefore, any end of the year exam is not a true reflection of what that student is capable of. It is also important to note that teachers and staff are not immune to these adverse impacts, and even the best teacher's health and cognitive function may be impacted.

This section focuses on children specifically because of their rapid biological growth and immature immune systems, which makes them more susceptible to pollutants found in their air, water and dust compared to adults. For example, a child breathes 50 percent more air, has greater hand-to-mouth contact, larger pupils that increase sensitivity to daylighting, and greater body surface-to-volume ratio limiting their ability to cope during extreme heat compared to adults. All these biological features mean that if a teacher and a student were exposed to the same amount of a harmful substance or environmental condition, the student would experience a more extreme physiological response.

Early in programming for health it is important to identify any vulnerable child populations. It is essential to make sure the environment is designed for all users. Vulnerable students may include:

- students with disabilities (mobility, auditory, visual),
- students living in homelessness or unstable housing conditions,
- students experiencing food insecurity,
- English Language Learners,
- students with unreliable transit, and
- racial minorities.

These students may not engage with the built environment as intended and special provisions can be made such as tailored wayfinding that accounts for differences in language proficiencies, vision (e.g., blindness, color blindness, other visual impairments) and culture (e.g., symbology and graphics used). Even improving signage may increase student's psychological safety, reducing stress and anxiety. For students experiencing homelessness or housing instability, a school may choose to include additional amenities such as private showers, laundry and additional storage for personal items. These amenities may improve a student's focus and sense of stability and decrease bullying.

To start programming for child health in schools, an evidence-based approach is useful. The Harvard Chan School of Public Health—supported by more than 30 years of public health and building science research—has developed a conceptual framework for considering different environmental conditions. Their *9 Foundations of a Healthy Building* highlights the role of ventilation, lighting and views, acoustics, air quality, thermal health, moisture, dust and pests, security and safety, and water quality. During K-12 school programming, additional considerations include walkability, ergonomics, food environments and access to health services (nurses offices). Promoting walkable interior spaces can help support a holistic approach for reducing childhood obesity and create opportunities for spontaneous interactions between teachers and students. Ergonomics in schools can account for students' body size, use of technology and posture. Food environments can be designed in a way to "nudge" students toward healthier options and include opportunities for a greater discussion about sustainability and health. Lastly, it is estimated that more than half of U.S. public schools do not have a school nurse available every day. Ensuring that primary care is available on-site can reduce worsening health conditions, limit the spread of infectious diseases and facilitate the administration of medicine (e.g., inhalers).

Examples of programming for child health:

- *Furniture selection:* Building materials and furniture can contain harmful chemical additives that are not covalently bonded and can migrate out of the product into dust. Over time, exposure to this chemical laden dust can result in problems with hormone regulation, developmental disorders and even cancer.
- *Types of heating and air handling systems:* Access to air conditioning can reduce cases of heat stress that reduce student focus and academic performance. Easy to maintain, affordable mechanical ventilation can limit the spread of communicable diseases, improve attention span, reduce allergies and asthma and support better test performance compared to air handling systems that are not operated as intended or poorly maintained.
- *Surfaces (flooring, ceiling, desks):* Careful selection can reduce the need for harsh chemicals and cleaners that adversely affect and potentially injure students, teachers and staff, especially custodial workers. Floor finishes, ceiling materials and wall finishes can have significant impact on space acoustics. Hard, non-absorptive materials can increase reverberation and decrease acoustical quality making it harder for students with hearing limitations or cognitive disabilities to understand information being presented.
- *Placement of windows:* Access to daylight can trigger the circadian rhythm and help regulate student's alertness and sleep quality. The effect of glare and brightness can also influence visual acuity.

Physical Safety and Learning

Safety is a major factor in planning schools. Every child and every teacher deserves a safe environment. School shootings have been too frequent in our society. Safety officials from the community are critical sources of information. Those officials should have clear communication pathways to the school administrators and to the programmers and designers. The school community needs to understand that a safety plan is being developed and to have input into its development. If teachers do not feel they are in a safe environment that concern will be telegraphed to their students. If parents do not feel that the children are safe their children will not feel safe.

Designers must contact local officials and open lines of communication between the planning team, municipal leaders and the school administration. They should discuss the school's existing protocols and key concerns about any new development. This is not a singular conversation but rather an ongoing discussion held throughout the programming, design and construction processes.

During the programming process the focus is on opening the conversation, understanding the community's current approach to school safety, learning about potential site issues, and setting goals and parameters for the future safety plan. Site issues may include likely entry points for emergency vehicles, widths of access drives and key approach points, as well as specific neighborhood concerns. It is also important the community be aware of basic safety design strategies that will be employed. These may include:

- planning landscaping to minimize hiding areas,
- providing a single primary entry point with a supervised, locked vestibule,
- planning for clear lines of site and visibility throughout the site,
- minimizing unsupervised hiding spaces within the school,
- ensuring the classrooms have secure areas of refuge,
- ensuring that appropriate portions of the building can be locked off from one another to minimize movement during an event,
- providing technology for access and building lockdown, video cameras for visual supervision and recording, and
- ensuring appropriate glazing in high-risk areas requiring natural light.

Many key elements of the safe school will not be fully determined during the programming stages. For instance, the technology ultimately employed to synchronize cameras, access cards and computerized lock downs will probably not be figured out at this initial stage. What is critical is to allow the school community to raise questions and concerns so the design team can understand the goals and begin to consider the most effective ways to create a safe school environment for that community.

It is also important to convey that, as you are creating a school that is safe from outside intrusion, it is also important to avoid making it feel like a prison or a bunker. In most instances the elements put in place to protect the students should be invisible. Schools should be designed to foster compassion, creativity and joy. Emotional safety and physical safety are closely intertwined. If a school building does not appear welcoming, students and families will not feel welcome.

Social and Emotional Safety and Learning

Our brain evolved in part by discovering patterns and recognizing information that would help us stay alive. When we can successfully see patterns, solve problems or grasp a new concept, the brain releases positive feedback that stimulates us to want to take on more challenges. The spark of insight caused by acquiring new knowledge feels good and that, in turn, translates to an increased desire to acquire additional new insights.

Conversely, when problem solving is not successful, perhaps the knowledge required to solve the problem is not available, not enough time is allowed, or stress levels are simply too high, the interest in problem solving will be diminished.

Stress occurs when we sense an imminent or perceived threat, whether mental or physical. With that perception, our bodies will tend to shift into a fight or flight mode. An increasing release of adrenaline and cortisol prepare our muscles and cardiovascular systems to respond and take action by increasing heart rate, respiration and blood pressure. Under these conditions, survival is prioritized, and learning can be diminished. The relationship between learning and stress is complex, but stress can impair memory formation and new learning can also be impaired by stress. Long-term stress with the continuous neurobiological response it causes can damage parts of the brain that focus on cognition.

The balance within a classroom may be hard to obtain. Educationally, a learning challenge is good and can be highly motivating to undertake and highly satisfying to overcome, but too much stress can diminish the motivation and turn the satisfaction into despair. Not only is the initial learning not achieved but the delight and emotional engagement needed to take on new problems are diminished or lost.

Many students have stress outside of the school that can impact their ability to learn. Often that stress is beyond the potential of the teacher or the school to mitigate, but there are ways that school and specifically a school building can be a refuge for many students and help them diminish the impact of stress on their lives. While much of the emotional engagement comes through the child's relationship with the work and the teacher, a building design can help reduce stress or at least not add to it. Students need to be able to find their way easily within the building and understand where they physically belong. Wayfinding systems and graphic landmarks can help orient oneself as do frequent windows allowing visual connections to the out-of-doors. Endless windowless corridors can be overwhelming for anyone, let alone a child. Visual clutter and disarray appears to increase stress with some students. Designing school elements like windows, seating, graphics, shelving and counters in keeping with the student's height helps to reinforce that this is a place meant for them. At the same time, ensuring accessible or universal design for all means users with diverse abilities are able to move through and make use of the building comfortably.

The Natural Environment and Learning

Edward O. Wilson, the great biologist and author, popularized the concept of biophilia. His hypothesis was that humankind felt an innate and genetically determined love for the natural world. There is a growing body of evidence suggesting that experiences with nature support cognitive function, physical health and psychological wellbeing. Students randomly assigned to classrooms with views of greenery perform better on concentration tests than those assigned to purely "built" views or windowless classrooms [1]. Enjoyment and engagement have been reported to be higher during outdoor-based learning activities than parallel indoor activities [2,3]. Natural light has been shown to have a positive impact on learning and there is even some evidence that design elements that integrate patterns or images from nature can also have a positive impact on learning. Connecting students to nature both in and out of school buildings is an important key to effective learning and should be a significant component woven through the programming process.

There is another reason to assure that awareness of the natural environment is woven through the programming process. Schools are typically designed to stand for at least 50 years. School construction like all construction is a carbon-intensive effort both in the construction and over its life of operation. Decisions regarding water use, waste mitigation, landscaping and recyclable and healthy materials all play into the creation of a sustainable facility. The community should be aware of the environmental impacts and, ideally, be open to mitigating some or all of that impact. The school building itself can play two significant roles: the structure and its operations are an excellent learning tool for students, and sustainability choices made for the building can serve to educate the public.

The Community and Learning

The community can also play a role in student learning. At a basic level, creating a school where parents feel they are welcome reinforces their connections with their children and with teachers and provides another layer of emotional security for most children. Many schools provide dedicated parent information or resource centers within the school to encourage parent participation.

Children also benefit by feeling they are part of the larger community and many schools achieve this quite effectively through inviting the community into the school after school hours to make use of gyms and theaters. Many communities hold civic functions in their cafeterias and libraries. Ties to the community can also be reinforced through graphics and imagery that invoke the local history, heroes or natural resources.

There are other reasons to consider the community when designing schools as well. As demonstrated in many communities across the country during the pandemic, schools often serve as resource centers, providing meals, access to technology or even shelters during emergencies. In some communities the school functions as the primary public connection with families.

Any given school is part of a school district's larger ecosystem. Planning of a school needs to be considered as part of the district's overall PreK-12 educational plan. This may mean studying the community demographics, ethnic and racial distribution, transportation systems including pedestrian and bike access, and grade configuration. Climate change and sea level rise now are important factors when considering the potential of a new school site. Air pollution and noise have significant negative impacts on a child's learning and there is increasing research suggesting that access to green space can have a positive impact. Every community is different and these differences can and should affect school planning as well as the final design.

Part 2: Visioning and Planning

Visioning Process—Setting Goals

The programmer needs to understand the client's specific needs for their students, educators and community, but it is also important for the client to understand the impact that the physical building can have on learning, on the community and on the greater environment. Goals in each of those three areas should be established and clearly understood so that decisions about how best to meet specific needs flow out of clear and agreed upon objectives. The necessary dialog to articulate goals can be initiated through a visioning process. A visioning process most typically involves a broad cross section of the community including educators, administrators, and students. These stakeholders all come together to consider how teaching and learning will take place, the role the schools will play within the community and the role the building will play in the larger natural environment.

Many educational administrators considering a new building or a significant overhaul of an existing building already have a clear understanding of their pedagogical goals. For them, a visioning process is an opportunity to share and explore that understanding with the design team and the entire community as well as an opportunity to think broadly about how a new building will help support those goals. However, for many educational administrators, the visioning process is a fresh opportunity to come together with fellow educators and community members to brainstorm about the future of teaching and learning, to provoke new thinking, and to establish new shared goals for learning, for the community and for the natural environment. Regardless of where the group is starting, the Vision Process leader has an opportunity to provoke new ways of thinking about learning and about the relationships between physical space and learning in a new facility.

That process provides groundwork for thinking broadly about the whole child. A successful visioning process will consider and establish:

- shared teaching and learning goals,
- shared community goals, and
- shared sustainability goals.

Once these goals are established the process can move to the implication of those goals on the nature and quality of spaces that are needed, the relationships among spaces and with the out-of-doors, and the role the building will play in sustaining its community and our shared natural environment

Setting Learning Goals: Weymouth Middle School

The visioning process is a series of exercises and conversations to provoke and explore different types of pedagogy interspersed with examples of different ways that teaching and learning take place. The opportunity to plan a new Weymouth Middle School elicited enthusiasm from both educators and parents. Weymouth is a traditional blue collar community with a history of manufacturing. Located just south of Boston, its demographics are changing as a younger, professional class moves in. While the existing school was appreciated, this seemed to be an opportune moment to look to the future and set new goals. A visioning process of four meetings was developed. A group of approximately 40 people representing educators, community members, parents and students was invited to attend the sessions.

At the first session, the Superintendent and the Middle School Principal presented current initiatives and innovative programs to give the audience a sense of what was currently underway. The visioning facilitators then provided some background on the neurological research impacting teaching and learning and examples of project-based, themative and exploratory models that had evolved from the available science. The group then worked together and in smaller groups to think about possible educational missions and possible learning goals for the future middle school.

The preliminary outcomes from the first meeting were quite interesting. Student engagement, keeping students emotionally engaged with their learning, was a clear priority. Viewing a child holistically, where engagement might come for some through math and for others through art was recognized. From a school that was just beginning to integrate hands-on problem solving came a commitment to learning that was hands-on and real-world-based with an emphasis on interdisciplinary science, technology, engineering and fine and performing arts. Unusual for a middle school was seeing career preparation in school as a tool for engaging and empowering student learning. There was also a clear understanding of wellness and of social and emotional

WEYMOUTH MIDDLE SCHOOL VISIONING GOALS

Educational	Community	Facility
New School should... • support fine and performing arts • foster wellness • begin to prepare students for future careers • promote learning that is hands on and engaging • support STEAM programs and interdisciplinary learning • allow students the opportunity to learn by solving problems • support social and emotional growth of students • encourage students to feel empowered and responsible for their own learning 5	New School should... • provide spaces that support town-wide community needs • reflect the town of Weymouth's commitment to education • inspire school pride amongst students	New School should... • provide different environments for different activities • allow occupants to feel a sense of ownership in their space • be able to adapt to the future and new methods of teaching and learning • be durable and low maintenance • allow for students to move around and be active • have places for outdoor learning • prioritize safety • feel open, inspirational, and full of natural light • provide spaces for students to interact and work together • support equity and be accessible to all students • include the most up to date technologies

FIGURE 7.1 Visioning for the school based on educational goals, community goals, and hopes for the facility itself. Image courtesy of HMFH Architects.

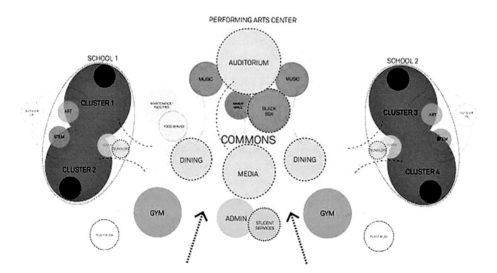

FIGURE 7.2 A loose, conceptual model of the school environment created as part of the programming process. Image courtesy of HMFH Architects.

growth as an integral part of the learning. Their draft goals after the first session are given in Figure 7.1.

Over the next two sessions these ideas and their implications for learning, for education and for spaces within a school building were discussed in more depth and then small groups were asked to graphically illustrate the outcomes (Figure 7.2).

The diagram shows some of the conceptual outcomes of the process and captures much of the thinking around how children learn and many of the learning goals that were discussed during the visioning. In the diagram, the 1,400 student school is divided almost entirely into two smaller schools, an upper 7th and 8th grade school and a lower 5th and 6th grade school, allowing students a comfortable, familiar and clearly recognizable homebase within the larger school. In this case each of the smaller schools has its own art, music, gym, outdoor classroom and dining space as well as its home academic area. Just as importantly, each school has its own counselors and administrators fostering clear support for the health and wellness of the students and for their families within their own small school. These moves were intended to provide a sense of security and welcome for the students and their parents. In addition, they allow teachers to get to know and more deeply engage the students in their small school.

Each school is further divided into two grade-level clusters, each with interdisciplinary teaching teams collaborating with their groups of students. The teams, with dedicated project areas, are intended to encourage project-based learning across the traditional disciplines. The history teacher teaching ancient Greece can easily engage the math teacher in the importance of Pythagoras in geometry. Measuring for, and building a model of a Greek temple can reinforce both the math and the history lessons. This opportunity to reinforce important concepts through multiple strategies and perspectives helps to develop and reinforce neural pathways along the way. It can also support complex problem solving, which might not otherwise have been part of the history lesson.

Each cluster has designated STEM/Vocational space. In this move, Weymouth is doubling down on both hands-on learning and real-life learning as strategies to foster student engagement in learning.

Through the planning and early design phases of the project the goals did not change but many of the strategies evolved. Ultimately the school became a 6–8th grade school with three small schools, one for each grade level rather than two. The STEM/Vocational spaces turned into major focal points for the school, visually and physically demonstrating their importance with the educational plan. They are tied into high school career strands so students can continue their interests as they move into secondary school. Throughout the evolution the goals served as a North Star reminding them of the basis of their hopes and aspirations for their students.

None of these concepts are solutions in and of themselves. They are put in place as opportunities to provide teachers and students an infrastructure that supports teaching and learning. They each require enormous teacher commitment, pedagogical development and dedication to begin to have an impact.

Setting Community Goals: St John New Brunswick Elementary School

A new or newly renovated school has the potential to play an important civic role within the community. Articulating that role can be a huge step in building support for the school during the planning phases but, more importantly, maintaining community support and providing critical resources and addressing critical needs for students and community members throughout the school's lifetime. These opportunities will shape the nature of the facilities, the site, the entrance and how the public moves through the facilities. The visioning process is the time to articulate and prioritize these opportunities.

St John, New Brunswick is a community which is currently in the initial planning stages for a new elementary school within its urban core. Their visioning process brought together educators, parents, non-profits, health and social services organizations, and civic leaders to consider the school building as a true community center. The process led to a commitment to public/private partnerships that will provide space and services within the school such as early education, after school care, family health and mental health services, and a community event space with a kitchen. Their gym and playground will be used after school and on weekends by neighbors and community groups. Through the visioning process it became clear that they see their new school as more than a learning environment. They see it as a core component in building and strengthening the economic future of their citizens and their community. And, central to that, is assuring that the students and their families have a full range of services, commonly referred to as wrap-around services, through their neighborhood school. The economic health of the community is tied directly to the health and wellbeing of their students.

This approach is particularly important as many communities, particularly urban communities, consider how to assure greater equity where systemic racism has too long shaped educational and health outcomes. Too often urban schools have been subjected to higher levels of air pollution and noise, older facilities with neglected systems and less access to green space. Each of these attributes correlates with lessened academic achievement.

Needs evolve over time. Many schools became daily food distribution centers and technology access points during the pandemic. As climate change ushers in a higher frequency of severe weather incidents we are seeing more and more schools being used as temporary emergency shelters or as short-term warming or cooling centers. In all communities it is critical to leverage the planning for a new school to bring resources such as gyms, community centers, health care, emergency shelters and food distribution centers into the conversation. In many communities the school auditorium is the only place where community members might see a live performance.

Setting Sustainability/Environmental Goals: The Fales School

When planning a school, a community should also be thinking about the larger environment. Buildings through their construction and operation make up about 40 percent of global CO_2 emissions. While we commonly think of designing energy-efficient buildings, and perhaps even using renewable energy sources, we often are not aware of other impacts, for instance, the energy used to manufacture and transport materials to the site is significant. If all buildings were built wisely and durably with energy efficient systems and envelopes, minimal water use, minimal waste, and using healthy materials that are not carbon intensive in their production, then their CO_2 contribution and other impacts environmental would diminish significantly. Very directly, CO_2 emissions can be detrimental to student health and learning. The characteristics of an energy-efficient school, well-balanced natural light, indoor air quality and temperature control all contribute to student health and wellbeing, which, in turn, improves student learning.

Establishing environmental goals early in the process will have greater impact than adding them after major decisions have been made.

Key goals should be established around:

- energy use,
- water use,
- waste reduction,
- materials used both for student health and also for material use to minimize carbon production, and
- building's use as a learning tool.

The Fales School Sustainability Visioning Process was a separate process from the educational visioning process. It quickly became clear that the community was very dedicated to exploring the extent to which the new school building might become a zero net energy building. Establishing this purposeful and attainable goal early in the project gave the Fales team the opportunity to prioritize specific site planning strategies that were crucial to the achievement of the goal. The building is partially sunk into the ground, reducing its energy use. Roofs were sited to take advantage of south facing roofs for photovoltaics and north facing clerestory windows that reduced interior lighting requirements. The goal is integral with the planning and outcome of the project, which is currently expecting to produce more energy than it requires to operate.

Programming a school building is also a wonderful opportunity to teach students and the community about carbon emissions, water use and waste, and how by working together reductions can take place. Many schools choose to integrate environmental studies into their curriculum in which case the building cannot only be a learning tool during design and construction but can continue to be an environmental learning tool in its operations.

Conclusion

School planning today is very different from ten years ago. Neurological and health-based research points toward specific approaches for effective teaching and learning. This, in turn, impacts school design. While many teachers are consciously employing the research, many educators and most community members are unaware of the implications of teaching modes on school buildings and on school buildings' role within the greater community. Understanding the body of knowledge and its effect on education is critical to the design of schools. Helping educators and community members employ that knowledge during the planning process will assure the school is designed for the way it will ultimately be used.

The school planning process is complex and multi-dimensional. We are planning places that will stand for upwards of 50 years. Understanding how these buildings can help to support teaching and learning, as well as strengthen communities and contribute to mitigating climate change is a key aspect of school planning.

References

1. Li, D., Sullivan, W. C. (2016, Apr.) Impact of Views to school landscapes on recovery from stress and mental fatigue. *Landscape and Urban Planning.* doi:10.1016/j.landurbplan.2015.12.0152.
2. Skinner, E., Chi, U. (2012, Jan.) Intrinsic motivation and engagement as "Active Ingredients" in garden-based education: Examining models and measures derived from self-determination theory. *The Journal of Environmental Education.* 43(1): 16–36. doi:10.1080/00958964.2011.596856
3. Alon, N. L., Tal, T. (2015, Apr.) Student self-reported learning outcomes of field trips: The pedagogical impact. *International Journal of Science Education.* 37(8): 1279–1298. doi:10.1080/09500693.2015.1034797

8
PROGRAMMING FOR WELL CERTIFICATION ON A UNIVERSITY CAMPUS

Robin Z. Puttock, RA, LEED AP BD+C, WELL AP and Angela Loder, PhD, WELL AP

> Our understanding of health as a multi-dimensional phenomenon is enhanced when we widen our perspective to include user participation, multiple scales, and rigorous standards of evaluation. The authors show how this was done with the involvement of architecture students in evaluating three new buildings planned for the campus of the Catholic University of America in Washington, DC using the WELL Building Standard. This experimental pedagogical activity can serve as a precedent for future community programming and health evaluations.

A sociologist at Cornell named Stephen Sweet encouraged his students in 2002 to observe and learn from their campus as a microcosm of society. During the spring semester of 2021, architecture and environmental studies students at the Catholic University of America (CUA) were encouraged to do the same. CUA currently has three significant design and construction projects underway: a dormitory, a dining commons and a classroom building. Recognizing this as a unique opportunity to analyze how different university building programs can contribute uniquely to the wellbeing of students, a new course was developed by the School of Architecture and Planning at CUA to partner students (the user) with the University Architect's office (the owner), and members from all three of the design teams (the designer). The course is called *Human Centric Evidence Based Design for WELLbeing* and features a foundation in both the evidence-based WELL Building Standard and the methodology of data gathering and case study analysis related to the built environment's effect on human wellbeing. Students use their growing knowledge of the WELL Building Standard's concepts of Air, Water, Nourishment, Light, Movement, Thermal Comfort, Sound, Materials, Mind and Community [1], which will be further elaborated upon below, to analyze the data gathered from peer interviews and apply it to a semester-long case study assignment. This chapter presents the themes that have started to emerge during this multi-disciplinary and multi-programmatic process.

The Catholic University of America

The Catholic University of America is located on 176 acres in Northeast Washington, D.C. and is the home to about 5,700 students and workplace for about 800 faculty. There are 12 individual schools within the University, including a School of Architecture and Planning. CUA was

DOI: 10.4324/9781003164418-11

founded in 1887 and its first building, Caldwell Hall opened in 1889. The last building to be constructed on CUA's campus prior to this recent design and construction surge was Opus Hall which opened in 2009. There are 50 buildings on campus now comprising over 2.3 million gross square feet. The campus is almost 75 percent green space within a fairly dense urban area of Washington, D.C. The topography of the campus varies a good deal which provides some challenges for accessibility and universal design, but also provides the opportunity for green space preservation and active design strategies [2]. One more aspect of this campus design that specifically lends itself to programming for wellbeing is, as the National University of the Catholic Church [3], CUA draws inspiration from Pope Francis' encyclical, *On Care for our Common Home, Laudato Si'* which states, "it is not enough to seek the beauty of design. More precious still is the service we offer to another kind of beauty: people's quality of life" [4].

The WELL Building Standard

The WELL Building Standard was first introduced in 2014 by the International WELL Building Institute (IWBI) and is currently the culmination of over a decade of research into the many ways that the built environment can "enhance, rather than hinder our health and wellbeing" [5]. In general terms, the WELL Building Standard is a rating system

> "premised on a holistic view of health: human health as not only a state of being free of disease—which is indeed a fundamental component of health—but also of the enjoyment of productive lives from which we derive happiness and satisfaction [6]."

As we all know, there are many rating systems related to health and wellbeing available today. The questions that all of them have to face are: How do you create standards when the research is unclear or shifting? How do you balance the need for adaptable, globally applicable standards with specific contexts and populations? What do you include, and what do you leave out [7]? In addition, and perhaps most related to this chapter, how do you educate the next generation of architects, planners and designers to understand and apply these standards? These questions are at the heart of IWBI's approach to research and the WELL Building Standard. The WELL Building Standard was selected for this course because as of the date of this writing, there are almost 6,000 WELL certified and/or registered projects in 67 different countries. These projects comprise over 829 million square feet. It is clearly a system that is gaining momentum in the industry and fluent knowledge of it will serve the students well in their future career paths.

Using the socio-ecological model [8] and a holistic approach allows IWBI to draw on the best-available evidence that links design, policy and built environment strategies to human health and wellbeing outcomes for the WELL Building Standard. The evidence supporting each feature is substantiated by a combination of peer-reviewed scientific literature and academic research, existing design standards, laws or codes, and best practice as identified by researchers, industry experts, and public health and other relevant professionals. Each feature is based on the latest evidence and has been chosen based on its potential impact on human health and wellbeing, as well as its feasibility for implementation given current market and technology conditions [9].

Results from post-occupancy surveys and indoor environmental testing, as well as regular addenda updates, will also help to contribute to further understanding which features are most effective, globally applicable and most commonly implemented. It can also help identify which features may need to be adapted for a global market. This requires a flexible, adaptive approach to translating research to practice, and ongoing feedback from stakeholders, subject matter experts, and the projects themselves [10]. The combination of best available research, and design and policy best practice, along with continual testing and feedback, enables the International WELL Building Institute to continuously improve and update WELL features based on current, cutting-edge research and practice to support human health and wellbeing [11].

The goals of the ten WELL concepts are described in the Building Standard as follows [12]:

- *Air*: to ensure high levels of indoor air quality across a building's lifetime through diverse strategies that include source elimination or reduction, active and passive building design and operation strategies and human behavior interventions.
- *Water*: to address aspects of the quality, distribution and control of liquid water in a building. It includes features that address the availability and contaminant thresholds of drinking water, as well as features targeting the management of water to avoid damage to building materials and environmental conditions.
- *Nourishment*: to require the availability of fruits and vegetables and nutritional transparency and encourages the creation of food environments where the healthiest choice is the easiest choice.
- *Light*: to promote exposure to light and aims to create lighting environments that are optimal for visual, mental and biological health.
- *Movement*: to promote movement, physical activity and active living and discourages sedentary behaviors through environmental design strategies, programs and policies.
- *Thermal Comfort*: to promote human productivity and ensure a maximum level of thermal comfort among all building users through improved HVAC system design and control and by meeting individual thermal preferences.
- *Sound*: to bolster occupant health and wellbeing through the identification and mitigation of acoustical comfort parameters that shape occupant experiences in the built environment.
- *Materials*: to reduce human exposure to hazardous building material ingredients through the restriction or elimination of compounds or products known to be toxic and the promotion of safer replacements.
- *Mind*: to promote mental health through policy, program and design strategies that seek to address the diverse factors that influence cognitive and emotional wellbeing.
- *Community*: to support access to essential healthcare, workplace health promotion and accommodations for new parents while establishing an inclusive, integrated community through social equity, civic engagement and accessible design.

The University Campus

Almost 20 million students were enrolled in American universities in the Fall 2020 semester, belonging to 1,400 four-year institutions and 2,600 two-year community colleges [13, 14]. These university campuses vary in size, population, demographics, academic focus and are in rural, suburban and urban areas of the country. However, as multi-scaled places for living, working and playing, one opportunity remains constant across all university campuses: the potential for universities, as microcosms of society, to foster wellbeing among students, faculty and staff. This impact of wellbeing can be considered at the urban scale, the building scale and on the human scale.

The word "university" is derived from the medieval Latin word "universitas" meaning "a community regarded collectively" [15]. The concept of "community" is a significant component to human health and wellbeing. The World Health Organization (WHO) defines "community" as "a specific group of people, often living in a defined geographical area, who share a common culture, values and norms, are arranged in a social structure according to relationships which the community has developed over a period of time" [16]. The WHO goes on to define "empowerment for health" as "a process through which people gain greater control over decisions and actions affecting their health." And finally, the WHO has defined "community empowerment" as "individuals acting collectively to gain greater influence and control over the determinants of health and the quality of life in their community, and is an important goal in community action for health." Based on what we know of college campuses, they certainly fall under the domain of "communities" and therefore, it is only a natural progression to consider how we can incorporate "community empowerment" in the health and wellbeing of the students, faculty and staff on these campuses. This is the focus of this chapter.

The Unique Opportunity for Programming

It is rare for universities to build new buildings, especially three new projects at the same time. At CUA during the Spring 2021 semester, a unique opportunity presented itself that was a perfect laboratory for joining pedagogy, a research methodology and professional practice in the communication of fundamental evidence-based standards that contribute to human health and wellbeing in our built environment. That semester, three new campus buildings were currently in the advanced stages of planning, design and construction; a dormitory, a dining commons and a classroom building. The School of Architecture and Planning was eager to capitalize on the available learning opportunities of a university landscape undergoing such significant infrastructural changes. The course director saw meaningful potential in engaging with the University's Office of Facilities Planning and Management, whose multi-disciplinary mission at CUA is Stewardship: Taking care of the University's Places and Spaces [17].

Dormitory

The dormitory, amidst the design process by Perkins Eastman at the time of this publication, is a four-story, 100,000 square foot facility housing 350 students. Its schematic design phase is complete, and the design development phase has been placed on a temporary hold due to the COVID-19 pandemic. The design of the facility, currently targeting LEED Silver certification, was influenced by the CUA 15-year masterplan developed in 2012. The masterplan proposed view corridors be maintained and created, especially ones terminating with a view of the Basilica of the National Shrine of the Immaculate Conception, CUA's immediate neighbor and the largest Roman Catholic Church in North America [18].

The design of the dormitory deviated from the masterplan in that it introduced a chapel in the middle of the two wings, both to separate the male students from the female students, and to separate the two quadrangles (quads) into two different programmatic spaces, one an active Green space and the other a passive Green space to be used for quiet contemplation. The designers believed the students should be provided with options to support wellbeing—both physical and mental [19].

Understanding the importance of natural ventilation, emphasized during the COVID-19 pandemic, and the importance of acoustical comfort, the designers included operable windows in all occupied spaces and placed the dorm rooms primarily on the west side of the building which faces the two quads and not the east which is the location of a busy street and metro line.

Finally, CUA placed an emphasis on dormitory amenities that support student wellbeing such as community gathering spaces, kitchens, lounges, group study rooms, quiet study rooms and the chapel. Though these spaces are often what attracts potential students to a university, these spaces are expensive square footage to include in the program and reflect a commitment of the university to the wellbeing of their students as they don't produce direct revenue for the university [20].

Dining Commons

The dining commons is a two-story, 35,000 square foot facility serving 635 students. Also designed by Perkins Eastman and targeting LEED Silver certification, the building is currently under construction at the time of this writing and scheduled to open in Fall 2022. The University program emphasized the need for a variety of spaces and experiences for the students in relation to dining spaces and community feel.

The designers felt it was critical to offer the students both indoor and outdoor dining experiences [21]. In addition, the design provides a variety of spaces on the interior to dine, including an intimate hearth area and a grand dining room with plenty of clerestory light. The main entry sequence invites the student to pass through an exterior garden sequence, culminating in the main interior entry comprising a significant healthy food display.

Perhaps the most unique feature in support of wellbeing of the facility is the way that it addresses the significant topography of the site. The masterplan suggested that the students could move around the building and travel up the hill as they headed to the north portion of the campus. However, the design of the dining commons provides a grand sallyport collegiate gothic stair and associated exterior elevator under and through the building so the students can engage with the design of the building as they navigate the topography. The stair is wide and well lit as the architects recognize the role it needs to play as a gateway between the north and south parts of the campus. The architects expressed their desire for it to be a "joy to experience" [22].

Classroom Building

Finally, the new Conway School of Nursing classroom building, designed by Robert A. M. Stern Architects and Ayers Saint Gross will be a four-story 106,000 square foot building. At the time of publication, it had completed the design development phase and was scheduled for opening in Fall 2024. This classroom building is contracted to achieve both LEED Gold and WELL Gold. The School of Nursing's Dean Patricia McMullen stated that "this project should embody a holistic approach to nursing that includes body, mind, spirit. We need to address all parts" [23].

CUA describes this program as a natural choice for a WELL-certified building due to the population that it serves, as both an educational environment and one that serves the healthcare industry [24]. As a result, several programming decisions were made to promote the wellbeing of its occupants. These include a visible and aesthetic main stair incorporating artwork and lighting features. The student lounge is located adjacent to the exterior oak garden with a Heritage Tree, which encourages both a view connection and a physical connection for the students with the outdoors. A large commons area was included as the main entrance lobby with the goal of bringing the community into the building, either for formal or for informal events. This is designed to be another connection to the exterior, specifically to the grand entrance gateway fountain.

Another programming decision that was inspired by the WELL Building Standard was the restoration space in the building. It was designed to be a quiet place of reflection complete with individual lighting control, thermal control, a variety of seating options and configurations, natural materials and plenty of spaces for privacy. This space was a joint vision of the owner, designer and users with some influence from the WELL Building Standard, which outlines the appropriate square footage for a space like this, based on the occupancy of the building.

Interestingly, the building program did not include all of the spaces that are recommended by the WELL Building Standard. For example, the WELL Building Standard encourages a fitness facility space for its occupants. However, because this building is on a university campus with fitness amenities in other buildings, the decision was made to not include this space to achieve this specific WELL "point."

The interviews with the CUA design teams and the owner's representatives yield some interesting themes. First, the primary goal of the University is designing buildings and sites that promote the wellbeing of their occupants, using the WELL Building Standard as a best-practice reference as it includes evidence-based design from hundreds of credible sources. However, it is important to note that these standards should not be followed "blindly" as a simple exercise in earning points in a rating system. For example, adding a fitness facility in a new building on a university campus might not be the best use of resources when a fitness facility is located in an adjacent building on campus. The University's holistic mission should prevail when it comes to decision-making. For university campus design specifically, outside forces typically prevail, meaning that donors tend to lead the way. Twenty years ago, for example, donors started to demand their alma maters actively demonstrate how their campuses promoted environmental stewardship. At the time of this writing, there is a growing movement demanding emphasis on occupant wellbeing. So much of what is being programmed currently on CUA's campus during this active period of design and construction is, as the university architect has stated, "just common-sense design—designing for the well-being of our students, faculty and staff is just good design" [25].

Human Centric Evidence-Based Design for WELLbeing

Human Centric Evidence Based Design for WELLbeing is the new course that has emerged from this unique opportunity on CUA's campus. The course uses the WELL Building Standard as the textbook, with the goal of all students passing the WELL Accredited Professional Exam at the end of the course. This is a valuable credential for professionals who specialize on the ways that the built environment affects human health and wellbeing. The standard itself is gaining exposure at an exponential pace, partially due to the COVID-19 pandemic and the launch of the WELL Health-Safety Rating for Facility and Operations Management.

The class comprises many majors including architecture, environmental studies and net-zero design, and ranges from second-year undergraduates to third-year graduate students. The students learn about the philosophy behind the WELL Building Standard, as well as the evidence and practice-based research that it is built upon. Students become familiar with the ten concepts of the WELL Building Standard: Air, Water, Nourishment, Light, Movement, Thermal Comfort, Sound, Materials, Mind and Community through reading about and discussing precedents related to each of the concepts over the course of the semester. Each week a nationally recognized guest speaker on the built environment and wellbeing presents their research to the class. A wide variety of perspectives is shared from academia, owners and professional practice, including architects, engineers and contractors.

In addition, what makes this course unique, the thread that weaves the course together, is the case study assignment inspired by the three projects on CUA's campus. It is critical to take advantage of the opportunity to have students at CUA not only learn the content of the course but also to apply it to, and have a voice in, what will become their own personal built environment. In order to understand the power of the application and of the "community empowerment" of the voices of the students, one must first understand the WELL Building Standard itself.

The Case Study

From the onset, it was clear that the pedagogical success of the *Human Centric Evidence Based Design for WELLbeing* course would rely on the successful integration of both the understanding of the WELL Building Standard and its application to the actual design of the built environment. This cannot be achieved by simply studying a building standard or a rating system. There needs to be a real-world application, a personal connection for the students. An opportunity for empowerment. What could be more personal than the environment where the students live, work and play? What could be more empowering than the opportunity to present your thoughts and ideas to the people who are making the decisions? The design and construction projects on CUA's campus have been an excellent laboratory for this class to conduct its research and make its recommendations.

The semester-long case study for this course follows a loose interpretation of the scientific method as a methodology: make an observation, ask a question, propose a hypothesis, make predictions, test the predictions and iterate [26]. For most of the students in the class, this methodology comes quite naturally as most are designers and problem solvers. Design thinking is a skill that design schools such as CUA integrate into their curriculum from the very beginning. For this case study assignment, students first gained a foundational understanding of how the built environment affects human health and wellbeing. The students quickly realized that most of what was being taught was already inherently known by them. Natural daylighting and views to nature are good, sitting at a desk all day without moving is bad. The new content that was delivered to the students included specific evidence-supported ways that the design of the built environment could change health outcomes for the better, focusing on the three building programs that CUA was introducing into their campus with new facilities: the dormitory, the dining commons and the classroom building.

Next, the students gathered data from their peers in a student preference survey distributed to over 100 fellow CUA students, composed of 20 written response questions soliciting qualitative feedback about favorable and unfavorable built environments on campus. In addition, the survey solicited four sketches, again, of favorable and unfavorable built environments on campus. The goal of soliciting different forms of feedback, visual-spatial as well as linguistic-verbal, was not only a nod to Howard Gardner's work [27], but was also designed to allow for analysis which would lead to three-dimensional design solutions.

After the data gathering portion of the case study, the students began the data analysis phase. Students were encouraged to consider the following prompts as they analyzed the survey data: "Which WELL Concepts were referenced most often in the responses? Think about why this might be." "Is there a correlation between the program of the space and the responses?" and "How does any of the above apply to how we as designers should program spaces on college campuses? (i.e. What spaces should have access to daylight? What spaces should be adjacent? What spaces can be loud?)." Students were tasked with formulating a theme encompassing what they gleaned from the data and to create a layered diagrammatic analysis in both sketch form and with tables and charts. In addition, students were to identify existing precedents on university campuses around the world that successfully demonstrate the themes that emerged from the analysis for the three program types: dormitories, dining commons and classroom buildings. For example, one student team identified the importance of stair design as a significant component of active design, which is included within the Movement feature of the WELL Building Standard. Another student team studied the importance of adaptability of spaces, particularly as they related to the Mind Concept. Finally, one particularly innovative team studied Light and Sound and added Space to develop a new take on a psychrometric chart (Figure 8.1) to theorize

Programming for WELL Certification

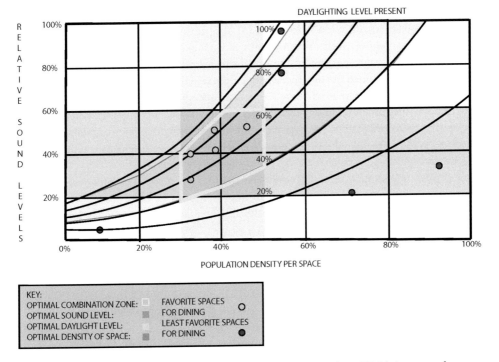

FIGURE 8.1 Student work in *Human Centric Evidence Based Design for WELLbeing* maps the convergence of ideal soundscape, population density, and lighting quality. Image courtesy of CUA students Nolan B, Sean D, Tim L, Madison S, and Holly T.

wellbeing in each program space in terms of these three features when compared to the student survey data.

The next step in the case study analysis was to build upon the wellbeing themes and select at least one building on CUA's existing campus for each of the three building program types for further study. For this next phase of analysis, the students used 3M's Visual Attention Software (VAS) to understand the wellbeing implications of each building program type as designed. To understand the impact of a VAS analysis, the students needed to first understand the evolutionary biological science behind it. In layman's terms, the brains of human beings have evolved to house a mechanism to allow the visual system to select specific information that is biologically required from the environment for survival [28]. For example, it is known that humans see red before we see green. Theories have been suggested that this is so early humans could see red apples in a field of greenery that would provide sustenance [29]. It is also known that humans see edges first, which may be to provide valuable information regarding escape routes [30]. This information is received subconsciously, or precognitively, in the first three to five seconds. After five seconds, what we see is part of our cognition. According to neuro and data scientists, "VAS simulates the first glance phase before gender, age, culture, and viewer tasks impact the viewer's attention. If viewers see your content during this first glance, it's more likely that they will engage with it consciously later" [31]. For the purposes of this course, the focus is on determining what we, as human beings, see in the precognitive moments. It is during this these first seconds, it is theorized [32], that what we see governs our behavior, can cause us to linger in a space and make positive memories that we will consciously associate with that space [33]. However, it is postulated that the reverse is also true, that if we do not precognitively "see" an environment, this lack of a frame of reference can make us feel anxious or unsafe [34].

Using the theories identified in Ann Sussman's and Justin B. Hollander's book *Cognitive Architecture* as described above, students ran photos of each existing CUA building type through VAS to identify what aspects of the building and site design are visible to human precognitive sight, meaning what human beings receive through visual inputs prior to conscious vision. Working under the premise that what we see in our precognitive sight affects our wellbeing as described above, the students could identify what humans see on a first glance when encountering each built environment. The students were able to analyze which environments contributed positively to wellbeing and which did not. These analyses were compared with the student preference survey data and the themes and hypotheses were tested.

For example, one student team hypothesized that occupant social comfort was affected by the programming of the space (dormitory, dining commons or classroom). What felt comfortable in one program, such as the community feel in a dormitory actually felt crowded in a

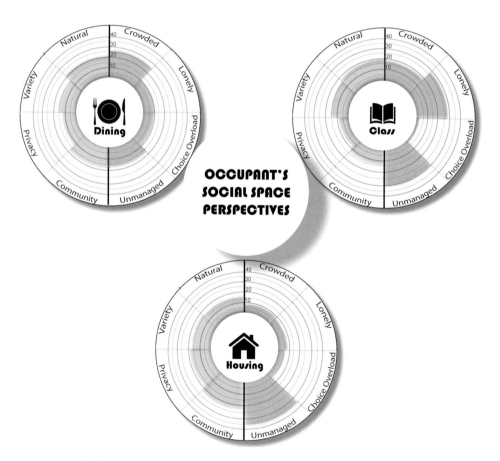

FIGURE 8.2 Student work in *Human Centric Evidence Based Design for WELLbeing* illustrates the variance of characteristics desired between categories of social space. Image courtesy of CUA students Claire B, Claire D, Brianna H, and Julianna O.

dining commons or in a classroom. This hypothesis was supported by the data as shown on the student chart in Figure 8.2. Another conclusion cited by this same student team was that a variety of seating was seen as comfortable in classrooms and dormitories, but was often considered uncomfortable in dining commons. The data stated this was due to choice overload already in those spaces. A future VAS analysis of examples of all three of these spaces might show both the gaze sequence and the areas of interest which have the potential to prove or disprove the student hypotheses. This will be part of the second half of the semester case study work.

Armed with evidence, research assistants of the course director were able to expedite their case study work ahead of the rest of the class in order to produce documentation for this book chapter by press time. These students, working closely with the course director, ran VAS analysis on photos of existing buildings on CUA's campus, specifically looking at active design elements as their case study focus. After analyzing the VAS reports of the existing condition photos of interior and exterior stairs of all three building programs on CUA's campus, this research team then created Photoshop "Re-inventions" to hypothetically improve upon the existing designs of the buildings and sites on CUA's campus. These "Re-inventions" were once again run through 3M's VAS software and the results were analyzed. Did the "Re-inventions" invite precognitive vision to the spaces the student-designers wanted to highlight, for example, the stairs in the active design? It is clear from Figure 8.3, that the Photoshop "Re-inventions" allow humans to see the stairs in their precognitive sight and therefore are more at ease and can actually make favorable memories in that space. It is thought that, in this case, the human being is more likely to take the stair and be active as opposed to staying home or taking the

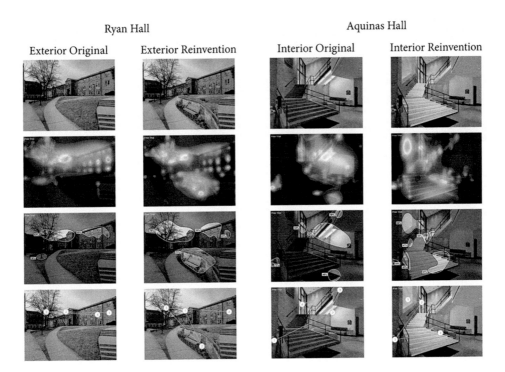

FIGURE 8.3 Student work in *Human Centric Evidence Based Design for WELLbeing* suggests changes to spaces across campus based on VAS analysis. Image courtesy of CUA students Evan D, Megan D, Erin O and James G.

elevator. This additional movement, a concept in the WELL Building Standard, can contribute to improved wellbeing.

The last phase of the case study was to build upon the application and empower the students to be a part of the design of their community. Expanding beyond suggested design "Re-inventions" to existing work, the students were now provided the opportunity to propose "Re-inventions" to the design work that was then "on the boards" at CUA. About midway through the semester, the design professionals chosen to shape the campus of CUA (dormitory, dining commons and classroom building) accompanied by CUA's University architect and her team, presented their work to the students. Students, who were emboldened with their newly acquired knowledge of both the WELL Building Standard and its application to existing campus building types, asked a multitude of questions to the design professionals during the presentations. The students knew that the final part of the semester-long case study assignment would be to prepare and propose "Re-inventions" to the design professional teams on each of the building types. The students will have an opportunity to shape their campus community. The professional design teams have been invited to one of the last classes of the semester to act as the design jury for the "Re-inventions." The director of the course is optimistic that the students will have a voice and their ideas will be *well* received.

Conclusion

It was the goal of the course *Human Centric Evidence Based Design for WELLbeing* to take full advantage of the unique opportunity that presented itself at CUA with three simultaneous design and construction projects and to provide a call to action to the students of CUA. Hopefully, these students will be empowered to use their voices, and their new understanding of the WELL Building Standard to communicate with design teams who are shaping their own built environments to foster human health and wellbeing. This is a critical and timely topic, highlighted by the COVID-19 pandemic. The time is now to provide the knowledge to the next generation of designers to "create spaces that inspire; spaces that are inclusive; spaces that allow us to flourish; spaces that help us become happier and healthier people" [35].

References

1. International Well Building Institute. (2018). *WELL v2.* https://resources.wellcertified.com/tools/well-v2-or-q4-2020/
2. Ibid.
3. The Catholic University of America. (n.d.). About Us. https://www.catholic.edu/about-us/index.html
4. Pope Francis. (2015). *Laudato Si': On Care for Our Common Home* [Encyclical].
5. International Well Building Institute. (2018). *WELL v2.* https://resources.wellcertified.com/tools/well-v2-or-q4-2020/
6. Ibid.
7. Loder, A. G. W. (2021). Translating Research to Practice. *Guidelines for Prevention and Preparedness, Resilience and Recovery: A Foundation for Action.* International WELL Building Institute pbc.
8. Center for Disease Control and Prevention. (2013). *Social Ecological Model.* https://www.cdc.gov/violenceprevention/about/social-ecologicalmodel.html
9. Loder, A. G. W. (2021). Translating Research to Practice. *Guidelines for Prevention and Preparedness, Resilience and Recovery: A Foundation for Action.* International WELL Building Institute pbc.
10. Ibid.
11. Ibid.
12. International Well Building Institute. (2018). *WELL v2.* https://resources.wellcertified.com/tools/well-v2-or-q4-2020/

13. Moody, J. A. (2019, Feb.). A Guide to the Changing Number of U.S. Universities. *US News and World Report*.
14. National Center for Education Statistics. (2020). Back to School Statistics. https://nces.ed.gov/fastfacts/display.asp?id=372#College_enrollment
15. Oxford English Dictionary. (1989). University. *Oxford University Press*.
16. World Health Organization. (1998). Health Promotion Glossary. https://www.who.int/healthpromotion/about/HPR%20Glossary%201998.pdf
17. (D. Nauta-Rodriguez, personal communication, March 11, 2021).
18. The Basilica (n.d.). https://www.nationalshrine.org/rectors-welcome/
19. (M. Bell and C. Calleri, personal communication, March 11, 2021).
20. (D. Nauta-Rodriguez, personal communication, March 11, 2021).
21. (M. Bell and C. Calleri, personal communication, March 11, 2021).
22. Ibid.
23. (L. White, personal communication, March 11, 2021).
24. Ibid.
25. (D. Nauta-Rodriguez, personal communication, March 11, 2021).
26. Khan Academy. (n.d.). *The Scientific Method*. https://www.khanacademy.org/science/high-school-biology/hs-biology-foundations/hs-biology-and-the-scientific-method/a/the-science-of-biology
27. Gardner, H. (1983). *Frames of Mind*. New York: Basic Books.
28. 3m. (n.d.). *The Science of VAS*. https://vas.3m.com/scienceofvas
29. Ibid.
30. Sussman, A. and Hollinder, J. B. (2015). *Cognitive Architecture: Designing for How We Respond to the Built Environment*. New York: Routledge, Taylor & Francis Group.
31. 3m. (n.d.). *The Science of VAS*. https://vas.3m.com/scienceofvas
32. Sussman, A. and Hollinder, J. B. (2015). *Cognitive Architecture: Designing for How We Respond to the Built Environment*. New York: Routledge, Taylor & Francis Group.
33. Sussman, A. (2020, October 13). Eye Tracking Architecture to 'See' Human Nature. *Geneticsofdesign.com*.
34. Sussman, A. and Hollinder, J. B. (2015). *Cognitive Architecture: Designing for How We Respond to the Built Environment*. New York: Routledge, Taylor & Francis Group.
35. International Well Building Institute. (2018). *WELL v2*. https://resources.wellcertified.com/tools/well-v2-or-q4-2020/

PART 3
Streetscapes

9
PLACEMAKING
Programming Urbanism for Human Engagement

Robert S. Tullis AIA

>The science of place is rooted in our embodied cognition, the instinctually crafted perceptions of safety, liveliness, containment, and engagement. The author has synthesized the insights of theoreticians and investigators of the public realm, identifying the essential aspects of successful urban spaces, and illustrating how our perception of space is tied to cultural narrative as well as social imperatives.

We are a social species. This characteristic is part of our DNA. We instinctively feel a need to gather simply to connect with others. And we do so in buildings and city spaces. It has been estimated that in the developed world we spend 90 percent of our time in the built environment. Much of that time is spent inside buildings, but we also spend time outside; walking, sitting, conversing, dining, shopping or recreating in the urban public realm. Urban spaces have always been important in the civic life of cities and societies. But, as Ann Sussman [1] has pointed out, we evolved in places without buildings and our cognitive facilities evolved not expecting to see buildings. So urban spaces are most successful when they are designed in concert with *basic principles of human perception and behavior*; when they promote human health, happiness and emotional connectedness; and when they encourage or incubate interaction and thus become a theater for human events. This chapter discusses human factors in the programming of such spaces, both their use and their form, and how the identity of "place" and significance accrue to well-designed and attractive urban public spaces.

As other chapters in this book point out, programming with respect to human factors is important for individual buildings and their interiors. But it must also be applied to the design of exterior spaces, primarily those of the city and town, to create a successful and civic public realm, or as Jan Gehl called it, "life between buildings." This chapter will suggest a methodology for such programming based on specific tenets:

- that building design should always take into consideration (as Renaissance architects like Leon Battista Alberti advocated) the form of the exterior spaces produced by it,

DOI: 10.4324/9781003164418-13

- that exterior public space is most successful when it is designed (as Aldo Rossi maintained) as a distinct and memorable *locus solus* that functions as a theater for human events,
- that research (from Camillo Sitte through Kevin Lynch and Jan Gehl to recent brain study) on human relationships to urban public space should guide its design, and
- that when space transforms into distinct "place" (as Yi Fu Tuan and other phenomenologists theorized) a bond between the human being and urban form takes place.

I maintain that we should strive to design the public realm so that our urban spaces have a greater likelihood of *making this transformation* and *creating this bond*. And that we don't have to guess why good public spaces are successful and attractive. Extensive research has been conducted on place characteristics, their spatial form, human behavior in them, human perception of them and our emotional reactions to them. This research informs the contents of this chapter. While the names of the researchers and theorists cited above and others referred to below are often well-known, the specifics of their work are not widely applied by designers today. Our public realm, quality of life and civic identity suffer as a result.

Pope Francis wrote

> "Given the interrelationship between living space and human behavior, those who design buildings, neighborhoods, public spaces and cities ought to draw on the various disciplines which help us to understand people's thought processes, symbolic language, and ways of acting. It is not enough to seek the beauty of design. More precious still is the service we offer to another kind of beauty: people's quality of life, their adaptation to the environment [2]."

And as Winston Churchill more famously said, "We shape our buildings, and thereafter they shape us.[1]"

What Is Place and Placemaking?

Often when buildings are designed, little attention is paid to the urban spaces that they create. We may think that some are successful by happenstance, or perhaps we wonder why we instinctively prefer some places and not others. We all have our touchstone references for distinctive, memorable and beloved urban spaces. For streets, a good example is Barcelona's Las Ramblas. For squares, it's the Italian piazza, Florence's Piazza della Signoria, for example. Why do these places work for so many? Is there something inherent in their form, in their activity, in their DNA, that makes them resonate? How is it that they somehow *transform from space into place*? What, fundamentally, is the dynamic of placemaking?

To explore these questions we must first define *place* and *placemaking*. Places can exist at many scales, big or small. Your bedroom is a place and North America is a place. But for our definition, we will focus on *exterior public spaces that can be experienced as a single entity, taken in by the human senses as a single experience*. Piazzas or squares are the best example, and they have been used for centuries as elements around which districts or cities are organized, and they have functioned as the shared physical resource for the civic engagement of communities (Figure 9.1).

Scale of our focus: exterior public spaces experienced as a single entity

Place de Toscane, Val de Europe, France
Photo from SkyscraperCity.com

FIGURE 9.1 Image courtesy of SkyscraperCity.

What is placemaking? One answer is that all you need to change space into place is human activity, and the term is used by organizations that plan community-building events in public spaces. This event-based approach is usually called "creative placemaking." While valuable for its social impact, this approach shows little concern for architectural form. The definition of "placemaking" for our purpose is *the creation of a legible space within the city fabric, one that has the power through its form and use to be memorable and attractive to people, and thus have identity and meaning.* By means of this power, space becomes place; not merely the voids between structures left over when the building design is done.

Placemaking's three-legged stool therefore begins with both use *and* form. The third synergistic element has been variously called image, meaning, emotion, memory, identity or even authentic relationship to context. Christopher Alexander called it "the quality without a name." It is the "je ne sais quoi" that attempts to describe how humans relate to space. Today it's often called *sense of place*. Let's begin our discussion with activity and use, and then examine the physical form that serves as the home of those activities. As we do, let's also note the human factors of place design and some of the research on the relationship between human beings and place, just a smattering of what designers should know. We'll conclude with a brief introduction to the theory of Situated Cognition and what neuroscience has to teach us about the interaction of our mind, body and environment (Figure 9.2).

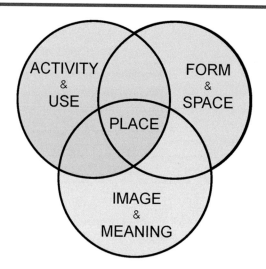

FIGURE 9.2 Image courtesy of Robert Tullis.

Activity and Use

So, what are the activities that we are designing for? What's our program brief, if you will, for active urban public spaces? Let's apply a little rigor to our discussion. There are three major categories of human activities in such public spaces: *un-programmed activities, semi-programmed activities and programmed activities.*

Un-programmed activities are those that people initiate on their own, as part of their individual use of the space. Things like strolling, talking, sitting, relaxing. They are the most prevalent and numerous activities in the public realm. For these to occur regularly, the characteristics of the space must resonate with human predispositions. The space must feel friendly, offer spatial definition and be occupiable in a way that meshes with how we instinctively behave.

Some researchers have focused on such human behavior in public open space, setting up cameras to record it, counting people, diagramming their movements. William Holly Whyte's work in the mid-1970s is the most well known [3, 4]. Holly Whyte posited that the presence of unprogrammed activities is the "yardstick" for measuring successful places. If a space allows or fosters these behaviors, if people feel comfortable enough to engage in them, then its design is good. If a space is unused, people instinctively see it as uncomfortable, and there is something wrong with its design.

Whyte found that people tend to *sit* in well-defined edge locations, such as steps, walls and ledges even if they are in the mainstream of the plaza's travel paths. Whyte found that when people *stand* on a plaza, they tend to station themselves near fixed objects such as a bollard, flagpole or statue. What he found people rarely do is choose the undefined middle of a large space. These are examples of what another researcher, Jan Gehl [5–7], termed *the edge effect* and of what thinkers from Camillo Sitte [8] to Christopher Alexander [9, 10] have observed. Alexander wrote, "If the edge fails, then the space never becomes lively" [11]. From biological research we now know this to be an evolved edge-hugging trait called **thigmotaxis** [12].

Whyte observed people's tendency to stop and chat in the midst of the most active pedestrian traffic paths and their tendency to sit where they can face others walking by. The see-and-be-seen aspects of this social interaction are consistent with another biological human instinct proven by brain research that we unconsciously and constantly scan for faces. Whyte observed what he called a process of **triangulation**, in which some external stimulus provides a linkage between people and prompts strangers to talk to each other as if they know each other. And he famously concluded "What attracts people most, it would appear, is other people" [13]. Jan Gehl refers to this proclivity when he cites two Nordic sayings, "Man is man's greatest joy," and "People go where people are" [14].

Both the edge effect and our tendency to scan for faces strongly correlate with geographer Jay Appleton's *prospect and refuge* theory; that humans prefer physical environments that meet a basic human psychological need for both opportunity, where one can survey the surroundings, and safety, where one's back is secure [15]. Appleton says that recognizing this evolved and innate human desire gives us the means to understand successful and enduring *place aesthetics,* and the ability to predict them. And it gives us the ability to successfully design places with such qualities. As designers, we must ask ourselves if our buildings form exterior spaces with the right characteristics for unprogrammed activities to occur.

Semi-programmed activities are similar to unprogrammed activities in that they are self-initiated, but they require the availability of some specific facility. Civic facilities like post offices and libraries generate semi-programmed activity. In the days before cell phones, a bank of phone booths always correlated with popular places. Today, public Wi-Fi incubates semi-programmed activity. As do public toilet facilities, especially for those with infants. And don't forget pets; dog parks attract a crowd as can public watering stations. We have all witnessed the triangulation effect of strangers stopping to pet someone else's dog and striking up a conversation. Sometimes simply the setting out of things can encourage semi-programmed activity. Public chess games are an example; all that's needed is a table. Boston's Post Office Square encourages use of its lawn by making seat cushions available at lunchtime, and offers a "reading room" that's just a rack of general interest books and magazines. People spontaneously played the pianos set out in Boston's squares during a "Play Me, I'm Yours" program. Anything that encourages people to sit and lengthen their stay will do.

Some of the most prevalent semi-programmed activity is retail-based; public behaviors like window shopping and newsstand browsing. The king of retail-based semi-programmed activity is al fresco dining. It animates exterior public spaces at many times of the day and people spend long periods of time there. Diners watch the passers-by and they watch the diners. Everyone is drawn by food and drink.

In addition to purpose-specific facilities, designers should incorporate more general design elements proven to encourage semi-programmed activity, particularly in retail environments. Whenever possible, wide and zoned sidewalks should be provided; we can use the acronym SHOP to define these zones. The sidewalks should have clearly delineated Storefront, Hallway, Outdoor amenity and Parking zones. The outdoor amenity zone should be populated with trees and distinctive lighting, seating, trash receptacles, protective bollards, bike racks, public art and the like.

Facades should provide soft edges with lots of nooks and crannies to facilitate edge-hugging. Jan Gehl emphasizes that these edges should consist of smaller vertical facades or multiple bays on larger ones, so that there is variety, diversity and an iterative beat to the changing experience as the pedestrian walks along the edge. Horizontal facades are generally not well suited for retail. People's average walk rate and average blink rate means that new visual information should be presented every 15 to 25 feet. And in the retail world there's something known as the "five second rule." A storefront has five seconds to tell its "merchandise story'" or the pedestrian will be past the door before their subconscious tells them to turn in [16]. Arcades, canopies, and awnings should be provided as elements of an *armature of connection and passage* (discussed in more detail later), or should be encouraged by tenant design guidelines. Quality signage and low-sill storefronts with a minimum of 70 percent glass should also be mandated by tenant guidelines to encourage inside-outside human interaction. As a practical matter, designers should think of the base-building architecture that defines storefronts as an empty stage on which multiple different sets can, and will, be built over time to tell different "merchandise stories" and to incorporate different and distinct "trade dress." Changes due to the lifespan of stores or restaurants or leases shouldn't negatively impact the human relationship with the more permanent structure of the retail edge condition (Figure 9.3).

Programmed activities are those that require a license, sponsor or organizer. Included in this chapter is a programming pyramid, developed from a similar diagram by Biederman Redevelopment Ventures, the company responsible for the renovation of NYC's Bryant Park, its fabulously successful operation, and consultation on a variety of other good programmed public spaces. It shows four categories of programmed activities to consider when planning retail-oriented mixed use projects or civic spaces. When planning for programmed activities, suitable physical space, surfaces and utilities must be pre-engineered into the urban public realm.

Daily Characteristics are the foundation; things that people who visit the public space will find every day, like street performers and distinctive vendors. These are key to encouraging people to habitually engage with a space. What elements can designers use to support daily characteristics? The acoustic qualities of recessed arcades might be considered to support musicians. Natural grade changes can be leveraged to create a stage area that doesn't look vacant when there's no show. Jan Gehl posits that 12 feet is the comfortable human "public distance," a distance we subconsciously choose if we want to hear a street performer, but at the same time indicate we don't want to be part of his show. And sure enough, we typically find that a 12 foot radius circle

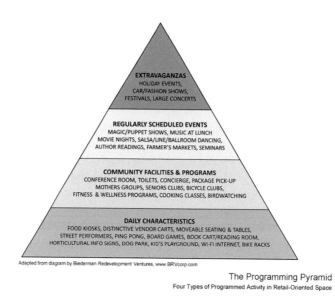

The Programming Pyramid
Four Types of Programmed Activity in Retail-Oriented Space

FIGURE 9.3 Image courtesy of Dan Biederman, BRV.

defines the front row. Architects wouldn't dream of designing, say, a baseball diamond with less than 90 feet between bases, but we mis-design exterior public social spaces (or never consider such human factors as part of their program) all the time.

Community Facilities and Programs are closely related to daily characteristics, allowing a space to host gatherings like mother's groups, senior's fitness groups, bicycle clubs, etc. Playgrounds for kids and meeting rooms for adults are examples. If the place can act as the "home" for community interests, then the participants are more likely to build a role for it in their life and frequent it even when their group isn't meeting there. Such gathering spots must be considered part of an un-enumerated program of uses and activities.

Regularly Scheduled Events include weekly farmer's markets, Friday movies in the park, or Wednesday dance classes. Retail places can leverage the merchants: a bike shop can be a race's starting line, a kitchen shop can sponsor cooking classes, a wine shop can host a tasting event. Surfaces and utilities are important design considerations, especially for food-related events. Try to double-purpose street and plaza space. An office parking lot can be used on weekends for a market, or a row of parallel parking spaces can be reserved for licensed food trucks during the lunch hour. Hard paving allows the space to be hosed down when the trucks drive off. Good delivery access and trash removal are a major consideration, as are electrical power and drainage.

Extravaganzas are things like Christmas tree lightings, winter skating, summer concert series, spring car shows or fashion shows, and Fourth of July fireworks. Siena's Palio is the classic example of a major extravaganza held in a distinct place, the Piazza del Campo. Again the forward-looking provision of appropriate surfaces and utilities should be part of the program, perhaps enumerated specifically for extravaganzas. A concealed and sound-isolated location for a portable chiller and an underground route for glycol lines to the central location is needed to stage an ice rink. And buried electrical and sound lines in a pavement hatch are needed for the all-important Christmas tree.

But you can't just have the extravaganzas; you need to foster and sponsor activities at all four levels in order to appeal to multiple people at multiple hours of multiple days throughout the year. In a successful public open space, people will be attracted if they feel that "something's always going on." It's important for designers to think about these activities and uses and to provide physical opportunities for them as well as facilities that support them in ways that humans can instinctively relate to. When the space sustains liveliness, it becomes memorable and acquires social significance, and perhaps most important, emotional and cultural meaning.

In addition to our categorization of activity as unprogrammed, semi-programmed and programmed, Jan Gehl posits that human activity can be sub-divided into *necessary, optional, and social* categories [17]. He says that necessary activities like commuting to work or shopping for basics happen regardless of the quality of the environment, but that optional activities like dining out are greatly influenced by a quality environment, and social activities like meeting friends for drinks and dinner are dependent on multiple people perceiving that an environment is of high quality. Holly Whyte quantified that the five most-used New York City plazas in his surveys had 45 percent of their users visiting in groups while the five least-used plazas had 32 percent in groups [18]. He noted that when people visit in groups it's because they have all agreed to, and that therefore use by groups is an index of selectivity.

Optional and social activities in the public realm also last longer. Gehl maintains that the *frequency or number* of activities and their *duration* in time are both influenced by good design. He says that life between buildings, successful and vibrant urban public space, is a product of the number of activities times the duration of those activities. The notion of *stasis* is important here. It's not how many people move through a public space, but the amount of time that they spend in a space, that gives it vitality.

If you want stasis, you must design places for people to sit. In his studies of public plaza seating, Whyte logged the amount of time each person sat. One might assume that the majority of in-and-outers account for the bulk of the total time spent sitting, but that was not the case. He found that only one quarter of a plaza's total sitting time was spent by those who sat for less than ten minutes, three-quarters by those who stayed 11 minutes or more, half by those who stayed 21 minutes or more [19]. Whyte developed his research on the subtopic of *"sitability,"* or how the availability of places to sit, their location, and their physical types and sizes encouraged sitting or incubated the human predisposition to sit. In addition to documenting the human preference for edge conditions he famously advocated the use of moveable chairs, finding that the ability to move a chair gave people a subconscious but satisfying feeling of ownership over the seat. The lesson for designers who want to encourage optional and social activities? Both Gehl and Whyte preach, "Design for the person who's going to sit awhile" [20].

But we are also a walking species; we have evolved to walk. Our hunter-gatherer ancestors likely walked 5–10 miles a day. Many of us still walk a mile or more daily. City spaces and streets from ancient times through the early Renaissance were designed around people who walked everywhere, or in the case of the military, mustered, drilled, and marched. With the advent of personal use of the horse and carriage and even the streetcar, cities still functioned at a pedestrian pace. It was only with the widespread use of the automobile that city design became detached from the speed and scale of walking. For our placemaking focus, we should come full circle to examine the design characteristics that support this basic unprogrammed activity, specifically the act of walking within a defined urban place. In the age of computer apps like Walk Score, we generally refer to these characteristics as contributing to a place's *"walkability."*

In the Form and Space part of this chapter, we will touch on how the subconscious relates walking to *spatial proportions* and to the presence of an architectural *armature,* and how pedestrian movement involves *serial vision* in architectural composition. But for now let's examine the basics of the activity of walking.

According to Jeff Speck [21, 22] there are four characteristics that an environment must offer to have walkability. The walk must be useful, safe, comfortable and interesting. By *useful*, Speck means that there must be reasons to walk; the necessary, optional and social activities that Jan Gehl categorized. They must be compact, best provided in close proximity to each other in mixed use environments. And within the quarter mile-5 and half mile-10 minute walk circles that relate the speeds at which we walk to the distances we are willing to walk. And they must be well-connected, with access to parking, sidewalks, bike lanes and bike share, transit nodes, and the like (Figure 9.4).

By *safe*, he means both perceived safety and real safety. Perceived safety is the presence of physical characteristics of place that cue a person to feel safe, like well-lit and clear views (Oscar Newman also wrote about these in 1972s *Defensible Space*). Real safety is the presence of things like street trees and parallel parking that protect pedestrians from traffic, narrow streets and small corner radiuses that slow car speeds. And no "swoopiness," the stream-form designs that typify limited access roadways, where drivers are subconsciously cued not to look for pedestrians. By *comfortable*, he means walks along good edges with places to sit and stand and lean. Walks that offer prospect and refuge aesthetics through good spatial definition and zoned sidewalks of sufficient widths.

To be *interesting*, Speck says there must be signs of humanity, the presence of other people assured by uses that are active at different times of day and by distributed entries that pulse people onto the sidewalks at different places. Walks with continuity; no missing teeth in the street wall. Walks with visibility; with lots to look at through open facades and storefronts. Walks with sequence; a cadence of different stimuli tied to our walk and blink rates. Jan Gehl and Chris

Placemaking **117**

"A GENERAL THEORY OF WALKABILITY"

To be successful, an environment must offer four characteristics. The walk must be:

1	USEFUL	Reasons to walk Mixed uses Compact Connectivity	Necessary, optional, social behaviors (Gehl) Live, Work, Play, Shop, Institutions 5 minute and 10 minute walk circles Access to parking, bike lanes/bike share, transit
2	SAFE	Perceived Safety Real Safety	Defensible Space characteristics (Oscar Newman) Street trees and parallel parking Narrow streets/lanes, small corner radiuses (slows car speeds, necessitates small blocks) No "swoopiness" (stream-form designs)
3	COMFORTABLE	Prospect & Refuge (Jay Appelton) Spatial Definition	Good edges (Edge Effect, Jan Gehl, Chris Alexander) Container ratios Zoned sidewalks
4	INTERESTING	Signs of Humanity Continuity Visibility Sequence	Uses active at different times of day, distributed entries No missing teeth Open facades, storefronts Cadence, vertical proportions, walk and blink rates Serial Vision (Gordon Cullen)

FIGURE 9.4 Image courtesy of Jeff Speck—Walkable City, 2012.

FIGURE 9.5 No place to stand in Houston: The pedestrian is the least important sidewalk occupant. Image courtesy of Robert Tullis.

Alexander teach us about the importance of establishing intermediate destinations, eye targets that break the route into "digestible segments" and lead the pedestrian along [23, 24]. As we'll see, Gordon Cullen teaches us how to shape building placement to make the walk interesting and connected.

In all of these characteristics, we should note that the human factors of vision and perception link pedestrian movement with *seduction and discovery*. That when we feel curious, intrigued or even seduced to walk forward to discover something that is hinted at but not quite cognitively complete, we are likely to do so. And that when discontinuity or obstructions break the spell, we will stop, turn around, or otherwise abandon walks that do not fall into Jan Gehl's necessary activity category. As shown here in Houston, that city's history of near total disregard for the pedestrian experience leads traffic engineers to make room on the sidewalks for nearly everything except the human being! As placemakers interested in design that anticipates and facilitates human activity in urban places, we should do better (Figure 9.5).

We have discussed the broad categories of unprogrammed, semi-programmed and programmed activities; and we've distinguished those that are necessary, optional and social activities. During this review we've noted how good design, using an awareness of human factors, can leverage them to support this program brief. Human factors like the edge effect, the importance of soft edges with vertical proportions and an iterative beat, our face-scanning tendency, triangulation and our attraction to other people, prospect and refuge spatial characteristics, instinctual social distance, the importance of stasis, and characteristics that encourage people to sit and to walk. Now let's turn more completely to the second leg of placemaking's three-legged stool, the form of the public realm and some design methodologies that can help.

Form and Space

Just as our programs for building interior spaces specify physical characteristics needed to support their functions, so too should the programming of exterior urban spaces address those that support the desired human activities. Edward T. White [25] posited that the formal design of a place can prohibit, impede, discourage, allow, promote or create activities. Imagine these levels of activity-support as a range on a VU meter. He wrote "Activity is created by a place when *human nature* meets *environmental opportunity* to bring about *human behavior*." Those not comfortable with the notion that design can "bring about" or create activity can substitute the word "encourage" or "incubate." Regardless, when we design public open space we should be trying for the positive side of White's range, leveraging human factors with supportive architectural and spatial form (Figure 9.6).

So, what formal elements can provide the environmental opportunity that meets human nature to bring about (encourage, incubate) human behavior? In discussing form as it applies to placemaking, there are two major categories: *solids and voids,* or elements and space.

Solids: Architectural Elements

Let's first talk about the solids. All architectural form begins with these primary elements: point, line, plane, and volume [26]. Points within the city are nodes and physical markers, usually vertical. A well-known example of the use of points in urban placemaking is Pope Sixtus V's plan for Rome, in which obelisks were set up to mark important nodes in the public realm to serve as targets for future or reconfigured streets and piazzas. Lines are often treated as an axis, as in Rome's Piazza San Pietro or Paris' Champs de Mars. Lines can lead forward in a certain direction, as at Louis Kahn's Salk Institute, or can be felt in the tension between two point markers,

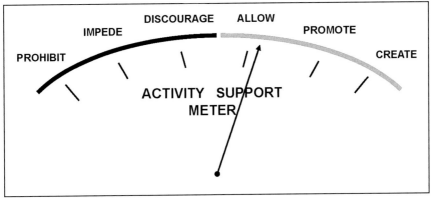

"Activity is created by a place when **human nature** meets **environmental opportunity** to bring about **human behavior**."
Edward T. White

FIGURE 9.6 Activity and Use: Design of a space to support human activity. Image courtesy of Robert Tullis.

as at Place Stanislas in Nancy France. Planes are often walls, and are usually the definers of an edge condition. Their edges can be exposed or articulated to imply a thin depth as at Florence's Piazza Santo Spirito or a thick depth like the "colonnade" at Rafael Moneo's Murcia City Hall. Volumes are most easily recognized as solid objects in space, with perceived mass, weight and independent identity. Their independent nature can be heightened by their physical separation as at Piazza Maggiore in Sabbioneta, scale difference as at Bramante's Tempieto San Pietro in Rome, or decorative contrast with other structures as at Campo Santa Maria Nova in Venice.

Note that the functioning of point, line, plane and volume in city design are (or should be) related to *basic principles of human perception and behavior*; that *how* these forms are perceived by people leads directly to *whether* they support human activity within civic life, and *why* they do. Kevin Lynch, in his influential book [27] focused on human perception, how people *perceive and remember* city spaces and urban patterns. Lynch documented how, to understand and navigate through a city, people first and foremost create a cognitive map, a "generalized mental picture of the external physical world," based on their experience [28]. He discovered that the map is the result of a *two way process* between individual and environment; the environment suggests distinctions and relations among the various physical parts of the city, and the observer selects and organizes them in a personally meaningful way. Lynch discovered that people use five distinct components of a city when forming images of it in their mind; *paths, edges, districts, nodes and landmarks*. If these are the components that literally make city spaces memorable, then it makes sense that we should use them to help create memorable social places. And to evaluate our designs to assure their legible definition.

How can designers use these basic solids in placemaking? Three useful design methodologies, *typology, mannerism and armature* can help with the answer.

In *typology*, architectural elements within the city fabric are abstracted to become just that: elements. No longer are buildings seen as specific architectural solutions to specific programmatic needs of a specific owner or client, designed by a particular architect with a particular style or approach, at a particular time for a particular site. Instead they are seen as formal constructs that play a certain role in urban design (examples of axes, edges, focal points, deflectors, paths, portals and places) overlaid onto place-design problems to help develop and test solutions. They are *types*. Next, these types become devices or tools to fulfill certain functions, like chess pieces that each move in a distinct way according to rules. The associated notion is that architecture behaves somewhat like language; just like nouns, verbs and adjectives are arranged according to a grammatical set of rules to form sentences, so too are buildings of different types arranged to form places, districts and cities. A good reference for the use of typology in urban design is Colin Rowe and Fred Koetter's 1978 book *Collage City*.

A more personal and referentially Italian theory of urban typology is Aldo Rossi's 1966 book *The Architecture of the City*. Like *Collage City*, it's a critique of the modern movement's effect on the city and focuses on architecture's role within urbanity and the effects of time, history, memory and meaning. Rossi felt that modernists had thrown the baby out with the bathwater when they rejected history in their quest to banish historicism. Rossi says that a city must be understood and valued as something constructed by man over time. Of particular importance are *urban artifacts which withstand the passage of time*. In contrast to modernism's anti-monument polemics for instance, Rossi argues that the city remembers its past through monuments, and that memory and monuments give structure to the city. He asserts that over time, the built city embodies the collective memory of its people, and that such memory is therefore associated with places and objects. He believes that such "effects and facts" are the data of the city, "analogues" with which new but timelessly meaningful places can be built.

Rossi gives an interesting example, citing Canaletto's c. 1756 painting, Capriccio Palladiano. In it Canaletto advances the notion of the Italian ideal city by painting an entirely realistic and convincing but fictitious (analogous) city space. In the center he paints a design by Palladio for Venice's Rialto Bridge that was never built. Flanking it Canaletto paints two buildings by Palladio that actually exist, but in a different city (Vicenza). Rossi says that this scene "nevertheless constitute[s] an analogous Venice formed of specific elements associated with the history of both architecture and the city... [It] constitutes a city we recognize even though it is a place of purely architectural reference" [29]. This leads to Rossi's most important idea for us; that of the "locus solus," or *singular place*. The city as theater for human events isn't just a site that can accommodate and give meaning to events and rituals, it is an event itself. The singularity of a place is recognizable in the distinct "permanences" that mark the events that have *or can happen* there. Unlike the modernist's "zeitgeist" (the spirit of the times), Rossi's "locus solus" is the spirit of the place (Figure 9.7).

As a design method, typology relates to human factors because it employs and reassembles architectural elements based on the functional role assigned to them by human perception (and their familiarity as historical artifacts recognized among people). Typology assumes that we intuit that a door is for moving through and a colonnade is for moving along. Typology rejects an urge for abstraction and engineered "total design" solutions, and instead embraces pragmatic, episodic, eclectic and *specific* forms that are rooted in human experience. As a planning technique it advocates looking at precedents as a referential point of departure, a benchmark or yardstick if you will, for composing the spaces between buildings (more on composing urban *space* in a moment).

Mannerism, as a placemaking design methodology, is sort of an extension of typology, but relates more specifically to the edges of urban spaces, to the parts of the buildings that define them. Mannerism, for our definition here, is the manipulation of expected architectural norms to produce a compositional tension or instability that emphasizes solid-space relationships and

FIGURE 9.7 Cited by Rossi as an example of an Analogous City. Capriccio Palladiano, Canaletto (Giovanni Antonio Canal) c. 1756.

draws attention to the variant elements. Mannerism, as we are using the term, facilitates the treatment of different parts of the building and facades *distinctively* and allows emphasis to be put on certain parts and facades in response to their immediate exterior context rather than in response to the interior functions they contain. By using a mannerist approach, the building design becomes more about *place than project*.

History is full of examples, particularly the late Renaissance and Baroque periods. Michelangelo's manipulation of the building facades facing the Campodoglio and Da Cortona's manipulation of the forms defining the piazzetta at Santa Maria della Pace are two well-known examples from these times in Rome. But let's look at a specific 20th-century example; the 1989–1990 buildings at 38 and 64 Sidney Street in University Park at MIT, Cambridge, MA. Both were designed by Koetter Kim & Associates (led by Fred Koetter, co-author of *Collage City*) as the first components in their University Park masterplan and design guidelines. The masterplan extends a street-and-block pattern through the available land and places interconnected open spaces along a major and minor axis so that the various parks and courtyards read like voids carved from the mass of surrounding **urban fabric**. These two buildings face, shape, and define four distinct urban spaces, two side streets, and a service street. Their facades are individually and hierarchically manipulated (we'll call them A, B, C and D walls) to relate to these exposures, not to coalesce into a uniform wallpaper-like skin of a free-standing object nor to solely express the buildings' internal use.

Their A-walls face the largest public central park. They are composed of a series of grand order piers, and are articulated as having *depth*, an implied ten foot zone of metal and glass behind the piers. This zone doesn't really exist inside (all homogenous lab/office space to the core) but is imposed on the building for mannerist reasons. This sets the A-wall apart as a grandly scaled independent element, giving it a heightened importance commensurate with its position in the urban grid, and it gives the A-wall's piers the independence needed to break free of the building mass. For at the center of the composition the last piers are run past the ends of the buildings, detaching from them to form a gateway at the next public space, the plaza between.

Note other mannerist tricks employed at the A-walls. The narrow flanking windows in each bay are recessed to emphasize the figure quality of the middle windows and the object quality of the piers. The entry bays are emphasized not by varying the piers (which owe fealty to the scale of the park and thus shouldn't be changed) but by fully recessing the entire window and not just the narrow flankers. And note how the facades don't end at a solid brick pier as you might expect, but rather that the glass "zone of depth" appears to extend out laterally from behind the piers, punctuating the separation from simpler perpendicular walls lining the plaza (Figures 9.8 and 9.9).

These are the C-walls, third in the hierarchy of facades. At the plaza, and at the side and service streets, both buildings are sheathed in simpler flat walls with punched openings. Raised stringcourses are the only architectural articulation here, and they are employed to keep your eye moving horizontally along to the corners where the action is.

While most of the rear C-walls face the service street, the inner 30 feet of each face a secondary public space on the masterplan cross-axis, Landsdowne Quadrangle. So here a B-wall is employed, separated from the plaza's flanking C-walls with a vertical slot. The B-wall picks up characteristics borrowed from the A-wall but slightly "dumbed down." The architecture is telling us that this space is important, not as important as the central park, but important enough to be defined by a special face (Figure 9.10). (In plan, the ground floor entry lobbies are offset to get the rear entry doors centered in the B-walls.)

At the southeast corner of 64 Sidney's service street is a small roundabout street, called Pilgrim Circle. Here the interstitial C-walls are completely interrupted and replaced by the insertion of a special composition, a D-wall whose whole purpose is to define and give distinct identity to the circular urban space. Note the mannerist moves here. The D-wall is separated

38 & 64 Sidney Street
A Walls, facing primary street and park

View along Sidney Street
showing the gap at the main cross-axis

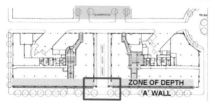

Mannerism and Facade Composition
The A Walls

FIGURE 9.8 Image courtesy of Robert Tullis.

Placemaking **123**

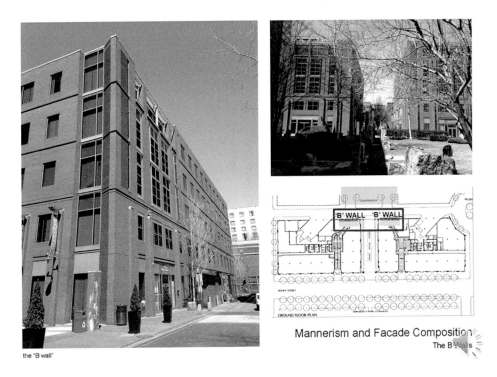

FIGURE 9.9 Image courtesy of Robert Tullis.

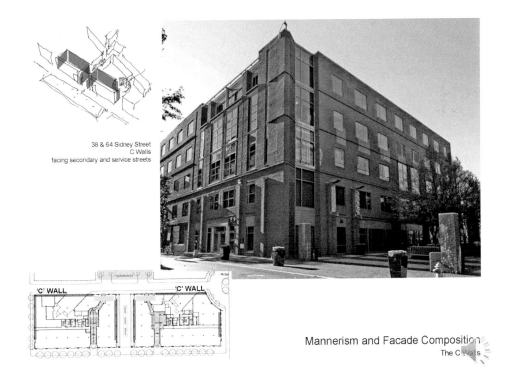

FIGURE 9.10 Image courtesy of Robert Tullis.

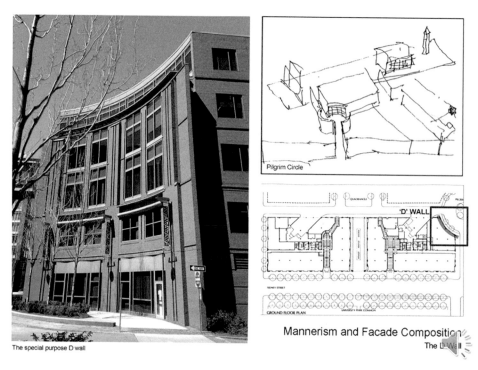

FIGURE 9.11 Image courtesy of Robert Tullis.

from the building with glass slots and its end piers are run completely past the corners of the mass, which is held back at the attic story to complete the illusion of a detached element that embraces the roundabout. These winged ends set up a threshold condition that heightens your sense of passing into a distinct space. Use of such a mannerist approach to building design, especially the manipulation of the edge forms and facades to define exterior spaces, shows how to *put place before project* (Figure 9.11).

The concept of *armature* comes from William Mac Donald's *The Architecture of the Roman Empire, Vol. 2, An Urban Appraisal*. The Romans extensively used armature in their architecture and urbanism. In his concluding chapter entitled "Form and Meaning," MacDonald writes, "The buildings need to be seen not as isolated archeological or typological examples, but as essential, interdependent parts of urban configurations, members of civic families rather than of functional or stylistic groups" [30]. He goes on to say,

> "Partly this Roman order arose from a powerfully developed sense of the importance and the necessity of strongly stated boundaries… In mature architecture this evolved into systems of orderly control, not only of axes and vistas, but of the definition of a building overall. This definition was in large part the product of a keen sense of boundary functions in Heidegger's terms [Martin Heidegger, the 20th century German existential philosopher], who speaks of the boundary as not that at which something stops but … that from which something begins its "presencing." A concept of possessive location, of the clear and indisputable definition of place, was crucial to the nature of Roman architectural order [31]."

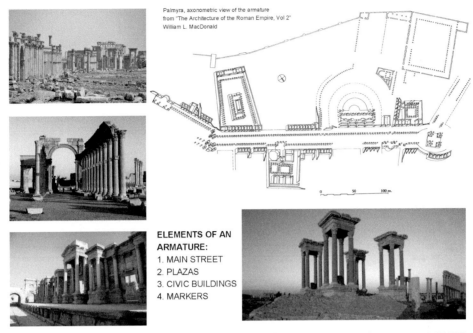

FIGURE 9.12 Printed with permission of Yale University Press.

These two related concepts, Heidegger's notion that a boundary is where something *begins to assert its presence*, and MacDonald's notion that through "possessive location" comes an indisputable *definition of place*, together address the apparent dichotomy of figure and ground (Figure 9.12). So how does MacDonald think the Romans accomplished this possessive location? He writes, "Order was realized by defining and relating structural and spatial relationships exactly, by holding them together in rationally conceived frames" [32].

> "Their deep concern for the concept of place, of fixed and well-marked centers, is shown by numerous formal devices and hundreds of buildings… Urban content [was] derived from contextual relationships among public buildings and from the architecture of connection and passage [33]."

Examples of *an architecture of connection and passage* from the ancient cities of Palmyra and Djemila are colonnade-lined streets, arches at thresholds and bends, fountains and way-stations at important nodes, and stairways at grade changes. They are the structures that people passed through, moved along, or paused at on their way to and from the plaza and civic destinations. They are the *signs* that people *read* to aid the legibility of place; "the definitive frame of the town's formal essence." And they are the solid formal components that should be part of our programming of human-centered public open space. The concept of armature has great applicability to our concern with making legible and memorable urban places, and it functions at a local and experiential scale, which is the scale of our concern. In more contemporary architecture, Charles Moore's Kresge College, a precinct within the University of California at Santa Cruz, is an example of the armature along a linear plan, and Leon Krier's "Res Publica—Res Economica—Civitas" diagram is a guide to using armature within a gridded plan [34] (Figure 9.13).

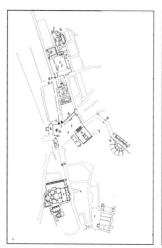 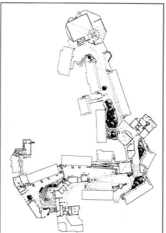 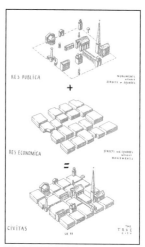

THE ANCIENT ARMATURE
Djemila, city plan
Source: William L. MacDonald
The Architecture of the Roman Empire, Vol. 2

THE ARMATURE ALONG A PATH
Kresge College, UCSC, 1972
Charles Moore and William Turnbull
Source: GreatBuildings.com

THE ARMATURE IN A GRID
Leon Krier Ideogram
Source: Krier, The Architecture of Community

The Armature
An Architecture of Connection and Passage

FIGURE 9.13 Printed with permission of Yale University Press.

Voids: Architectural Space

Let's transition from talking about solids to talking about voids, or *urban architectural space*. Typology, mannerism and armature, as ways to classify, manipulate and arrange solid forms, intersect with concepts of urban space in *the human being's act of moving through the space amongst the solids*. Here we can apply Gordon Cullen's concept of *serial vision*. Cullen's 1961 book *Townscape* is all about the visual influence of movement and time as a determinant in the creation of distinctive places. He developed a design theory of sequential experience that accompanies pedestrian movement, through linked squares and streets and across perceived thresholds. He contends that spaces seen episodically and together "give a visual pleasure which none can give separately" [35]. Cullen coined terms like *closed vista, deflection, narrowing and projection/recession*, to describe the effects one gets while walking, and he encouraged designers to use them in orchestrating the placement of solid forms in the city. He writes, "We discovered that the human being is constantly aware of his position in the environment, that he feels the need for a sense of place and that this sense of identity is coupled with an awareness of elsewhere" [36]. Cullen's methodology (like Ed White's and Camillo Sitte's, below) is primarily aesthetic and visual, as opposed to rational. The important touchstone here is human perception during movement through distinctive urban spaces (Figure 9.14).

Edward T. White [37] has posited that humans perceive all public spaces to have the role of either path, portal or place based on *our reading of their proportions*. Paths are linear spaces with attenuated proportions, portals are constrictions or transition points between paths and places, places have more equilateral proportions (often squares, root two rectangles or golden section rectangles) with stability of shape. White maintains we then have *expectations of how to act* in them, either to move along, pass through, or stay in. From the standpoint of human behavior,

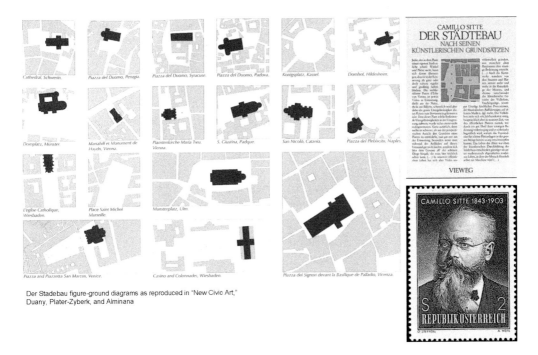

FIGURE 9.14 Image courtesy of Andres Duany.

it's useful to think of the spaces we design in these categories, and to understand that they have distinct symbiotic relationships to their use by pedestrians.

Nineteenth-century Vienna architect Camillo Sitte is the godfather of research on urban space. In his landmark 1889 book *Der Stadtebau* "City Planning According to Artistic Principles," Sitte focused on the design of popular and beloved piazzas and squares, trying to understand what physical features made them so. He presented his findings using the graphic technique of figure-ground analysis. Looking at these, we note how the piazzas and the streets leading to them appear to be outdoor rooms carved from the surrounding building mass, and that they have defined shapes. This is, of course, what architects refer to as *figural space*, volumes *of* space rather than *free space*, volumes *in* space.

Sitte distilled six principles for planning good city squares:

- integration of the sculptural mass of buildings with the open space,
- proper siting of monuments in the space that leaves its center open,
- defined enclosure and controlled access points that frame views in and conceal views out,
- pleasing proportions of the open space,
- avoidance of overly simple and boring plan shapes, and
- harmonious grouping and composed relationships of linked spaces.

Particularly important is the principle of *enclosure and thresholds*, and Sitte calls it "this most important and really essential prerequisite of any artistic effect" [38]. He makes his most famous forensic observation, known as the "turbine plaza," when he writes "that by leading the streets off in the fashion of turbine blades, the most favorable conditions result, namely that from any point within the plaza no more than a single view out of it is possible at a time" [39].

Recent research adds quantifiable and measured data to surveys like Sitte's. From these efforts we learn that the sense of *enclosure* so important to Sitte is strongly felt at height-to-width *container ratios* (an Ed White term) of 1-to-2 and 1-to-3 and that it dissipates at ratios of 1-to-5 and 1-to-6. Taller/tighter is better. Jan Gehl relates the way humans see and hear to the size of spaces in which we feel comfortable. It's no surprise that spaces feel most comfortable when we can see details and people across the way, satisfying our need to scan for faces. Spaces in the size of stadiums (300 feet, sometimes called the "social field of vision") are the outer limit of human recognition, and those the size of theaters (75–100 feet, sometimes called the "emotional field of vision") allow us to effectively relate to other humans as distinct people. We can also compare the "good piazzas" that researchers have identified and find that they share similar sizes and proportions. Gehl notes that typical European rectangular squares average 230 feet x 330 feet, Camillo Sitte states in *Der Stadebau* that the largest plazas in ancient cities average 190 feet x 470 feet, the average of all plazas documented in Robert Gatje's *Great Public Squares* is 265 feet x 410 feet, and those falling between the mean and average in Josh Simoneau's *Civic Intimacy* are 320 feet x 450 feet. This is a relatively tight range of sizes and proportions; clearly something is going on here. Although Sitte's research is over 125 years old and some spaces he analyzed are a thousand years old, the principles he identified still apply to human experience of our public realm today. There are rules, and good spaces follow them.

This leads to a discussion of the two fundamentally different types of urban space; *free space* and *figural space*. In *Collage City*, Rowe and Koetter humorously exemplify the two with a juxtaposition of Florence's Piazza Uffici (a defined void seen as figure, a volume *of* space) and Le Corbusier's Unite d'Habitation (a defined solid surrounded by a continuous void, a volume *in* space). Rowe and Koetter wryly observe that one is the jelly mold for the other!

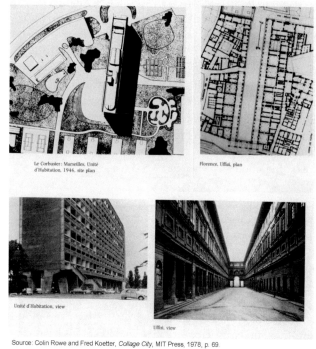

FIGURE 9.15 Printed with permission of MIT Press.

Let us consider more placemaking-appropriate free space examples than Corb's freestanding building. Sometimes we think of the difference between free space and figural space as the difference between Greek space and Roman space (Figure 9.15). At the Agora and Acropolis, we see an assemblage of buildings defined as solid volumes in free space that resonates as a distinct place. The building placement may look random when viewed in plan, but it's carefully calculated by *a system in which man is the center*. The space between buildings is treated as a continuous field whose function is to present building forms to a human on the ground, and they're dramatically presented in oblique two-point perspective. This view practically insists that we walk toward them; it's really all about movement. (Roman spaces are more about stasis.)

C.A. Doxiadis' famous diagram shows that when viewed from the "gunsight" of the Propylea's defined entrance portal, the buildings on the Acropolis fan out to fill one's cone of vision, creating a particular type of visual enclosure. Buildings are either completely hidden or the entirety of each building is visible in three-quarter view. No buildings are partially covered. One angle, typically near the center of the visual field, is left open, compelling movement toward the distant landscape. This route is the sacred way. It is often the generative force in Greek placemaking. In Athens, it evolved from the Panathenaic procession, a yearly parade which began in the Elysian Fields cemetery of heroes, traveled through the public Agora marketplace and climbed the Acropolis until, passing through the Propylea portal, it reached the temple of Athena at the top. Over time the route became a major street, and it dictated the design of both the Agora and the Parthenon. It could be argued that it actually influenced the Greek conception of space. The notion of a processional route as the generative force in the establishment of a street with delineated and episodic *armature* components along the way has come down through history to influence some major streets that serve as important examples

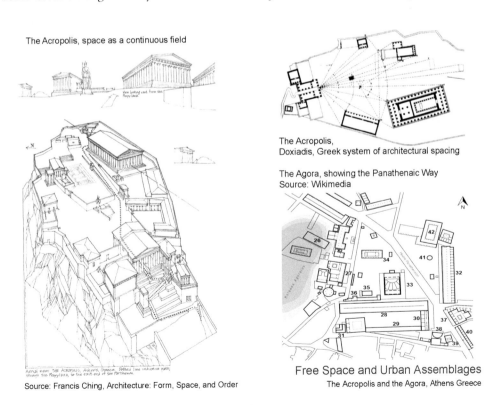

FIGURE 9.16 Printed with permission of John Wiley & Sons.

for many placemakers today, most notably Barcelona's Las Ramblas, London's Regent Street and Florence's Via Romana-Santa Maria-Calimala-Roma (Figure 9.16).

Abstract modern versions of free space often lack such a direct relationship to man's place in it. In 1980, for Volume 1 of the *Harvard Architectural Review*, Stephen Peterson wrote an article titled "Space and Anti-Space" that quite succinctly describes the nature of free space and figural space and then talks about the differences these conceptions of space can have on the creation of places in the city. Peterson first writes "The form in which space is presumed to exist is the framework of our perception of the world." He goes on to say that "Modern architecture and contemporary society in general have accepted the destruction of volumetric space … and this fact conditions all our current conceptions of meaning and form." Peterson writes that modern architectural space is assumed to be a slice of the continuum, "conceived to be a free element in nature, a found resource. It is thought to be transcendental, abstract, continuous, vast, and with no form." He quotes art theorist and psychologist Rudolph Arnheim, who wrote "Space is experienced as the given which precedes the objects in it. In the absence of such objects, space would still exist, as an empty boundless container."

Peterson says this concept of space as a natural phenomenon becomes romanticized with a kind of implicit animal character. He writes,

> "One can imagine a typical modern interior in these terms, as an attempt to make one's own particular piece of wild natural space feel at home. The informal arrangement of walls and the lifting of all the furniture off the floor allows the free and "natural" movement of one's own house space. Like a domestic pet, it is allowed to roam freely throughout the interior."

This image of space as a pet wandering though Meisian free-standing walls and furniture humorously captures the perceived "behavior" of free space. But Peterson laments, "Being indefinite, it cannot carry meaning and must remain the background condition for form. It can no longer be imagined as a medium of design." For the rest of the article he will refer to modern, free space as "anti-space" and to the more traditional, figural alternative as "space." He writes that,

> "Space [figural space] *can* be man-made, not found; it *can* be willfully created; it *can* be made to have form; it *can* be figure as well as ground. [Figural] Space is not a natural phenomenon, … [it] has value; it is charged with presence. It [has] properties which are tangible: scale, proportion, and size. Its shape *can* be measured and its limits defined."

Peterson writes that historically, the two types of space derive from different world views. He says that the development of one-point perspective in the early Renaissance led to a focus on *volumetric figural space* in between objects and surfaces. Its singular vantage point and vanishing point combined the principles of an underlying geometric order with the framework of its appearance to the individual in society, one common to all persons and *implying a social agreement* about the perception of figural space. Free space derives from a post-Copernican view of an open and infinite universe in which universal truth was less certain. Fueled by romanticism, "the individual vision replaces man's general vision as the framework for interpretation… [Figural] Space itself loses value since the correctness of composition is determined by the picture it makes for each individual (the picturesque)."

For placemakers concerned about creating *civic spaces and communitas*, these observations about individualized frames of reference associated with free space versus communal frames of reference associated with figural space are captivating. This is not a nostalgic preference for the historic over the contemporary. In fact, the immediate juxtaposition of space and anti-space can be one of a designer's most expressive tools. The point is that if you think about the nature of space, you will design the nature of space. If you don't, you leave it to chance. Echoing Jan Gehl's "Life, space, buildings; in that order please" [40]. Peterson concludes, "Urbanism is achieved by designing space first, the monument and dwelling unit last. The context of the city must be actively designed, not passively responded to as circumstance. Architecture must assert its responsibility to form urban space" [41].

Sense of Place

This leads directly to the third leg of placemaking's three-legged stool, that "je ne sais quoi" or "quality without a name" that is the human-to-place interaction or the bond of memory-emotion-meaning that today we refer to as "sense of place." Architects have been debating the importance of memory, emotion, and meaning in design for ages; from Plato and Aristotle's earliest thoughts that *place provides the basis for existence* [42] through the post Industrial Revolution modernist schism between engineering and architecture and between thinking and feeling [43]. We will not review this history here, but rather we'll pick up the narrative in the late 20th century, at the advent of three influences:

- the 1970s questioning of modernism by certain architects,
- the 1980s rise of phenomenology and kinesthetic approaches to architectural environments, and
- the 1990–2000s development of neuroscience and brain research.

Modernism (as it relates to city design) advocated separating people and cars on the ground plane, separating homes from the ground in slab-like high rises and separating life functions into different parts of the city. But because modernism's urban utopia had failed to materialize by the 1960s despite the great changes that transportation engineering, mega-projects, and functionalist zoning had made on city design and city spaces, some architects started to re-examine and re-embrace earlier thought. Aldo Van Eyck, for instance, *emphasizing human interaction* in what seems to be a Giedeon reassessment wrote, "Whatever space and time mean, place and occasion mean more. For space in the image of man is place, and time in the image of man is occasion" [44].

This reassessment led to a focus on *kinesthetics* and *place dialogue*, the role of the human body and our five senses in relationship to a place-oriented architecture. In their 1977, book *Body, Memory, and Architecture*, Charles Moore and Kent Bloomer refer to "a feeling of being bounded, possessed and centered" within sympathetic buildings and say that it "must apply to the city as well if the city is to belong to its constituency" [45]. They refer to the 1966 book *The Senses Considered as Perceptual Systems*, in which psychologist J.J. Gibson focused on *how our senses process environmental information*. Gibson maintains that senses are not just receptors, but that they project out to gather experience; they are aggressive, information seeking mechanisms [46]. In Gibson's orienting system, we gather information to make distinctions about up vs. down, front vs. back, order vs. randomness. These relate to gravity and the ground plane, to our body posture, to our position relative to three-dimensional objects. Nikos Salingaros contends this out-reaching nature of our senses makes us information processing machines. We are compelled to constantly scan our environment and *engage with it as an informational field*. Spatial information plays a fundamental role in human functionality; we require it in order to sustain us. Sensory feedback we get fulfills a need for emotional nourishment, or in the case of poorly designed spaces, it does not.

And in their section on the perceptual dimension of urban design, the authors of *Public Places, Urban Spaces* write

> "The period since the 1970s has seen increasing interest in examination of people's ties to, and conceptions of places. This has often drawn on "phenomenology" which ... aims to describe and understand phenomena as experience, wherein human consciousness takes in "information" and makes it into "the world." Thus, while the meanings of places are rooted in their physical setting and activities, they are not a property of them, but [rather] of human "intentions and experiences." Hence, what "the environment" represents is a function of our own subject"ive construction of it [47]."

Landscape scholar J. B. Jackson, in his 1994 book *Sense of Place, Sense of Time*, wrote, "A sense of place is something that we ourselves create in the course of time. It is the result of habit or custom... A sense of place is reinforced by what might be called a sense of recurring events" [48]. Architect Donlyn Lyndon emphasized this when he wrote,

> "It is not the designer who creates the sense of place. It is the user or observer. The designer merely sets out opportunities for others to use; to make distinctions, to perceive connections, and to take advantage (or not) of the structure of thought that is there."

Leave it to the architect in this group to hint at something helpful for placemakers when he writes that the designer "*sets out opportunities.*"

At the dawn of the new millennium, these musings have combined with neuroscience to give validity to what is a paradigm shift for architects and placemakers, the emergence of the concept of *situated cognition*. In her 2017 book *Welcome To Your World, How the Built Environment Shapes Our Lives*, Sarah Williams Goldhagen writes that situated cognition (sometimes also called embodied cognition or grounded cognition)

> "holds that much of what and how people think is a function of our living in the kinds of bodies we do [and in the environments we do]. It reveals that most—much more than we previously knew—of human thought is neither logical nor linear, but associative and nonconscious... What the new paradigm of embodied or situated cognition reveals is that the built environment and its design matters far, far more than anybody, even architects, ever thought that it did [49]."

She defines cognitions as "the many processes by which people understand, interpret, and organize sensory, social, and internally generated data for their own use," or incidences of the human thought process. By situated (or embodied or grounded) the science means that we are situated in (1) our body, (2) the natural world and (3) the social world. Cognitions are the product of *a three-way collaboration of mind, body, and environment* [50]. Goldhagen writes,

> Cognitions do not emerge in tension with the corporeal self, as was thought for centuries, nor from a disembodied mind. Instead ... the brain and the body together facilitate the operations of the human mind, which depends on their architecture for its very existence and for its modes of functioning [51].

Neuroscience experiments reveal interesting results:

- Memories are consolidated, or prepared for long-term storage, in the brain's hippocampus, which works with "place cells" in other parts of the brain to facilitate navigation of spaces.
- In forming memories, the brain uses the very same place cells, encoding an experience along with meta-data about where it happened. Amazingly, un-coding also works in reverse, so that seeing the place reminds you of the experience [52].
- Sensory perception is always *preparation for action*. Our motor neurons and our capacity for *narrative* are involved. So when we look at a door, we also think about how it opens and how we might move through it [53].
- Sight activates *haptic* parts of the brain, so we don't need to actually touch surfaces to have them activate tactile-sense brain cells. Surfaces, textures and colors are therefore important, because all we need to do is look at them and we imagine what it would be like to touch them [54].
- People walking undifferentiated and bland street-fronts are quiet, stooped and passive. Those at complex and active street-fronts are animated and chatty. Skin conductance as a measure of arousal is higher [55].
- Mid-density *fractal patterning* in surrounding edges and facades seems to resonate with people. Such patterning (or ornament) is an important component of how humans perceive not only figurative objects, but space itself [56, 57].
- Eye-tracking experiments show we are drawn to parts of buildings with such patterning, and our visual fixations last longer. Our eyes are also drawn to patterns that can be construed as faces, and that have the vertically oriented left-right symmetry of faces. Because of our body's experience in gravity, nature has pre-set our preference for an up-down vertical orientation. Because our field of vision takes about the same amount of time and effort to process 12 inches vertically as it does just less than 18 inches horizontally, we are predisposed to favor information fields with golden section or root two proportions [58].
- People think more creatively and respond better to abstract concepts when seated in rooms with high ceilings or blue-painted ceilings. People in red rooms or exposed to red light suffer diminished problem-solving skills and reduced capacity to engage in social conversation. Humans respond to sharp, irregular, angled forms with discomfort and even muffled fear [59, 60].
- And a place-oriented favorite, the "beautiful room experiment," in which people found angst and distress in the photos of faces when they viewed them in a room that resembled a janitor's closet and found happiness and joy in the same faces when viewing them in a room resembling a private library! [61]

There are many more findings and they are all fascinating.

Conclusion

What all this tells us is that the notion of *human nature meeting environmental opportunity* is important, and that designers should:

- consider human pre-dispositions toward architectural form and space as the implicit and underlying program for the buildings and urban places we design, and

- set out opportunities with which our "hard-wiring" can engage, using all the devices and methods discussed in this chapter (and more), in order to
- create places which provide a legible information field that promotes emotional nourishment, that incubates the behaviors we seek, and that rests on the integration of form, activity, and meaning; our three legged stool.

And probably most importantly, that *the public realm should be designed as thoughtfully as the buildings that form it*. It should not be simply the residual area left over when the design of the buildings is done. We must think of the public realm as an intrinsic part of the design program of our individual buildings (particularly those in towns and cities). And think of these exterior spaces as the theater for human events in our culture, where people come together on a social and civic basis, importantly different from our relationships within private buildings. They should resonate with human beings, and thus *transform from space into place*.

As placemakers, we should design urban spaces that are in tune with our lives, that respond to us, and that make us feel responded to. If we do, our public realm will promote human health, happiness and emotional connectedness.

Note

1 In his speech to the House of Lords, 1943, requesting that the Parliament buildings be rebuilt exactly as before it was bombed.

References

1. Sussman, A. (n.d.). geneticsofdesign.com
2. Doordon, D. (2015). *Laudato Si': Care for our Common Home*. University of Notre Dame School of Architecture. https://green.nd.edu/news/student-perspectives-notre-dame-cares-for-our-common-home/
3. Whyte, W. H. (1980). *The Social Life of Small Urban Spaces*. New York: Project for Public Spaces.
4. Whyte, W. H. (1988). *Rediscovering the Center City*. New York: Doubleday.
5. Gehl, J. (2008, published in Danish 1971). *Life between Buildings*. Copenhagen: The Danish Architectural Press.
6. Gehl, J. (2004). *Public Spaces, Public Life*. Copenhagen: The Danish Architectural Press.
7. Gehl, J. (2010). *Cities for People*. Washington, DC: Island Press.
8. Sitte, C. (1889, translated 1965). *Der Städtebau* (City Planning According to Artistic Principles). Collins & Collins trans. New York: Random House.
9. Alexander, C. (1979). *The Timeless Way of Building*. New York: Oxford University Press.
10. Alexander, C., Ishikawa, S., & Silverstein, M. (1977). *A Pattern Language*. New York: Oxford University Press.
11. Ibid.
12. Sussman, A., & Hollander, J. (2015). *Cognitive Architecture*. New York and London: Routledge.
13. Whyte, W. H. (1980). *The Social Life of Small Urban Spaces*. New York: Project for Public Spaces.
14. Gehl, J. (2010). *Cities for People*. Washington, DC: Island Press.
15. Appleton, J. (1975). *The Experience of Landscape*. London: John Wiley & Sons.
16. Gibbs, R. J. (2012). *Principles of Urban Retail Planning and Development*. Hoboken, NJ: John Wiley & Sons.
17. Gehl, J. (2010). *Cities for People*. Washington, DC: Island Press. 21.
18. Whyte, W. H. (1980). *The Social Life of Small Urban Spaces*. New York: Project for Public Spaces. 17.
19. Ibid. 72.
20. Ibid. 73.
21. Speck, J. (2012). *Walkable City*. New York: North Point Press.
22. Speck, J. (2018). *Walkable City Rules*. Washington, DC: Island Press.
23. Gehl, J. (2010). *Cities for People*. Washington, DC: Island Press. 127.
24. Alexander, C., Ishikawa, S., & Silverstein, M. (1977). *A Pattern Language*. New York: Oxford University Press. 120.

25. White, E. T. (1999). *Path Portal Place, Appreciating Public Space in Urban Environments.* Tallahassee, FL: Architectural Media Ltd.
26. Ching, Francis D. K. (1979). *Architecture: Form, Space, and Order.* New York: Van Nostrand Reinhold.
27. Lynch, K. (1960). *The Image of the City.* Cambridge, MA: MIT Press. 6.
28. Ibid.
29. Rossi, A. (1966, in English 1984). *The Architecture of the City.* Cambridge, MA: Oppositions Books.
30. MacDonald, W. (1986). *The Architecture of the Roman Empire, Vol. 2, an Urban Appraisal.* New Haven, CT: Yale University Press. 250.
31. Ibid. 251.
32. Ibid.
33. Ibid. 256–257.
34. Krier, Leon (2009). *The Architecture of Community.* Washington, DC: Island Press.
35. Cullen, G. (1961). *Townscape.* New York: Reinhold Publishing Corp. 7.
36. Ibid. 12.
37. White, E. T. (1999). *Path Portal Place, Appreciating Public Space in Urban Environments.* Tallahassee, FL: Architectural Media Ltd.
38. Sitte, C. (1889, translated 1965). *Der Städtebau* (City Planning According to Artistic Principles). Collins & Collins trans. Random House. 170.
39. Ibid. 172.
40. Gehl, J. (2010). *Cities for People.* Washington, DC: Island Press. 198.
41. Peterson, S. K. (1980). *Space and Anti-Space.* Cambridge, MA: Harvard Architectural Review, Vol. 1.
42. Cresswell, T. (2015). *Place, an Introduction* (2nd ed.). Chichester: Wiley Blackwell.
43. Giedion, S. (1941). *Space Time and Architecture.* Cambridge, MA: Harvard University Press.
44. Carmona, M., Heath, T., Taner, O., & Tiesdell, S. (2003). *Public Places, Urban Spaces.* Oxford: Architectural Press.
45. Bloomer, K., & Moore, C. (1977). *Body, Memory, and Architecture.* New Haven, CT: Yale University Press.
46. Ibid. 33.
47. Carmona, M., Heath, T., Taner, O., & Tiesdell, S. (2003). *Public Places, Urban Spaces.* Oxford: Architectural Press.
48. Jackson, J. B. (1994). *Sense of Place, Sense of Time.* New Haven, CT: Yale University Press. 151–152.
49. Goldhagen, S. W. (2017). *Welcome to Your World, How the Built Environment Shapes Our Lives.* New York: Harper Collins. xii & xiv.
50. Ibid. 47.
51. Ibid. 47–48.
52. Moser, E., & Moser, M. B. (2014) *Mapping Your Every Move.* Cerebrum: Dana Foundation. From www.dana.org
53. Goldhagen, S. W. (2017). *Welcome to Your World, How the Built Environment Shapes Our Lives.* New York: Harper Collins.
54. Ibid.
55. Ellard, C. (2015). *Places of the Heart.* New York: Bellevue Literary Press.
56. Bloomer, K. (2017). *Fundamental Process Podcast.* Feb. 28, 2017.
57. Salingaros, N. (2013). *Fractal Art and Architecture Reduce Psychological Stress.* JBU- *Journal of Biourbanism,* Vol. 2 (2), pp. 11–28.
58. Sussman, A., & Hollander, J. (2015). *Cognitive Architecture.* New York and London: Routledge.
59. Goldhagen, S. W. (2017). *Welcome to Your World, How the Built Environment Shapes Our Lives.* New York: Harper Collins.
60. Hiss, T. (1991). *The Experience of Place.* New York: Vintage Books.
61. Ibid.

10

PROGRAMMING FOR THE SUBLIMINAL BRAIN

Biometric Tools Reveal Architecture's Biological Impact

Justin B. Hollander, PhD, Gideon Spanjar, PhD, Ann Sussman AIA, Frank Suurenbroek, PhD, and Mengfei Wang

> The use of **biometric monitoring** allows researchers insight into the processing of environmental data by our central nervous systems. As a result we can determine precisely which stimuli cause arousal or draw our attention. This technology is used widely by commercial interests but is not commonly used to improve the public realm. Our authors hope to change this.

How do people actually experience their surroundings? Why do they feel better, even happier, walking down one street than they do another? Why do some buildings and city squares always invite lingering and public gathering while others do not? Along with aspects such as density, function and location, architecture implicitly influences our behavior, but how? To program for health and wellbeing in architecture these questions require answers.

And now we have new technologies that can help us answer them. These tools reveal architecture's impact on us and help us to "see" the hidden mechanisms that drive our actions in built environments. These findings reveal biological processes in real time and can help us better understand what people need to "see" in order to feel safe and secure in a setting, to promote individual and collective wellbeing, and ultimately to deliver more successful programming in architecture.

Marketing professionals, technology companies and car manufacturers are familiar with these advanced research technologies, using them to discover what attracts people, and to manipulate human behavior to increase consumption [1]. What about using these tools to improve the public realm? In the fall of 2020, we had the opportunity to explore employing some of these state-of-the-art tools to look at the urban experience subliminally. Our team, led by researchers from the Sensing Streetscapes project at the Amsterdam University of Applied Sciences, included researchers from the Tufts School of Urban and Environmental Policy and Planning (UEP) and the Human Architecture + Planning Institute (theHAPi.org) in Greater Boston. We sought to build on the international interest in creating healthy built environments by better understanding the impact of buildings on people, with the ultimate goal of improving the public realm.

In this research, we used eye-tracking—a biometric tool that marketers, web designers and retailers frequently rely on to learn how people actually see things. Eye-tracking measures the

DOI: 10.4324/9781003164418-14

conscious and *unconscious* eye movements people make as they take in their surroundings This appraisal process then informs subsequent movement and behavior.

The mobile eye-tracking glasses (Tobii 2) used in this study, recorded people's visual attention as they moved down urban streets. Mobile eye-tracking is lauded for delivering "robust eye tracking and accurate gaze data while giving users the freedom to move and interact naturally." Advanced eye-tracking software can create powerful visualizations of data collected. These include "heat maps" that aggregate data to show where people look during the first moments they take in a scene, and where their gaze frequently returns often without awareness. Heat maps elegantly record and document the unconscious visual scanning behaviors that influence our motion and overall perception of place.

To further understand the human experience this "Sensing Streetscapes" study paired eye-tracking glasses with galvanic skin response (GSR) monitors that measure autonomic nervous system (ANS) arousal to track how the body instantly and subliminally responds to visual stimuli. We used software by iMotion to both collect and aggregate the data from the eye-tracking and GSR sensors. In the Boston pilot study, to help gauge the positive or negative emotional quality of the human experience, we also combined these metrics with preference studies asking respondents to note which streets they liked being on most, and where they felt at their best.

Testing Technology & Streets in Boston and Amsterdam

We set up the study wondering whether it would pick up differences between car-centric urban areas and streets and urban areas that have been designed with a pedestrian focus. Could these tools capture and record meaningful differences? What would they show us about our subliminal behavior on distinctly different streetscapes?

A wide array of classic studies in urban design and architecture have analyzed design principles of great streetscapes. Jane Jacobs [2] noted that "buildings on a street equipped to handle strangers" called for orienting structures toward the street to contribute to the requisite number of "eyes upon the street" needed to promote people's sense of safety. Jacobs also stressed the importance of edge conditions in designed streetscapes. Gehl, Alexander etc. emphasize the importance of balance in the visual complexity of streets, whereas Montgomery et al. make the case for pedestrian-focused streetscapes. Moreover, a rich body of existing literature explores a multitude of variables at play in any quest to create more walkable streets. These studies are mainly based on observation and self-reporting. What might the measurements of unconscious visual behavior unlock? What are the physical stimuli that elicit our response? And how does this play out within different kinds of streetscapes in high-density settings and different urban cultures?

The Selected Streets in Boston

In the Boston Sensing Streetscape study, we selected two very well-known streets: Newbury and Boylston. We needed ones that would be easy to find volunteers to walk down two days after a contentious political election in the U.S. (Thursday, November 5th, 2020). Newbury is particularly famous as attractive for pedestrians while Boylston, wider and more car-centric, is less so. Both form part of Boston's dense commercial core.

A mile-long, Newbury Street is lined with historic 19th-century brownstones (most from the 1860s), three to four stories, that contain many shops and restaurants above street level. It is two-lane and one-way, with parked cars on either side. Boylston, a major east-west thoroughfare a block away, features 19th- and 20th-century buildings, many multi-story, including the

138 Justin B. Hollander, PhD et al.

52-floor Prudential Center, built in 1960. Boylston Street is one-way, three-lane and also lined with parked cars on both sides. Gloucester Street, linking the two, is lined with 19th-century brick architecture, mostly low-rise like Newbury, three-to-five stories, and also features two one-way lanes, lined with parked cars on either side.

Boylston and Newbury streets, less than 1/10 of a mile apart, are known for having sharply different identities and ambiance. We wondered: would this show up in biometric studies and preference testing? What measurable differences would be found?

The Selected Streets in Amsterdam

In Amsterdam, we chose the South Axis of the Zuidas, the city's financial district, as our pilot location (Figure 10.1). Contrary to the Boston pilot study location, the Zuidas with its high-rise building typology is a new type of streetscape in Amsterdam. The development of the district started around the millennium and was strongly influenced by the regionalization of the city and the globalization of urban networks. The Zuidas was designed as a new financial and multimodal accessible district. It was inspired in part by Canary Wharf in London and the grid of Manhattan.

FIGURE 10.1 Streetview of Newbury, Gloucester, and Boylston Streets, the site of a Sensing Streetscapes study. Image via Sensing Streetscapes.

Currently, the district is in a new phase of development with a plan to build more dwellings for a more balanced mix of commercial and residential use. Part of this plan is to enhance the pedestrian network to improve the attractiveness of the Zuidas as a living environment for citizens.

For this research, we selected three types of streets in the Zuidas: Gustav Mahlerlaan, a car-centric main road, George Gerswinlaan, a parallel pedestrian centric road in the residential area, and the connecting residential road Peter Schatstraat between these two. The Gustav Mahlerlaan is a central tree-lined avenue with sidewalks on both sides. Most business and residential towers are approximately 30-80 meters in height, with a few rising to nearly 100 meters. The street has well defined edges and most of its buildings use retailers, cafes, bars, shops, supermarkets and other ventures to activate the ground floor. The George Gerswinlaan has a more residential design with building blocks starting at 20 meters. The narrow street has spacious sidewalks featuring greenery and raised flower beds. On either side of Peter Schatstraat are large residential towers, one standing nearly 90 meters high (Figure 10.2).

FIGURE 10.2 Streetview of Gustav Maherlaan, Pieter Schatstraat and George Gershwinlaan, the site of a Sensing Streetscapes study. Image via Sensing Streetscapes.

Results: Heat Maps & Gaze Paths

Collecting biometric data on human subjects is at once revealing, overwhelming and ultimately humbling. It gives us a glimpse of the vast amounts of stimuli we are constantly absorbing and responding to, mostly without our awareness or control. With these remarkable tools we find ourselves in a new era, "The Age of Biology," as described by the OECD (Organization of Economic Cooperation and Development) in 2013. This term distinguishes the 21st from the 20th century, "The Age of Chemistry and Physics," which brought us plastics, radar, computers, and the 19th, "The Age of Engineering," which led to railroads, telephones and marvels of the first iron bridge and tower construction [3].

Our findings, reflecting unique possibilities in our Age of Biology, occurred on three levels: (1) how our unconscious visual behavior in streetscapes happens—and the way it differs in different streetscapes and urban settings; (2) what frontiers for new research these findings suggest; and (3) how biometric technologies might be used to inform programming and design.

Boston Heat Maps: Aggregated Eye-tracking Data

In our Boston study we successfully gathered eye-tracking data from four participants who walked down the selected streets one-at-a-time, for six-to-eight minutes each, wearing mobile eye-tracking glasses. To gauge how they absorbed each street each participant was instructed to stop at a specific location on each street, called an EMA (or Environmental Maintenance Assessment point), and take in the scene. The heat maps below aggregate the eye-tracking data collected by combining the "fixations" or focal points of the participants' focus. These heat maps, capturing the participants' *gaze path* data over 20–30 seconds, glow reddest where they looked most, fading to yellow then green where they looked least, and show no color at all in areas ignored. The heat map below is from an individual respondent at one of the EMAs (Figure 10.3).

Examining the heat maps we were struck by how much time and effort people spent looking at cars and other people. While our study's intent was to explore the impact of buildings, we

FIGURE 10.3   Looking out onto Boylston Street from a sidewalk patio, [participant 2] focuses on cars and people. Image via Sensing Streetscapes.

realized these can be tricky to isolate. The reddest areas, where subjects fixated most initially, tended to fall on people and cars rather than architecture. Green areas where they focused less fell on cars and people, too. Overall, it was remarkable how much energy and time they spent gazing toward sidewalk and road conditions, always glancing at things that were moving, and how much less time was spent looking up at buildings. The results suggest the brain works hard to ensure the path ahead of us—where we are about to move our body—*is safe*, directing eye movement without our awareness to do so.

Observe, below, how a string of discrete focal points carefully follow the line of parked cars on Boylston. Even when not moving, the cars grab visual attention (Figure 10.4).

With about 50 percent of our brain matter involved in visual processing [4], what we look at matters, even subliminally, because it takes up so much of our brain's energy.

Boston Gaze Paths: Aggregated Eye-tracking Data

Mobile eye-tracking also yields revealing videos showing the *gaze path* the eyes follow, with yellow dots representing the *fixations* where the eyes *stop to take in specific stimuli*, and the lines between them, *showing the movement between fixations*, called *saccades*. With videos we thus can

FIGURE 10.4 On Boylston Street, [participant 7] fixates mostly on or around parked or moving vehicles. Image via Sensing Streetscapes.

"see" the sequencing the brain has the eyes take, which until relatively recently most architects and planners would likely never have seen before.

The videos can be combined over short intervals to create images that aggregate the brain's efforts taking in specific stimuli. In the images below, for instance, recorded in 10-second spans, we observe how the participant focused on a nearby car. Note the thoroughness of this endeavor, how multiple fixations are made around the entire vehicle, although the car is at some distance (Figure 10.5).

People, as mentioned previously, have an amazingly magnetic effect on us. Eye-tracking can help us see how we are drawn to look at them subliminally everywhere, all the time. Note how, in the scene below on Newbury St. the participant creates a gaze path of tight fixation circles directly around the group walking toward her (Figure 10.6).

Seeing these results brings to mind the famous Nordic proverb "Man is man's greatest joy," frequently cited by the Danish planner Jan Gehl. With eye-tracking studies you actually "see" how people-focused we are, and come away appreciating the truth behind the ancient saying in new ways.

Views to the Street and Pavement

The study's gaze-path videos also proved revealing because they showed so much asphalt and concrete. We didn't expect this; but it makes sense! Because of the way we evolved to hold our head when walking, at about 10° to 15° looking toward the ground, the videos in Sensing-Streetscapes show large amounts of pavement, sidewalk and roadway. Most images created in each video show 50 percent or more of a scene as asphalt, concrete or brick; sky or building elevations rarely appear as much.

The finding, reminding us of the way we walk, helps us understand why the quality of sidewalk and its paving patterns is extremely important if we want to build streetscapes that invite people along them and contribute to a happy public realm. (See Appendix, online, for bar charts showing how much more time people spent looking at cars, people, pavement than architecture.)

FIGURE 10.5 A 10-second gaze path shows the participant's subliminal focus on a parked car on Newbury Street. Image via Sensing Streetscapes.

FIGURE 10.6 A 10-second gaze path shows the participant's subliminal focus: a group of people approaching. Image via Sensing Streetscapes.

Amsterdam Heat Maps: Aggregated Eye-tracking Data

In Amsterdam six volunteers wearing mobile eye-tracking glasses and GSR followed the route at their own pace, in parallel with the Boston pilot study. They were all familiar with the Zuidas neighborhood.

The participants were asked to stop at each of the five designated Environmental Maintenance Assessment locations (EMAs) and take in the environment. The EMA's were strategically chosen to be locations where the panorama of the street unfolds or where a pedestrian may encounter a distinctly new situation and naturally pause to (re)orientate herself—approaching a square, the entrance of a new block, or turning a corner. The heatmaps of each EMA (see below) show the aggregate eye fixations of all participants (Figure 10.7).

Amsterdam Gaze Paths: Aggregated Eye-tracking Data

Individual gaze path images show how people and distant views, with their potential traffic, drew the eye. When scanning buildings, many people's areas of interest tended to focus only on ground floors. Participants' focus tends to remain directed toward the streetscape in front of them. The street pavement, new or in good condition and with few people on it, might explain why, in contrast to the Boston pilot-study, the gaze paths show slightly less focus on pavement (Figure 10.8).

Tracking Nervous System Arousal

Biometric studies gain power by adding metrics. In this Sensing Streetscapes study we combined eye-tracking with Galvanic Skin Response (GSR) to monitor participants' nervous system responses to visual stimuli on city streets. GSR technology records changes in sweat gland

FIGURE 10.7 Aggregated eye-fixations of 6 participants on Gustav Mahlerlaan show how little we focus on the buildings in our paths. Image via Sensing Streetscapes.

FIGURE 10.8 The gaze path of [participant 6] shows increased focus on building facades. Image via Sensing Streetscapes.

activity and skin conductance (or the continuous variation in the electrical characteristics of the skin) that reflect the intensity of our emotional state, also known as level of emotional arousal. GSR can help us "see" the immediate impact of visual stimuli on the body and nervous system.

It is important to note, however, that GSR tracks only the intensity of an emotional experience, not its quality (i.e., positive or negative, happy or sad).

Boston: GSR

The GSR signals recorded here showed us immediately how the body is always interacting and responding to its environment. In these studies (with iMotions biometric software) the GSR data appear as a timeline running below the eye-tracked image (see next page):

Participants fixating on people regularly caused increased arousal (Figure 10.9). Remarkably we observed this happening even when a viewer fixated on *a photograph of a person* seen through a first-floor window. Cars, whether parked or moving, loud noises and being talked to also increased

FIGURE 10.9 Focusing on people causes a small GSR peak. Note how GSR arousal peaks occur throughout the participant's walk and how arousal amplitude is continually shifting over time. Image via Sensing Streetscapes.

FIGURE 10.10 Viewing an image of a person inside a building generates a peak. Image via Sensing Streetscapes.

arousal. In the Boston study, we observed the tallest peaks happening when participants were touched by the researcher who removed the GSR sensors at the study's end (Figures 10.10 and 10.11).

One of the unexpected findings of the pilot-study was the emotional arousal stimulated in people as they took in cars, as can be seen in the image above. (Note the vertical line, in the timeline above, showing a peak rising as an observer's fixations surround around a car.) More research needs to be done here, but the pilot-study suggests that car-free streets and walking/biking routes may be healthier for people because they trigger less arousal of the nervous system.

FIGURE 10.11 Focusing on a car generates a small arousal peak. Image via Sensing Streetscapes.

Boston: Preference Studies

The preference studies volunteers completed after the walk enable further evaluation of the GSR collection, indicating how arousal levels may link with positive or negative emotional experience. Boston participants all indicated preference for Newbury over Boylston Street suggesting correlation between the lower arousal levels there. Alternately, these findings suggest a connection between rising average peaks per minute in Boston and a greater experience of stress in urban streetscapes.

Why do people enjoy Newbury over Boylston? The human nervous system can walk there with less arousal (stress).

Amsterdam: GSR

Mobile eye-tracking and GSR were also combined in the Amsterdam pilot study. We found that a wide array of stimuli could trigger visual responses and arousal.

In Amsterdam, we noted peaks fell into five categories: conversation (before the walk), traffic or the crossing of a street, looking at people, finding the EMA point, and hearing sounds. GSR peaks in relation to buildings were rare. One exception occurred when a participant scanned a glass building and caught the reflection of the sun in the distance. Unexpected or sudden sounds or scenes played the dominant role producing peaks, along with rattling bikes or sudden shouts.

Discussion

"You can take a person out of the Stone Age…but you can't take the Stone Age out of the person," the psychologist Nigel Nicholson famously observed [5]. Our behavior is more hardwired than we realize.

Mobile eye-tracking glasses create videos that dramatically reveal the limits of human perception, bringing them into full view. Combined with GSR they reveal how visual stimuli instantly are experienced by the human nervous system. They show us how when walking down a busy and stimulus-rich street the brain takes in too-much stimuli for the conscious brain to "see."

Assessing the relationship between real-time individual bodily behavior in streetscapes and their design can prove challenging. We observed how high-density settings, where cars are not present, tends to trigger more visual attachment to the environment. In contrast, the presence of cars absorbs large amounts of human attention, apparently decreasing the amount of possible attention for streetscape design attributes.

Along with new technologies available in our "Age of Biology," we may now also import other critical neuroscience discussions into the field of architecture. What role does peripheral vision play when people walk down an urban street? Can buildings offer comfort if people are not looking directly at them?

This relates to another well-known observation about how our brain deals with multiple stimuli in public spaces. "Simmel's Mask" refers to our biological capacity to shut out the multiplicity of inputs in public spaces in order to focus on a selected few. In what respect does a streetscape with a human scale produce a comforting and/or interesting context for the pedestrian? In Amsterdam, we saw attention focused on buildings with balconies that project into the streetspace. At the same time few cars and limited numbers of people on the street may have enhanced study participants' ability to take in this surrounding architecture.

On the other hand, even on Boston's Newbury street—famous for its brownstones design rhythm and definition—participants focused on humans, making few fixations on the surroundings. Could we argue that this streetscape provides enough comfort that pedestrians were able to focus on other elements, like people? Or are we actually stumbling upon another discussion from neuroscience: Do we look at people in a positive light, or do we first scan them to assess for threat, or are we actually always doing both?

Based on our first explorations, we can hypothesize that a streetscape with a human-scale like Newbury St., helps us feel secure and safe in a space, creating optimal conditions for checking out people, minimizing stress and remaining at ease and with an open mind. In contrast, streetscapes with a significant presence of cars, traffic and little definition between car- and pedestrian spaces put us on edge. When there is anticipation of threats, one may expect more intense visual scanning and arousal.

If these hypotheses hold true, the relationship between the built environment and pedestrian wellbeing may be linked further. A streetscape with a human scale in high-density environments might enable a stress-reduced context, allowing people to more easily focus on others. Hence, environments that eschew the human scale and allow for the unfiltered presence of cars might produce more anxiety responses, limiting the contextual efficacy of "Simmel's mask."

Further research is needed to elaborate and test these kinds of hypotheses. Studying how cars impact us, even when parked, appears particularly germane.

Conclusion

As books like Leonard Mlodinow's *Subliminal, How Your Unconscious Mind Rules Your Behavior* [6], and others now report that, in the 21st century, we find ourselves in a new position to study and grapple with the hidden ways humans actually evolved to function, and how streetscapes truly set the stage for our behavior and wellbeing.

Programming for health and wellbeing in architecture today requires the incorporation of these new understandings. More than ever before we have the capacity to not just explore our biological nature, but to embrace it, programming more appropriately for people by acknowledging the human, unconscious processes steering our behavior. Too often, in the last century, we have ignored these, to our detriment. Prioritizing cars over people and ignoring the impact of architecture on humans, we created places that were—and still are—alienating and isolating, rather than comforting. Places where people unconsciously don't really want to be, where it is difficult to walk, linger or feel like you belong.

Sensing Streetscapes studies in Amsterdam and Boston, using biometric tools, brought some of our prime human subliminal behaviors into full view, letting us see the complex biological systems at work when we do something routine, like walk down a city street. They dramatically reveal how this simple action is anything but. These new biometric technologies are not only valuable for a new line of research, they can also prove to be powerful new tools in the hands of designers to create more user-experience-based designs.

As the Nobel-prize winning neuroscientists, Mary-Britt and Edvard Moser, report: "The most advanced surveillance system you will ever find is built into your own brain and nurtured by evolution" [7].

The Sensing Streetscapes eye-tracking results reveal this sophisticated "surveillance system" at work in real time, tracking how people's eye movements took in their surroundings subliminally and how often study volunteers focused on cars, people and pavement, without awareness or conscious control. The studies also showed dramatically that nervous system arousal levels, tracked with GSR, spike instantly, without awareness when taking in a car, people, hearing a sound, and when crossing a street.

The challenge is to bridge the well-known physical elements of great streetscapes from the literature—and get a deeper understanding of how these elements do indeed interact and create the best living and walking conditions for pedestrians. This is especially important in this time as urban areas grow denser and more new high-rise developments appear. Moreover, we have an opportunity to move beyond our own fixation on classic "great places" such as historic city centers or emblematic environments such as Manhattan and historic Boston—and maybe even the Zuidas in Amsterdam. We need to understand the relations between humans and the conditions of streetscapes everywhere in a city.

Programming for health and wellbeing implies building the city of tomorrow, frequently in new high density settings. In doing so, we shape the conditions of individual and collective human experience, and lay the cornerstone for a resilient social fabric.

Acknowledgments

This research has been made possible by funding from the Dutch Research Council: NWO-SIA RaakMKB. This collaborative research between Boston and Amsterdam is part of the larger research project "Sensing Streetscapes" from the Chair of Spatial Urban Transformation (bouwtransformatie) at the Amsterdam University of Applied Sciences (see: www.sensing-streetscapes.amsterdam). We thank our researchers Lyske Gais de Bildt, Zoë Jonker and Jolanda Tetteroo.

Boston researchers received additional support from iMotions and are very grateful for it. At iMotions, we particularly thank Nam Nguyen, neuroscientist, for helping us run the study in Boston, and Francesca Marcionne, neuroscientist, for helping us set it up.

References

1. Johnson, M. A. and Ghuman, P. (2020). *Blindsight: The (Mostly) Hidden Ways Marketing Reshapes Our Brains*. Dallas, TX: BenBella Books, Inc.
2. Jacobs, J. (1961). *The Death and Life of Great American Cities*. New York: Random House.
3. OECD. (2012, Nov. 12). The 21st Century: The Age of Biology. OECD Forum on Global Biotechnology. Paris. https://search.oecd.org/sti/emerging-tech/A%20Glover.pdf
4. ImageThink. (2012). Is it True or False that Vision Rules the Brain? https://www.imagethink.net/true-or-false-vision-rules-the-brain/
5. Nicholson, N. (1998, Jul.-Aug.). How Hardwired Is Human Behavior? *The Harvard Business Review*.
6. Mlodinow, L. (2012). *Subliminal, How Your Unconscious Mind Rules Your Behavior*. New York: Pantheon Books.
7. Moser, E., & Moser, M. B. (2014). Mapping Your Every Move. *Cerebrum: The Dana Forum on Brain Science, 2014*, 4.

11
THE FUTURE OF CODES AND THE ARCHITECTURE PROFESSION

A. Vernon Woodworth FAIA

The history, evolution and goals of **building codes** are inadequately covered in the curriculum of architecture schools. Due to the centrality of these documents to our professional obligations and practice increased focus is warranted. The American Institute of Architects (AIA) agrees, and has drafted an ambitious plan to transform how codes are written and enforced. This plan calls for a switch to "performance-based codes," whereby goals are established and outcomes are monitored. This is a dimension of evidence-based design that may change the role of the architect in the built environment.

Construction codes were among the earliest written laws. The Code of Hammurabi, ascribed to the sixth King of Babylonia (1792 BC to 1750 BC), includes specific punishments for losses due to faulty construction. By Roman times construction regulations focused on preventing fire spread between buildings. With the density that cities require conflagration became a threat equal to earthquake, storm and volcano in its potential for devastation. Density also facilitated the transmission of infectious diseases. Approximately one-third of the population of Athens lost their lives to an unnamed plague between 430 and 426 BC. In AD 165 Roman troops returning to the capitol brought with them a disease that resulted in the death of as many as five million. In 541–542 AD a disease that became known as the Plague of Justinian resulted in the death of between 20 and 40 percent of the population of Constantinople. This plague was the first known outbreak of what became known as the "Black Death," a scourge that, from the Middle Ages to the 18th century, would periodically reduce the population of cities by up to 50 percent. It was in the 15th century during an episode of Black Death in the Republic of Venice that quarantine in isolation wards known as lazarettos for seafaring visitors was introduced. The word quarantine means "to keepe fortie dais from companie," namely "if one comes from infected places" [1].

The origin of modern building codes is often traced to the Great Fire of London which, over the course of four days in September 1666, destroyed the medieval core of the city, some 700 acres within the old Roman wall. Over 13,000 houses were destroyed and tens of thousands of residents were displaced. The subsequent Rebuilding of London Act of 1667 insured that existing streets were widened and that replacement structures were built of non-combustible materials. A second Rebuilding Act in 1670 raised additional funds for street widening and church rebuilding. Size limits imposed on residences were intended to address overcrowding. The fact that the Black Death had taken the lives of 80,000 Londoners just a year before the Great Fire and that no reoccurrence took place afterwards has been understood by some to suggest that the Fire relieved the City of the density and infestation that provided the scourge's incubation medium. Whether true or not, this suggestion has served to reinforce an understanding of the relationship between public health and the built environment.

Sanitation and waste management have been constant challenges over the course of urban development. Adequate ventilation is essential to minimizing risk of respiratory tract infection. Safe drinking water is a precondition for a healthy community. While evidence shows that the earliest urban settlements of the Indus Valley contained urban sanitation systems of considerable sophistication and efficiency, close to 800 million people today live without such systems worldwide [2]. Rats seem to love cities as much as people do, spreading disease as efficiently as any other factor. And the social distancing requirements imposed by the current COVID-19 pandemic have called into question the future of urban life. Add to these considerations the challenges imposed by environmental degradation and global climate change and the scope of the problem begins to become clear. Health and wellbeing in the urban environment are subject to the quality of infrastructure, the cleanliness of air, access to nature and a stable ecosystem that can maintain its equilibrium amidst dense human habitation. Climate change, novel viruses and increasing population migration all illustrate that public health has become a global phenomenon, without geographic boundaries. Our remedies for vulnerability must be universal and effective, enhancing long-term outcomes and promoting healthy populations. Anything else is merely a stop-gap effort. In this equation the contribution of our urban environments will be fundamental.

Architecture's Role in Environmental Health

History shows that the design of our physical environment holds critical consequences for the health of our communities. With this established, it becomes incumbent on the design professions to take responsibility for the health impacts of the built environment.

Architects are pledged to "advance our nation's quality of life and protect the public's health, safety and welfare" [3]. With the discovery that the buildings we design are major contributors to greenhouse gas emissions, this mission statement has undergone an expanded interpretation. Prior to this revelation the profession had been collectively content to meet the minimum standards of building and other codes. There have been multiple contributions of architects and their professional association, the AIA, over the years that have raised awareness or improved practice, but energy and construction codes continue to establish the baseline under which the vast majority of buildings are designed, built and operated.

At their 2018 Convention, the AIA adopted a new initiative intended to change the role of architects in the ecology of minimum construction standards. The resulting White Paper, titled *Disruption, Evolution, and Change*, marks a bold move to position the profession in a role analogous at the environmental level to that of a physician. Here is the opening statement from the paper:

> "We stand for protecting communities from the impact of climate change. Global warming and man-made hazards pose an increasing threat to the safety of the public and the vitality of our nation. Rising sea levels and devastating natural disasters result in unacceptable losses of life and property. Resilient and adaptable buildings are a community's first line of defense against disasters and changing conditions of life and property. That is why we advocate for robust building codes and policies that make our communities more resilient [4]."

Central to this initiative is the role of architects in the development and application of building codes. As stated in the White Paper, "the relationships among the designer, building codes and standards, enforcement, and building performance outcomes must also fundamentally change in order to address this current era of growing hazards" [5]. The AIA identifies the slow pace of codes in addressing novel technologies and challenges, as well as a projected decline in the availability of qualified personnel in the regulatory professions, as reasons for this observation. The solution identified is adherence to "holistic health, safety, and welfare" (HSW), through a new standard of professional practice "that delivers buildings designed to meet the highest levels of energy efficiency, consistent positive health and safety outcomes for building occupants, and life cycle designs and resilience as integral design strategies to protect the general welfare of the public" [6]. The report refers to "growing bodies of knowledge in resilience, equitable design and advanced building performance" as the basis for a new definition of HSW, the long-standing minimum definition of an architect's responsibilities. "Disruption, Evolution, and Change" makes the case that architects are the primary stewards of environmental health, safety and welfare, and therefore responsible for leading the way to a sustainable and equitable future.

Looking Forward: Stewardship

To accomplish this ambitious goal the White Paper lays out a multi-year action plan intended to establish a "new regulatory trajectory." Central to this plan is the adoption of collective responsibility for code development and enforcement, based on the recognition that the profession of building official is challenged by inadequate training and a shortage of qualified individuals. As stated in the White Paper,

> "A staff shortage in jurisdictions across the country has forced local governments to rely on outside plan reviewers, who are most often not architects and do not possess architects' specialized expertise. Today's marketplace has opportunities for architects to assume these roles, engaging in peer reviews and promoting their enhanced knowledge. By filling this gap, architects would collectively take responsibility for code compliance as a profession, which they have already done as individuals, while taking advantage of opportunities for valuable work in the void that is growing in code enforcement infrastructure [7]."

This incremental infiltration of the code enforcement community would coincide with aggressive involvement in the code development process and advocacy for performance-based design as the future of regulatory standards. The plan is laid out in five-year increments, concluding in 2038 by which time "architects will be prepared to assume responsibility as the primary stewards of code compliance consistent with their legal and ethical obligations within holistic HSW" [8].

Beginning with the 2021 International Energy Conservation Code (IECC) an optional Zero-Energy Appendix will be available for adoption. Inclusion of this opportunity to require zero-net energy for all new construction in a nationally adopted code was based in large part on advocacy by the AIA, and represents the most significant development in energy codes since the introduction of mandatory thermal resistance values in the 1970s. Subsequent to this action through a time honored participatory process the International Code Council (ICC), in response to lobbying from construction industry interest groups, internally altered the status of the IECC by changing it from a code to a standard. This change in status will result in a different and less equally representative development process, in which industry participation will be enhanced. This development from an organization that has, by default, become the arbiter of building performance in adopting jurisdictions, indicates the extent to which change is needed. The time has come to remove special interest considerations from the code development process. While the AIA's White Paper was drafted before this development, its message has become more urgent as a result. In the absence of federal mandates, if health and wellbeing are to become mandatory outcomes for environmental alterations it is the profession of architecture, along with allies in the fields of design education, accrediting and registration, and construction, that must lead. Given the pressing need to act immediately, the timeline for implementing the goals of the AIA White Paper may be too generous.

Reproduced here are the milestone summaries for each projected five-year milestone

> **2023**—Architects will demonstrate the expertise and engagement with professional colleagues in the industry that recognize not only their pre-existing legal and ethical responsibility for compliance with all building codes, but the skills and ability to act as industry leaders designing all new construction and major renovation projects to above-code standards and based on holistic HSW.
>
> **2028**—Architects will be designing all projects under high standards of performance and, using increasingly accurate feedback and data to validate decisions, will be fully engaged in determining and developing even higher levels of performance.
>
> **2033**—Architects will assume the lead on development, application and implementation of high-performance buildings that meet the needs of our clients, meaningfully integrate communities and recognize a world cognizant of a brighter future for mankind.
>
> **2038**—Architects will be prepared to assume responsibility as the primary stewards of code compliance consistent with holistic HSW.

Within the expanded descriptions of the targets for 2023 are steps involving the development of performance-based codes, goals for net zero energy and carbon, embodied energy, water use reduction, building/community resilience and hazard risk reduction. Building performance reporting is emphasized, with the goal of "100 percent transparency…by requiring buildings to display performance metrics reflecting their 'asset performance rating', 'operational performance rating,' and 'disaster performance'." An aspect of this requirement would involve the development of a national methodology and database "to track predicted project energy performance during design and provide a standardized reporting format for measuring progress against a consistent and normalized baseline" [9].

By 2028 the AIA's code advocacy will extend to **regenerative buildings**, buildings that are restorative of the environment, resilient buildings/communities, improved wellness through buildings, and support of physical and mental health" [10]. The efforts to improve sustainable outcomes would also be extended to existing buildings. By 2033 the profession will routinely exceed all prescriptive expectations by determining "how our buildings should perform using outcome-based goals, technical performance data, technology innovation, and the creativity of architects and engineers to utilize the best building science appropriate for each project" [11]. Architects' responsibilities will extend past the certificate of occupancy, because "Performance validation by definition is a post-occupancy function; the architect must become the focal point for review and resolution" [12]. This is a logical extension of a move toward performance-based design. As described in their summary of goals at this step, the intent is to "establish an outcome-based performance code as a national standard that minimizes amendments by state and local jurisdictions" [13].

With the fruition of this agenda by 2038 architects will be stewards of the built environment. This will manifest through:

- increased rigor of an architect's education and experience relative to building codes and regulations,
- integrated automated digital code checking into the design process,
- transition to outcome-based performance building codes and standards,
- the architect becoming established as the primary interpreter of a design's code compliance, and
- comprehensive peer review, third-party commissioning, and outcome evaluations confirm the values in the holistic HSW that may raise the standard of care for architects [14].

Transformative Impact Is Within Reach

A transition of this magnitude is akin to a paradigm shift in the regulatory environment as it relates to construction. With the release of this plan followed closely by the worldwide COVID-19 pandemic the ability of the AIA and its members to deliver on its goals remains to be seen. The profession can, however, learn from other transformative efforts in its recent past. In 1975 the AIA Task Group on Building Regulation issued a report entitled "One Code: A Program for Building Regulatory Reform." The report advocated for a single national code to replace a patchwork of conflicting regulations. By the 1990s the three existing model code groups joined forces to establish the International Family of Codes, first published in 2000, culminating a process recommended by the AIA 25 years earlier.

Another valuable precedent is the growth and impact of the U.S. Green Building Council's "Leadership in Energy and Environmental Design" (LEED) rating system. LEED was formed in 1993 with the goals of defining "green building through establishment of a common standard of measurement," promoting whole-building design practices, recognizing sustainability accomplishments in the construction industry, stimulating "green competition," raising consumer awareness and transforming the building market. Intentionally and effectively employing the dynamics of market transformation to effect changes in the construction industry has become LEED's lasting legacy.

A final source of inspiration for the AIA's ambitious agenda can be found in the development of the International green Construction Code (IgCC). In a process initiated in 2009 the International Code Council convened a committee to "initiate a code development project regarding a green code for commercial and high-performance buildings" ("History of the IgCC," iccsafe.org). With initial support from the AIA, ASTM International and the Illuminating Engineering Society (IES) a draft green code was created melding the categories from the LEED rating system with the mandatory requirements of a building code. Simultaneous efforts by ASHRAE, undertaken in conjunction with the USGBC, to create a sustainability standard (ASHRAE 189.1) ultimately led to a joint publication of both documents with the ASHRAE standard constituting a compliance option for the IgCC. While adoption has been sluggish this effort did create a model which can be used in crafting future mandatory language regarding sustainable construction. By extending the jurisdiction of a building code to "Site Development and Land Use," "Material Resource Conservation and Efficiency," "Water Resource Conservation, Quality and Efficiency," "Indoor Environmental Quality and Comfort" and "Commissioning, Operation and Maintenance," the IgCC extended the scope of any previous code, as well as the jurisdiction of building officials and the responsibilities of design professionals.

These three examples illustrate how positive change can occur in construction practices and regulations. To facilitate the expansive goals of the AIA White Paper, "Disruption, Evolution, and Change," strong alliances must be forged, entrenched bureaucracies must be galvanized, and long-standing attitudes must be discarded. Opposition from within as well as from outside the design professions can be anticipated. To overcome these obstacles an industry-wide commitment to evidence-based design and careful post-occupancy evaluation of design outcomes is required.

Architects have always had the advancement of "health, safety and welfare" in their mandate as professionals. With the proliferation of disciplines addressing urban design and planning, landscape architecture, interior design, and specialization in hospital and healthcare design, this mandate has become diluted, and minimum code requirements have become the standard. As the AIA White Paper recognizes, changing this equation requires a revised definition of both HSW and the architect's role. By embracing evidence-based design and outcome evaluation architects can display the scientific rigor and commitment to improved outcomes needed to earn a greater level of responsibility. With the findings of neuroscience regarding our innate responsiveness to environmental cues architects now have a scientific basis for the determination of healthy outcomes. While architecture has previously been described as the "mother of all arts," suggesting a primary role in fashioning the aesthetic experience of the built environment, it may in the future become a force for healing and regulation, for individuals, groups, societies and the ecosystems that sustain them.

While the use of biometric monitoring to evaluate design decisions is in its infancy it is conceivable that such techniques may become an essential, even a required aspect of the design process. If we know how to evaluate human responses to design, why would we not employ this ability consistently to ensure the most healthful and effective outcomes? The same is true of our expanding understanding of biophilia, as well as sustainable building technologies. Our understanding of costs and benefits with regard to construction standards is shifting as the consequences of current practices become more evident. It is only logical that new practices and requirements will evolve to address these consequences. Architects can, and should, be the change agents in this evolving transformation of industry practices.

References

1. Weekley, E. (1967). *An Etymological Dictionary of Modern English*. Dover Publications.
2. Neiderud, C. (2015). *How Urbanization Affects the Epidemiology of Emerging Infectious Diseases*. Taylor & Francis.
3. American Institute of Architects. (n.d.). Where Architects Stand: A Statement of Our values. https://www.aia.org/resources/50766-where-architects-stand-a-statement-of-our-va
4. American Institute of Architects. (2018). Disruption, Evolution, and Change. https://content.aia.org/sites/default/files/2019-06/ADV19_Disruption_Evolution_Change.pdf
5. Ibid. 7.
6. Ibid.
7. Ibid. 17.
8. Ibid. 19.
9. Ibid. 21.
10. Ibid. 22.
11. Ibid. 23.
12. Ibid.
13. Ibid.
14. Ibid. 24.

PART 4
Region

12
PROGRAMMING IN THE BIOREGION

Philip Norton Loheed AIA, NCARB, Assoc ASLA
with A. Vernon Woodworth FAIA

Planning is programming at the city or regional scale. Jurisdictional boundaries are more or less arbitrary in relation to the goals of the planning process. The authors argue here that the most effective scale at which to plan for health and wellbeing is the **bioregion**, an area of shared values and recognizable identity. A bioregion can be made up of multiple ecosystems, but there is a commonality of natural and cultural features that binds the region in systemic coherence. A schema for advancing bottom-up planning in the bioregion is advanced, and a plea made to revert to one-planet living as a precondition for a sustainable future.

The Case for Programming in the Bioregion

The human understanding of place is related to our means of perception and evolutionary priorities. Chief among these priorities is survival, with reproduction following closely behind. Hunter-gatherers worked in groups to forage, evolving social skills that allowed for cooperation and communication, as well as rudimentary technologies to enhance their effectiveness. Wayfinding was a critical skill, such that recognition of environmental patterns was a trait favored through natural selection. Knowledge of places rich in resources would be transferred through generations, with genetic repercussions. Humans, like all mammals, are territorial. We have evolved to respond to our environments in specific ways that promote survival and prosperity, and we compete to this day in the Real Estate market for pride of place, views, and location, location, location.

The science of ecology recognizes a watershed as the smallest example of an **ecosystem**, defined as "a biological community of interacting organisms and their physical environment." Humans evolved within specific environmental conditions in east Africa, adapting in ecosystems that may all have ultimately been part of the Nile River watersheds. Our ancestors exhibited resilience by expanding from this original context into other ecosystems, employing the cunning and ruthlessness of the hunt in combination with the patient attention to detail of the gatherer. With the advent of trade and permanent settlements the area of territorial identification became simultaneously more defined and more fluid, with less correspondence to ecosystems. An area of cultural identification and commercial interdependence is greater than a watershed or an ecosystem. In this article the term **bioregion** is used to describe such an area.

According to the World Wildlife Fund a bioregion is "an ecologically and geographically defined area that is smaller than a biogeographical realm, but larger than an ecoregion or an ecosystem." A bioregion is independent of the artificial boundaries that define a municipality, state, commonwealth or country, although the history of such boundaries may have bioregional roots.

With the recent explosion of technological innovation and resource consumption human population has exceeded the natural limits of our ecological context. The industrialization of human production and the development of the service economy have established a new level of human dominance that overlooks the economies of scale imposed by ecological limits. Our current rate of resource consumption exceeds the capacity of planet earth to support us. Our only hope of survival is a return to **"One Planet Living"** whereby resource consumption is reduced to a sustainable level. There are many implications to this requirement, but a prerequisite is acknowledgment of bioregionalism as an efficient and sustainable economic, cultural and environmental boundary. In addition, trade relationships can be evaluated at each bioregional boundary—exploring the relationship of the region to the planet, by comparing, for example: "locally sourced food" to "borrowed from others," indices of sustainability and resilience can be created and tracked (Figure 12.1).

Planning within the limits of a bioregion has multiple advantages for systems health and dynamic equilibrium. It is self-evident that cities are not and cannot be self-sufficient. However cities no longer have defined contributory regions that provide the resources necessary for their health and prosperity. Economic incentives favor mass production of food and other necessities without regard for regional distribution patterns or ecosystems health. By incentivizing bioregional production and distribution a closer approximation to the checks and balances of natural systems can be achieved. When the imperative of preparing for the impacts of climate change is considered, bioregional planning becomes essential. Flooding, intense heat, air quality and sea-level rise cannot effectively be addressed at the level of the jurisdiction or the watershed alone. A comprehensive and multi-pronged approach is required, encompassing a coherent and integrated series of regions.

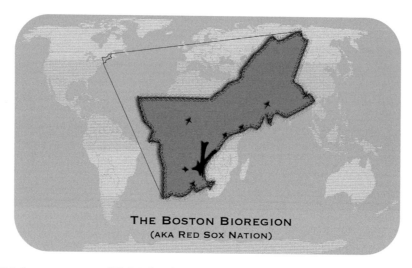

FIGURE 12.1 Image courtesy of Phil Loheed.

At the heart of regional identity in the human sphere is our legacy of tribalism and territoriality. A few brief millennia of empires and nation/states cannot erase these cognitive and behavioral patterns. The legacy of tribalism informs our political systems, education opportunities and land-use policies. One of the most visible identifiers of a bioregion is affiliation with a specific sports team, essentially a tribal identification that any anthropologist would recognize as such. But what do sports teams have to do with biological or geographic boundaries?

Our history of competing social groups selected for facial recognition. As groupings grew beyond a scale of intimacy, other mechanisms for kinship identity evolved. Culture supplanted kinship as the defining property of a group. Cultural identity requires frequent reinforcement and definition. This became a primary responsibility of leaders. Games, healthy competition, spectacles and ritual all played a role. If rural inhabitants of northern Maine and urban dwellers in Boston can both identify as members of Red Sox Nation the potential for a bond is established. This bond can be used to generate motivation for common activities, for instance, subscribing to cable stations or buying a specific brand of beer. A politician can generate approval and support just by attending a sporting event and being caught on camera. The cultural dimension of a bioregion is the key to its effectiveness as the fulcrum for meaningful transformation and renewal.

At any scale we must be able to experience emotionally our connection to a specific population and territory to be willing to act on its behalf. If a neighborhood has a problem, be it crime, trash, access to transportation or gentrification, a neighborhood group is the appropriate scale at which to initiate solutions. It is the identity with place that drives people to act. If the preservation and **regeneration** of natural systems, or the development of **resilience** to events driven by climate change, become priorities, the "bio-hood" is the scale at which these matters are most effectively addressed. Neighborhoods are not just about place, as the incorporation of the word "neighbor" implies. A neighbor is someone you can maintain a casual relationship with, perhaps extending to borrowing a cup of sugar or a landscape tool, and with whom you can discuss matters of common interest. The closer you are to a neighbor the more interdependent you may become. Similarly, in a "bio-hood" familiarity with natural systems and the impacts of development create affinities between disparate residents for the sake of mutual goals. Bio-hoods can work with the help of non-profits, government agencies, and philanthropic institutions to address immediate issues such as water pollution, flood management, land conservation, and habitat protection. But the bio-hood scale cannot meaningfully improve access to public transportation, plan for evolution to a sustainable economy, or manage retreat due to sea-level rise (Figure 12.2).

The complexity and scale of our resource and climate dilemmas call for the development and strengthening of place identity beyond jurisdictional boundaries, bio-hoods and specific ecosystems. The existence of tributary economic areas with associated support from cultural and educational institutions has innate potential to address these dilemmas at a meaningful scale. And importantly, existing geographic and cultural identification can support the enhancement of bioregional efficacy. An important element in bioregional cohesiveness is expressed by the concept of "economies of scale" applied in social and environmental contexts. One coastal community addressing flooding and sea-level rise will not be as effective as several contiguous communities. Urban run-off into rivers and streams is likewise a problem that must be addressed regionally. Air quality can be affected by conditions at a great distance, and resource distribution is a universal concern for the sake of equity and resilience. Goal setting and mobilization require consensus and investment, and both will be based on the recognition of common good in the goals established. This is the rationale for a bioregional approach to planning, whereby

FIGURE 12.2 Image courtesy of Phil Loheed.

natural and social systems are most effectively integrated into the dynamic equilibrium necessary for health and wellbeing.

Environmental Management Is the Human Mandate

A big-brained species with a proclivity for violence and an insatiable appetite for dominion seems an unlikely candidate for the role of steward. Yet we have job experience to draw upon. The successful hunter-gatherers did not passively reap nature's bounty. Extensive knowledge of environmental conditions was a precondition for prosperity. The creative use of fire to manage woodlands resulted in enhanced productivity of desirable species and the ecosystem as a whole. The agricultural revolution actually diminished our meaningful contribution to ecosystems health by reducing **biodiversity** and destroying habitat, and the Industrial Revolution promoted our role to that of ecological executioner. But humans became farmers only 10,000 years ago, whereas we had been successfully manipulating the natural environment as hunter-gatherers for 60,000 years before that. We still enjoy our gardens, and prize landscaping. Nature is still the context in which we continue to most reliably find beauty and meaning. We love our pets, spending billions annually for their companionship. We have the skills, honed over millennia, to celebrate and enhance natural systems, and we now have the incentive to use these skills to avoid extinction, a primary evolutionary motivator.

Yet humankind evolved from hunter-gatherer to farmer over thousands of years. We have decades, at most, to regain the balance of our social and economic systems within the context of a challenged biosphere. To meet this challenge a new sense of shared identity and purpose is required. Political parties, faith traditions, national origin, and economic status are all insufficient factors for the development of these motivators. However our instinctual connection to place and identification with tribal energy can provide the basis for transformation.

The leitmotiv of the industrial age was exploitation. In a future of sustainability we will revert to a culture of cultivation. Incubating, nurturing, attending to and overseeing will replace extracting, mechanizing, poisoning and exploiting. Success will be defined by systems health, not by personal wealth or status. This transformation has been underway for half a century already, although in fits and starts, with little progress to report. But people are now beginning to connect the dots between economic wellbeing and environmental health. A stock portfolio will soon yield its reassuring quality to the measurable reduction of CO_2 emissions. Those who care about the lives of their children and grandchildren will give less consideration to their college tuition and more attention to global temperature increase.

Nevertheless the impacts of climate change will continue to unfold for hundreds of years, regardless of the activities that we initiate tomorrow. To avoid the worst-case scenarios of social upheaval and resource conflicts strong common purpose and resolve is required. Existing governmental entities are either too limited to undertake meaningful action, or too unwieldy to respond effectively. The scale of robust response is regional, a potentially self-reliant economic and ecological area of mutual interest and identification. Let's take water supply as one example. A reliable supply of fresh water is a precondition for survival. Such supplies are threatened by watershed degradation, salt water infiltration, drought and excess demand. A bioregion provides the appropriate scale at which each of these issues can be addressed. Because development in one city, town, or county can degrade water supplies in multiple adjacent jurisdictions, concerted action is required to safeguard supply. The same argument holds, with different variables, for energy production, habitat protection, wetlands preservation, food supply, production and distribution of goods and services, and cultural innovation. Foremost among the cultural innovations required is the cultivation of stewardship as the highest human aspiration. Environmental resilience is a precondition for human resilience, but the opposite is also true. We must commit by taking full responsibility for environmental consequences before our current trajectory of demise can be altered.

Human Health Is Environmental Health

A rudimentary understanding of evolution and ecology informs us of the inseparable nature of organism and environment. Yet our cultural and economic development has obscured this relationship through the establishment of artificial constructs, like ownership and nations. The power of these artificial constructs is evident now in a collective failure to acknowledge and act on multiple indications of impending environmental collapse. A species that undergoes rapid population growth at the expense of other species and the quality of water and air will soon face drastic consequences. For humans these consequences include increased respiratory and immune-deficiency illnesses, malnutrition, heat strokes, vulnerability to cross-species infection, as well as depression, anxiety and social disruption. With the paralyzing consequences of the COVID-19 pandemic humanity has come face to face with its vulnerability and fragility. Health is no longer an individual matter, and no longer the responsibility of the medical profession alone. Health is a systemic condition, whereby organic systems interact for the mutual benefit of **dynamic equilibrium**.

Ecosystem health is achieved through species diversity and a food chain that acts at all scales of efficiency. Energy transfer is at the core of the system dynamic, with multiple pathways for this transfer to occur. Complexity of energy interchange is an essential ingredient of ecosystem resilience. We evolved based on our opportunistic responses to environmental contexts, finding different ways to obtain and prepare nutrition, creating social arrangements that enhanced survival behaviors, and problem solving with neural networks that reinforced memory, stimulated intuition and developed logic.

Our success may be our undoing. With a relentless urge for mastery we have occupied the top of the food chain, insisting that we are made in God's image, without regard to the most basic of truths: that we are part of a larger network of systems on which our survival depends. The time has come to outgrow our intra-species tribalism and our inter-species destructiveness if we are to avoid a pitiful future of decline and disarray.

To this end our bioregional imperative is the protection and restoration of ecosystems. Nature is our most precious resource. Any business owner knows to keep an accurate inventory of all elements in the supply chain. Species populations, biodiversity, and habitat are the key metrics of environmental health. Our social and cultural priorities as expressed by policies and pundits must pivot to enhanced sensitivity in these arenas. What would it be like to have an Environmental Health Index (EHI), along the lines of a stock exchange? People could buy shares in, for instance, estuary restoration. The EHI would reflect levels of investment and use data collection on salinity, plant and marine species, etc., to numerically reflect the health of estuarine habitats within a given bioregion. Newscasters would report on the day's EHI movement, and a "good day for the EHI" would bring everyone a sense of security regarding this "leading environmental indicator" and its implications for our collective future. Investment opportunities could include sectors in biodiversity, air and water quality, carbon sequestration and offsets as well as energy efficiency improvements. Funds would be distributed impartially to non-profits, start-ups and NGOs based on objective quantification of their effectiveness and potential.

What benefit would investors realize from such a scenario? At the very least, an effective system would streamline the bewildering array of charitable requests from conservation organizations. Donors interested in habitat protection could focus their gifts on a fund that would "invest" through the most effective channels, including existing non-profits. But beyond increasing the efficiency of voluntary funding for environmental matters there would continue to be tax credits for qualified investments, and recognition to investors. Bioregional EHI's could compete for government subsidies by demonstrating higher levels of investment and results. This is just one thinly sketched opportunity to create a cultural and economic structure that would support environmental health. If we can dream up and implement ways to package mortgages for profit and speculate on pork belly futures, surely we can find a way to incentivize an outcome that would provide benefits for all.

Another dimension to the bioregional approach, touched on above, is the affirmation of place identity. By emphasizing the interconnectedness of people within a defined economic and environmental region a sense of common purpose is more readily developed. Because of our instinctual connection to place there is a health dimension to this dynamic. Although not eligible for third-party payments the condition of "homesickness" is universally recognized. We have evolved to define our identity according to place. Travel is an industry that supports and exploits the values of exploration and discovery, novelty and excitement. But there is a cost in environmental and cultural quality to this industrialization of the imagination. Bored or depressed by where you are in life? Why not change the scenery for a few days or a week? Spew some contrails into the atmosphere and live it up on some foreign shore! Your hard-earned money is diverted from your hometown to an economy that creates permanent service workers of the local populace and emphasizes transience over cultural development.

Investing in the home-place is more in accord with our survival interests. What if the money for that big vacation were to be invested in conserving open space, or restoring wetlands, within a bike ride of our homes? We would then enjoy the fruits of our investments throughout the year, year after year! Our neurons could then fire reliably with the pride that stewardship provides, rather than constantly seeking the stimulation of diversion and novelty promoted by tourism.

However we choose to address our environmental dilemma, we must do so in accordance with our instinctual nature. This means understanding how we as homo sapiens have evolved and adapted in relationship to natural systems and physical places. We have to understand that cultural conditions reinforce neural wiring and can be altered to better suit our common interests. And we have to act within the laws of nature as well as the laws of mankind. Most importantly, we must come to see how our fates are intertwined, and act accordingly.

Risk Assessment/Goal Setting

Having established the value of the bioregional approach we can now proceed to the meaning and practice of programming in the bioregion. A first step is to identify the systems at risk, the stressors that put them at risk, and the steps necessary to restore and maintain operability. These systems can be natural or man-made. For flood management, ecological productivity, and aesthetic value, marshes and wetlands perform better than any engineered system. The economic value of wetlands must be factored into the equation of their preservation, restoration and recreation. But sea-level rise will jeopardize remaining coastal wetlands, and adjacent areas are

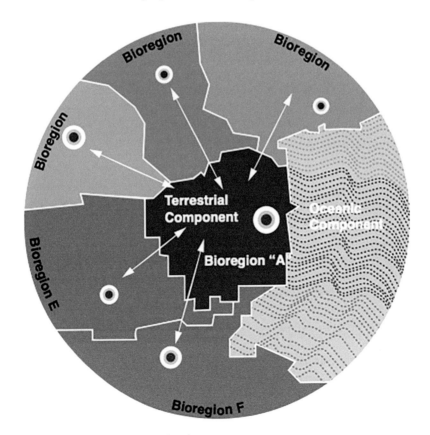

FIGURE 12.3 Image courtesy of Phil Loheed.

inevitably over-developed due to our human proclivity for dwelling by the water. A concerted effort to enhance wetlands preservation will require expenditure of financial and political capital. To undertake such an effort the real value of these vital ecosystems must be made clear to all stakeholders, including residents who may have to sacrifice their waterfront homes for the greater good (Figure 12.3).

Risk assessment is not a reactive activity. Our vulnerability to disease and social disruption due to environmental conditions has been amply illustrated over the past several decades. During this same time period various disconnected efforts to confront the implications of sea-level rise, temperature increases, CO_2 emissions and air and water pollution have sprung up, foundered or prospered, in varying degrees. But no systematic evaluation of environmental risks and the strategies and costs for mitigation has been attempted. By establishing the bioregion as the context for such an evaluation we make this effort definable and therefore possible. But regional planning requires a commitment by all jurisdictions and their populations. Again, education is the path to consensus and action. Because all residents of a bioregion have access to and rely upon common resources, our interdependence must be acknowledged.

Even within a discrete bioregion the implications of a comprehensive assessment of risks from climate change is a tall order. Falling back on our earlier analogy to the world of business, our role as environmental stewards requires a full inventory of assets and threats. With natural resources understood as our primary source of health and wellbeing we can begin to strategize priorities and investment strategies to protect these resources.

Categories for resource evaluation would certainly include the following:

- food security,
- fresh water supply,
- biodiversity and habitat protection (including wetlands protection and restoration),
- resource allocation and social resilience,
- jobs,
- affordable housing,
- public transportation,
- stormwater management,
- coastal development/vulnerability,
- climate change relocation programs/opportunities,
- biohood awareness and organization,
- heat mitigation, and
- carbon sequestration.

There are interrelationships among many of these categories, and certain elements necessary for each. Education and communication are universal necessities. Jobs, public transportation, and affordable housing are inextricably intertwined. But how can we prioritize the multiple investments that such an inventory is likely to indicate as necessary?

One approach is to evaluate the cost benefits of differing scenarios within each category. If planting trees supports heat mitigation, carbon sequestration and jobs the immediate returns seem to warrant the necessary investment. But what about the need for retreat from coastal properties at risk from storm surge and sea-level rise? The cost of abandoning properties (usually at the top of the market in terms of value) and relocating homes and businesses may have a more immediate priority and a greater social cost, while draining resources from other priorities. In such cases a multi-pronged approach is warranted. First and foremost, we can no longer afford to subsidize insurance for such properties, resulting in repeated claims and building back at greater scales of opulence and risk. But we can also limit development through zoning regulations, and incorporate resilient strategies into zoning and **building codes**. And we can aggressively enforce the wetland protection ordinances that were adopted to protect habitat and limit vulnerable development.

The development of regional planning over the past half-century has been largely hampered by jurisdictional boundaries and the lack of consensual delegation to a regional authority. Because habitats and watersheds are independent of jurisdictional boundaries this has delayed the implementation of sound environmental strategies at a meaningful scale. With the publication of Ian McHarg's *Design with Nature* in 1971 we were provided a methodology for sustainable development. Using overlays of population and resource mappings McHarg showed us how to avoid vulnerable ecosystems and focus development in more suitable locations. Using students from his program in Landscape Architecture at the University of Pennsylvania for data collection McHarg provided common sense guidelines based on ecological principles for the New Jersey shore which had suffered extensive damage to properties on its barrier islands in the mid-1960s. These guidelines, which spanned several jurisdictions governed by development interests and shortsighted politicians were largely ignored. In his book *The Geography of Risk* Gilbert M. Gaul describes the enabling role of the Federal Emergency Management Agency (FEMA) in providing insurance to these vulnerable settlements, which have repeatedly been rebuilt at ever-larger scales and levels of density after multiple storm events. During Superstorm Sandy in October 2012 communities on Long Beach Island alone suffered $1 billion in damages. The meaning of the phrase "barrier islands" has once again been ignored. Long Beach and other islands along the New Jersey Shore have been built back and properties are selling for record prices. Without a change in FEMA insurance policies and land-use regulations that incorporate reasonable risk assessment this cycle of destruction and rebuilding will not be recognized for the folly that it is.

Risk assessment will have different implications for different socio-economic groups, for different ethnic populations, and for different age groups. In addition to determining what is at risk, a thorough inventory will also assess who is at risk. Due to the essential nature of social cohesion as a fundamental aspect of resilience, all potential risks to health and wellbeing for all residents must be addressed. A study by the Urban Land Institute has confirmed that urban areas previously subject to "red-lining" also experience extreme temperatures during heat events, up to 13 degrees higher than adjacent neighborhoods. Having systematically constructed a built environment of discrimination and exploitation we must now face the consequences, and recognize our responsibility to mitigate these consequences.

Programming for Resilience

Resilience is the ability to withstand disruption and challenges to the functioning of natural and human systems. Our ability to predict such challenges and disruptions far exceeds our willingness to prepare in advance for such events. So programming for resilience runs up against the same challenge as risk assessment in a bioregion: the need for consensus and political will. The solution to this problem is sound analysis and careful planning by scientific and policy bodies. To generate political will the economic impact of proposed investments in resilience should be contrasted with the potential costs of not acting. To the extent that individual jurisdictions within a bioregion will share in the benefits of resilience strategies, they must also be willing to share in the costs.

But such top-down planning has limited appeal. To this end politicians, town councils, city councils and bio-hood groups will have to work together with policy organizations on the establishment of priorities, timetables, revenue allocation and effectiveness monitoring. Creative economic incentives can be incorporated into zoning codes and development policies. Risk communication will ensure awareness of the bases for decision-making. Consensus will emerge from a committed effort to shape the future, and a common understanding of the need for urgency.

Restoring Habitat, Food Chain and Biodiversity

A narrow view of resilience is the protection and ensured operability of infrastructure: electric service, water and sewer, natural gas, food supplies and transportation networks. These are indeed essential for short-term survival, during a storm or a heat wave. However the challenges we face as a result of sea level and global temperature rise are long-term threats to living systems equilibrium. For these threats we require a resilience strategy that protects natural systems, the fundamental source of our health and wellbeing.

Ecosystem stability is a function of diversity, the complex web of energy transfer that creates a stable and dynamic network of living beings. Biodiversity requires a healthy food chain and adequate habitat for all species within the food chain. In conjunction with an inventory of natural resources an understanding of critical habitat for all stages in the food chain can emerge. To the extent that this habitat is intact, measures to preserve it can be implemented. To the extent that this habitat is eroded an analysis of cost/benefit for habitat restoration programs can be undertaken. Such an analysis will balance the initial cost of purchasing and restoring property to a natural state with the long-term benefits of ecosystem productivity. Our interest is not in food production necessarily, or even in preserving nature for recreational or biophilic purposes. A healthy ecosystem performs numerous environmental functions that we take for granted, from carbon sequestration and water filtration to disease protection. The relationship of habitat degradation to trans-species transmission has been established, through recent global virus outbreaks. Habitat loss also results in the loss of potential sources of medicine, described by Eric Chivian in his essay "Species Loss and Ecosystem Disruption":

> "Over the course of millions of years of evolution, species have developed chemicals that have allowed them to fight infections, tumors, and other diseases; to capture prey and avoid being eaten; and to prevail over competitors in the struggle for territory. These chemicals have become some of today's most important pharmaceuticals."

The author goes on to describe how Taxol, the top-selling cancer drug in the U.S., is a natural product of the Pacific Yew, once treated as a trash tree by logging interests. When we claim that nature is healing, we may be more right than we can know.

Of highest priority for a sustainable future is a return to "One Planet Living." This is a concept introduced by "Bioregional" in 2002, and incorporated in the design and construction of the BedZED ecovillage. Their approach seeks to reduce carbon emissions and consumption by changing peoples' behaviors through design. A focus on wellbeing as a principal outcome results in enhanced physical and emotional health with reduced environmental degradation. One Planet Living is central to a successful Bioregional culture, whereby self-sufficiency in essentials and economic activity is a priority. This will require changes, not just in individual behavior, but also in corporate and cultural values. A significant and central achievement of humanity is the power of the marketplace, wherein planned obsolescence and a hunger for more drive patterns of consumption. Technology and the centralization of resources are creating a new cyber-marketplace where the individual preferences of every consumer can be tracked, analyzed, and catered to (as I write this my portable speaker is playing songs from a collection created by algorithms based on my music preferences). This new marketplace can be tweaked to reduce material consumption (I no longer buy vinyl, cassettes, or CD's), but new metrics must be introduced to make this meaningful. Can Amazon decarbonize on its own, or is governmental involvement required? Should consumer products have the equivalent of a value-added tax based on carbon footprint?

The issue of One Planet Living is political and moral, as well as cultural. Human society evolved from tribes to empires based on efficiencies in resource distribution, defense and governmental functions. The provision of "bread and circuses" was largely sufficient to maintain the social order. Today's global civilization likewise relies upon a steady diet of consumer goods and entertainment to keep the peace and allow the machinery of the marketplace to keep running. One Planet Living is a threat to this existing system of economic/social equilibrium. Achieving consensus that our existing expectations and consumption levels are unsustainable is not the goal of government, industry, media or even the academic and scientific communities. Until a concerted effort to bring this topic to the forefront of political consciousness occurs we will continue to undermine our chances for survival.

Programming for Sea-level Rise

Touched on above is the difficult, in fact painful, need to plan now for permanent alterations of our shorelines as a result of the inevitability of continued sea-level rise. As with One Planet Living, our cultural and economic priorities are currently resistant to facing this reality. We have discussed how the costs and benefits of remedial efforts can be evaluated as a prelude to decision-making. Many communities have introduced zoning regulations to limit development in vulnerable areas, and wetland preservation is regulated through national, state and local legislation. These initiatives will not be sufficient if the social costs of disrupted lives and destroyed property are to be avoided. A rational approach would involve managed retreat, including restrictions on all construction within a buffer zone and provisions on sale or transfer of property. A model could be the program established to phase out obsolete septic systems at point of sale by requiring the seller to upgrade to new standards. This approach depends upon the establishment of workable resilience strategies or the provision of replacement value to the seller. Purchasing buildings that are at-risk will be necessary. Prioritizing properties that can be used to create wetland buffer areas would have multiple benefits. We will need these buffers as storms increase in intensity and existing coastal wetlands disappear. And it is worth repeating that wetlands are among the most productive ecosystems on the planet (Figure 12.4).

FIGURE 12.4 Image courtesy of Phil Loheed.

Managed retreat requires a masterplan. There is a process of global urbanization taking place that is unlikely to be slowed by climate change or pandemics. Because the majority of cities worldwide are located on waterways, their vulnerability to climate change impacts, including land-based and coastal flooding as well as sea-level rise, poses significant threats to ongoing wellbeing. Resilience strategies must be baked into all development going forward, including relocation programs and aggressive protection and creation of nature-based buffers.

Social Programming

The mechanisms of the marketplace are insufficient to manage the goals outlined above. The issue of political will has been raised repeatedly, but it is public opinion that drives political will. While sound strategies are well known and available to mitigate all but the consequences of runaway climate change, the groundswell of public opinion needed to implement these strategies has yet to emerge. There will be both winners and losers as certain geographical locations, climate zones, and neighborhoods fare better or worse than others. How will we collectively respond? While outpourings of generosity and support routinely occur in the wake of natural disasters, such as Hurricane Katrina or the earthquake in Haiti, we are comfortable with extreme inequity, chronic hunger, and environmental racism on an ongoing basis. Can we consent to the reallocation of resources for the common good, a concept completely alien to our underlying cultural values? Will an understanding of our common interests override the drive that informs every aspect of our current economic and political trajectory?

Our position in this chapter is that this can, and must, happen, by means of the formation of a bioregional identity with the health of ecosystems and social structures at its heart. With an emphasis on community and the mutual support of all individuals and entities within this community a new sense of value and identity can emerge. We must learn to emerge from an era of status and position as the defining metric of self, returning instead to a shared identity with our place, both natural and handmade. By devoting ourselves to the health of our communities and our environment we can gain a sense of purpose and meaning that a life of consumption and self-indulgence can never provide. There is no program yet for this leap of faith, but the need is present, so, following the law of supply and demand, we are confident that a way will be found.

The Problem of Data

We close with a note on big data. Sorry, the term requires capitalization: BIG DATA! A utopia based on cyber-omniscience might be an attractive thought, but the reality, as with all utopian schemes, is neither achievable nor necessarily desirable. Certainly the impact of Geographic Information Systems (GIS) has revolutionized regional planning, and this and other technologies are likely to prove essential going forward. But an effective decision-making process will always require human judgment and values. The challenges posed by climate change and the evaluation of options in response do require an aggressive attention to data on all aspects of our environment. But it is one thing for my phone to decide which song I might like to hear next, and a completely different matter to determine the allocation of resources in managed retreat from a coastal area. Technology allows us to extend our senses and the impact of our decisions. Increasingly we are allocating our decisions as well to technological processes. A computer can more reliably manage load-shifting on an electricity grid than a human, but it is not able to develop social programs, or weigh political considerations. The concept of bioregionalism relies on the good will and mutual respect of all residents in the preservation of natural and imposed systems. The program has yet to be invented that can create these conditions of cooperation in living beings. For that, we can only rely on ourselves.

13
REGENERATIVE DEVELOPMENT AND DESIGN
Nature and Healing

Bill Reed AIA and A. Vernon Woodworth FAIA

> Nature is a regenerative force, having evolved to ensure maximum energy capture and transfer. We can adapt our development patterns to regenerate natural systems if we are willing to change our behaviors and our sense of selves. Ritual is a human means for transforming individual and group identity that can be employed to create common goals and mutual understanding when managed by a skilled facilitator. Ritual is a tool developed by all human societies to promote regenesis, a new connection to the spirit and the community, that allows us to move forward with new vision and purpose.

In an ecosystem all parts function as a living and dynamic whole. Darwin's amazing insights into evolution emphasize the interplay of species and environment through natural selection as the fundamental dynamic of the life force. But what happens when a species evolves to the point that, through the development of technology and brain functioning, the interplay of species and environment is disrupted? Symptoms include unchecked population growth, deteriorating environmental conditions, unregulated externalities and disruption in natural systems such as nutrient and water cycles, the fundamental engines of the seeming paradox of dynamic stability and evolutionary processes. Ultimately the biosphere is altered, resulting in a cycle of decline in habitat viability that becomes self-reinforcing, like a negative feedback loop. The catastrophic term for this condition is "collapse."

Because of the interdependent nature of all living systems no piecemeal approach can arrest this deterioration of ecosystem integrity. In Albert Einstein's words "no problem can be solved from the same level of consciousness that created it." "Regeneration" is a term used to describe a state of consciousness and being that is able to engage a continuous process of rebirth, of understanding and engagement with the dynamic and evolutionary system of life. Regeneration is first and foremost a developmental practice, an evolutionary practice, a process that requires us to be self-aware, a process of internal becoming. Because we are not outside of the processes we wish to heal, a reductionist approach that differentiates between a subject and an object cannot succeed. We achieve this by cultivating awareness of our interior states, and how who we are impacts our relationship to interpersonal, societal and environmental systems. A truly sustainable condition requires us to develop an awareness and connection to our surroundings that has largely been obscured by external analytic static. This conscious cultivated state of self

DOI: 10.4324/9781003164418-18

and interpersonal connection provides the foundation to engage the underlying living forces that flow through our beings and the world we inhabit.

Ecosystem development is characterized by the capture of solar energy for biological purposes of succession and diversification, resulting in ever-greater stability and resilience. How, and why, does this occur? In his novel *Lila, An Inquiry into Morals*, Robert M. Pirsig explores this question:

> "The Second Law of Thermodynamics states that all energy systems run down like a clock and never rewind themselves. But life not only "runs up", converting low-energy sea water, sunlight and air into high energy chemicals, it keeps multiplying itself into more and better clocks that keep "running up" faster and faster. Why, for example, should a group of simple, stable compounds of carbon, hydrogen, oxygen and nitrogen struggle for billions of years to organize themselves into a professor of chemistry? What's the motive? If we leave a chemistry professor out on a rock in the sun long enough the forces of nature will convert him into simple compounds of carbon, oxygen, hydrogen, nitrogen, calcium, phosphorus, and small amounts of other minerals. It's a one-way reaction. No matter what kind of chemistry professor we use and no matter what process we use we can't turn these compounds back into a chemistry professor. Chemistry professors are unstable mixtures of predominantly unstable compounds which, in the exclusive presence of the sun's heat, decay irreversibly into simpler organic and inorganic compounds. That's a scientific fact. The question is: Then why does nature reverse this process? What on earth causes the inorganic compounds to go the other way? It isn't the sun's energy. We just saw what the sun's energy did. It has to be something else. What is it? [1]."

Resilience is the ability of a system to maintain functional integrity in the event of environmental disturbances. Resilience can be understood in terms of health, although it more specifically refers to dynamic properties such as energy interchange and adaptive potential. Resilience is certainly a primary factor in the evolutionary process, informing the survivability of individuals, species and ecosystems equally. It is also a very different dynamic from competitiveness which emphasizes aggressive behavior and dominance. The competitive model implies limited resources and inevitable conflict, while resilience implies interconnected cooperation in a community of common interests. It seems fair to say that the competitive model of evolution bears a distinctly human stamp, while resilience resembles the dynamics of the way life really works.

Individual resilience is a factor of community integration. We have evolved as social beings reliant on one another for survival from birth. Being cut off from the group is a threat to survival. The cultural adaptation of specialization has reinforced this dynamic and made possible the development of civilization with all of its rewards and discontents. The stages of social development involve the family, peer group and a larger purpose or role. These are the fundamental elements of personal identity. It is human nature to take the priorities and worldviews of each stage as one's own, and to identify with these throughout the lifecycle. Yet our cultural environment is subject to change and, despite attempts by dominant groups to maintain the integrity of their worldviews, survival can only be assured by adaptation, a process that is able to participate in the evolutionary dynamic. With clear evidence that current patterns of consumption and development are upsetting the equilibrium of the biosphere the resilience of modern civilization is being put to the test. Awareness is engendering anxiety, and denial is resulting in a political version of "acting out," whereby destructive behaviors are engaged in as a defense against painful truths.

Under the circumstances our collective response requires individual transformation. Because the viability of a civilization is based on the perception of a static or mechanical worldview of stability and continuity, transformation is inherently threatening. Cultural and religious rituals have traditionally sought to contain this threat by providing a context in which transformation can be undergone by means of a sanctioned procedure. But there is no currently vital sanctioned ritual for the emergence of ecological consciousness. Therefore it is incumbent on us to create one.

Design professionals often think of the programming process as a necessary task that precedes the creative process. This perspective misses the human dynamic that is both part of and essential to programming. There are a number of different stakeholder groups in any building project. Programming involves reaching an understanding with as many of these groups as possible regarding the goals and outcomes of the endeavor. This could be a perfunctory audit of statistical variables, however such an approach will yield only drab consequences. Engaging the client and the community in deepening an understanding of their evolutionary role and potential holds much greater value. Facilitating a conversation between the client and the community sets up a dynamic process of discovery of the nature of the larger system they live within and that can result in a collective unifying vision of how to engage this system in a value-adding process. Bringing to this dialog a deep understanding of the natural forces that enliven a site and its environs will open the potential for a project that contributes to the on-going health and resilience of the community.

The potential inherent in this approach occurs as follows: the programmer, through self-examination and education, comes to an understanding of process and people that allows her to relate deeply to the site, to the user groups, and to the natural and social communities that will be impacted by the project. By gathering the stakeholders into a process of communication and exploration she facilitates the uncovering of consensual values and aspirations, allowing all parties to shed their defensive identifications with protective worldviews, and move toward an empathic connection with the full dynamic potential of the site as well as the value that it and its inhabitants can add to, and receive from, the larger lifeshed they are nested within. The creativity unleashed in this interaction is the essential ingredient of a successful project. Transformation moves from the individual programmer to the user groups and then to the design, the project and the community.

This approach suggests that the process of programming can function as a social ritual whereby a group process renews bonds of affinity and creates goals that function as symbols of aspiration and identity. Anyone familiar with the community process surrounding planning initiatives and development proposals is aware of the extent of emotional energy generated by these events. The containment and transformation of emotional energy are the essence of the ritual process. Our current process pays only lip service to the true mandate of community building, whereby bonds are strengthened and resilience is reinforced. Only the skilled guidance of a deeply committed facilitator can enable this outcome. If this facilitator is also the author of the project program, the chances for a regenerative outcome are greatly enhanced.

A recent experience of Regenesis Group in community engagement around a 4,500,000 square feet mixed-use development in Vina del Mar, Chile, provides an illustration of this process. The Developer, Inmobiliaria Las Salinas, sought to build on a brownfield site that they had operated for years as a refinery in a coastal garden city that has degraded significantly over the last 30 years due to social fragmentation, cultural decline from the accommodation of mass tourism, degradation of ecological system health, automobile dominance in the fabric of the region, disenfranchised neighborhoods and political intractability.

The project was in danger of being derailed by a multitude of local groups united in opposition to it. Regenesis Group undertook an intervention that began with the collective creation of a Story of Place. Over an initial two-week period Regenesis investigated the patterns of life in the Vina del Mar and Valparaiso region, engaged and co-learned with the municipal government, the developer, and most of the community activist groups, to co-discover the processes and inter-relationships that helped create the city they loved. The unfolding of this "Story of Place" helped to establish a common foundation of understanding from which it was possible to help the citizens paint a vivid picture of the potential of Vina del Mar. By reflecting on the place's long history as a thriving and sustainable contributor to the region, the Story of Place articulated key patterns of health and resilience that, once restored, would enable the Vina del Mar to regenerate itself as a whole socio-ecological system.

The result was remarkable. Every group learned the seriousness of the developer in wanting to help the community align around united action. At first both the developer and the community were tentative, but as the process unfolded an alignment emerged whereby the community and developer (1) realized that the developer was serious about the development process as a way to transform their own practice and relationship with the community, (2) began to engage and collaborate with each other and the developer, (3) realized that ecological health in the region could be improved with highly leveraged interventions, (4) understood that the community would receive social, economic and environmental benefits that would improve the quality of life in the region, and (5) a partnership of trust was being formed and a process implemented that would reconcile additional concerns as they arose.

Ninety-five percent of the participants shifted from an extremely negative perspective (they had universally called the developer "the enemy") to being gratefully engaged. They were excited about the potential to bring back the health of the city. They were willing to commit to work together to find synergistic solutions. Likewise the developer became willing to adapt their masterplan in order to create new potential in the community, such as restored ecological habitat connectivity, social re-integration, the quality of the formerly extensive tree canopy, and the restoration of a severely degraded estuary. The core issue that the developer had to make a profit was made clear and accepted by all stakeholders.

A commitment of time and good will by all parties is required to achieve these results. The consequences can extend far beyond the boundaries of the site. Because the various groups were willing to put aside their differences and work together, momentum was generated that has coalesced around actively engaging issues of mobility, ecological connectivity, coastal restoration and interest in restoring the Margamarga Estuary, 80 percent of which had been filled to create a parking lot.

The Regenesis intervention found common ground in a story of place that all stakeholders could buy into. The implicit assumption introduced was that the issues were not confined to the boundaries of the site. Once the focus was widened to a regional perspective the individual parties could emerge from behind their defensive "us vs. them" positions to find common ground. The narrative informing thought and behavior moved from adversarial to cooperative, and ultimately to symbiotic. In other words, there was a realignment of the energy pattern that informed these relationships toward the natural dynamics that underlie healthy ecosystems: renewal, reciprocity and resilience.

The importance of the time dimension cannot be underestimated. Change is always a matter of process, and process requires time. Major rituals often are undertaken over days or weeks, with discrete intervals emphasizing specific dimensions. Psychotherapy requires an ongoing relationship, identifying dysfunctional beliefs and behaviors, and taking the bold steps necessary to dismantle these. The reason for this is the myelination process neurons require to establish new neural pathways. Myelin is a substance that attaches over time to the axon of a neuron to facilitate electrical communication with other neurons in its network. Production of myelin as part of the establishment of a new neural pathway is the fundamental building block of the learning process.

This is why it takes the consistent engagement of a design team and community leaders and the real-time application of reconciling principles to begin to understand what it means to be in a mutually beneficial relationship with each other and an ecosystem. During the Vina del Mar project, two months into the process at the third workshop, the development manager, who was still quite worried about what he would have to "give up," made his first personal discovery. He actually stopped the meeting and announced that he "got it." "Got what?" we asked.

> "Reciprocity. I've been holding the idea that we could only be in a transactional relationship with the community, trading this for that. This is a dance of relationship, a development of understanding of what's important, at the core, for all the players."

This was a breakthrough experience for a key individual in the process, made possible by repeated exposure to a novel interactional framework, and his own willingness to allow his habitual thought framework to be challenged.

Establishing a new neural network in the context of a community-wide activity is a precise and succinct definition of the dynamics of the ritual process. Ritual is at least as fundamental a human act as making art or language, or worship. Ritual enables renewal, a proscribed context for change which allows the overall social structure on which we depend for mutual survival to be both maintained and refreshed. To be refreshed is to be revitalized, reborn in spirit, regenerated.

In practical terms regeneration means to contribute to the value-generating processes of the living systems of which we are part. Without adding value—with a conscious awareness of the ongoing, co-creative and emergent processes of life—systems degenerate, like the chemistry professor on the rock. The imperative in any design process is to intentionally develop the understanding required to participate in improving the resilience of the relationships at work in ecosystems, human social systems, businesses, families and so on. Without a process of continually adding value to living systems sustainability is not possible.

It is difficult for a reductionist culture to understand that working with the complexity of a living system is possible in the first place. This is likely due to a difficulty in conceiving how a living system can be addressed without a reduction to manageable parts. This is where working with pattern understanding comes into play. For practitioners familiar with working with patterns, it is actually easier to assess living patterns and reach definitive conclusions from these distinct patterns than it is to try to make sense of thousands of pieces. A living system—or place, or watershed, or community—is a "being" or "organism." It is necessary to be in relationship with it. If we are not, then abuse, neglect or misunderstood interventions are the result. The nature of such a relationship is a big leap for the design and building industries. The land is not simply dirt that we build upon. Various aboriginal peoples had this understanding. Everything in space and time, including the consciousness of "who" they were, was inextricably part of the whole. The Navajo term for mountain refers to a

> "whole set of relationships and the ongoing movement inherent in those relationships. These relationships include the life cycles of the animals and plants which grow at different elevations, the weather patterns affected by the mountain, as well as the human's experience of being with the mountain. All of these processes form the dynamic interrelationship and kinetic processes that regenerate and transform life."

Since this motion of the mountain is not separate from the entire cosmic process, one can only really come to know the mountain by learning about "the kinetic dynamics of the whole."

All this is not to say that working in pieces and parts with quantitative measurement is wrong. It is just the wrong place to start. As Wendell Berry observes, "A good solution is good because it is in harmony with those larger patterns, solves more than one problem, and doesn't create new ones." He goes on to explain that health is to be valued above any cure, and coherence of pattern above almost any solution produced piecemeal or in isolation. Adopting one or two green or "sustainable" technologies into a green building practice while ignoring the underlying principle of regeneration is ultimately not effective and, at worst, produces unintended and counterproductive consequences. Western and Eastern medicine practices may be a useful comparison. Neither is right nor wrong in itself. Green design, as it is practiced in a mechanical manner, can be compared to working on the heart or intestinal system as a specialist might- curing the particular issue but not addressing the overall systemic nature of the cause, whether it is diet, environment, stress or genetics. Integrative design, an organized process to find synergies among building and living systems, has an analogy in integrative medicine—many specialists getting together to diagnose and address relatively complex causes and effects.

Regeneration might be compared to naturopathic and Eastern medicine—cranial sacral therapy, acupuncture and so on—these practices start with the energetic patterns of the whole body. While not necessarily more effective in all cases, it is always better to start with the nature of the larger environmental influences and interrelationships before solving for the symptom or cutting the body open.

From the perspective of health-supporting architecture and planning our responsibility is not to design "things" but to positively support human and natural processes in order to achieve long-term quality of life—that is, evolution with the necessary corollary of positive potential for all life. Programming can set the agenda and establish the goals by identifying the larger environmental influences, ensuring that the resulting building, inhabitants and stakeholders will connect and contribute rather than detract and degrade. There are current designs and policy practices that approach this nature of interrelationship with the places we inhabit. Ecosystems have been seen to recover their health and demonstrate even greater levels of potential than imagined-deserts being turned into food-producing gardens with minimal water use; water being brought back to the desert by appropriate planting and techniques of slowing run-off; damaged, low-diversity and desertified ecosystems brought back into full flower along with increased animal and plant habitat by replicating preindustrial conditions; urban areas brought back to civility and habitability through attention to the nature of human and natural patterns in each unique place. Examples include Jane Jacobs' work in New York City neighborhoods as noted in *The Death and Life of Great American Cities*, in which she uses the term regeneration for her work. Alan Savory's work in creating new health in damaged ecosystems is another example. Regenesis in Santa Fe, New Mexico, looks at the socio-ecological whole and unites disparate sectors into interactive systems participating in healthy evolution.

The key is to start from what is core to the life of the client and to the place and culture in which you are working. This discovery process of relatedness—between stakeholders and the whole living organism of the subject place—is the source of compassion and care, from which springs the energy to effect creative change. Programming can involve unearthing these relationships and facilitating this compassion through a guided process that weaves a story of place into the fabric of the project, myelinating neurons and binding participants in a narrative of renewal.

Reference

1. Pirsig, R. M. (1991). *Lila: An Inquiry into Morals*. Bantam: London. 144–145.

14
PROGRAMMING FOR HUMAN HEALTH IN A CHALLENGED CLIMATE

John Gravelin, Eleanor Hoyt and Jim Newman

Resilient design for new and existing buildings is poised to become a new service subset within the practice of architecture. The authors are at the forefront of this effort and have explored the social and environmental dimensions of resilience as well as the practicalities of flood proofing, **Passive Survivability**, and the like. The extent of meteorological disruption caused by climate change will depend upon the effectiveness of our carbon reduction strategies. Somewhere in the range of potential consequences, no one can say precisely where, are tipping points that will signal systems failure and environmental collapse. The extent of our intrinsic resilience in terms of emergency response, community cohesiveness, and preparation by design may provide the difference between survival and destruction.

Architects and designers are challenged with managing a range of risks in a cost-effective manner related to our existing building practices. The scope of this mandate is all-encompassing. Architects and designers are now responsible for providing robust building and habitat systems, managing the emergency processes associated with life-safety and wellbeing in a challenging climate, and facilitating an equitable social system that can support all citizens under all circumstances.

Resilient design offers many positive human health benefits, from saving lives and property during hurricanes to relieving the chronic stress of hotter, longer summers. Resilience provides the new standard by which we must design and build for a changing climate.

The urgency of a resilient built environment is such that we will soon need a standardized code of resilient design. We can no longer afford to allocate resources to buildings and communities that will not withstand the increasing frequency of climate hazards. A resilient code would streamline emergency efforts, create a standardized emergency methodology for both first responders and occupants to understand and interact with during times of duress, as well as improving climate-hazard awareness among everyday citizens.

In a culture of resilience everyone has a role, and every step taken toward programming systems can and will save lives and property.

DOI: 10.4324/9781003164418-19

The Power of Adaptation

The ability to adapt to and recover from difficulty is an asset in any organization, industry or aspect of everyday life. In architectural practice, resilience refers to the ability of an environment to provide for basic human needs to occupants during unexpected or extreme conditions. While building resilience can be discussed in terms of design strategies or facility improvements, community strength, human health and life-safety are at the heart of every conversation about dealing with hazards and risks. By improving the resilience of our designs, we are enhancing the ability of occupants to adapt and recover, and to move forward with strength and determination from adverse conditions.

Our global climate is changing and the hazards we face are changing too. Countries around the world have experienced acute examples of climate change from destructive hurricanes to severe droughts and devastating wildfires. Through resilient design we are working to ensure that our built environment can adapt to these changing forces by supporting community strength and keeping our people and our future generations safe.

The Role of Resilience in Design

Designing for resilience in our built environment is not a singular approach. It employs existing standards and architectural concepts for sustainability, Passive Survivability and community building to develop a new perspective for enhanced human health and safety.

Building codes in the U.S. provide the minimum benchmark for all architectural practice, and a design that does not meet the building code is, by definition, illegal. While there are national and international codes, there are also state, city and local codes that dictate a community's response to regional and environmental priorities. Some building codes mandate sustainable and resilient designs; however these standards have not been adopted in many parts of the country.

According to the Brundtland Commission's Report in 1987, sustainable development is defined as development that "meets the needs of the present without compromising the ability of future generations to meet their own needs." In architecture, *sustainable design* aims to achieve this goal. There are rating systems, codes and standards that embrace many different approaches to realize a "sustainable" building.

The U.S. Green Building Council (USGBC) has developed the Leadership in Energy and Environmental Design (LEED) rating systems, through which buildings can receive public ratings for employing sustainable strategies. The LEED rating system has recently incorporated strategies for resilience. To become LEED Certified, every building must achieve certain minimum sustainability characteristics, which are scored. While one building may focus on 100 percent renewable energy, other buildings may focus on indoor air quality (IAQ) to increase occupant health, or environmentally friendly materials to reduce the overall carbon footprint. The new resilience strategies in LEED now give scores for hazard assessment and resilience planning.

Passive Survivability encompasses design principles that support the continuous habitability of buildings during extended power outages or interruptions in heating and cooling systems. The goal of Passive Survivability is for buildings to support occupants passively, without functioning active systems. This is a simple goal. The design strategies supporting Passive Survivability can be complex. Passive Survivability is key to resilient design because it is based on the specific vulnerabilities of occupants in relation to their particular climate and hazards. Minimum building codes and sustainable design requirements are integral to Passive Survivability.

Community Strength Building includes strategies at the building scale that support the strength of community residents and systems. Buildings can reduce community strength by using up community resources (such as open space or storm water system capacity) or they can enhance community strength by adding capacity to systems or supporting community needs. An important determinant of a community's capacity for resilience is the extent of interdependence and redundancy of systems and relationships.

Resilient design embodies building codes, sustainable design, Passive Survivability and community strength building, in ways that designers can ensure the provision of basic human needs for today and the preservation of social systems for tomorrow in the face of environmental stress. Ideally a resilient building can absorb climate change stressors and provide opportunities to enhance human health and community strength into the future.

Programming for Resilience

In architectural programming, the needs of building owners and building occupants are translated into space requirements, functional criteria and project goals. Programming for resilience builds off existing methods by considering the needs of owners and occupants during unusual or emergency conditions, in addition to everyday design circumstances. These unusual conditions are not only unique to every building and community, they are continually changing. Architectural programmers must anticipate how changing environmental conditions will influence future owner and occupant needs so as to enhance resilience in our built environment.

Programming establishes goals and seeks to identify and maximize capacity. By establishing resilience as a goal in the programming stage, a defined capacity for response to environmental stress can be established as a design requirement. To improve the resilience of a project, a designer must *understand hazards, assess vulnerabilities,* and then *develop strategies* to reduce those vulnerabilities.

Building codes came into existence and have continued to evolve over time based on real-life events, in a continual process of evaluating cost/benefit and minimum standards of life-safety. Through this process risks to occupants and communities based on fire or structural failure have been lowered significantly. Codes have the ability to address resilience as well. Such efforts are in their infancy, but are likely to increase as the severity of climate events increases.

In the meantime, resilient programming can be integrated into the research and goal-setting process of standard programming by identifying potential hazards and vulnerabilities related to climate events. A general approach to resilient design, using identified hazards and risks, can also help to strengthen the built environment in preparation for unforeseen events by anticipating cascading failures. Environmental health, social health and individual health are increasingly being understood as interrelated. The responsibilities of the design professional have always included the maintenance and preservation of individual health, as well as respect for the principles of social health. Now the dimension of environmental health has been added to the mix, and resilient principles have become integral to achieving the stability required to sustain social systems and personal health in times of crisis.

Understanding Hazards

There are many hazards across many climates to consider when programming for resilience. Here we look at three common hazard categories but encourage the reader to explore others that may be relevant to their community:

- **Flooding:** Flooding is a broad hazard that can come from multiple sources. Coastal communities or projects located close to water bodies can experience general flooding during storm events with excessive precipitation or high winds over time or flash flooding with heavy precipitation during a short time period. Localized flooding, which is rarely found on flood maps, can occur in almost any urban setting where impervious surfaces and poor drainage systems result in excess stormwater with nowhere to go. Whether a building is exposed to riverine flooding, storm surge or inadequate stormwater management, flooding can put both occupants and building systems at risk.

- **Severe Storms:** Severe storms also come in many forms. Hurricane and coastal storms bring high-level sustained winds, heavy precipitation and even tornadoes. In coastal areas, storm surge from a Category 1 hurricane can raise water levels by four or five feet. A Category 5 hurricane can bring storm surge of up to 20 feet. Severe thunderstorms can occur almost anywhere and similarly bring strong winds, hailstorms, flooding and lightning. In addition to building damage, severe storms often result in loss of power. According to the National Hurricane Center, a "moderate" or Category 2 hurricane is expected to cause "near-total power loss with outages that could last from several days to weeks."
- **Extreme Heat:** While seemingly less dramatic than a hurricane, extreme heat is one of the most deadly climate hazards faced by the U.S. Heat-related illnesses can impact anyone, but seniors, children, and people with respiratory issues are at highest risk. As our climate changes over the next century average temperatures are expected to rise, increasing the number of days which exceed 100 degrees. With these increasing temperatures also come increasing frequency and duration of heatwaves. These increasing temperatures will be felt across the country, but the effects may be more severe for individuals who rely on public transit or work outdoors with limited access to shade or air conditioning, and those who live in urban environments where dark-colored pavement and buildings contribute to urban heat islands.
- **Other hazards to consider:** Hurricanes and Coastal Storms, Severe Thunderstorms, Wildfire, Drought, Winter Storms, Earthquakes, Tornados.

These different climate related hazards result in types of vulnerabilities that lead to distinct types of damage to buildings and infrastructure. Flooding can compromise envelope (a building's exterior shell that repels outdoor elements) and roof systems, infiltrate basements, damage mechanical systems and introduce moisture and mold to interior spaces. Wind from severe storms can damage siding and roofs and extreme temperatures can overload a building's cooling capacity.

Many of these hazards also result in a loss of power to building systems, whether locally when severe wind damages a utility pole, or regionally when a city's cooling demand during an extended heat wave (or power shut-offs due to wildfire danger) closes down the electrical grid. Without power, a building may lose the capability to maintain habitable indoor temperatures. An occupant on an upper floor of a high-rise building with electrical water pumping systems may no longer have access to potable water. And without power or the ability to charge cell phones, occupants may lose their ability to communicate with others, including emergency service providers.

Additional health concerns arise when floodwaters interact with overloaded sewer systems and introduce contaminated material into indoor spaces, or when repeated flooding prevents building materials from drying, promoting the growth of mold and indoor pollutants.

Hazard Mitigation Plans

A good place to start gaining an understanding of potential hazards and vulnerabilities for a specific building site is the local hazard mitigation plan. In the U.S., federal funding from FEMA is available for cities, counties, and states to develop these plans. Within them, each municipality must identify all potential environmental and human-induced hazards that may face their communities as well as investigate any associated vulnerabilities. Hazard mitigation plans are required to rank hazards by risk and thus can be used by designers for identifying and prioritizing hazards applicable to their projects.

It is important to note that hazard mitigation plans are primarily based on historical information. Hazards and vulnerabilities are usually based on past occurrences of events and disasters and may not fully consider how conditions may change in the future. Many areas of the U.S. now have vulnerability assessment reports that specifically address future hazard scenarios. While there is a general understanding of the impacts of climate change, such as rising sea levels and temperatures, the severity of these impacts will vary by region. The coastal communities of Miami may be most concerned about sea levels rising over the next 20 years, whereas increasing urban temperatures are likely more important to the residents of Chicago. Increasing drought conditions in California elevate concerns for wildfires, while Texas residents will focus on preparing for another deadly storm like Hurricane Harvey in 2017.

Designing buildings and systems that can physically withstand or adapt to hazard exposure is a key part of a resilient designer's job. It is, however, perhaps even more critical to design buildings that ensure every occupant has the capacity to withstand or adapt to such exposure in safe and healthy ways that are relevant to the buildings' uses.

Assessing Vulnerabilities

Once hazards are understood, it is time to develop an understanding of how the identified hazards make your building, occupants and community vulnerable. Vulnerability is defined as the ways in which the generalized hazards lead to failure or loss of function in a specific location and building.[1]

When Hurricane Sandy hit the east coast in 2012, many owners and occupants experienced firsthand the risks associated with flooding. This type of event can result in disastrous impacts including loss of utilities either from shutdown or from systems being submerged by floodwaters, damage to critical systems as a result of flooding of below-grade equipment, and damage to building interiors due to water intrusion bringing debris and infiltrating non-waterproof materials. These impacts resulted in the loss of functionality of systems such as heating and cooling, telecommunications, fire equipment, sump pumps and elevators. In many of these circumstances loss of key services lasted for two weeks or longer forcing occupants to either evacuate or shelter in place for an extended period of time.

Similar impacts should be considered for each identified hazard. How will this design function in extreme heat? How will occupants remain cool without access to air conditioning?

Heat and Human Health

While flooding is commonly viewed as the deadliest hazard, consider that three times as many people died from a heatwave in Phoenix, Arizona than during Hurricane Harvey. Heat waves are brutal, prompting people to wonder if certain cities are "livable." Phoenix, Las Vegas and others along the sun belt are feeling the heat. Heat-related deaths are mostly caused by dehydration. Exposure to sun and a high dew-point can prove very stressful to the human body, especially for children and the elderly. A common cause of heat-related deaths is a lack of awareness or understanding of a heat index—moisture and temperature as a metric for exposure. The warning signs for heat stroke are very subtle, and dehydration can lead to passing out quickly—especially for people working or doing physical activities. People who don't have access to air conditioning are extremely vulnerable to heat exhaustion, especially when temperatures don't cool off during the night.

Cities across the country and the world are experiencing hotter and more prolonged heat events throughout the course of the year. Heat waves can impact communities in many different ways. Railroad tracks literally melt and bind in heat. Rolling blackouts and brownouts occur when the electric grid is strained by excessive cooling loads. Fires spread, well, like wildfire. What's more, barring the limiting of carbon emissions on an international scale, heat waves are anticipated to become much worse.

Warming temperatures across the globe are causing abnormalities in the annual seasons and climate. Long-term impacts such as invasive species, algae blooms, vector-borne illnesses and droughts only exacerbate the degradation of human health in a changing climate.

Cities like Phoenix and Philadelphia have programs to provide relief from the heat. Planting trees, installing spraygrounds, and providing shelters to provide cooling to the public are some of the ways that can save lives from heat stroke. While the vulnerability of heat isn't as exciting as the drama that unfolds from hurricanes, we must not forget that heat waves are associated with more violence (as seen in New York City and Chicago), and strain our social and urban infrastructure. Heat is now becoming a chronic stressor, meaning that heat is an ongoing stressor for human health.

Resilience focused programmers and passive survivalists are currently designing to mitigate heat impacts. Orienting buildings and glass facades away from solar exposure, creating atriums and large natural and passive ventilation chambers help provide cool environments with minimal energy intensity and mechanical cooling. Buildings that can provide their own cooling will be livable if electricity is lost. Even installing awnings over openings can reduce several indoor degrees and help people without natural cooling. Specifying materials that can absorb the solar energy during the day and releasing the heat at night also helps provide comfortable environments.

In urban settings, understanding where the heat island temperature density is can play a crucial role for municipalities and housing authorities to allocate funds for trees and low-cost cooling strategies. Pockets within the city, particularly paved surfaces with little vegetation that are exposed the entire day, are literally hotter than other parts of the city—even a block down the street lined with trees or shaded by buildings. These microclimatic anomalies change wind patterns, insect habitat, bird flight patterns and humidity with cascading consequences.

Increased average heat drives the demand for air conditioning with additional environmental consequences. And for populations unable to afford effective air conditioning, the health implications are more pronounced, underlining the social consequences imposed by climate change.

Social Vulnerability

Buildings are designed for people. Whether a single-family home or a large commercial office building, building design is focused on the needs of people. When faced with an external stressor, such as a natural disaster, people can respond in a variety of ways. But there are a number of variables that can be used to identify populations who may experience the impacts of such a stressor disproportionately. These variables of social vulnerability [2] describe an individual or community that is more likely to be negatively affected by a natural disaster and less likely to be able to recover from the event afterward.

The **Social Vulnerability Index** is a metric from the Centers for Disease Control that considers a number of socioeconomic and demographic parameters (e.g., age, poverty, unemployment, lack of vehicle access and high school graduate rate) at the census tract level. These parameters are aggregated to describe the collective vulnerability of a population under four themes: socioeconomic status, household composition, race/ethnicity/language and housing/transportation.

Different groups of people may experience greater vulnerability to climate-related hazards due to a lack of access to critical resources and emergency services. Having access to transportation, food or medical services as well as the ability to visit an emergency shelter or community center will have a big impact on occupant health and safety in emergency situations. In general, residents or workers with lower incomes, fewer resources or decreased social connectivity, fare worse in emergency situations than those with higher incomes or more resources. Planning and programming with lower resourced communities and individuals in mind can help reduce these disparities (Figures 14.1 and 14.2).

ACCESS TO COMMUNITY RESOURCES

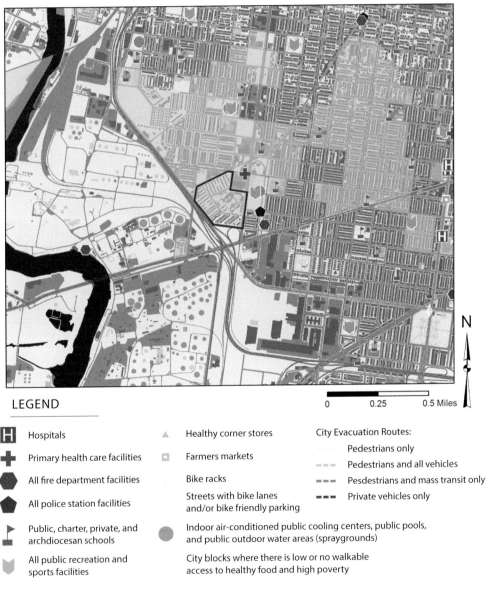

FIGURE 14.1 Distribution of resources such as hospitals, fire departments, healthy food outlets, and access to air conditioning are closely related to social vulnerability. Image courtesy of Linnean Solutions.

184 John Gravelin et al.

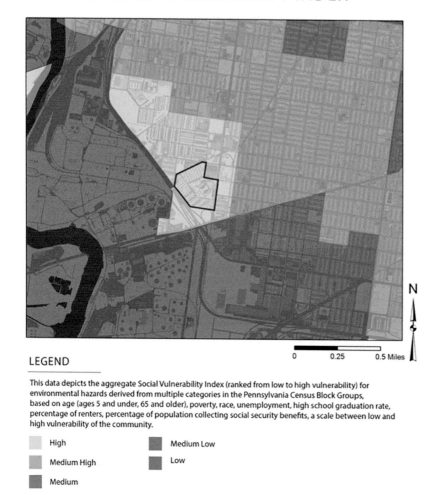

FIGURE 14.2 Individual characteristics impact vulnerability to environmental hazards as well. Image courtesy of Linnean Solutions.

Developing Strategies

New and existing buildings will differ in their vulnerabilities and their applicable resilience strategies. When starting from an early design phase, one of the most effective strategies may be asking the question: *Should this program go in this place?* While architects may not have much control over site location, assessing site vulnerabilities and posing the question to the broader ownership and design team can spark a valuable conversation and help to weave the concepts of protection, adaptation, backup and community resilience through the life of the project.

Protection

Common resilience strategies are focused around increasing protection of a building in the face of extreme weather conditions. This can mean taking measures to keep water out of a building during flood conditions or actively removing water that has infiltrated during heavy rains. This might also mean adding shading to a building façade to protect specific functions and occupants from heat.

Wet or dry?

Unwanted water infiltrating a building often results in damage whether due to flood conditions, heavy rain or utility backups. The natural response to preparing for such a condition is to attempt to keep water out often by sealing exterior openings and cracks or installing flood proof doors. This strategy, called dry flood proofing, can be effective in certain situations by preventing damage to critical systems and deterring mold growth. However for some buildings, particularly older buildings, dry flood proofing can cause enormous hydrostatic pressure against the structure as floodwaters are actively diverted. For this reason dry flood proofing is not recommended by FEMA for residential buildings. Alternatively, wet flood proofing describes measures that allow water to enter a building in a safe and controlled way. By utilizing flood proof materials and properly protecting mechanical equipment, water can be allowed to actively flow through a building, preventing hydrostatic pressure build-up and avoiding structural damage.

Adaptation

Our climate is changing which means the everyday environment we inhabit is changing. Adaptation strategies look for ways to help our buildings and our occupants to be better suited to our new and changing environments. One primary element of this adaptation involves maintaining comfortable and habitable spaces as extreme temperatures become more intense and more frequent. In our buildings, this can take the form of improved envelope efficiency including high-performing windows, increased exterior insulation or vegetated or light-colored roofs. These improvements come with the co-benefit of energy efficiency on non-extreme days. There is also great opportunity to design programs that encourage adaptation such as elevating mechanical equipment out of basements and allocating space for them either on an upper floor or on the roof. Similarly, elevating occupied spaces and designing floors at risk for flooding to house parking or storage reduces the impact of a flood event.

A building doesn't need to be in a flood zone to experience severe flooding during a storm. Developed areas with a high percentage of impervious surfaces often lack enough permeable ground that can absorb and infiltrate stormwater during rain events. Many urban areas have municipal stormwater systems in place to remove excess rainwater. But those systems are often old and lack the capacity to handle projected heavier rains in the future. Some systems are already undersized. In many cities, combined sewer and stormwater systems are still in place, which allow stormwater to combine with municipal wastewater when dedicated storm drains are full. Residents experience the unfortunate impacts of a combined sewer system when at-capacity wastewater pipes are overloaded with heavy rainfall and overflow into basements and low-lying streets. Adaptation strategies for buildings in such areas might include runoff reduction strategies such as green infrastructure and other nature-based stormwater management measures that increase the amount of permeable surface area or temporarily store rainwater to allow sewer systems to recover over a period of time. These strategies are often closely tied to a building's program through dedicated rain gardens or bioswales, vegetated roofs or permeable pavement systems.

> Cities and urban areas tend to experience higher temperatures than the rural or suburban areas surrounding them. This is due to a city's high percentage of dark-colored and impervious surfaces such as roofs and asphalt, and the lack of a tree canopy. Darker materials absorb radiation from the sun during the day and then slowly release heat during cooler hours. This is referred to as the urban

heat island effect and results in elevated surface temperatures putting residents at higher risk of heat-related impacts and altering microclimate conditions.

Shading is an age-old adaptation strategy for reducing exposure to elevated heat. Effective shading can be achieved in a number of ways and typically in a cost-effective manner. Just as sitting under a tree during a hot summer day provides us with relief, we can apply the same concept to our buildings. Strategically siting or orienting project elements to take advantage of surrounding buildings or trees (or planting more trees) can reduce the amount of direct radiation absorbed by a building's façade and thereby lower the project's cooling demand. This also makes it easier to maintain cooler temperatures indoors in the event of a power outage. Similarly, architectural elements designed as exterior shading devices around glazing such as overhangs or louvers directly reduce the amount of solar radiation entering a building through its windows. While it may be tempting to design interior devices such as curtains to give residents control over their shade, remember that interior shades do not prevent solar radiation from entering through the window, making them far less effective than exterior or glazing-integrated devices.

Backup Power

Power is critical to occupant health and safety, and designing backup power systems can ensure the functioning of crucial systems. Extended loss of power can have detrimental impacts such as a disruption in cooling capacity during a heat wave or a loss in communication systems in an emergency. Power outages can also make our indoor spaces dangerous or uninhabitable due to a lack of lighting in hallways and stairwells or a loss in pumping power to deliver potable water to upper floors. Programming and planning for backup power including identifying generator and fuel locations, as well as establishing what systems will be connected, not only reduces the impact of an extended power outage but can also make it easier to repair and recover afterward. Other critical services such as emergency lighting and access to potable water can be integrated into a backup power strategy. Emergency lighting is required by code to last only 90 minutes, just long enough for occupants to evacuate. But what if evacuation is not feasible? Or occupants have been instructed to shelter in place? Designing battery-powered or solar-powered long-lasting emergency lighting in critical areas such as stairwells or around the building exterior can allow occupants to remain safe for longer periods of time. Similarly, strategies for Passive Survivability include storing a supply of potable water on site or designing a space for occupants to access potable water during an emergency.

Community

Perhaps the most powerful strategies to improve the resilience of buildings have less to do with design and more to do with our sense of community. Neighbors are an incredible resource for both emergency support and emotional strength. Programming for community resilience includes designing and planning spaces that encourage community interaction, enable relationship building and provide equitable access to critical resources. Integrating community resilience spaces into our designs not only dedicates space for emergency response and recovery, but also creates opportunities to engage with community members during non-emergency times.

Resilience hubs take community spaces to the next level, not only serving as gathering space for emergency and non-emergency times, but also providing key resources that will allow for safely sheltering in place such as access to potable water and back-up power for cell phones and medical devices [3]. These spaces, as well as other opportunities for connection like a community garden, will allow neighbors to connect, build relationships and support each other when needed.

The U.S. Centers for Disease Control and Prevention lists "social isolation" [4] as a risk factor for heat-related illness. The implication of social isolation was illustrated during the 1995 Chicago heat wave where hundreds of deaths were concentrated in areas where residents didn't have nearby contacts, didn't know their neighbors and lacked access to community support.

A major component of resilient design involves understanding the role a building will have in a community setting. It is one thing to implement a resilient solution, such as solar-paired battery systems, but it is also necessary to understand the function of this system within the community context, and how it will be used during emergencies. A resilient building should be able to not only provide shelter to occupants during a storm, but also to fulfill its role in the community during and after a storm.

Programming for Climate

To illustrate how one can think of programming in response to understanding climate conditions, think of designing for a building in the arctic. The location is isolated, cold, with a lack of sunshine, and limited resources. How many people will need to occupy the building? What are the time intervals by which resources can be shipped? What is the main fuel source? These questions aren't typically asked when building in the U.S. because the infrastructure is present to support these complex needs, but these are common considerations among isolated communities around the world.

The first step to consider when programming for resilience is to prepare for community self-sufficiency while interacting with the local climate. Ideally food, water, shelter and waste must all be processed locally and sustainably. This means that a maximum degree of efficiency must be achieved with a minimum of waste.

Weather, Climate and Natural Disasters

To understand how to become resilient, it is important to distinguish between different types of climate-related hazards, and to plan for the appropriate responses. There's a lot of confusion around the difference between normal, seasonal weather and unprecedented climate-change related phenomena. For example, it would appear that our society forgets or doesn't accept the fact that hurricanes, floods and fires are naturally recurring instances of our global climate.

The fact that our current building standards and other designed safety systems haven't been able to withstand normal environmental conditions is a concern and suggests most of our built environment isn't prepared for climate change. Hurricanes are rated on the Saffir Simpson Scale based on sustained wind speed and categorized by damage to structures, Category 1 being the least severe and Category 5 the most severe. After the deadly hurricanes of 2017, there were motions to create a Category 6 hurricane, calling attention to an ominous trend of increasingly devastating events. If our society isn't prepared for everyday storms, how are we prepared for a Category 6 hurricane?

One consideration alongside the increasing number and strength of storms is the fact that human development has increased, while undeveloped land available to manage the shocks and stressors of climate events is physically decreasing. As a result natural hazards that primarily impacted the local ecology now pose a greater risk to our cities, homes and beloved places.

Resilient planning therefore also extends to the preservation of wetlands and other floodwater storage areas, to the preservation of green space and tree canopy for the mitigation of urban heat island effect, and to a micro-grid energy delivery network employing sustainable technology.

A key challenge when designing and programming for "resilience" is properly establishing the flood standard to design for. While this can be challenging enough (financially), there are other liability and equity issues—the fact that a community on one side of a river has flood walls and that the other doesn't will result in flooding of the lower community. Who decides where the flood prevention stops? When FEMA and the National Flood Insurance Program (NFIP) offer public comments on the proposed flood maps, which typically increase the areas susceptible to flooding the public responds in outrage over the notion that they will require flood insurance protection. Often a major political battle over where the exact lines of the flood zones should be placed results, literally a "fight over inches"—and this all boils down to the climate data that informs the mapping.

Resilient Buildings: New vs. Existing

The existing building stock presents particular challenges when programming for resilience. Many coastal communities already experience "sunny day floods"—areas that are flood prone during high tides due to rising sea levels. Existing coastal communities face the greatest climate change burden because some buildings and infrastructure simply won't be able to withstand certain types of flooding. Buildings once protected by natural wetlands, flood barriers, bayous and levees now realize that the design standards from years ago are outdated. Without massive infrastructure upgrades, some locations will simply be uninhabitable in the face of climate change and sea level rise.

Cities face the greater challenge of valuing properties in the face of climate change. Climate experts have claimed that housing prices near coastlines are dramatically overpriced, but if this is true, the notion that once prime market real estate is devalued because of climate hazards has yet to be fully realized. Most coastal cities have a history of expanding into the sea with landfill, continuing to this day. Waterfront property is sought after by developers around the world—what will stop this phenomena from occurring in the future?

Existing buildings do have resilient strategies that they can implement to avoid property damage and loss of life. Buildings in flood zones can design wash-out floors—first floors whose walls can wash away by the force of the water while maintaining the structural integrity of the core. While sacrificing first-floor walls for every storm is not sustainable, the ultimate question of how long an existing building can financially endure the damages lies in our current flood insurance policies.

Building and Zoning Codes That Require Resilience

A number of municipalities in the U.S. have already instituted resilience requirements through building codes, zoning codes or municipal ordinance:

- building codes that focus on the life-safety aspects of resilience,
- zoning code amendments and overlay districts that define areas of more stringent application of resilient strategies, and
- comprehensive zoning code amendments that add overall resilience to the goals of the zoning code.

The effort in New York City after Superstorm Sandy is a good example of a sustained effort to adjust building codes to address occupant safety in relation to natural hazards. In the aftermath of Sandy, the Urban Green Council convened a task force (The Building Resiliency Task Force) for the City to examine building codes and local laws. Since that initial work, New York City has made a number of code changes addressing raising buildings, flood zone data sets, temporary flood barriers, backup power, backflow prevention, and a host of other specific topics. This work continues through the efforts of the Special Initiative for Rebuilding and Resiliency and the NYC Buildings Department [5].

A number of municipalities across the U.S. have adopted zoning amendments or resilience overlay districts to use the project entitlements process to increase resilience. The cities of Boston, Cambridge and Somerville in Eastern Massachusetts have all adopted flood overlay districts to add requirements for current and future flood potential. Boston has taken the process several steps further by requiring all projects within the flood areas defined in the Boston Sea Level Rise Flood Hazard Map to delineate a development resilience plan which the Boston Planning and Development Authority reviews. Requirements include raising habitable space out of flood levels, moving equipment out of flood levels, managing water intrusion in lower building levels and emergency planning. Washington D.C., San Francisco, and numerous other cities have adopted similar requirements. Cities on the West Coast of the U.S. adopted earthquake requirements, on which many of the flood requirements are modeled, over 20 years ago.

The City of Cambridge, Massachusetts is also developing a more comprehensive resilience-focused zoning amendment that will adjust development requirements to increase flood resilience, reduce heat island effect and increase rainwater management. The Cambridge Zoning for Resilience Task Force is considering a "Cool Points" model that works through incentives and requirements to reduce heat island effect in the City and increase flood resilience [6]. This model is based on a combination of "Green Score" zoning ordinances in Somerville, Massachusetts and Seattle, Washington and the comprehensive "Resilience Quotient" model from Norfolk, Virginia [7].

Programming professionals need to understand what types of uses and occupancy are allowed within the resilience requirements. The deeper step is for programming to support the resilience goals of each municipality by enhancing the arrangements and types of uses, such as adjusting outdoor space uses to provide cooling effects of trees and green space to the public rights of way, as is incentivized in the Cambridge Cool Points system.

Beyond Buildings

Capacity Building and Situational Awareness

Capacity building for resilient programmers refers to integrating multiple, seemingly small-scale solutions into everyday practices. For example, conservation efforts undertaken toward reducing energy, water and resource consumption builds capacity by reducing resource demand during emergencies.

Capacity building is also referred to as strengthening institutional and organizational processes to streamline responses to emergencies. Large organizations have internal chain of command structures to provide situational awareness among their community. If there are strategies to provide redundant communication channels, to practice emergency responses and to constantly improve upon these structures, the organization will manage emergencies more efficiently—and can perhaps extend their internal resources to others.

Situational awareness refers to the real-time processing of information to effectively respond to emergencies. This practice is mostly used by first responders. Situational awareness is only as effective as the inherent capacity built into an organization. First responders can receive information throughout an entire emergency, but if they don't know how to respond they will fall short of their community's expectations. The inverse is also true—an organization can have an incredible emergency procedure in place, but if they don't have real-time information to respond to they will be rendered helpless.

It is important to understand the distinction between building capacity and situational awareness because architects are primarily building capacity among the built environment and its community to prepare for and adapt to climate change. Situational awareness is primarily used during the emergency itself, and is a critical tool for emergency response.

All of the tiers of resilience, from building codes to regenerative design, inherently build capacity because they help people and communities to prepare for and overcome the obstacles that arise during emergencies. For example, a building in a flood zone may have removable flood barriers to install in doorways and entrances around a building. This builds capacity to prevent flood damage. The building owners must use situational awareness to know when to install the flood barriers to prevent the damage, and building owners must be educated on how to install barriers.

In essence, most critiques of a poorly managed emergency can be distilled to a lack of built-in capacity and/or a lack of accurate or real-time information. On a community scale these are not easy tasks to be responsible for. However it is crucial to acknowledge that planning and preparing for storms, floods, wildfires and heat is psychologically the first step toward managing risks.

A lack of disaster planning and preparedness can be seen in the devastating impacts of the last few years' hurricanes, earthquakes, fires, heat waves and droughts, all occurring at unprecedented levels. The purpose of this chapter is not to promote fear, but to understand the common characteristics of hazards and the patterns in community responses in order to prepare for and respond to these patterns by reimagining our built environment.

Resilient design planners focus on hurricanes because they are the epitome of a subset of hazards (coastal flooding, inland flooding, structural damage, evacuation), and, in turn, they lead to other cascading hazards such as loss of power, loss of communications, disrupted travel, disrupted supply chains, etc. Hurricanes can impact large geographical areas—crossing many international borders—and can have a prolonged lifespan of over two weeks. Hurricanes are powerful and getting more powerful, and our society must adapt to them.

Media coverage commonly highlights the devastation following hurricanes, which typically gives the impression that there was nothing anyone could do to mitigate the damage from such a terrifying storm. The irony is that the U.S. has a "hurricane season" in which hurricanes are anticipated every year. What is unprecedented is the greater frequency and increasing strength of these hurricanes due to warming ocean temperatures and a shifting jet stream. The goal is to make sure that we have the capacity to anticipate and plan for these expected disruptions in our architectural and engineering communities and within our governments and corporations.

How We Treat Each Other

Resilience needs to include everyone, otherwise we are not resilient. Communities that are underserved by infrastructure or services will always be more vulnerable to climate risks. Emergency aid is essential for people who are already burdened with daily stressors. Considerations must be managed to provide resilience responses centered on the people who need help the most.

A common theme emerging in relation to flood mitigation is how to limit damage upstream without compromising communities downstream. A town in Missouri is blaming increased flooding on levees installed in Illinois. The town in Illinois has financed flood protection from the Mississippi River, but has shifted the floodwaters to an adjacent town without the means to finance flood protection strategies. Therefore, the town that enabled resilient strategies only considered themselves—not their neighbors. This is not a sustainable solution because it simply shifts the risk from one town to another.

Social equity considerations are important for designers because sustainable and resilient investments need to serve everyone—not just those with the means to participate. This is an ever-present tension in the dynamic of real-estate investment and gentrification. Investment helps to grow cities and to provide safe living conditions, but this is often done at the expense of displacing established communities. Because new construction is expensive, low-income communities can't afford the costs and have to move out of rising rental areas. This dynamic is beginning to unfold around resilience, where wealthy communities are protecting themselves while adding to the risks for adjacent poorer communities, leading to unequal distribution of risk and a reduction of resilience at the larger scale. The metaphor of the weakest link in a chain defining the strength of the chain is relevant to resilience at different scales. The resilience of a region is only as strong as the least supported individual or community.

The Power of National Resilient Standards

National resilient standards would benefit FEMA aid processes, lower tax-payer and subsidized flood insurance from bankrupting local communities, and ultimately reduce vulnerability to communities to help rebuild after storms with less difficulty. Implementing resilient "REACH" codes can enable faster recoveries and finance physical insurance policies for communities around the world.

National standards would benefit first responders by designing and programming emergency preparedness features similar to how fire codes have helped firefighters quickly understand complex life-saving systems and use them when needed. A national resilience code would inherently benefit building occupants by providing guidance for strategies and construction to withstand emergency conditions. A national resilience code would benefit multiple tangential processes to buildings that impact human health—by consuming fewer fossil fuels, by reducing exposure to unhealthy air quality and by preventing strained public life-safety systems from failing.

Specific building typologies should have more robust emergency features and functions streamlined specifically to help their needs. Emergency shelters and predetermined public buildings should be routinely provided with features to help communities during times of stress. As a global society, we have never been more technologically prepared to withstand environmental emergencies. We must act now to create resilient communities while we have the ability to do so.

Bringing it All Together

People and organizations around the globe, from municipalities and public housing authorities, to private companies, and even the military, are endeavoring to prepare for a changing climate. A culture of preparedness is emerging. This is the time to regenerate our social, economic and environmental systems for the future—we must come together as a society to understand and plan for tomorrow's changed world. Everyone has a role to play, and we must all be on the same page when preparing for, responding to and adapting to climate change.

Programming for Resilience Now

Although resilient design embodies complex technical, social and political challenges, some solutions are much easier than we might imagine, while others are difficult. Solutions such as enabling carbon-free commutes like riding bicycles are not new, but we understand and value the environmental and health benefits of active and carbon-mitigating tactics. Cities around the world, driven by cultural demand, are understanding that safe roads help lessen traffic congestion, help support public transit and provide fun and healthy activities for tourists and residents alike. Strategies such as installing bike lanes can be viewed as a carbon-mitigation resilience tactic, and while restriping roads may be a political struggle for the transportation authorities, restriping roads is easy and can transform a once dangerous roadway into a safer and more livable place.

We need a common-sense resilience perspective that can offer many benefits for a low cost. Land use and zoning policies may offer low cost options for achieving many benefits by discouraging development in areas with extreme hazards. Building common ground is an important factor in developing resilient systems. We know that tree-lined streets generate higher property values, provide comfortable temperatures and enhance overall life experience. Urban and suburban reforestation can be a strong shared goal. We must find common talking points to advocate for resilient strategies like trees in ways that build shared understanding. We all want the same things—safe and healthy places that enhance our lives.

Simple, innovative solutions have never been more accessible. While many strategies to enhance resilience are complicated and expensive, keeping climate change in mind in the development process can expose simpler options. For better or for worse, change is exponential. Extreme weather events can transform a city overnight, but so too can proactive planning. Resilience understanding can open us up to fresh solutions and fresh relationships to nature, with each other and with ecosystems.

Note

1 A site analysis is a critical step in architectural programming. This is equally true when programming for resilience. Using available geo-spatial data, a designer can begin to evaluate which hazards are of greatest relevance to a project site and what the associated vulnerabilities may be.

   Data
   The FEMA Flood Hazard Layer is a common place to start, allowing for an assessment of the 100- and 500-year flood zones. Similar local or regional flood data may be available for hurricane storm surge and projected sea level rise.

   Some states and major cities are beginning to develop mapping programs for extreme temperatures and urban heat islands. While not available everywhere, these maps can be used to identify sites that may experience elevated temperatures compared with regional or state averages. As a rule of thumb, developed urban areas and areas with primarily dark-colored surfaces tend to experience higher temperatures than more rural areas with more abundant tree cover.

   Local open data programs may provide access to additional data such as wetlands and waterbodies, land use and impervious surfaces, or past storm events.

   Flooding outside of flood zones
   A map is just a model and all models are mere generalizations. FEMA flood maps are a tremendous resource providing valuable spatial flood data covering the majority of the United States. However, FEMA maps are based on past flood occurrences and represent only a piece of the larger flood picture for any project site. This is becoming more and more relevant as sea levels rise and storm events become more intense. Storm analysis following Hurricane Harvey in Houston found that flood zones accounted for only half of the area hit by floodwaters in September of 2017. Approximately 40 percent of the buildings that were flooded were in an area "of minimal flood hazard" meaning those properties were unlikely to have flood insurance [1]. While such maps are a good place to start, climate projections describing future conditions, as well as first-hand experience from local planners or residents, are also critical to consider.

References

1. Fessenden, F., Gebeloff, R., Walsh, M. W., & Griggs, T. (2017, Sept.). Water Damage From Hurricane Harvey Extended Far Beyond Flood Zones. *The New York Times*.
2. Agency for Toxic Substances and Disease Registry. (n.d.). CDC's Social Vulnerability Index. https://www.atsdr.cdc.gov/placeandhealth/svi/index.html
3. Schoeman, L. (2015). *Ready to Respond: Strategies for Multifamily Building Resilience*. Enterprise Community Partners.
4. Centers for Disease Control. (2017). Heat-Related Illness. *Picture of America Report*.
5. Special Initiative for Rebuilding and Resiliency. (2013). A Stronger, More Resilient New York. https://www1.nyc.gov/site/sirr/report/report.page
6. Cambridge Community Development Department. (2017). Climate Resilience Zoning. https://www.cambridgema.gov/CDD/Projects/Zoning/climateresiliencezoning
7. Homewood, G. M. (n.d.). Planning for Resilience in Norfolk. https://www.hrpdcva.gov/uploads/docs/03_Presentation_Norfolk_Zoning_Ordinance.pdf

15
THE POST-PANDEMIC CITY

Lawrence A. Chan FAIA

City-scale design interventions are rare but valuable opportunities to enhance health and wellbeing for an entire urban population. The author has had the opportunity to lead multiple such interventions, and here shares helpful insights into the potential revitalization of cities in the post-pandemic era.

The COVID-19 coronavirus pandemic that began in January 2020 has transformed people's lives and activities globally, especially in cities where the majority of the world's population currently live, work, shop, recreate, socialize and move about. News since early 2020 from around the world has reported that people and nations were unprepared or hesitant in responding to the COVID-19 outbreak, which has contributed to both the spread of infections and the longevity of the pandemic. The eventual impact around the world has affected how people behave and interact, both in public and in private, and how they might view cities, buildings and the open spaces around them.

Concerns about air quality—which we rely upon for health and wellbeing—has accelerated, especially since microscopic traces of COVID-19 can linger for hours [1] in the air left by the unprotected breaths, coughs, sneezes, spoken words, laughter, shouts and exhausted cigarette smoke from infected persons or asymptomatic carriers of the coronavirus. Preventive measures, advocated by the Center for Disease Control and the World Health Organization, include wearing protective face coverings and maintaining social distances of six feet or more [2], but are not adequately followed due to indifferent and lax governmental response [3], non-compliant citizens, deniers of the pandemic's threats [4], and adherents of conspiracy falsehoods [5].

For the majority of the population that has been wary of COVID-19, the concerns about healthy air and wellbeing have heightened awareness about social distance and urban air quality. People who feel threatened by the potential for infection and the urgency to comply with prevention protocols have brought new meaning to keeping others from invading their "personal space" [6]. There may be tendencies to ask for "some elbow room" from those around them, to unconsciously draw "lines in the sand" to keep people away, or perhaps to emotionally demand someone to: "Get outta my face!" Space is no longer an imaginary "Final Frontier" but the all-encompassing lifeline for relief and respite. It is where one goes *outside*—encompassing open spaces, parks, plazas, squares and tree-lined boulevards, among others—in search of remedies

DOI: 10.4324/9781003164418-20

from lockdown and confinement to home, especially since the air outside has improved during the pandemic due to dramatic reductions in traffic and air pollution [7]. The reviving value of open space may once again inspire another renaissance in city planning and **urban renewal** programs that promote urbanity and the quality of city life, and simultaneously contribute to global initiatives to combat climate change.

In the words of Richard Sennett,

> "The exposed, outer life of the city cannot be simply a reflection of inner life. Exposure occurs in crowds and among strangers. The cultural problem of the modern city is how to make this impersonal milieu speak, how to relieve its current blandness, its neutrality, whose origin can be traced back to the belief that the outside world of things is unreal. Our urban problem is how to revive the reality of the outside as a dimension of human experience [8]."

Pandemic and City Life

The significant absence of city vibrancy—reduction in traffic, abandoned small businesses, shuttered civic and commercial venues for communal activities, streets empty of people—has diminished the *raison d'être* of cities as exciting places to live, work, and enjoy social and cultural activities. The distribution of newly developed vaccines may eventually help end the pandemic and revive life in cities. However, full recovery may fall behind—if not regress—as more virulent mutations of COVID-19 have been emerging [9] and people are returning prematurely to pre-pandemic activities without sufficient precautions [10]. Moreover, scientists acknowledge that vaccines will not eradicate COVID-19 due in part to a high rate of vaccine hesitancy [11, 12], conspiracy theories and misinformation on social media [13] and ongoing mutations that will transition the coronavirus as a seasonal disease similar to, but more severe than, the flu [14, 15].

Unknown severity of future coronavirus outbreaks suggests that current impingements on urban life may reoccur during each incident and create a long-term negative impact on city vibrancy. As a preemptive measure, it would be wise to reaffirm the characteristics and qualities that make cities great—their density, cultural and ethnic diversity, and overall contribution to society—and (re)program how cities can flourish once again after the immediate danger is over. Whether there may be a need to adapt to regular COVID-19 outbreaks, social distancing, frequently washing hands and working from home, "cities are worth fighting for" [16].

Through thousands of years, cities have been exemplars for human settlement and activities, such as gathering together with or for a common purpose; living and working together based on common beliefs, values, needs and goals; sharing skills and knowledge; and economically pooling individual resources. Cities have served as seats of power; as centers to administer governance; as repositories to collect and advance knowledge, conduct scientific research, provide medical treatment and disseminate education; as exchanges to trade goods and services; as institutes to promote and celebrate culture and the arts; and as sanctuaries for community, worship and social interaction. Over time, cities have physically evolved and resiliently responded to maintaining and enhancing urban life against disruptive changes, such as population growth, excessive congestion, economic development, natural disasters, devastations from war, infrastructural improvements and infectious diseases.

The unique impact of the pandemic has created new challenges for cities to be hospitable, safe and attractive, for which architects and planners can contribute important and innovative solutions. While *indoor* spaces are physically constrained by physical structures, *outdoor* spaces—especially streets, parks, and other public places—have fewer constraints to provide physical,

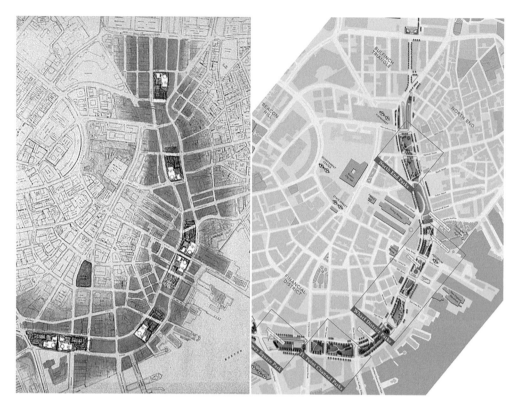

FIGURE 15.1 A comparison between "Two Avenues Linked by Seven Squares," using Copley Square as a precedent footprint, proposed by Chan Krieger & Associates, 1989, left, and the existing Rose Kennedy Greenway, right. Images courtesy of Lawrence A. Chan FAIA and The Greenway Conservancy.

social and mental relief. In locations where sufficient outdoor spaces are lacking—particularly in city centers—cities may draw from past and recent precedents to create more open space, such as:

- *Adding City Open Space Through Renewal*—where a large malfunctioning infrastructure project, such as Boston's 1950s elevated John F. Fitzgerald Expressway, was supplanted with an underground improvement in the 1990s, and covered with a greenway in 2007 (Figure 15.1).
- *Adding City Open Space Through Reassignment*—where a specific block or street of a city is converted as new civic space, such as Boston's Post Office Square, in which a multi-story public garage was demolished and rebuilt underground and a heavily landscaped park was created at street level in 1990 [17]; or where a city street, such as Washington Street in Boston's Downtown, is entirely closed to create a pedestrian mall; or where a street is partially reduced in width to create broader pedestrian open space, such as the conversion of Shanghai's Zhongshan East 1st Road alongside the Bund Esplanade (*Figure 15.2*).
- *Adding City Open Space Through Extension*—where a city expands outward for new development and open space—notably, numerous suburban examples from Llewellyn Park,

founded in 1853 within West Orange, New Jersey, to Summerlin, founded in 1990 within Las Vegas—that are linked to the city center by transportation systems, such as public transit, commuter rail, and new roadways that also provide access to recreational and other urban or semi-rural areas beyond a city's boundaries.

- *Adding* **Satellite Cities**—where a state or private entity builds a new town outside the official limits of a major city to fulfill growth, such as Milton Keynes in 1967 beyond the outskirts of London, and Columbia, Maryland, also in 1967, between Washington, D.C. and Baltimore, Maryland.

Adding City Open Space through Renewal

The John F. Fitzgerald Expressway—more commonly known as the Central Artery—and its underground replacement, often referred to as the Big Dig [18], were highways that twice affected Boston physically, socially and environmentally. The original Expressway was emblematic of the mid-20th-century highway and urban renewal movement that prioritized access and movement of internal combustion vehicles through a city, heartlessly clearing away old buildings and dense neighborhoods that were designated as "deficient" by the Boston Redevelopment Authority. Precedents included the creation of new boulevards through slum clearance in 19th-century Paris, but the end result in Boston was not as beneficial to pedestrians as it was in Paris. Built in 1951 and completed in 1959, the elevated Central Artery highway was so successful in transporting vehicles through the city that its estimated operational capacity was reached within one year of completion. Its performance and benefit then diminished steadily over the next 30 years until it was replaced [19].

Chan Krieger & Associates (in practice 1984–2010) was hired by the Boston Redevelopment Authority in 1989 to develop a masterplan for the 27 acres of newly uncovered land after the elevated six-lane Central Artery highway was demolished and replaced by an eight- to ten-lane underground tunnel. The proposed concept (*Figure 15.1*) [20] was to redevelop the corridor like a zipper, where new city blocks would be periodically interspersed with seven new civic squares. The scheme was conceived firstly to repair the previously destroyed urban fabric of the city; secondly to reestablish five of the historic squares that were previously erased by the original Expressway; and thirdly to reinforce cross streets lined with small businesses to engage pedestrians and reactivate the streetscape between Downtown and Boston Harbor. However the re-creation of civic squares that are exemplified by Boston's Copley Square and Post Office Square proved much less compelling when compared to the unique opportunity to create a new 27-acre linear park to replace a much-loathed elevated highway abutment in the heart of the city.

An early critique of the completed Greenway was that the sparsely attended corridor [21]—which is as wide as the length of a football field in some locations and marginally planted with small trees—was less park and more a wind-swept median framed by two busy, three-lane surface avenues predominantly lined with office buildings with little or no commercial street functions to engage or attract pedestrians [22]. As an impressive open space asset for Boston the Greenway should be a valuable place for passive recreation, fresh air and respite during the COVID-19 pandemic, especially with minimum traffic that normally framed the surrounding streets. However casual and periodic observations of the Greenway suggest that the park is as uninhabited as before in contrast to other linear open spaces in Boston such as the Charles River Esplanade, Commonwealth Avenue Mall in the Back Bay and Boston Harborwalk that runs parallel to the Greenway just one block to the east.

A major benefit of the Rose Kennedy Greenway is in providing an urban "lung" [23] in the heart of Boston, but its emptiness suggests that open space alone may not be successful without attractive complementary features. The Charles River Esplanade and Boston Harborwalk have the advantage of facing waterfronts with long distance views, but the design and location of Commonwealth Avenue Mall suggest a more successful formula for a linear urban park than the Greenway. In comparing the latter two spaces, the Greenway is relatively broad, between 120 and 180 feet wide, interspersed with broad gaps of paved areas, thinly lined with small trees, and flanked by two busy, three-lane traffic streets, during normal times prior to the pandemic, that wind through a 250–300 feet wide corridor along the eastern edge of Downtown flanked by high-rise buildings. In contrast, the linear park on Commonwealth Avenue is 100-feet wide, continuously bracketed by lawns and large shade trees, and embedded within a relatively narrow 200-feet boulevard framed by low residential buildings that offer a sense of intimacy, and where the 2-lane side streets include street parking that slows traffic speed, buffers pedestrians along the sidewalk and shortens pedestrian crossings.

Residents who live along "Comm Ave." and from adjacent neighborhoods actively populate the park at all times of the day and weekends. In contrast, the Greenway may find an occasional office worker during the lunch hour, children on periodic daycare or day trip outings or wandering tourists passing through while destined toward Boston Harbor. The termini of the Greenway are also feeble with a small uninspiring installation in Chinatown at the southern end, and an unresolved and limp splay into North Washington Street at the northern end. In comparison, Commonwealth Avenue is anchored on its eastern end by Boston Public Garden, and intertwined with Olmsted's Emerald Necklace at The Fenway on its western end.

The value and use of parks, open spaces, streets, bicycle paths and other pedestrian areas have risen in demand during the COVID-19 pandemic, especially to facilitate exercise, social distancing and respite for those who are confined to home. Many times, it is a challenge to find desirable open spaces in densely developed areas of a city or to create new open spaces. So, the lesson that may be drawn from the Greenway is that when the rare opportunity arises, special care must be considered to locate, design and reinforce the new space that would enhance its success and use. When free land is not available to create new open space, several cities around the world have resorted to converting streets to fulfill the need for additional pedestrian space.

Adding City Open Space through Reassignment

In dense urban areas, "open space" is disproportionately allocated to, and dominated by, vehicles and traffic most often resulting in a scourge on a city's quality of life [24]. In exemplary historic cities there has often been a complementary interplay between buildings and open space, "but with the city of modern architecture, of course, no such reciprocity is either possible or intended" [25].

One expedient method to add much-needed pedestrian and/or open space in a city during the pandemic has been the conversion of vehicular streets for "safety and wellbeing" and for "much-needed exercises and fresh air" [26]. In some cities, the successful closing of streets for pedestrians and bicycles has been so well received that at least one city is planning to permanently convert nearly 20 miles of its streets after the pandemic [27].

Precedents in Europe with district-wide street closures and a reduction of vehicular traffic have been successful and popular with local citizens [28] to the extent that some cities have entirely closed their city centers to all non-essential vehicular traffic [29], or converted parking spaces for pedestrian and bicycle use [30]. Such initiatives would not only provide more open space but also improve air quality in some cases by as much as 40 percent [31].

During its 26-year practice, Chan Krieger & Associates was commissioned to help several major cities across the U.S. and abroad to re-envision downtowns and waterfronts to improve and expand pedestrian space and access. The list includes Boston, Buffalo, Cincinnati, Dallas [32], Des Moines, Detroit, Knoxville, Louisville, Minneapolis, New Orleans [33], New York [34], Pittsburgh [35], Shanghai [36]. Shenyang, Washington, D.C. [37] and Worcester. The widening and redesign of Shanghai's Bund Esplanade (*Figure 15.2*) is similar to Boston's Big Dig, where a 10-lane riverfront drive is replaced by a four-lane surface boulevard and six-lane underground tunnel, and where the abandoned six-lane surface road has been reallocated for the extension of the subway system underground and a park and pedestrian open space at street level [38].

One distinguishing difference between the Bund Waterfront Park and the Rose Kennedy Greenway is that Shanghai's vacated-roadway-converted-to-a-park was merged to one side of the street rather than situated freestanding in the middle of the newly narrowed roadway. Thus the added benefit in Shanghai was the widening of the existing historic Bund Esplanade that is located on the roof of a one-story garage/levee along the length of the Huangpu River. While retaining the structure of the garage/levee, the entire Bund Esplanade was demolished, redesigned, rebuilt and integrated with the former roadway lanes to create a new linear park along the one-mile riverfront [39, 40]. One significant change was the conversion of the street-side of the garage for retail uses and restaurants—features that engage pedestrians and vitalize the edge of the elevated Esplanade similarly to many historic European squares and piazzas but conspicuously rare, if not absent, along the Rose Kennedy Greenway and Boston's City Hall Plaza.

FIGURE 15.2 Rendering of the Bund Riverfront Park & Esplanade, Shanghai, construction completed May 2010, designed by Chan Krieger Sieniewicz, architects, and Klopfer Martin Design Group, landscape architects. Image courtesy of Lawrence A. Chan FAIA.

In a city the conversion or closure of traffic lanes to reinforce and expand the pedestrian realm will not only help to increase sidewalk widths and expand bicycle networks, but will also provide multiple ways to enhance city life with attending benefits: promoting the value, use and efficacy of public transportation and reducing vehicular traffic, pollution, and the use of fossil fuels will also help mitigate climate change. Converting and reusing obsolete public garages will help open up opportunities for residential, commercial or business occupancies. Distributing parks and open spaces more equitably across the city will serve social and environmental justice. Providing more open space, landscape and trees to advance air quality, fresh air and opportunities to exercise and keep social distance, will help facilitate health and wellbeing. Each of these strategies could also enhance the identity and economic value of the context surrounding the newly created civic spaces.

Nevertheless the dramatic human toll of COVID-19 has instilled some fear about living in cities, and in several cases prompted people to either temporarily leave the city for less dense environments, or to permanently relocate and live in the suburbs or countryside. While the debate about leaving the city for "greener pastures" is as old as European immigrants escaping to the New World after Christopher Columbus' discovery, the escape to less congested areas would be leaving behind the greater resources, redundancies and amenities that distinguish cities from their suburban and rural counterparts. Moreover, since the virus can be spread by infected and asymptomatic people [41], any type of travel—whether between large cities and small towns, or between countries—can easily transmit and spread infections to a wider area and aggravate the inabilities of less populated settlements or areas without sufficient resources, to repel, treat, manage and control outbreaks [42, 43].

Adding City Open Space through Extension

The suburbs outside city centers have been natural expansion zones for cities to grow and for the city dwellers with wealth to have country homes. By the 1850s, the development of the suburbs as planned communities in the U.S. began with the 1853 founding of Llewellyn Park in New Jersey as designed by Alexander Jackson Davis. The emerging suburban development model was further romanticized by Frederick Law Olmsted's landscape plan of Riverside, Illinois in 1868 [44].

Suburbs have attracted people who look for relief from the demands of, and dissatisfactions with, city life. For people who want to leave, the disadvantages of city living may include small apartments in close proximity to neighbors that instill a lack of privacy; the high cost of living; congestion of people in public places; and the difficulty or inability to own a car to offer greater independence for travel and more freedom to move about. To "leavers," the advantages of the suburbs may include more open space, landscape, fresh air and better health away from the confines and congestion of cities; more opportunities to afford and own a piece of land and a free-standing home with private open space; and greater proximity and ease of access to recreational areas such as regional parks, beaches and resort areas. What is undeniable, and beyond the scope of this essay, is the systemic racial bias that has historically impeded equitable access to the suburbs for people of color [45].

There is no direct correlation between density and the spread of infections to sufficiently implicate cities as being more hazardous to one's health during a pandemic. On the contrary, several European and Asian cities are denser and more populated than the densest cities in the U.S., and have had fewer infections and deaths [46, 47]. A number of sources have concluded that the greater number of infections and deaths in the U.S. when compared to other nations has been more related to a culture of individual freedom manifesting itself as irresponsible behavior toward health warnings and skepticism of scientific advice to prevent the spread

The Post-Pandemic City **201**

of infections—such as social distancing, not gathering in groups and widely available testing [48]—and the congested living conditions of nursing facilities, substandard homes of poor families or low-wage earners, homeless shelters, jails and detention centers [49, 50].

Although the suburbs can provide room for city growth, they can also lead to a loss of unique open space surrounding the city—open spaces that may have been precious elements of a natural ecosystem that, when eradicated or abused, could lead to environmental decline and detriment to the city. For example, loss of wetlands may prevent hindrance of rising seas and storm surge if the city is located near the ocean. Sewage discharge and illegal dumping of toxic effluents can pollute rivers, lakes and underground water. Loss of farms may diminish access to locally grown, farm-to-table fresh food. Loss of natural areas could threaten wildlife sanctuaries and endemic species, and lead to potential zoonotic infections [51]. Damage to some natural environments may be irreversible—such as the deforestation of the Amazon [52] and the tropical forests preserves of Borneo, Indonesia, and Malaysia that substantially contribute to climate change [53]. As cities around the world accommodate growth, it is more urgent than ever for state and federal agencies to develop sustainable strategies that save and protect valuable forests [54], and implement more stringent regulations regarding how and when to use or not use available land for development of suburbs and outlying fringe areas.

In 2006, Chan Krieger & Associates advised the city of Shenyang, in northeast China to prepare a masterplan for the city's projected growth. The city originally proposed to double

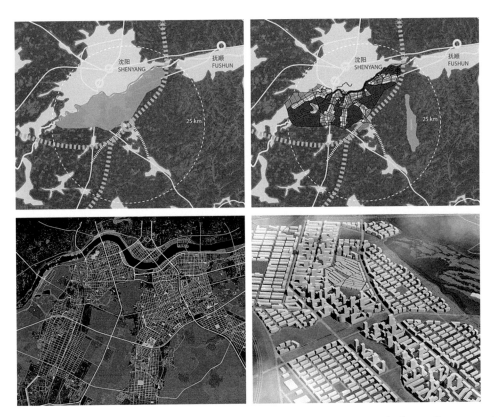

FIGURE 15.3 Shenyang 2006 masterplan by Chan Krieger & Associates, clockwise from upper left: (a) original government uniform development plan; (b) proposed land use plan, with plan of Manhattan Island (in red) for scale comparison; (c) conceptual aerial rendering of building mass and landscape distribution; and (d) conceptual masterplan detail of street and open space plan. Image courtesy of Lawrence A. Chan FAIA.

its size by developing uniformly across the Hunhe River together with radial highways to connect adjoining towns and the new international airport. Chan Krieger proposed an alternative concept that concentrated development along five Manhattan-sized transit-oriented corridors with capacity to fulfill the needs of the projected growth, while simultaneously preserving existing valuable agricultural land and natural areas (*Figure 15.3*). The objective was to balance urban development with preservation of agricultural and natural areas that would provide higher air quality for health and wellbeing, help to mitigate climate change and maintain food security.

Some of the advantages identified in the Shenyang masterplan included the efficient and sustainable use of land; equitable and flexible distribution of population; transit-oriented development to reduce the need and use of highways, thus reducing pollution and promoting better health and wellbeing; opportunities to equitably distribute and provide easy access to open space and parks from all neighborhoods; preserve and integrate existing **riparian corridors** and other natural features to enhance development areas; maintain valuable agricultural land to ensure food security; maximize access to, and use of, existing natural areas for recreational opportunities; and promote biodiversity between urban development and natural preservation to help combat climate change.

Many cities around the world have mature suburbs that have been significantly developed in a widespread pattern not unlike what was originally proposed by the City of Shenyang—a condition commonly derided as "sprawl." As suburbs become bigger and denser, and former open spaces are lost, it often becomes more difficult for cities to accommodate population growth and new development while maintaining equitable basic services and amenities and upgrading aging infrastructure. For some states and countries, a solution to address growth pressures is to build a satellite city.

Adding Satellite Cities

Aside from historic examples of new settlements, utopian communities, Garden Cities and 19th- to 20th-century new towns, the contemporary era of satellite cities are clean-slate responses by some countries to accommodate growth when it overwhelms the resources of a major city to effectively provide for current and future populations—particularly in the collective zone comprised of South Asia, East Asia and Southeast Asia, where 55 percent of the world's population lives [55]. A developing country such as Malaysia that has ambitions to advance economically has concluded that a state-of-the-art new city can help the nation to instrumentally expand the country's budding industries in technology, services, tourism and healthcare, and attract foreign investments from, and collaborations with, companies and institutions from more developed countries [56].

In 2015, the author was hired as an independent planner by the Malaysian government to assemble a team to develop a 25-year masterplan for a new city (*Figure 15.4*) [57] to relieve the pressures of growth of Kuala Lumpur (KL) and its surrounding suburbs. The new city—sited on an aggregate of 27,500 acres of plantation land currently used for the cultivation of palm oil trees—is earmarked for two million people and 1.5 billion square feet of development and embedded in a large 592-square mile special economic zone—Malaysia Vision Valley, in the adjacent state of Negeri Sembilan. At 43 square miles, the new city will be almost as large as Boston (48 square miles) and less than half the size of KL (94 square miles). However, the new city would be significantly denser (46,500 people per square mile) in comparison to Boston (14,300 people per square mile) and almost two-and-a-half times the density of KL (19,080 people per square mile.)

The Post-Pandemic City **203**

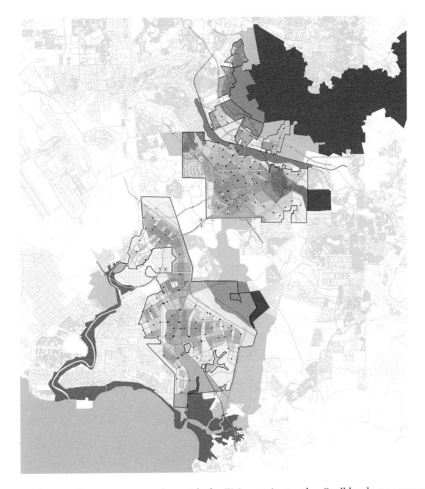

FIGURE 15.4 Twenty-five-year masterplan with the "Mountain-to-the-Sea" landscape greenway for a New City in Malaysia Vision Valley, State of Negeri Sembilan, Malaysia, 2017. Image courtesy of Lawrence A. Chan FAIA, principal master planner.

A major starting point for the new city masterplan was to depart from traditional Malaysian development of highway-connected single-use silos in order to deemphasize vehicular traffic, reduce the use of fossil fuels, and shift the focus toward sustainable development with diverse mixed uses and functions that are integrated with public transit, generous landscape and pedestrian open spaces. Six design principles[1] were established to help guide recommendations[2] for phased development.

The overall goal for the new city in Malaysia Vision Valley is to provide growth capacity for Greater Kuala Lumpur by creating a pedestrian-oriented, walkable, vibrant, automobile-independent, sustainable city that is based on dense transit-oriented development prototypes rather than low-scaled "Levittown" precedents. The plan aspires to maximize the preservation and augmentation of landscape assets—especially forest preserves and riparian corridors—for human enjoyment and access; to help reverse the detrimental effects of climate change; to promote air quality for health and wellbeing; to reserve or re-establish natural buffer zones between human settlements and wildlife sanctuaries; and to create exemplary living and working environments that enhance urbanity and a high quality of life—all values that preceded the COVID-19 pandemic but have since reenergized interests and emphasis as a consequence.

The Threat of Zoonoses

The World Health Organization has indicated that COVID-19 is a zoonosis—a "disease or infection that is naturally transmissible from vertebrate animals to humans," either from infected wildlife to agricultural animals and then to humans, or directly from infected wildlife to humans. A number of highly infectious outbreaks over the past 100 years can be traced to wildlife origins, including COVID-19 (bats), Ebola (bats or infected non-human primate), Hendra (bats or infected horses), Henipa (bats), HIV/AIDS (monkeys), MERS (camels), Nipah (bats or infected pigs), SARS (bats or infected civets) and Spanish Influenza (birds).

Scientific knowledge about COVID-19—officially called SARS-CoV-2 and at least three newly discovered more virile mutations—is still incomplete. In addition to previously known-to-date infected animal carriers, scientists have also found COVID-19 infections in other animals, including, cats, dogs, ferrets, gorillas, hamsters, lions, minks, several varieties of monkeys, pumas, snow leopards, tigers, and tree shrews. Although it is still not yet revealed if the latter group of animals—and perhaps others yet to be discovered—when infected, can transmit the virus to humans [60], public health officials remain concerned about the dangers of COVID-19 after discovering that tigers and lions that recently tested positive for the virus were infected by infected zookeepers [61, 62]—a reverse zoonotic infection known as zooanthroponosis or anthroponosis [63]—that increases the unknown about COVID-19 and its ability to spread among mammals, both human and non-human. An even greater concern is finding more contagious mutations of the COVID-19 in animals that can lead to newer variants among animals, including domestic dogs and cats, and then jump to infecting people again [64].

Since the discovery of coronaviruses can be traced to the 1920s, the increasing occurrences of outbreaks may be explained by a 2016 report by the United Nations Environment Programme (UNEP) that warned that

> "The emergence of zoonotic diseases is often associated with environmental changes or ecological disturbances, such as agriculture intensification and human settlement, or encroachment into forests and other habitats. Zoonoses are also opportunistic and tend to affect hosts that are already stressed by environmental, social, or economic conditions [64]."

The UNEP report is further supported by a 2019 report by the Royal Society released just one month before the COVID-19 outbreak that found that

> "Exploitation of wildlife through hunting and trade facilitates close contact between wildlife and humans…provide further evidence that exploitation, as well as anthropogenic activities that have caused losses in wildlife habitat quality, have increased opportunities for animal-human interactions and facilitated zoonotic disease transmission [65]."

Together, both the UNEP and Royal Society reports suggest that one radical preventive remedy would be for human settlements to withdraw from, and reestablish natural buffers around wildlife sanctuaries. This dramatic initiative would not only help to reduce potential zoonotic incidents but also help to rebalance the biodiversity between human settlements and wilderness areas, and restore the natural landscape to mitigate climate change. As an additional measure some cultural practices, such as the hunting, procurement, farming, sale and consumption of wildlife—including known infected species such as badgers, bats, civets, crocodiles and pangolins would need to be effectively restricted, policed, managed and permanently banned [66]—such as the example set by the Chinese government after the outbreak of COVID-19 by shutting down all farming of wildlife for food and instructing farmers to dispose animals in a way that did not spread disease [67].

A consequence to a redistribution and separation of human settlements and activities from wildlife sanctuaries could be a greater flow of human migration toward available non-wildlife land and existing settlements—potentially encouraging sprawl in the former movement, and increasing congestion in cities in the latter movement. Cities would then be faced with a multifaceted challenge including accommodating additional density; creating and maintaining sufficient open space; increasing infrastructural facilities; and adapting preventive protocols against future infectious outbreaks.

Environmental Remediation

Each of the four case studies discussed above provides some example strategies to help cities recalibrate urban living conditions in reaction to human experiences during the COVID-19 pandemic; namely, confinement to work- or learn-from-home situations; insufficient or inconvenient access to public open space and parks; limited distribution of local neighborhood services; and lengthy commuting distances between employment centers and affordable residential areas, especially for essential workers who cannot work-from-home. Open space plays a key role in helping to solve some of these issues by striving to improve quality of air, health and wellbeing, and to help recapture the vitality and urbanity of cities, including:

- *Public open spaces* that provide fresh air, sunlight and visual delight in congested areas of a city, but have greater value when they are well designed and populated with people. Although the Rose Kennedy Greenway (*Figure 15.1*) is an impressive civic space and achievement, the wide traffic lanes and office buildings surrounding its windswept, minimally treed edges results in a space that is less people-oriented and successful than Commonwealth Avenue Mall, where the latter is more intimate and quiet, is surrounded by slower and fewer traffic lanes, and attracts people throughout the day, especially residents who live nearby and along both its maturely treed edges.
- *Streets* that can be readily converted into public open spaces, especially in neighborhoods and communities lacking in parks, playgrounds, landscape, civic spaces and safe generous bikeways. Streets can be dedicated pedestrian zones as demonstrated by Boston's Downtown Crossing and found in numerous European cities, and wide streets can have traffic lanes reassigned to adjacent sidewalks to create linear parks as demonstrated by the widened and redesigned Bund Esplanade in Shanghai (*Figure 15.2*). A key consideration to apply when subtracting traffic lanes from a traffic corridor to create pedestrian and bicycle space is to reassign the space to one or both sidewalks rather than creating an isolated island between two vehicular traffic lanes like the Rose Kennedy Greenway.
- *Suburbs* that are earmarked for growth where transit-oriented development integrates buildings with existing open land would be more sustainable than simply expanding a city's footprint, as demonstrated in the Shenyang masterplan (*Figure 15.3*). Benefits gained include preservation and enhancement of existing natural assets, such as agricultural land and forests; efficient use and distribution of infrastructure; reduction of vehicular traffic and pollution; and better air quality for health and wellbeing.

- *Satellite cities* can relieve the congestion of large metropolitan areas with features that include a comprehensive transportation network, development that reinforces adjacent existing context, and stewardship of surrounding natural assets, as demonstrated by the masterplan for a new city in Malaysia Vision Valley (*Figure 15.4*). Benefits gained include the creation of an exemplary ecological settlement with state-of-the-art technology and infrastructure; reduced congestion in the host city/metropolitan area; opportunities for the host city to transfer uses to the satellite city in order to renew, renovate or upgrade the existing city; and preservation of the natural landscape and wildlife sanctuaries that would help to reduce the effects of climate change and potential incidents of zoonotic infections.

The stewardship of natural landscapes and wildlife preserves is not only relevant to mitigating climate change but will also reduce human interventions that harm the land and soil, human and animal life, and environmental biodiversity. Activities such as the desecration and reduction of natural preserves through deforestation, soil erosion, toxic chemicals in agriculture, mining, landfills, unprocessed sewage, litter, groundwater contamination, destruction of wildlife habitats and careless wildfires [68] contribute to environmental damage, global warming and climate change that lower the Earth's ability to absorb carbon dioxide. These activities endanger all life, including endangered species of endemic animals, plants, and insects, animal migration patterns, and human and community health with increasing incidents of zoonoses. Together with the release of plastic into the world's oceans, the effect of human activities has been decreasing global health and wellbeing in the air that we breathe, the water that we drink, and the food that we grow, harvest and eat.

Rising global temperatures have also been an impetus for human migration, adding pressure on cities and urban areas to accommodate population growth, decrease food security, and increase water use and waste production. Record levels of unbearable heat, inadequate rainfall and unseasonable drought conditions, crop failures, swarming pests that scavenge meager food production, rising seas along coastal areas, and increasing occurrences of natural disasters, are some of the results of climate change that have made many regions uninhabitable, and together with abject poverty, have resulted in increasing mass migrations toward more climate resilient countries to further increase challenges for existing cities and settlement areas that are already coping with providing sanctuary and adequate living conditions for current citizens, recent steady influxes of migrants from conflict zones [69, 70], and the growth of poverty areas [71, 72].

Ironically, the pandemic and its effect on global industries and national economies have resulted in a profound reduction in vehicular and airplane exhaust emissions but not other forms of air pollution [73]. The evidence suggests that rather than return to pre-pandemic operations, nations should take the opportunity to leverage and sustain the environmental gains during the pandemic as an ongoing endeavor to mitigate climate change [74]. Thus, resolving the conjunction of two diametrically different conditions—environmental gains and diminished city vibrancy due to the pandemic—is one of the great challenges ahead for countries to reevaluate, recalibrate and resuscitate the sustainable characteristics of a healthy Earth and vital city life [75].

Enhancing City Attributes

Cities have had many attributes to attract people throughout history. The attributes include a variety of opportunities in goods, services and leisure; diverse opportunities for education and employment; an array of social and civic support services; alternative and redundant medical care; rich collections of cultural institutions and entertainment venues; a broad network of communication and resources—locally, statewide, nationwide and/or worldwide; and diversity of people and ideas for social interaction, creativity and innovation. The high densities that support these qualities not only make cities vibrant and attractive, they also provide advantages for cities to more quickly and effectively adapt to changes and challenges, such as threats and incidents of infectious diseases and outbreaks due to the depth and redundancy in medical facilities, trained personnel, institutional knowledge and databases, and other support services available in cities more than remote areas [76].

Based on recent estimates, 55 percent of the world's population and 83 percent of the U.S. population currently live in *cities* (broadly defined by the United Nations to represent urbanized areas); and in 30 years' time, by 2050, the estimates will respectively increase to 68 percent worldwide and 89 percent in the U.S. [77]. Thus, future pandemics—which are likely to reoccur due to the alarming progress of coronavirus mutations—will continue to disrupt our cities and city life unless new preventive, pre-emptive measures are adopted, such as designing and planning environments and procedures to more effectively respond to future outbreaks; enforcing modified behavior to avoid contracting and spreading infections; and relocating or withdrawing human settlements from, and practices that engage, with wildlife sanctuaries in order to reduce incidents of zoonoses.

The Post-Pandemic City?

The significant reduction of vitality in cities during the pandemic has raised greater awareness and appreciation of public open space. With city properties predominantly privately owned and fully developed, the most abundant source for new public open spaces will be through reprogramming city streets or traffic lanes for pedestrian use and enjoyment. Since city streets and sidewalks are public, the conversion of city streets may be the most expeditious way to acquire new pedestrian space because streets are plentiful, relatively malleable into a variety of shapes and uses, universally shared, mostly loved (but occasionally despised), can be positioned either in the foreground or background, and like a favorite accessory, capable of complementing almost anything adjacent to it.

Public open spaces allow more latitude and opportunities to maintain social distancing, offer more diverse environments for people to enjoy away from their homes and workplaces, and provide opportunities for time alone and mental wellbeing. Although our journey through the COVID-19 pandemic has not yet ended, we can only speculate on how buildings might change in response to COVID-19 and future infectious variants, and how the ongoing and evolving collateral negative effects will influence future city life, social behavior and the global economy.

One opportunity for innovation within city limits can be found in the vastness of office building vacancy. Space in offices has been vacated due to increased social distancing requirements, increased work-from-home capacities, as well as unfortunate layoffs. For some businesses, work-from-home has been so successful that companies are considering full adoption of the solution after the pandemic [78]. If widely implemented, the accustomed character of central business districts would be dramatically altered by empty or marginally occupied office buildings [79], closed small businesses, and, subsequently, empty streets with little human activity. One potential solution in response to vacant office buildings would be to reprogram them for alternative uses—particularly for residences [80, 81]—in a similar manner to the way in which former 19th-century industrial warehouses have been retrofitted.

Physically, the wide spacing of structural elements and the generous floor-to-floor heights of office buildings would provide great flexibility and potential to convert the buildings for residential use with unconventional housing amenities, such as larger floors and taller ceilings with extra space for working from home and home schooling; generous daylight, especially buildings that are predominantly clad with glass; centralized HVAC systems that can ease maintenance, repairs, and installed with commercial-graded air filtering systems; multiple speedy elevators to facilitate social distancing; rigorous telecommunications capabilities; commercial-grade, high-capacity services, such as building security, loading docks, waste collection and fire protection; commercial-grade amenities, such as athletic facilities, common rooms, restaurants and retail services; underground or adjacent garage; downtown location, often within walking distance to public transit; and great views from upper floors if the building is a skyscraper. Reprogramming office buildings for housing in downtown locations would also help cities to accommodate population growth, address the demand for housing in city centers, reduce the flow of commuter traffic into the city, maintain and improve the vitality of downtowns, offer opportunities to renovate and upgrade substandard housing elsewhere in the city, reduce human impulses to relocate to the suburbs and contribute a sustainable initiative to mitigate climate change.

Residential use in converted office buildings is just one of many possible uses. Large floor plates, tall ceilings and generous daylight can also be attractive for institutions, schools, commercial retail, restaurants, data centers, entertainment venues and recreational facilities. Vertical farming in reprogrammed empty office buildings is an alternative that can contribute to food security [82–84]. Another possibility is to convert the entire structure as a vertical forest "decked from top to toe in a verdant blaze of shrubbery and plant life, a breath of fresh air for metropolises" [85]. Incorporating all these possibilities together would be comparable to creating nodes of transit-oriented development within a city, and would help to steer cities and city living toward a more sustainable direction than before the pandemic.

Conclusion

In his memoir, published the same year as the worldwide onset of this pandemic, President Barack Obama shared the following sentiments:

> "(T)he pandemic we're currently living through is both a manifestation of and a mere interruption in the relentless march toward an interconnected world, one in which peoples and cultures can't help but collide. In that world—of global supply chains, instantaneous capital transfers, social media, transnational terrorist networks, climate change, mass migration, and ever-increasing complexity—we will learn to live together, cooperate with one another, and recognize the dignity of others, or we will perish [86]."

The COVID-19 pandemic is providing an unprecedented experience in the dawn of the 21st century that is having a profound effect on our cities and how we live in them. Countries around the world were unprepared for COVID-19, and individual unilateral responses to combatting it have been immature and barely adequate. COVID-19 is yet another wakeup call since HIV/AIDS in the 1980s on the dangers of zoonoses, and may be the penultimate warning for the world to better prepare for subsequent infectious outbreaks and pandemics.

The rapidly growing intense effects of climate change on the planet have demonstrated how things can get worse and accelerate quickly when we do not heed early warning signs during the dawn of their occurrence, do nothing during the afternoon stage, continue to vacillate at the dimming dusk of climate change, and thus face a greater task in trying to stop, let alone reverse, climate change during its dark evening. Only when the world diligently works collectively together throughout the night to develop effective strategies and act to ensure the safety and habitability of our cities, natural environments, and the Earth as a whole—from future zoonotic outbreaks and irreversible climate change—may we still have a chance to ensure the livelihood, survivability and ability for future generations to see and enjoy a new dawn [87].

Acknowledgment

The author would like to thank Pamela de Olivera-Smith, Keely Menezes, and Hubert Murray FAIA for their critical and patient reviews and keen edits of the author's drafts that helped him to improve his essay, with special thanks to Mr. Murray for ongoing stimulating conversations about urban design and urbanism.

Notes

1 *Development Plan for 27,500 Acres of Land in Malaysia Vision Valley:* Planning Principles [58]
   1 Promote synergy and mutual benefits between the new city and existing surrounding communities and historic settlements within and around the project's boundaries, including river corridors, mountain reserves, farms, indigenous villages, and habitats of endemic plants, birds, and wildlife
   2 Create a comprehensive and coordinated transportation network that will reduce the use of cars and fossil fuels, and integrate mobility modes for pedestrians, bicycles, buses, public transit, commuter rail—all linked to a central multi-modal transportation hub designated for a rail station serving a high-speed rail line planned between KL and Singapore
   3 Integrate and incorporate landscape as an integral component of development, expanding recreational amenities, protecting existing valuable landscape settings and cultural artifacts, and connecting major natural assets to create a 20-mile long "Mountain-To-The-Sea" greenway between the Bukit Galla Forest Preserve in the north and the Straits of Malacca in the south
   4 Promote and implement sustainable strategies, including water conservation, recycled waste, renewable energy, green architecture and land use, "smart" growth and state-of-the-art-technology
   5 Balance new development with open space and landscape to promote urbanity and an exemplary quality of life with an emphasis on transit-oriented development
   6 Establish a dynamic downtown that integrates the planned multi-modal transportation hub at the city center with it strategic location at the confluence of two major riparian corridors and the "Mountain-To-The-Sea" greenway

2 *Development Plan for 27,500 Acres of Land in Malaysia Vision Valley*: Urban Design Strategies [59]
   - All developed areas will be mixed-use, with integrated residences, convenient commercial services, and generous landscape and pedestrian open spaces
   - 50 percent of the residential development will be reserved for the workforce who live in the city, and 50 percent of all available housing will be affordable
   - Floor Area Ratio (FAR) will be limited to 6.0, and maximum height will be limited to 15 stories, with occasional special exceptions up to 30 stories in the central business district
   - An extensive public transit network—including light rail streetcars, rapid bus transport, and express rail lines to KL and the airport—to support the pedestrian environment with transit stops located within a five-minute walk from all development.
   - Conventional parking requirement standards are reduced by 50 percent to discourage the use of cars and land allocated for parking lots and garages
   - Buildings will have active pedestrian street frontages with arcades on the ground floor to protect pedestrians from the tropical sun and daily spontaneous rain showers
   - City streets will be limited to two to three traffic lanes each way, and integrated with street parking, public transit, bicycle lanes, generous pedestrian sidewalks and crosswalks, street trees for shade, and sustainable landscape features to minimize water runoff
   - At least 44 percent of the project land will be left natural or enhanced by additional landscape
   - Natural buffer zones will be established around existing indigenous village reserves and the Bukit Galla Forest Preserve, where access will be restricted to scientific research, academic education and limited eco-tourism
   - Existing hilly features, low lying areas, and riparian corridors will be included as landscape, converted for passive recreational use, or reinforced with water resources rather than the conventional practice of cutting down hills and filling valleys and stream beds

- Mountainous areas previously used for palm agriculture will be restored as permanent forest reserves
- The Bukit Galla Forest Preserve and the Straits of Malacca will be linked by a 'Mountain-To-The-Sea' greenway utilizing existing riparian corridors, forested mountains, iconic natural assets and topographical features, and new regional and local parks
- Development along the new city's boundaries will complement adjacent existing settlements and natural artifacts with inviting and inclusive compatible building types, uses and scale.

References

1. Harvard Medical School. (2021, Feb. 12). *Coronavirus Resource Center.* Harvard Health Publishing. https://www.health.harvard.edu/diseases-and-conditions/coronavirus-resource-center
2. Centers for Disease Control and Prevention. (2020, Oct. 5). *Science Brief: SARS-CoV2 and Potential Airborne Transmission.* Covid-19. https://www.cdc.gov/coronavirus/2019-ncov/more/scientific-brief-sars-cov-2.html
3. Wallace-Wells, D. (2021, Mar.). How the West Lost COVID: How Did so Many Rich Countries Get it so Wrong? How Did Others Get it so Right? *New York Magazine.*
4. Climo, L. H. (2020, Sept.). Pandemic Deniers, What's With Them? *Psychiatric Times.*
5. Swenson, A. and Klepper, D. (2021, Mar.). Nurses Fight Conspiracies along with Coronavirus. *Associated Press.*
6. Whitbourne, S. K. (2019, Apr.). 5 Things You Need to Know About Personal Space. *Psychology Today.*
7. Borenstein, S. (2020, Dec.). World Carbon Dioxide Emissions Drop 7 Percent in Pandemic-hit 2020. *Associated Press.*
8. Sennett, R. (1960). *The Conscience of the Eye: The Design and Social Life of Cities.* Norton. xiii.
9. Mandavilli, A. (2021, Feb.). In Oregon, Scientists Find a Virus Variant with a Worrying Mutation. *The New York Times.*
10. Renault, M. (2021, Feb.). Experts Warn against COVID-19 Variants as States Reopen. *Associated Press.*
11. Thompson, D. (2021, Feb.). The Surprising Key to Combatting Vaccine Refusal. *The Atlantic.*
12. Engber, D. (2021, Mar.). America Is Now in the Hands of the Vaccine-Hesitant. *The Atlantic.*
13. Ortutay, B. and Seitz, A. (2021, Mar.). Defying Rules, Anti-vaccine Accounts Thrive on Social Media. *Associated Press.*
14. Purtill, C. (2020, Dec.). How to End This Pandemic, and Prepare for the Next One. *The New York Times.*
15. Greshko, M. (2021, Jan.). COVID-19 Will Likely be with us Forever. Here's How We'll Live With it. *National Geographic.*
16. Novakovic, S. (2020, Mar.). Will COVID-19 Spell the End of Urban Density? Don't Bet On It. *Azure Magazine.*
17. Friends of Post Office Square. (n.d.). *History of Boston's Post Office Square.* Norman B. Leventhal Park. http://www.normanbleventhalpark.org/about-us/history-of-post-office-square/
18. Mass.gov. (n.d.). *The Big Dig: Facts and Figures.* Highway Division. https://www.mass.gov/info-details/the-big-dig-facts-and-figures
19. Bostonroads.com (n.d.). *John F Fitzgerald Expressway (Central Artery).* http://www.bostonroads.com/roads/central-artery/
20. Ferguson, R. (1994). *Urban Revisions: Current Projects for the Public Realm [Exhibition].* Museum of Contemporary Art, Los Angeles. 92–94.
21. Ryan, A. (2009, Oct.). Call it the Emptyway. *The Boston Globe.*
22. Keane, T. (2008, Jan.). The Grass Isn't Greener. *The Boston Globe Sunday Magazine.*
23. Levine, L. (2020, Jul.). *The Lungs of the City: Frederick Law Olmstead, Public Health, and the Creation of Central Park.* The Gotham Center for New York City History.
24. Florida, R. (2018, Jul.). How Cars Divide America. *Bloomberg CityLab.*
25. Rowe, C. and Koetter, F. (1978). *Collage City.* Cambridge, MA: The MIT Press. 79.
26. New York City Council. (2020, April 17). *Speaker Corey Johnson and Council Member Carlina Rivera to Introduce Legislation to Open City Streets during Coronavirus/COVID-19 Pandemic.* https://council.nyc.gov/press/2020/04/17/1939/
27. Baruchman, M. (2020, May). Seattle will Permanently Close 20 Miles of Residential Streets to Most Vehicle Traffic. *The Seattle Times.*
28. BBC News. (2020). Barcelona's Car-free Smart City Experiment. https://www.bbc.com/news/technology-50658537

29. Burgen, S. (2018, Sep.). 'For Me, This Is Paradise': Life in the Spanish City That Banned Cars. *The Guardian*.
30. O'Sullivan, F. (2019, Mar.). A Modest Proposal to Eliminate 11,000 Urban Parking Spots. *Bloomberg CityLab*.
31. O'Sullivan, F. (2018, Nov.). Spain Wants to Ban Cars in Dozens of Cities, and the Public's on Board. *Bloomberg CityLab*.
32. City of Dallas, Texas. (2003). *A Balanced Vision Plan for the Trinity River Corridor*. https://trinityriver-corridor.com/about/balanced-vision-plan
33. Kennedy, S. (2007, Dec.). New Orleans Waterfront Plan Takes Shape. *Architectural Record*.
34. New York Lower Manhattan Development Corporation and New York City Department of Transportation. (2004). *Chinatown Access and Circulation Study Final Report*. http://www.renewnyc.com/attachments/content/pdfs/Chinatown_Final_Report_2004-12-13.pdf
35. Riverlife Task Force. (2001). *A Vision Plan for Pittsburgh's Riverfronts*. https://riverlifepgh.org/wp-content/uploads/2016/10/Vision-Plan-For-Pittsburghs-Riverfronts-Web-version.pdf
36. Keegan, E. (2008). Chan Krieger Sieniewicz to Redesign Shanghai Riverfront. *ARCHITECT Magazine*.
37. District of Columbia Office of Planning. (2003). *The Anacostia Waterfront Framework Plan*. https://planning.dc.gov/publication/anacostia-waterfront-framework-plan-2003
38. Bassett, S. (2010). Better City, Better Bund: The Shanghai Bund Gets a New Life. *Topos*. 72. 68–73.
39. Gordon, S. (2011, Dec.). The Regeneration of Shanghai's Bund. *BBC*.
40. Skiffington, D. (2010, Jul.). Redefining the Waterfront: Redesign of Shanghai Bund Restores Grandeur to Famous Huangpu District. *World Architecture News*.
41. Guarino, B. (2021, Jan.). People without Symptoms Spread Virus in More than Half of Cases, CDC Model Finds. *The Washington Post*.
42. Mervosh, S. (2020, Dec.) Small Town, No Hospital: Covid-19 Is Overwhelming Rural West Texas. *The New York Times*.
43. Thornburgh, N. (2020, Mar.). The Rich Fled New York. Don't Be Like Them. *The Atlantic*.
44. Fein, A. (1972). *Frederick Law Olmsted and the American Environmental Tradition*. Doubleday Canada. 33–35.
45. Richardson, B. (2020, Jun.). Redlining's Legacy of Inequality: Low Homeownership Rates, Less Equity for Black Households. *Forbes*.
46. Keegan, M. (2020, Dec.). Why Cities Are Not as Bad for You as You Think. *BBC*.
47. Barr, J. and Tassier, T. (2020, Apr.). Are Crowded Cities the Reason for the COVID-19 Pandemic? *Scientific American*.
48. Pinsker, J. (2020, Mar.). The People Ignoring Social Distancing. *The Atlantic*.
49. Bassett, M. T. (2020, May). Just Because You Can Afford to Leave the City Doesn't Mean You Should. *The New York Times*.
50. Loh, T. H. and Lienberger, C. (2020, Apr.). How Fear of Cities Can Blind Us From Solutions to COVID-19. *Next City*.
51. World Health Organization. (2020). *Zoonoses*. https://www.who.int/news-room/fact-sheets/detail/zoonoses
52. Harvey, F. (2020, Mar.). Tropical Forests Losing Their Ability to Absorb Carbon, Study Finds. *The Guardian*.
53. Lustgarten, A. (2018, Nov.). Palm Oil Was Supposed to Help Save the Planet. Instead It Unleashed a Catastrophe. *The New York Times*.
54. Derouin, S. (2019, Nov.). Deforestation: Facts, Causes & Effects. *LiveScience*. https://www.livescience.com/27692-deforestation.html
55. Worldometer. (n.d.). Population: World. https://www.worldometers.info/population/world/
56. Economic Planning Unit, Prime Minister's Department, Malaysia. (2015). *Eleventh Malaysia Plan 2016–2020*. http://planipolis.iiep.unesco.org/sites/planipolis/files/ressources/malaysia_11thplan.pdf
57. Cheng, T. L. (2017). Visionary Push for Another Corridor. *The Star*.
58. Boston Design Group LLC. (2017). Planning Principles. *Development Plan for 27,500 Acres of Land in Malaysia Vision Valley, Negeri Sembilan*. 62–64.
59. Boston Design Group LLC. (2017). Urban Design Strategies. *Development Plan for 27,500 Acres of Land in Malaysia Vision Valley, Negeri Sembilan*. 142–161.
60. Centers for Disease Control and Prevention. (2021, Jan. 19). *COVID-19 and Animals*. https://www.cdc.gov/coronavirus/2019-ncov/daily-life-coping/animals.html
61. Goldstein, J. (2020, Apr.). Bronx Zoo Tiger Is Sick with the Coronavirus. *The New York Times*.
62. BBC. (2020, Dec.). Coronavirus: Four Lions Test Positive for Covid-19 at Barcelona Zoo. https://www.bbc.com/news/world-europe-55229433

63. Mandavilli, A. (2021, Mar.). Virus Variants Can Infect Mice, Scientists Report. *The New York Times.*
64. UN Environment Programme. (2016). Zoonoses: Blurred Lines of Emergent Disease and Ecosystem Health. *UNEP Frontiers 2016 Report: Emerging Issues of Environmental Concern.*
65. Johnson, C. K., Hitchens, P. L., Pandit, P. S., Rushmore, J., Evans, T. S., Young, C. C. W., and Doyle, M. M. (2020, Mar.). Global Shifts in Mammalian Population Trends Reveal Key Predictors of Virus Spillover Risk. *The Royal Society.*
66. Briggs, H. (2020, Feb.). Coronavirus: The Race to Find the Source in Wildlife. *BBC News.*
67. Doucleff, M. (2021, Mar.). WHO Points to Wildlife Farms in Southern China as Likely Source of Pandemic. *WBUR News.*
68. Kukreja, R. (n.d.). What Is Land Pollution? *Conserve Energy Future.* https://www.conserve-energy-future.com/causes-effects-solutions-of-land-pollution.php
69. Yahya, M. and Muasher, M. (n.d.). Refugee Crisis in the Arab World. *Carnegie Endowment for International Peace.*
70. White, B., Haysom, S., and Davey, E. (2013). Refugees, Host States and Displacement in the Middle East: An Enduring Challenge. *Humanitarian Policy Group.*
71. The Seattle Globalist. (2020, Sept.). Life in Kenya Slum Sheds Light on Growing Global Reality. https://seattleglobalist.com/slumrising/slumrising-partone
72. Ortiz, E. (2016, Aug.). What Is a Favela? Five Things to Know About Rio's So-Called Shantytowns. *NBC News.*
73. Plautz, J. (2020, Dec.). Did Covid Lockdowns Really Clear the Air? *Bloomberg.*
74. BBC Future. (2020, Mar.). Will COVID-19 Have a Lasting Impact on the Environment? https://seattleglobalist.com/slumrising/slumrising-partone
75. Environmental Protection. (2020, Mar.). COVID-19 and Climate Change: The Unexpected Pairing. https://eponline.com/articles/2020/03/24/covid19-and-climate-change-the-unexpected-pairing.aspx
76. Badger, E. (2020, Mar.). Density Is Normally Good for Us. That Will Be True After Coronavirus, Too. *The New York Times.*
77. United Nations Department of Economic and Social Affairs. (2018). 68% of the World Population Projected to Live in Urban Areas by 2050, says UN. https://www.un.org/development/desa/en/news/population/2018-revision-of-world-urbanization-prospects.html
78. Berliner, U. (2020, Jun.). Get A Comfortable Chair: Permanent Work from Home Is Coming. *NPR, All Things Considered.*
79. Haag, M. (2021, Mar.). Remote Work Is Here to Stay. Manhattan May Never Be the Same. *The New York Times.*
80. Hughes, R. (2020, Jun.). Remote Working: How Cities Might Change If We Worked from Home More. *BBC News.*
81. Haag, M. and Rubinstein, D. (2020, Dec.). Midtown Is Reeling. Should Its Offices Become Apartments? *The New York Times.*
82. Shead, S. (2020, Dec.). German Firm Says Indoor Vertical Farm in Singapore Will Produce 1.5 Tons of 'Leafy Greens' Every Day. *CNBC.*
83. Tatum, M. (2020, Oct.). Inside Singapore's Huge Bet on Vertical Farming. *MIT Technology Review.*
84. Krishnamurthy, R. (2014). Vertical Farming: Singapore's Solution to Feed the Local Urban Population. *Permaculture Research Institute.*
85. Phillips, T. (2017, Feb.). 'Forest Cities': The Radical Plan to Serve China from Air Pollution. *The Guardian.*
86. Obama, B. (2020). *A Promised Land.* Crown/Random House. xvi.
87. Global Footrpint Network. (2020, Jun.). Earth Overshoot Day Is August 22, More Than Three Weeks Later Than Last Year. https://www.footprintnetwork.org/2020/06/05/press-release-june-2020-earth-overshoot-day/

PART 5
Commissioning

16
PROGRAMMING AND COMMISSIONING
A Bookend Approach to Evidence-Based Design

A. Vernon Woodworth FAIA

Programming requires the clear establishment of goals for building operations. This is the first step as well in the commissioning process. While commissioning may ordinarily be used as a term referring to the testing and calibration of HVAC and electrical systems, its function of verifying intended outcomes can be extended to all aspects of the program. Effective evidence-based design involves both programming and commissioning, working together as methods for clear performance objectives and quality control.

The Programming-Planning Paradigm

What a program is for a building or facility, planning is for a city or region. Yet planning is often conducted at a scale below the threshold of the bioregion, and can easily be undermined by trends in the marketplace and mandates from state or federal levels. Furthermore transportation planning is likely to be largely divorced from land-use planning, and the dimension of ecology may not be planned at all. Much of the content of this volume is applicable at a scale greater than that typically implied by the term "programming." Regardless of how it is described or understood, the underlying commitment to a more intentional and comprehensive approach to environmental stewardship applies.

There is one aspect of a program which a city or regional plan does not include. This is the contractual potential of a program. A client willing to pay for a new building will want to guarantee that they get what they pay for. For this reason programmers interview clients and end-users and other stakeholders to reach defined goals and consensual objectives. While planning develops goals and objectives, there is rarely a client or agency that is effectively empowered to safeguard these. Political expediency may incentivize departure from long-term optimal outcomes. Decisions made in one arena to address one contingency may ripple out to impact other areas of administration. For planning to be equal in effectiveness and as useful as programming, it must have a consistent enforcement ability equal to that of an owner in a construction context. An owner can change their mind, but will usually stay true to a carefully crafted mission and set of general goals. When decision-making occurs in rotating election cycles consistency and commitment are imperiled.

DOI: 10.4324/9781003164418-22

Because the issues of health and wellbeing are fundamental to survival, and without jurisdictional boundaries, our agendas for planning must be given the priority they deserve, at the appropriate scale for maximum effectiveness. For the same reason sustainability and a fuller understanding of the biology of human experience must be incorporated into the scope of programming. Where every design or planning decision can have a health impact, on people or the ecosystem, then that impact must be identified and described if negative outcomes are to be avoided. Programming and planning turn this equation around to establish the outcomes from which subsequent design and planning decisions flow.

The intent of evidence-based design is to introduce the scientific method into the design process. To accomplish this effectively, enough information must be available to adequately inform the designer. A challenge, in programming as in planning, is knowing the right information and how much information is needed to achieve desired outcomes. Because the rigor of scientific inquiry has rarely been employed in design, this challenge may seem insurmountable. The solution to this dilemma is to evaluate and document the outcomes of design decisions. For the purposes of this essay we will include this evaluation and documentation under the general heading of "commissioning."

A Performance-Based Approach

With an increased emphasis on energy performance and efficiency, building commissioning has become a standard aspect of larger construction projects. Just as a new ship should not set out to sea without thorough calibration and testing of all systems, similarly with building energy systems, building envelopes, and multiple other aspects of a new structure, a thorough process of evaluation is required to ensure proper functioning. In its chapter on "Commissioning, Operation and Maintenance" the International green Construction Code (IgCC) requires a commissioning plan for site work, material resource conservation and efficiency, energy, mechanical systems, lighting, water resource conservation, and indoor environmental quality, listing a total of 52 specific commissioning items [1]. Certain items also require retro-commissioning, whereby systems are tested and adjusted again 1–2 years or more after occupancy.

Needless to say such extensive commissioning is not common practice, however a combination of efforts by design professions and conscientious owners is likely to introduce new standards for commissioning and post-occupancy evaluation. "Commissioning" is already a discrete service that is offered independent of engineering. So-called "third-party" commissioning guarantees greater objectivity and accuracy by removing the temptation to overlook errors that may imply liability. Just as a structural peer review may be required for more complex designs, third-party commissioning may soon become the norm for all but the smallest of buildings.

With an emphasis on programming for natural systems, sustainability and the science of health and wellbeing we can begin to imagine a concomitant commissioning process. In fact, commissioning is generally described as beginning in the earliest stages of a project, with documentation of intended outcomes. This is programming by a different name. So, if commissioning requires involvement at the earliest stages of a project, what is the involvement of programming at the project's conclusion? The point here is that programming and commissioning are two sides of the evidence-based design coin. Outcomes result from the documentation of intentions, the application of research and experience, and the testing and calibration of installations. This describes the process of performance-based design, an approach that the American Institute of Architects (AIA) has committed to as the future of architectural practice.

But is the architecture profession able to step up to this level of accountability? Post-occupancy evaluation (POE) has been given lip service for decades, but the realities of practice often make this an awkward exercise. Usually by the time a Certificate of Occupancy is issued all parties to a construction project are anxious to move on. While architects know they can learn from post-occupancy evaluation they may find it difficult to convince a client that the expense is necessary, and the potential for uncovering inadequacies is a further disincentive. A POE can ignite smoldering antagonism in the client-architect relationship, potentially leading to claims of errors and omissions. Why risk it?

Throughout the development of the IgCC similar concerns were raised by members of the architectural community. The expanded scope of code compliance created by this document raised the specter of greater liability exposure. By extending code-required commissioning into the post-occupancy phase this exposure expanded in duration as well as scope. Would clients be willing to pay architects for these services? Would insurance companies be forced to increase errors and omissions insurance costs? Similar arguments were raised by industry representatives objecting to the costs of increased regulation, and the enforcement communities concerned about how such a code impacted their roles and responsibilities. It was heartening to those architects involved in the development of this code that the AIA was a staunch supporter and patron of this process. The AIA has now taken the next step with the timetable and agenda laid out in "Disruption, Evolution, Change," a white paper advocating assuming the role of stewards of the built environment adopted at the 2018 Annual Meeting. A performance-based approach to code compliance lies at the heart of that agenda, and this can only be achieved by means of a careful articulation of goals along with objective verification of outcomes.

Supporters of POE emphasize the potential for creating a database of design practices along with their documented outcomes. With an enhanced ability to assess physiological impacts and the availability of remote data collection via cell phones and portable biometric devices this potential is approaching realization. The value of such a database to the design professions can hardly be overstated. A design practice relying on predetermined outcomes will offend the practitioners who self-identify as artists, while reassuring clients and other stakeholders who depend upon these outcomes. While artists use intuition and inspiration to achieve their goals, architects will now be asked to approach their responsibilities more like physicians, with full accountability for the health and welfare impacts of their design decisions. It is time for architects to assume the responsibility their practice implies, and also to receive the remuneration this deserves. An expanded definition of architectural practice that encompasses rigorous programming and extensive commissioning will benefit the health and wellbeing of the public at large and greatly enhance the role of the profession.

There will always be a role for creativity in architecture. When Renaissance painters came to understand the rules of perspective and began systematically applying a horizon line and vanishing points to their composition the results were revolutionary. Artists of the Middle Ages could not have imagined the impact of realistic three-dimensional images on two-dimensional surfaces. Similarly it is difficult for us to imagine the impact of a design practice capable of reliably predicting (and creating) physiological and psychological responses, enhancing learning, interacting, working and healing. As for sustainability, there is no question that so-called "green" building is in its infancy. All of the pieces are in place to create a built environment that functions within and enhances the natural systems of the biosphere. All that is lacking is the incentive to create established protocols and a knowledge base of effective practices. The best physicians are those that have mastered the techniques of their profession and can embody and channel the energy of the healer in their beings. Artists have traditionally had long apprenticeships intended to ensure technical expertise. Architects were once responsible for all aspects of the act of building, including many dimensions now delegated to consultants. The ultimate source of all creativity is the life force itself which any artist, designer or physician is hoping to channel in their work. There is nothing incompatible about attempting to enlist big data and a rigorous documentation process in this effort.

Insights from Occupational Environments

The workplace provides a valuable example of a context for evidence-based design. Through the middle of the 20th-century offices were private refuges or open bullpens. According to John Seabrook in his *New Yorker* article "Office Space,"

> "the cubicle evolved out of utopian notions of office flexibility and flow that were promoted in the sixties by Robert Probst, the head of research for the Herman Miller company. Probst grasped that office work was fundamentally different from factory work [2]."

Probst sought to enhance the workplace specifically for cognitive functioning with hinged partitions and standing desks. According to Seabrook

> "Probst's action-oriented designs may or may not have increased productivity and collaboration, but they did enhance the bottom line, allowing office managers to add more employees without having to move to a bigger space. As density increased, partitions collapsed into the smallest possible footprint: the ever-shrinking cube [3]."

This was clearly not the intended outcome. The programmatic goals were undermined by flawed implementation.

Seabrook goes on to describe a trend that spread from Silicon Valley of lower partitions and greater emphasis on inter-office communication and interaction. Ultimately this trend eliminated the cube, resulting in an "open plan" of adjacent desks. Dutch researchers have since identified the health results of this approach in a 2011 study on the associations between shared office space and sickness absences. Their publication concluded that

> "compared to cellular offices, occupants in 2-person offices had 50% more days of sickness absence…occupants in 3–6 person offices had 36% more days of sickness absence…and occupants in open-plan offices had 62% more days of sickness absence [4]."

If health and wellbeing are among the goals for a workplace along with productivity and efficiency, then clearly open plan office space is not the way to go. This conclusion has been reinforced by the COVID-19 pandemic, which has emptied out office buildings across the globe.

Now, with the clear demonstration provided by the pandemic that the physical office is no longer required for running a business it seems that the slate has been wiped clean, allowing us to reinvent our work behaviors. How do we create a work lifestyle that maximizes wellbeing as well as productivity? What will the post-COVID-19 workplace look and feel like?

Neuroscience and an understanding of the role of emotion in motivation and wellbeing are able to point us in the right direction. Creativity and learning require the elimination of excess stress, and this means that the central nervous system must perceive the workplace as safe. In their book *Creating Emotionally Intelligent Workspaces,* Edward Finch and Guillermo Aranda-Mena observe that "it is the perception of safety within the minds of employees that will determine how people respond to the workspace. An unpredictable and unstable setting will inevitably drain people's mental resources and inhibit creative thought" [5]. They go on to state that

"Our feelings of security may be threatened by noise, unfamiliarity and encroachment onto territory. What happens in an open plan work environment? We have learned to accept changing faces around us without feeling threatened. This is very different from our primordial reaction to unfamiliar surroundings that compromise our feelings of safety. We have learned to suppress this primitive response, but this does not occur without some drain on our physical and cognitive resources [6]."

Finch and Aranda-Mena follow Maslow's hierarchy of needs theory and his understanding of motivation to untangle the emotional components of the workplace. Maslow opined that the lower needs must be met before one can pursue those that are higher in the hierarchy. In ascending order he listed these needs as:

- physiology,
- safety,
- affection,
- esteem, and
- self-actualization.

Finch and Aranda-Mena go on to cite F. I. Herzberg [7] in which the author described physiology and safety as "hygiene factors." The workplace must address the hygiene factors, but motivation is generated by the higher goals of affection, esteem and self-actualization. Finch and Aranda-Mena describe these higher-level psychological goals as "achievement, recognition, responsibility and advancement." They go on to describe how our brains are wired for social interaction and cooperation, causing us to seek approval and to experience pain based upon rejection and criticism. They observe that social interaction "leads to the release of the brain chemical oxytocin which, in turn, leads to feelings of warmth and well-being" [8]. Here is the key to workplace wellbeing, originating from our nature as social mammals. We require interaction and validation for our emotional health.

This brings us to the thorny problem of technology. There is evidence that the neurological responses to biophilic environments can be reproduced using virtual reality, but do we get the same oxytocin response on ZOOM that we get in person? In terms of Maslow's hierarchy, can working from home supply the requisite affection and esteem, and promote our self-actualization? Writing before the COVID-19 pandemic Finch and Aranda-Mena concluded that "it is the transformative possibilities that arise from having people co-located that sets the office apart from other settings. The success of the office rests on its ability to leverage human input" [9]. If this is true then we have clear direction, a goal that we can plan for and measure. In-person work offers opportunities for spontaneous contact that can generate positive emotions of belonging and collaboration. A recent poll by the Urban Land Institute determined that 67 percent of those working remotely during the pandemic would prefer more opportunities for in-person contact and collaboration [10]. This may be indicative of our instinctual need for group interaction as a precondition of feeling safe.

Programming & Commissioning in Context

The programming goal here could be articulated as follows: "Provide safe and healthy workspaces in which co-workers can interact effectively and achieve their maximum creative potential." This goal can be "commissioned" by monitoring productivity, sick days taken, longevity of employment and the administration of surveys on job satisfaction. Increased air changes and filtration can reduce airborne transmission of viruses, daylight and fresh air have been shown to enhance cognitive functioning and health, as do views to nature. But it is the mutually reinforcing benefit of creative collaboration that will "leverage human input." Creating opportunities for this collaboration that feel safe is a primary challenge for designing the post-COVID workplace.

While the office real estate market has never experienced an event like this pandemic, the consensus is that this is temporary, and that, with some minor adjustments and increased flexibility for work from home, occupancy rates will eventually return to their pre-pandemic levels. This can happen with an increased appreciation for the health benefits which good design can impart. For instance, the design of interior spaces can boost the immune system. Studies have found that "**environmental enrichment**…can boost animals' immune systems, slow the growth of tumors, make neurons more resistant to injury, and stave off the cognitive decline associated with aging," according to Emily Anthes in her book *The Great Indoors* [11]. Environmental enrichment is provided by complexity, opportunity, and stimulation from both the physical and the social environment. An "enriched" environment provides measurable results in brain development and cognitive reserves. With this insight we can now amplify our primary programming goal for the workplace of leveraging human input by adding that the office should provide environmental richness, both physically and socially. Cognitive performance, health and a sense of wellbeing are the metrics by which this goal can be measured.

A variable of great importance in the enrichment of a work environment is the reinforcement of emotional intelligence. According to the formulators of the "ability model" of emotional intelligence this is "the ability to monitor one's own and others' feelings and emotions, to discriminate among them and to use this information to guide one's thinking and actions" [12]. While emotional intelligence may seem to be an inherent or learned ability related to individual histories and experience, physical circumstances can promote or undermine this ability. Finch and Aranda-Mena observe that "when it comes to perceiving emotions, environmental factors such as lighting, noise and occupant density can significantly impact on our ability to detect emotional signals." The authors go so far as to claim that "emotional dysfunction in the workplace is not the result of emotional inadequacies of employees. Instead (they) suggest that workplaces themselves create emotional dysfunction" [13]. Their recommendation is to seek to create an "emotionally intelligent workspace" in which "important human values can be cultivated." It is worthwhile to reproduce here the three categories of emotional triggers established by Finch and Aranda-Mena related to the built environment, and the office environment in particular:

- "*Instrumental*: Emotions arising from the functional or instrumental dimension are tied to levels of dissatisfaction. In other words, emotions are linked to hygiene factors. Eliminating dissatisfaction is always the goal, but going beyond this does not necessarily lead to satisfaction. It leads to a design philosophy of getting it 'right' and 'fixing it': eliminating negative emotions.
- *Aesthetic*: Emotions associated with the aesthetic dimension arise from the senses—we feel emotions as a result of direct interaction with minimal cognitive engagement. It is an immediate and spontaneous response. It leads to a design philosophy of 'creativity, play and interaction': stimulating positive emotions.
- *Symbolic*: Emotions arising from the symbolic dimension involve an interaction between the senses, cognition and memory. Seeing a place or an object triggers a memory or an association. We often use artifacts to trigger associations we want others to have about us. At a corporate level this might be described as branding. At an individual level, it might be

described as personalization. The resulting emotions typically reflect variations in culture and past experiences. It leads to a design philosophy of 'creating and communicating the right message'" [14].

A program for office space can, based on the nature and needs of the proposed occupants, establish goals based on each of these categories, and post-occupancy evaluation can assess how successfully these goals are achieved. This form of analysis of interaction with the built environment reaches into the most subjective dimensions of our spatial responses, providing insight that cannot be collected by technological means.

An emotionally intelligent building responds to the multiple needs and aspirations of its users. Expanding the scope of the term "commissioning" to include fine-tuning these responses can help fulfill the promise of programming for health and wellbeing. A promise with the potential to yield a significant return on investment in the form of greater occupant satisfaction, productivity and wellbeing.

References

1. International Code Council. (2018). *International Green Construction Code*. https://www.ashrae.org/File%20Library/Technical%20Resources/Bookstore/2018-IgCC_preview_1102.pdf
2. Seabrook, J. (2021, Feb.). Office Space. *Annals of Architecture, New Yorker*. 43.
3. Ibid.
4. Pejtersen, J. H., Feveile, H., Christensen, K. B., and Burr, H. (2011). Sickness Absence Associated with Shared and Open-plan Offices–A National Cross Sectional Questionnaire Survey. *Scandinavian Journal of Work Environment and Health*. 37(5): 376–382.
5. Finch, E., and Aranda-Mena, G. (2019). *Creating Emotionally Intelligent Workspaces: A Design Guide to Office Chemistry*. New York: Routledge. 27.
6. Ibid. 28.
7. Herzberg, F. I. (1966). *Work and the Nature of Man*. Cleveland: World Pub. Co.
8. Finch, E., and Aranda-Mena, G. (2019). *Creating Emotionally Intelligent Workspaces: A Design Guide to Office Chemistry*. Routledge. 28, New York, NY.
9. Ibid. 31.
10. Urban Land Institute. (2021, Mar.). The Future of the Workplace [webinar].
11. Anthes, Emily. (2020). *The Great Indoors: The Surprising Science of How Buildings Shape Our Behavior, Health, and Happiness*. New York: Farrar, Straus and Giroux. 6.
12. Salovey, P., and Mayer, J. (1990). *Emotional Intelligence: Imagination, Cognition and Personality*. 189. doi:10.2190/DUGG-P24E-52WK-6CDG
13. Finch, E., and Aranda-Mena, G. (2019). *Creating Emotionally Intelligent Workspaces: A Design Guide to Office Chemistry*. Routledge. 47.
14. Ibid. 53–54.

17

LIFE-ENHANCING HABITATS

Biophilia, Patterns and Wholeness

Gregory Crawford

Earlier chapters have made the case that we are drawn to living things by a deep instinct of identification and emotional connection. Christopher Alexander has been a pioneer in this realm for half a century. This chapter serves as an introduction to Alexander's work and a plea for inclusion of his insights into both architecture curricula and the programming process.

How do the images above make you feel?
Do you find yourself more drawn to one, than to the other?
Could you say that you find more beauty, more life, in one of the two images?

Furthermore, would you believe that people tend to agree? Indeed, when Christopher Alexander asked his class of 110 students during a lecture at the University of California in 1992, 89 said that the "Bangkok slum house" had more life; 21 chose to say that the question didn't make sense to them, or that they couldn't or didn't want to make a choice; no one said that the octagonal tower has more life (Figure 17.1).

FIGURE 17.1 The Bangkok Slum House and the Postmodern Octagonal Tower, one of the imagery comparisons taught by Christopher Alexander. Image via Alexander, 2002.

DOI: 10.4324/9781003164418-23

"Put simply, we have a natural hunger for beauty—because we have a natural hunger for the deeper, biologically relevant characteristics of places and things that we find beautiful. This works through information input and our neurophysiological system, which developed to process and interpret information and to discern its relevant and often hidden meaning beneath the obvious" [1].

Searching for the Quality

For several hours each and every day, for 20 years, Christopher Alexander compared objects, investigating the nature of this quality he calls aliveness [2]. In the first of his four book series, *The Nature of Order*, Alexander continues this comparative juxtapositioning, showing two images side by side, inviting the reader to identify in which of the two they find more life; buildings (as shown above), suburban roads, house edges, automobiles, bedroom dressers, parking lots, office building lobbies, fences and yet more curious comparisons. As one empirical way to get past the overlay of preferences to an objective assessment of the quality of a carpet, Alexander proposes a peculiar method:

> "(…) We must construct a question which is so concrete that it shocks the system, and forces a more direct, more true, and more accurate response [3]. The question asks: "If you had to choose one of these two carpets, as a picture of your own self, then which one of the two carpets would you choose?" … In case you find it hard to ask the question, let me clarify by asking you to choose the one which seems better able to represent your whole being, the essence of yourself, good and bad, all that is human in you [4]."

So, the issue is less about which of the two images is better, and much more about identifying an essence which is rooted in human feeling. What's more, Alexander asserts that we will likely find ourselves in agreement as to which of the two compared objects has more life.

> "…the different degree of life we observe in every different part of space is not merely an artifact of our cognition but is an objectively real physical phenomenon in space which our cognition detects. I claim that this quality is not merely the basis for a distinction between beautiful things and ugly things. It is something which is detectable as a subtle distinction in every corner of the world, as we walk about, in the most ordinary places, during the most ordinary events. It is a quality which changes from place to place and from moment to moment, and which marks, in varying degrees, every moment, every event, every point in space [5]."

Personally speaking, I am at times unarguably drawn to one image, while at other times I find myself groping to articulate what it is I am seeing exactly, attempting to make sense of the images, parsing the overt and subtle differences. I would like to suggest that both occasions are of significant value. Design courses do not intend to educate one in aliveness, how to find it, interpret it, classify it, discuss it, nor how to determine on what aliveness hinges, what it owes its existence to, how it can come about; and thus, as a designer/builder, how one can imbue spaces with it. At most, we gather that beauty is in the eye of the beholder, and we move on, thinking everyone is correct, no matter their opinion. Alexander, however, posits an entirely different notion of what beauty and aliveness are and what roles they may play in our lives.

> "Let us first consider the breaking wave. When we see waves in the sea, we certainly *feel* that they have a kind of life. We feel their life as a real thing, they move us. Of course,

in the narrow mechanistic view of biology there is no life in the wave (except insofar as it has seaweed or plankton living in it). But it is undeniable—at least as far as our *feeling* is concerned—that such a moving, breaking wave feels as if it has more life as a system of water than an industrial pool stinking with chemicals [6]."

Aliveness, as a quality, occurs and is experienced in everything around us; so-called inert materials such as wood and marble have it and even paper and machines have it, buildings have it, carpets, public squares, paintings, cups, hats, benches, laundry baskets have it; nothing is exempt from having it [7–9].

"Although we may not be able to define it exactly, I suspect that many people will agree that they see something like life in all these examples. I do not expect that we shall have perfect agreement about the examples. Still, we probably have something close to agreement [10]."

That this quality is omnipresent to varying degrees, tells us two things: one, that we can consider this quality according to a spectrum, in other words more or less, respectively per object; and two, that it tends to be easiest to determine the degree of aliveness when comparing just two of a kind.

If you would like to experience this for yourself, the team at Building Beauty has curated a comparative series online (Mirror of Self). Their results are consistent with Alexander's: the quality of beauty and aliveness are, generally speaking of course, objective. Now, if this is true, just what does it spell for the discipline of architecture; as such notions have been relegated to the domain of personal preference and taste, incomprehensible to scientific inquiry, and thus spurious at best, inconsequential at worst. "The possibility that the degree of life of different things and places and events is *objective*—not solely in the individual—implies that this 'felt' life has some part in the scheme of things that is truly enormous. If so, the existence of this felt life—existing as it must to some degree in every single thing there is—would be a discovery, an awakening, at an extraordinary level, perhaps comparable to the 16th-century discovery of the fact that the earth moves round the sun, or the 19th-century discovery of the electromagnetic nature of light" [11].

Christopher Alexander happens to be one of the few major figures in architecture who believes that front-loading human feeling is essential for both the profession at large and the impacts our built environment inflicts on society. A modern-day polymath and author of 20 books (with one in process), Alexander has paved an approach toward a life-enhancing design methodology. The 1982 debate with Peter Eisenman—considered by some as "perhaps one of the most aggressive public exchanges in the history of design" [12]—illustrates Alexander's position on architecture very clearly. What follows is a short excerpt:

EISENMAN: "I guess what I am saying is that I believe that there is an alternate cosmology to the one which you suggest. The cosmology of the last 300 years has changed (...) Precisely because I believe that the old cosmology is no longer an effective basis on which to build, I begin to want to invert your conditions—to search for their negative—to say that for every positive condition you suggest, if you could propose a negative you might more closely approximate the cosmology of today."
ALEXANDER: "The thing that strikes me about your friend's building [the town hall at Logrono by Rafael Moneo]—if I understood you correctly—is that somehow in some intentional way it is not harmonious. That is, Moneo intentionally wants to produce an effect of disharmony. Maybe even of incongruity."
EISENMAN: "That is correct."

ALEXANDER: "I find that incomprehensible. I find it very irresponsible. I find it nutty. I feel sorry for the man."

EISENMAN: "If we make people so comfortable in these nice little structures, we might lull them into thinking that everything's all right, Jack, which it isn't."

ALEXANDER: "If you were an unimportant person, I would feel quite comfortable letting you go your own way. But the fact is that people who believe as you do are really fucking up the whole profession of architecture right now by propagating these beliefs. Excuse me, I'm sorry, but I feel very, very strongly about this… But the fact is that architects are entrusted with the creation of that harmony in the world."

That architecture exerts unparalleled influence over our lives—shaping environments, experiences and mentalities alike—is central to the above debate; the built environment and human psychology are inextricably linked. In other words, architecture is as much—if not more so—about the human experience than it is about built space. The question thus becomes, what kinds of environments do we need, what kinds of experiences and mental states do we deserve? Eisenman proclaims we need jarring, disturbing environments which induce feelings of instability and awkwardness… because… life is not alright? But by prizing such abominations are we not simply promoting them? Architecture is certain to deliver and what is delivered is largely determined in the planning and programming phase of design. A great virtue of Alexander's approach is rooted in the human events and activities which represent who we truly are; built spaces which facilitate the multiplicity of human beings living their lives, as profoundly and intricately and accurately as possible.

As John Ruskin once put it: "Forms which are not taken from natural objects must be ugly" [13]. Or, as William Morris observed:

> "Everything made by man's hands has a form, which must be either beautiful or ugly; beautiful if it is in accord with Nature, and helps her; ugly if it is discordant with Nature, and thwarts her; it cannot be indifferent [14]."

Our path toward modernity has come with many, many trade-offs.

> "We believe, and have explained in *The Timeless Way of Building*, that the languages which people have today are so brutal, and so fragmented, that most people no longer have any language to speak of at all—and what they do have is not based on human, or natural considerations [15]."

It wasn't long ago at all, that people the world over knew their environments intimately, knew the proportions for their barns and living rooms, the materials they coexisted with, the personalities of the seasons. Alexander's life's work has been to reawaken the intimate relations of people in place, a fluency largely lost across the entire planet. Yes, we have vernacular architecture—a "style" resulting from a dynamic response process, as people adapted and refined their built environments in-situ. But why isn't this building process the norm? Why has vernacular architecture become so marginalized from modern building styles? And why does it appear to be so fanciful and dated?

> "Around the turn of the 20th Century a handful of designers and architects turned vehemently against living structure and visual manifestations of life itself. Any geometrical expression of living form and its accompanying complexity were condemned to extinction [16]."

Eisenman was actually defending spaces which cause dis-ease, an off-balancedness due to spatial incongruity. He furthermore argued that such environments constitute a relevant and correct design modality because it is a direct reflection of society, an ode to our problems, our feelings of anxiety and hopelessness; which, not so incidentally, are often experienced when confronting many contemporary structures. Eisenman argues that the dark aspects of our civilization ought to be acknowledged, perhaps even paid tribute to. But do we even understand the light aspects, the beautiful, life-enhancing way of building?

Having studied Alexander extensively and having interacted with his methodology personally and professionally, I am convinced that aliveness plays a vital role in framing one's quality of life, of cultivating a sensation of harmony, depth, health and wellbeing.

> "Design, in order to be truthful and useful to humanity, needs to accommodate both our anatomy and our neuro-physiological system. Uncomfortable utensils, furniture, and living spaces deny the former; whereas abstract, incoherent, ornament-shorn buildings and urban spaces deny the latter. Biological nature craves richly ordered structural information in our immediate environment, just as much as our neural system needs natural materials, patterns, and textures [17]."

Now then, suppose that we do in fact tend to agree about what is more or less alive; should we not prioritize aliveness in the design of our homes and urban spaces? Ought the designers and architects who create our built environments have a responsibility, a calling, to bring about this quality in our world? Safety notwithstanding, what other goal could possibly matter more? And lastly, how might we achieve this lofty target?

Patterns and *A Pattern Language*

A Pattern Language (1997) is often considered Alexander's seminal work. The book neatly deconstructs the broader built environment into constituents, called patterns, which interact and inter-operate.

> "Each pattern describes a problem which occurs over and over again in our environment, and then describes the core of the solution to that problem, in such a way that you can use this solution a million times over, without ever doing it the same way twice [18]."

Each and every pattern summarily describes what it is that makes a given element/feature/system *work*. However, a pattern is not a formula, it does not dictate what, exactly, must be done in order to meet a given need; a pattern describes an essence within a field of relationships. In this way, each application of a given pattern will look slightly different according to its context and particularities, leaving room for variety, nuance and personal touch.

Let's take the pattern SMALL PUBLIC SQUARES [19] as an example. The problem which SMALL PUBLIC SQUARES resolves is as follows: "A town needs public squares; they are the largest, most public rooms, that the town has. But when they are too large, they look and feel deserted" [20]. Thus, the instruction to realize this solution is:

> "Make a public square much smaller than you would at first imagine; usually no more than 45 to 60 feet across, never more than 70 feet across. This applies only to its width in the short direction. In the long direction it can certainly be longer [21]."

Life-Enhancing Habitats   227

61 SMALL PUBLIC SQUARES**

FIGURE 17.2 The Small Public Square gives life to a city when executed in proper proportion. Image via Alexander, 2002.

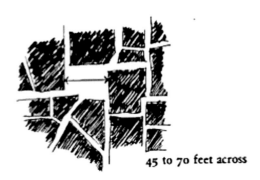

FIGURE 17.3 An aerial imagination of the ideal Small Public Square. Images via Alexander, 2002.

This pattern is a great example of spatial relativity. The size of a successful SMALL PUBLIC SQUARE rests on its dimensionality relative to the size of an average human being, the number of human beings who feel comfortable populating a particular framed space, the amount of distance individuals and groups require in order to feel both intimacy and safety, and the minimum dimensions the space needs in order to provide a sense of welcome, even while unpopulated.

In addition to the problem and solution statements, each pattern within *A Pattern Language* includes a visual aid in the form of a photograph (Figure 17.2) and another in the form of a sketch (Figure 17.3), a text of rationale as to why the pattern exists and lastly the ways in which this particular pattern tessellates with other patterns. An excerpt of rationale for SMALL PUBLIC SQUARES:

> "It is natural that every public street will swell out at those important nodes where there is the most activity. And it is only these widened, swollen, public squares which can accommodate the public gatherings, small crowds, festivities, bonfires, carnivals, speeches, dancing, shouting, mourning, which must have their place in the life of the town. But for some reason there is a temptation to make these public squares too large. On this basis a square with a diameter of 100 feet will begin to seem deserted if there are less than 33 people in it. There are few places in a city where you can be sure there will always be 33 people. On the other hand, it only takes 4 people to give life to a square with a diameter of 35 feet, and only 12 to give life to a square with a diameter of 60 feet. Since there are far far better chances of 4 or 12 people being in a certain place than 33, the smaller squares will feel comfortable for a far greater percentage of the time [22]."

And the final piece of information—the connection to other patterns—underpins one of the major virtues of the pattern methodology: no pattern exists in isolation.

Successful architecture is less about building spaces and so much more about building better relationships. Thus, a collection of patterns is assembled to form a language.

> "Each pattern can exist in the world, only to the extent that it is supported by other patterns: the larger patterns in which it is embedded, the patterns of the same size that surround it, and the smaller patterns which are embedded in it. This is a fundamental view of the world. It says that when you build a thing you cannot merely build that thing in isolation, but must also repair the world around it, and within it, so that the larger world at that one place becomes more coherent, and more whole; and the thing which you make takes its place in the web of nature, as you make it [23]."

In order to realize the pattern SMALL PUBLIC SQUARES, such a square would benefit from stemming off of a PROMENADE [24], a WORK COMMUNITY [25] and/or an IDENTIFIABLE NEIGHBORHOOD [26]. Likewise, ACTIVITY POCKETS [27] are able to form around the public square, strengthening it where people congregate, and reinforced shape can be achieved by associating POSITIVE OUTDOOR SPACE [28], HIERARCHY OF OPEN SPACE [29], BUILDING FRONTS [30], STAIR SEATS [31].

In total, *A Pattern Language* describes 253 distinct patterns; beginning with INDEPENDENT REGIONS [32] and ending with THINGS FROM YOUR LIFE [33], the 253 patterns includes such things as MOSAIC OF SUBCULTURES [34], NEIGHBORHOOD BOUNDARY [35], DEGREES OF PUBLICNESS [36], NECKLACE OF COMMUNITY PROJECTS [37], HIGH PLACES [38], TEENAGE SOCIETY [39], POSITIVE OUTDOOR SPACE [40], PEDESTRIAN DENSITY [41], A PLACE TO WAIT [42], SUNNY PLACE [43] and FILTERED LIGHT [44].

Any pattern language can provide a designer with a rolodex of maneuverable patterns to deploy within a given project. The selection chosen constitutes the "project language'" and can be used as a brainstorming and placement discussion platform. In this way, an architect or designer who is in service to a community can provoke the generation of patterns directly from the users and she can distill the design concept to begin to communicate in a common language.

Numerous pattern languages have since been created, in one way or another based on Alexander's original. As well, certain vocabulary, namely "Pattern" thinking has also gained traction among various design circles. Due to this larger broadcasting, the word has been adapted to fit many different contexts. While on one hand such adaptive diffusion is consistent with pattern thinking, on the other hand I find there to be a few misunderstandings. The most common misunderstanding I regularly encounter has to do with the disregard to the spatial predicate of a pattern. A pattern *exists in space*, and thus it must have a placement relative to other patterns. In other words, if you cannot sketch it, it's probably not a pattern.

My design team—Locus—has created a pattern language for regenerative settlement design, with a specific focus on application for temporary settlements, including refugee camps and informal settlements. We presented our work and authored papers for the 2017 Pursuit of Pattern Languages for Societal Change (PURPLSOC) conference, as well as the 2018 Portland Urban Architecture Research Lab (PUARL) conference. Our pattern language is one tool among four which together create a toolkit for regenerative design. The following images are of the front (Figure 17.4) and back (Figure 17.5) of one of our patterns, COMMUNITY UNITS.

COMMUNITY UNITS addresses scaling in a temporary settlement, with regard to both personal and group identity as well as service modalities. An individual is a resident of his city/settlement while simultaneously being a community member of his block/SHELTER CLUSTER; individuals will interface according to the pertinent scale among the COMMUNITY UNITS available to them. For example, consider the fact that every one of us is a global citizen while also a member of our distinct locality (house, village, town, city, bioregion); identities, responsibilities, and outlooks vary greatly across the scale. Accordingly, services including health services must be suitably sized according to the COMMUNITY UNIT it is attempting to serve. For example, SERVICE CENTERS are organized according to COMMUNITY UNITS: one would go to a neighborhood clinic for a routine check-up while a relatively more equipped and robust regional hospital will be frequented for more severe ailments.

One reason why pattern languages are often adapted to fit different contexts has to do with their innate flexibility to shift and adjust in order to accommodate new information and observations. This distinction is critical, as it underscores pattern theory as natively dynamic, rather than static. Living systems are able to flex, to evolve. Such a characteristic reflects the nature of the methodology: responsiveness. I argue that this dynamism is a prerequisite for a sense of user-agency to take hold; "person in place"' is a two-directional information flow. One must

FIGURE 17.4 Community Units: considering scale in settlement. Image via Locus Design Collective.

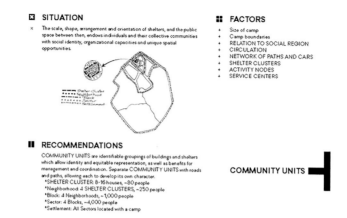

FIGURE 17.5 The shaping of our communities affects our ability to participate within them. Image via Locus Design Collective.

both be able to, but also feel personally invested in, modifying one's environment to suit their needs. I consider agency to be a critical ingredient toward successfully realizing wellbeing and expressivity through spatial personalization. It's difficult to imagine a more top-down system than that which produces the contemporary buildings that dominate today's landscape. Such uni-directional decision-making arrangements, vesting an elite group with the power of design, are extremely likely to result in spaces which are "used"—rendering the built environments mere commodities, and the users mere consumers.

If contemporary architecture represents the extreme end of directional decision-making, I suggest that tactical urbanism represents the other end of the spectrum. Tactical urbanism, also known as DIY urbanism, is a community-driven process which enables the sidestepping of bureaucratic red tape to take matters into the users' hands. Tactical urbanism, based on low-risk/high-reward design, disables involvement-inertia through temporary, low-cost installations where success is easily expanded upon. Citizens engaging in tactical urbanism might paint crosswalks and set cones at dangerous intersections (often at night), set chairs (or swimming pools) in parking spaces and plants at curbs, or reclaim ignored and underused areas including curb expansions. DIY urbanism can only occur when the inhabitants themselves are interacting with their built spaces in a continual modification to further improve their quality of life. Pattern languages offer tremendous value to such a process, due to their innate dynamism.

One way Alexander has instilled this dynamism is by considering each of the 253 patterns within *A Pattern Language* to be a hypothesis.

> "In this sense, each pattern represents our current best guess as to what arrangement of the physical environment will work to solve the problem presented. The empirical questions center on the problem—does it occur and is it felt in the way we have described it?—and the solution—does the arrangement we propose in fact resolve the problem? [The patterns] are therefore all tentative, all free to evolve under the impact of new experience and observation [45]."

We can read another nod to natural systems in these lines. *A Pattern Language* has been pre-wired to promote adaptation, not solely on a minutiae detail level, but in its entirety.

> "And yet, many of the patterns here [in *A Pattern Language*] are archetypal—so deep, so consideration deeply rooted in the nature of things, that it seems likely that they will be a part of human nature, and human action, as much in five hundred years, as they are today [46]."

Such an adaptable framework requires a great degree of humble confidence on the part of its authors, a stance towards one's work which acknowledges the degree of difficulty, and that such great feats are only accomplished with determination, time and varying points of view. In this respect, the pattern methodology has come quite close to emulating a true natural system, one which is innately predisposed toward a generative unfolding.

I hope I have conveyed some as to why we ought to consider human feeling—as a primary and multivalent driver in the designing of our built environments; and that there is a quality, present in all things, which can be called aliveness, that plays an active role in shaping our perceptions of our surroundings. If a given pattern represents a single resolved occurrence, a step toward harmony, then: what makes a pattern tick, to what does a pattern owe its relevance to? Part of the solution to this has to do with scale, and the way in which patterns relate to and enhance one another. With luck, we will step closer toward understanding this quality, which serves as the secret ingredient for evoking an increasingly elusive triumph of architecture: wellbeing, the invaluable and indispensable vibrancy when people and place chime in harmony.

Wholeness and Centers

If you would, please humor me by closing your eyes and allowing a place from your memory, a special place, a place that has a distinct personality, to come to mind…perhaps you've recalled a vibrant forest where the moss hung above a stream, a certain spot in Venice, a closet where you would paint in candlelight when you were young. Whichever place you have recalled, it will be unlike any other place in the entire world. This special place of yours is a great way to frame Alexander's notions of wholeness and centers; in large part this is because the image you've recalled is personal and thus you *feel* the wholeness. To feel the wholeness first-hand is inestimably more meaningful than any didactic lesson.

> "To start the discussion, I am going to describe a particular place which I like very much. In this example, we shall see that the wholeness in a part of space gets more life, or less life, according to the way the centers help each other. When centers help each other the wholeness has more life while when the centers are not helping each other the wholeness has less life [47]."

Alexander continues by recounting a time he spent with his family in Ravello, Italy: a small hotel's garden terrace, graced with a sea view. He goes on to name the various centers which formed the wholeness of the terrace. Now, his list could easily be interpreted to enumerate entities at various scales, often recognized as a list of elements, or perhaps of parts—things/items in space—yet Alexander chooses to use the word center. The previous example of the vibrant forest is itself a wholeness, a result of its centers, the moss and the stream; the certain spot in Venice has a wholeness so strong and distinct that the centers are likely to assert themselves in your mind without me even needing to name them; the closet's unique wholeness comes about by the candle (in the otherwise dark). Now, imagine the forest but this time without its moss and its stream; and the closet, but without the candle.

Part of the reason that "center" is a more accurate word is when a thing is set in space, its presence exerts a number of forces upon the space in which it has been set. And centers can be stacked, but in a very much more dimensional way than elements can be stacked. In this way, centers are able to help one another through mutual intensification; much the same way a symphony is composed of many singular instruments, a great space comes about by being more than the sum of its parts. And now, imagine the forest with birdsong, dappled light, a footbridge above the stream, the breeze-ruffled leaves; each additional center enhances the others, resulting in an even stronger whole. We only need to ask ourselves: "Does the inclusion of a given center help other centers, does it help the whole?" Alexander's garden terrace benefits tremendously by the columns which reinforce the divide between in and out, while their height, spacing, thickness and ornamentation all, in turn, further strengthen the columns. The result is an assembly, which is more commonly known as a system. And as with centers, the definition of a whole speaks toward a nest-ability, a cohesion toward harmony, whereas a system is more mechanical, much more a group of parts. In Alexander's garden terrace, the grapes help the view and the grapes help the tables; might the view help the grapes, in turn?

Incidentally, a whole can also be a center, and likewise a center can also be a whole; it is simply a matter of scale. For example, let us say there is a picnic table in a grove in our forest; the picnic table is a center within the grove, yet when we spread our picnic out upon it, the table becomes a whole. Space can be "thickened" with centers, with cohering assemblies of patterns, all in response to one another. With this approach, we can think in terms of density, stacking, nesting centers and further nesting centers.

What if our cities were planned and built in this way, what might they look like? If our built environments are, on a level, reflections of the human condition, then perhaps aliveness might begin to take shape once more, both within and outside of ourselves.

References

1. Mehaffy, M., & Salingaros, N. A. (2012). *Science for Designers: Intelligence and the Information Environment*. https://www.metropolismag.com/uncategorized/science-for-designers-intelligence-and-the-information-environment/.
2. Alexander, C. (2002). *Nature of Order; Book One: The Phenomenon of Life*. Center for Environmental Structure.
3. Alexander, C. (1993). *A Foreshadowing of 21st Century Art: The Color and Geometry of Very Early Turkish Carpets*. Oxford University Press. 28.
4. Ibid. 29.
5. Alexander, C. (2002). *Nature of Order; Book One: The Phenomenon of Life*. Center for Environmental Structure. 65.
6. Ibid. 32.
7. Alexander, C. (2002). *Nature of Order; Book One: The Phenomenon of Life*. Center for Environmental Structure.
8. Alexander, C. (1993). *A Foreshadowing of 21st Century Art: The Color and Geometry of Very Early Turkish Carpets*. Oxford University Press.
9. Alexander, C., Ishikawa, S., Silverstein, M., Jacobson, M., Fiksdahl-King, I., & Angel, S. (1997). *A Pattern Language*. Oxford University Press.
10. Alexander, C. (2002). *Nature of Order; Book One: The Phenomenon of Life*. Center for Environmental Structure.
11. Ibid. 77.
12. Rennix, B., & Robinson, N. J. (2017). Why You Hate Contemporary Architecture. https://www.currentaffairs.org/2017/10/why-you-hate-contemporary-architecture.
13. Ruskin, J. (1849). *The Seven Lamps of Architecture*. Smith, Elder & Co.
14. Morris, W. (1882). 'The Lesser Arts', in *Hopes and Fears for Art*. Ellis & White; originally a lecture titled 'The Decorate Arts: Their Relation to Modern Life and Progress', given in 1877.

15. Alexander, C., Ishikawa, S., Silverstein, M., Jacobson, M., Fiksdahl-King, I., & Angel, S. (1997). *A Pattern Language*. Oxford University Press. xvi.
16. Mehaffy, M., & Salingaros, N. A. (2012). *Science for Designers: Intelligence and the Information Environment*. https://www.metropolismag.com/uncategorized/science-for-designers-intelligence-and-the-information-environment/.
17. Ibid.
18. Alexander, C., Ishikawa, S., Silverstein, M., Jacobson, M., Fiksdahl-King, I., & Angel, S. (1997). *A Pattern Language*. Oxford University Press.
19. Ibid. 61.
20. Ibid.
21. Ibid.
22. Ibid. 312.
23. Ibid. xiii.
24. Ibid. 31.
25. Ibid. 41.
26. Ibid. 14.
27. Ibid. 124.
28. Ibid. 106.
29. Ibid. 114.
30. Ibid. 122.
31. Ibid. 125.
32. Ibid. 1.
33. Ibid. 253.
34. Ibid. 8.
35. Ibid. 15.
36. Ibid. 36.
37. Ibid. 45.
38. Ibid. 62.
39. Ibid. 84.
40. Ibid. 106.
41. Ibid. 123.
42. Ibid. 150.
43. Ibid. 161.
44. Ibid. 238.
45. Ibid. XV.
46. Ibid.
47. Alexander, C. (2002). *Nature of Order; Book One: The Phenomenon of Life*. Center for Environmental Structure.

18

EPIDEMIOLOGIC METHODS FOR EVALUATING ARCHITECTURAL DESIGN

C. Robert Horsburgh, Jr., MD, MUS

Evaluating the success of a design program involves definition of design objectives, a pre-specified methodology for evaluating the outcomes achieved and comparison with a control design. Naturally occurring conditions may provide control designs, or they may be part of the design process, for example in a redesign where before and after comparisons can be made. This chapter outlines some of the principles for implementing design evaluation using statistical principles and gives examples of the outcomes of such evaluations.

Epidemiology is the study of relationships between exposures and outcomes. It is widely used in medicine and public health to evaluate associations between clinical and behavioral characteristics and the occurrence of disease, but epidemiologic methods are applicable in evaluating relationships between many non-medical exposures and outcomes. In the design field, epidemiologic methods can be used to assess relationships between characteristics of the built environment and effects on users. The most common user effect outcomes studied are psychological states, such as stress and patient satisfaction, but health outcomes such as falls, aggressive incidents, wayfinding and post-surgical healing have also been studied.

Epidemiologic analysis begins with a hypothesis, for example, "exposure x is associated with outcome y." Hypotheses about building design can be generated by prior observation, theoretical frameworks or explicit design intent. Once a hypothetical association has been formulated, it can be tested using epidemiologic methods. Such testing involves several steps:

First, clear definitions of the exposure and outcome must be formulated. This is important because others must be able to attempt to replicate the analyses, since reproducibility is one of the hallmarks of reliable analysis. Building characteristics are often hard to classify, but substantial progress has been made in this area over the past decade, as the examples in this chapter will demonstrate. Second, sites where data are to be collected must be identified. Usually, these sites are selected based on the presence or absence of the specific characteristics of the built environment that are the object of study. However, it is also important to select sites with and without the characteristic of interest that are as similar as possible in other respects to reduce the need to control for *confounding* (see below). Third, data on users of the environment are collected with regard to the outcome of interest. It is important that the users whose data are collected are not aware of the hypothesis being tested, as otherwise the data collected may contain *bias*. Lastly,

DOI: 10.4324/9781003164418-24

the relationship between the exposure and the outcome are tested using statistical methods. These methods can indicate how likely it is that the relationship between the exposure and the outcome occurred by chance; if this is highly unlikely, then we conclude that they are associated due to some underlying relatedness. Epidemiologic studies cannot establish causality, but they can be used to build a case for a causal relationship.

A cardinal characteristic of epidemiologic analysis is comparison between exposed and unexposed groups, called *controls*. It is simply not possible to conclude that an association exists between an exposure and an outcome without studying both exposed and unexposed groups. Similarly, it is required that some study participants have the outcome of interest while others do not; if everyone has the outcome, including the control group, there can be no association between exposure and the outcome.

Bias is defined as "a systematic error in the design or conduct of a study that leads to an erroneous association between an exposure and an outcome" [1]. Bias can be introduced when selecting study sites or participants and when collecting information. Bias in collecting information is common and can occur when using study data collection instruments that have not been validated, when interviewers are not well trained (to avoid asking leading questions) and when respondents are aware of the study hypothesis and may give the answers that they believe the investigators want to hear.

Confounding is defined as "the mixing of effects between the exposure, the outcome, and a third variable that is termed the confounder... that distorts the association between the exposure and the outcome" [2]. There are several ways to control for confounding; the most important is to identify potential confounders and collect information about them, so that control can take place in the data analysis phase. Likely confounders are other exposures that are associated with the exposure of interest and other exposures that are associated with the outcome of interest. In the case of a prospective interventional study, participants may be randomized to exposures, which can theoretically control for confounders even if these are not measured.

Statistical methods are used to control for random error, which is the probability that the association between the exposure and the outcome occurred by chance. Once the frequency of exposures and outcomes are known, it is possible to calculate the probability of this association occurring by chance. By convention, a probability of 5 percent (1 in 20) or less is defined as being "statistically significant," although it is readily apparent that such a finding may occur once by chance if a study is performed 20 times. The measure of this probability is the "P value"; a P value of 0.05 is equivalent to a 5 percent probability that the association occurred by chance. Thus, while an association with a P value of 0.01 has only a 1 percent probability of having occurred by chance (even less likely than P=0.05), a chance occurrence is not completely ruled out.

Strength of association is another computed measure that is used to define the strength of associations between exposures and outcomes. Two measures are commonly used, the *Odds Ratio* and the *Risk Ratio*. These measures are similar, and both quantify the association in terms or a number (and a confidence interval). For example, a Risk Ratio of 2.5 indicates that the outcome of interest in the exposed group is 2.5 times more likely than in the unexposed group. A Risk Ratio of 1.0 indicates that the outcome of interest in the exposed group is no more likely than in the unexposed group.

As noted above, *Causality* cannot be definitively established in an epidemiologic study, but it can be inferred. The strength of the inference depends on a number of factors, most clearly set out by Sir Bradford Hill and referred to as "Hill's Criteria" [3]:

- strength of association (a higher odds or risk ratio is more likely to be causal),
- consistency (a causal finding should be able to be replicated by other investigators at other places and times),

- specificity (a single cause should lead to a single effect),
- temporality (the exposure should occur before the outcome),
- biological gradient (if there are several levels of exposure, a higher level should lead to more outcomes),
- plausibility (there should be a biological or social model to explain the causality),
- coherence (a causal interpretation of an association should not conflict with known facts),
- experiment (if tested by prospective experiment, the hypothesis is confirmed), and
- analogy (that the causal association is similar to other causal explanations).

In the following section five examples of application of epidemiologic principles to elucidating the effects of design features are presented. These five represent the best of the growing field of critical evaluation of outcomes of the design process.

View through a Window May Influence Recovery from Surgery

In this study [4], the investigator hypothesized that patients who were recovering from surgery would have a faster or more pleasant experience if the view from their hospital room looked out on a park. He found a hospital wing where half of the post-surgery rooms had a park view and half had a view of the brick wall of a facing building. He limited his study to examining women who were recovering from gallbladder surgery, an operation that is usually uncomplicated. He extracted all data from hospital records, so the data were all collected before he developed his hypothesis.

> Exposure: Room with view of park or room with view of brick wall
> Outcomes: Nurse assessment of patient attitude, amount of pain medication required, number of days spent in the hospital
> Site floor plan is shown in Figure 18.1.

Results were as follows:
  In addition, patients with window views of the trees spent less time in the hospital than those with views of the brick wall: 7.96 days compared with 8.70 days per patient ($P = 0.025$) (Figure 18.2).

The Relationship between Daylighting and School Performance

This study [5] was the result of a comprehensive evaluation of daylight in California Grade School classrooms in 1997 and 1998. The hypothesis was that the amount of daylight in classrooms would be associated with the performance of elementary school students on standardized tests.

> Exposure: Daylight in classrooms. The presence and size of windows and skylights in the classrooms, the size and tint of the windows and skylights, and the overall amount of daylight provided were assessed in each classroom. This provided a continuous exposure scale.
> Outcome: Improvement in standardized test scores over the course of the school year for students in classrooms with daylight assessment.
> Methods: Daylight score was assessed as a predictor of improvement in standardized test scores over one school year. Multivariate linear regression analysis was used to control for other influences on student performance.

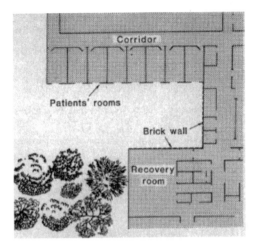

FIGURE 18.1 Floor plan from the widely-referenced Robert S. Ulrich study. Printed with permission of AAAS.

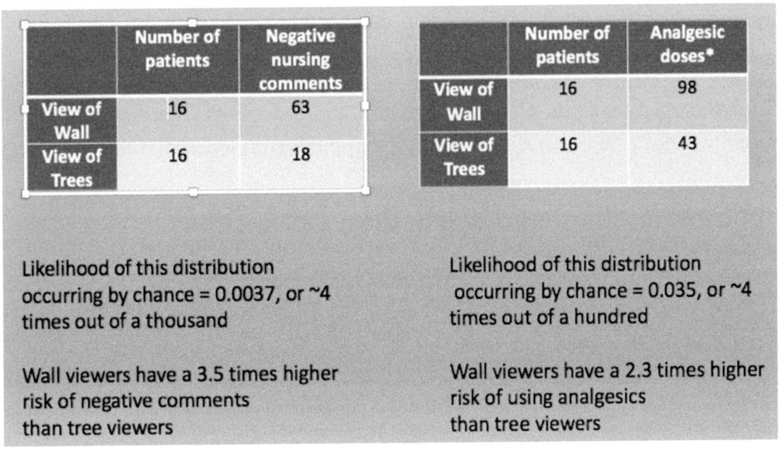

	Number of patients	Negative nursing comments
View of Wall	16	63
View of Trees	16	18

	Number of patients	Analgesic doses*
View of Wall	16	98
View of Trees	16	43

Likelihood of this distribution occurring by chance = 0.0037, or ~4 times out of a thousand

Likelihood of this distribution occurring by chance = 0.035, or ~4 times out of a hundred

Wall viewers have a 3.5 times higher risk of negative comments than tree viewers

Wall viewers have a 2.3 times higher risk of using analgesics than tree viewers

FIGURE 18.2 Those without tree views are more likely to give negative comments, as well as use more pain medication. Image courtesy of Robert Horsburgh.

Results: The findings demonstrated a 2.8 point improvement (26 percent) in reading test scores and a 2.3 point improvement (20 percent) in math test scores over the school year. Both comparisons were significant at P=0.001. The study controlled for other potential predictors of test performance, and the findings were subsequently replicated in two other schools.

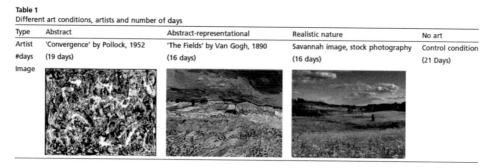

Table 1 Different art conditions, artists and number of days

Type	Abstract	Abstract-representational	Realistic nature	No art
Artist	'Convergence' by Pollock, 1952	'The Fields' by Van Gogh, 1890	Savannah image, stock photography	Control condition
#days	(19 days)	(16 days)	(16 days)	(21 Days)
Image				

FIGURE 18.3 The type of art on display impacts patient requests for anti-anxiety medication. Printed with permission of John Wiley and Sons.

Effect of Visual Art on Patient Anxiety and Agitation

This study [6] involved a prospective evaluation of the association between different kinds of art on the wall and the mental state of patients in an outpatient psychiatric waiting room. One of the three pictures shown below or no art was displayed on a rotating basis in the waiting room. Patients were allowed to request anti-anxiety medication and these requests were abstracted from hospital records.

>Exposures: Realistic nature image art, abstract-representational art, abstract art or no art
>Outcome: Medication requests by waiting patients

Results (expressed as the proportion of patients given anti-anxiety medications):

>Realistic nature image vs. no art: 13 percent vs. 32 percent (P=0.032)
>Abstract-representational image vs. no art, 24 percent vs. 32 percent (P>0.05)
>Abstract image vs. no art, 25 percent vs. 32 percent (P>0.05)

This study and the study on the effect of daylight in classrooms demonstrate the importance of natural surroundings and natural light on human performance and wellbeing (Figure 18.3).

Legibility of Interior Space and Wayfinding Satisfaction

In this study [7], the authors used a validated tool for assessing the legibility of floor plans and applied it to nine different nursing homes in the Hong Kong area. This tool, Space Syntax, provides an "Integration value" for each nursing home; a higher value means that the space occupied by the respondent is more integrated into the spatial system of the nursing home than a lower value; this, a higher score indicates complex layout, while a lower score indicates a simpler layout. They then conducted a survey in which a questionnaire was administered to the residents of these nursing homes. Residents were asked to rate their health status and also to rate their satisfaction with the wayfinding ease of their facility on a scale of "very satisfied" (+3) to "very dissatisfied" (−3).

>Exposure: Integration value of resident's room
>Outcome: Satisfaction with wayfinding
>Results: Both the exposure and the outcome were continuous, so a correlation coefficient was used to assess the relationship between exposure and outcome. The finding was that

the lower the integration value (i.e., the less complex the layout), the higher the resident satisfaction ($R^2=-0.71$, $P<0.001$). There was no relationship between resident health status and integration value.

The Location of Behavioral Incidents in a Children's Psychiatric Facility

This study [8] is a more complex design in which a condition is studied in an existing facility and then re-studied in a new facility of a different design. It has the advantage of the same staff and patient population and thus avoids the need to control for such differences. However, it is essential to allow a waiting period in the new facility, as there is a well-recognized honeymoon effect of moving into a new building. In this example, a definition of "negative incidents" including aggressive behavior, rape, suicide attempt, theft, injury, property damage, fire and intoxication was developed and applied to the old and the new facility. The majority of such events in the older facility occurred in the living rooms, so the new facility was designed with continuous staff supervision of the common rooms. The layout of the two facilities is shown in Figure 18.4:
The hypothesis was that the number of negative incidents would be decreased in the new facility.

> Exposure: new facility versus old
> Outcome: negative incidents
> Results: The number of such incidents per year did not change (157 per year in the old facility, 156 per year in the new facility), but the location did; in the old facility 42.4 percent of the incidents took place in the public spaces (hallways, day-rooms and entry), whereas in the new facility only 31.2 percent were in these spaces ($P=0.01$). However, this improvement was balanced by an increase in incidents in bedrooms, from less than 2 percent to 18 percent ($P<0.001$). Thus, the hypothesis was not confirmed, although the design change had the desired effect of reducing incidents in public spaces.

The study also documented the honeymoon effect: during the first six months of occupation, the number of incidents in the new facility was approximately 54 percent of the quantity that took place during the preceding year in the old facility; however, this number rose for the second six months.

Conclusions and Future Directions

These five examples show how careful selection of study sites and clearly defined study questions can be used to establish associations between design features and the experience of users. None of the studies is definitive, and all would benefit from additional studies to confirm or refute the findings in different situations and with different populations. In this way, it would be possible to come to some conclusions about how generalizable these findings are to the design process overall. Nonetheless, they represent an important first step in establishing a reproducible database of associations between exposure to design features and user outcomes.

As the results of study 5 show, negative findings can also be very informative; while the design change did not achieve the expected reduction in number of incidents, it did result in changing their location. This knowledge can inform future attempts to reduce negative incidents through design.

A critical feature of such studies is careful focus on specific design features and clear definition of expected outcomes. In reviewing the literature for this chapter, I found many studies that failed to produce useful results because they looked at outcomes that were too broad or too

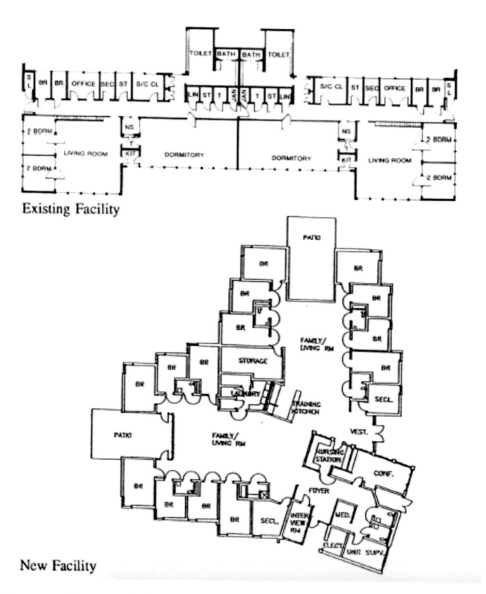

FIGURE 18.4 Changes to building layout affect negative incidents. Printed with permission of Springer.

loosely defined. Thus, while each individual result is only a very small step forward, when taken together, they can generate a powerful new scientific basis for design.

Another important feature of these studies is the inclusion of a control exposure. Post-Occupancy Evaluation (POE) is an essential activity for generation of hypotheses about design features. However, in the classic Post-Occupancy Evaluation a building is evaluated only with regard to whether it achieved its objectives, without attempting to determine whether its ability to do so was related to the specific design features. Having a control design that differs with regard to the feature in question and is evaluated for the same outcome allows the investigator to draw more definitive conclusions about whether the outcome was influenced by the design feature, and thus might be causal. In this respect, well-designed epidemiologic studies provide a major advance over Post-Occupancy Evaluations.

Developing a knowledge base of the effects of specific design features on user experience must become an essential part of architectural research. In most fields such research is largely undertaken by academic researchers, and the growing number of design research publications appears to indicate that a core of such researchers is beginning to develop at schools of architecture. Wider application of rigorous epidemiologic methods in such studies can be expected to improve the quality of results and accelerate progress in this area.

References

1. Aschengrau, A., Seage, G.R. (2018). *Epidemiology in Public Health, fourth edition.* Burlington, MA: Jones & Bartlett Learning.
2. Ibid.
3. Hill, A.B. (1965). The environment and disease: Association or causation? *Proceedings of the Royal Society of Medicine.* 48:295–300.
4. Ulrich, R.S. (1984). View through a window may influence recovery from surgery. *Science.* 224:420–421.
5. California Board for Energy Efficiency. (1999). Report. https://www.pge.com/includes/docs/pdfs/shared/edusafety/training/pec/daylight/SchoolsCondensed820.pdf
6. Nanda, U., Eisen, S., Zadeh, R.S., Owen, D. (2011). Effect of visual art on patient anxiety and agitation in a mental health facility and implications for the business case. *Journal of Psychiatric and Mental Health Nursing.* 18:386–393.
7. Tao, Y., Gou, Z., Lau, S.S., Lu, Y., Fu, J. (2018). Legibility of floor plans and wayfinding satisfaction of residents in care and attention homes in Hong Kong. *Australasian Journal on Ageing.* 37(4):E139–E143. DOI: 10.1111/ajag.12574
8. Shepley, M.M. (1995). The location of behavioral incidents in a children's psychiatric facility. *Children's Environments.* 12:352–361.

CONCLUSION

A. Vernon Woodworth FAIA

The approach to health and wellbeing suggested by the contributions to this volume is multidisciplinary and holistic. The intent, as stated in the Introduction, is to expand upon the fundamental goals for any and every given project, so as to include an evaluation of environmental impacts as well as an understanding of the physiological and emotional impacts of design choices. What we are doing is providing preliminary sketches for a sustainable future in which all people have access to nature, healthy food and clean water. Where we are regulated by the built environment, which imbues us with a sense of safety, meaning and wellbeing. These are fundamental goals for social health, a balanced and evolving system of reciprocity between individuals, organizations and ecosystems that is mutually supportive and fulfilling.

There is a general recognition in these contributions that a paradigm shift in human cultural behavior and self-understanding is in progress. Each contribution has its own perspective, and there is no overt correlation of content. However the need for change, and a firm commitment to a more balanced and equitable pattern of human cohabitation on a fragile planet, informs many chapters. Several chapters offer a deeper connection to the natural world and to our inner nature as the cornerstone of this change. Cultural trends in self-care, mindfulness, body-work and recovery from trauma may all be responding to the same impulse. The lesson imparted by an understanding of the dynamic of biophilia is that we require a communion with living patterns and energy to feel healthy and alive ourselves. A new car can't reach us at that level. Consumer goods can at best lull us into a numbed state of tranquility.

Most of all, we thrive on warm and familiar interaction with friends, acquaintances and loved ones. Our built environments had always been structured around this fact, up until the widespread use of automobiles. Our brains are structured to interact and communicate with others. Isolation is a punishment that can cause loss of brain mass, equivalent to trauma. This is true from the time we are born until we die, or lose the ability to interact. Recognizing this, we now know that it is critical to design all of our environments for optimal social interaction.

Change is a difficult process, but it is imprinted in our genetic makeup. By this I mean that human culture has developed effective mechanisms for change through the ritual process that enable us to transform our sense of self and our relationship to others. Ritual, like language, is a fundamental part of who we are as homo sapiens. With an understanding of the essential role of ritual in social change we can muster the resolve to sacrifice (a fundamental ritual dynamic) our

DOI: 10.4324/9781003164418-25

idea of being chosen for dominion over the natural world and begin our new role as stewards of environmental and social health. As much as we are identified with our belief systems, we are also quite familiar with the dynamic of change, and in fact superbly equipped to negotiate it.

A healthy system is a resilient system. This is true of natural systems, social systems and individual systems (such as the central nervous system). All systems experience stress, but each system has thresholds at which stress stops being an incentive for adaptation and starts being toxic. Design for resilience will become a priority as environmental and social stressors increase over the next few decades. Every design decision will be evaluated based on its ability to bestow resilience. For instance, rebuilding soil health is both a strategy for carbon sequestration and protection of groundwater. As such, it mitigates climate change while also adding resilience in case of flood or drought [1]. All it takes to rebuild soil health is planting a cover crop, preferably one that captures nitrogen. Currently only 6 percent of U.S. farmlands practice cover cropping, however in Maryland where incentives are provided to encourage this practice, 22 percent of farmland is planted with cover crops. A minor national policy to incentivize this practice could make a huge difference in the climate's rate of destabilization. In the meantime, every site condition can be evaluated for soil health, and every new project can include the goal to enhance this.

Health is beautiful, and beauty confers health. Neuroscience confirms this. If you need a justification for funding the arts or investing in good design, this is a good place to start. Yet it appears that the profession of architecture has lost sight of this fact, ignoring several millennia of institutional memory. The design professions are as responsible for health, safety and welfare as is the medical profession. Perhaps even more so.

Just as we need to widen the definition of our design practices to environmental and neurological health, so too must we look beyond the property lines of the site and ensure that our designs will facilitate the natural and social systems they inhabit. Contractual limitations and jurisdictional boundaries are not relevant to this responsibility. Fortunately, evidence is mounting that an approach that considers the bioregion and builds consensus among stakeholders will result in more successful projects.

The global trend toward expanded urbanization has already begun to transform cities into more celebratory environments. Yet there is so much more work to be done, to create social equity, to actively counteract the biases built into our structures, to heal the damage that the automobile has wrought, and to ensure resilience in the face of increased storm, heat and drought events. With the tools of big data and biometric monitoring the field of urban design is poised to come into its own as a force for healing. While these technologies may raise the specter of a top-down planning process, they in fact can promote an understanding of bottom-up human behavior, providing insight into our unconscious processes. The commercial sector has embraced neuroscience research, making it central to their marketing strategies from website and product design to movie trailers and book covers. The design professions can employ these methods in the interest of public health, for the common good, and for our mutual co-regulation.

Positive Stimulation: Neurological and Environmental

Neuroscience has shown us that our brains are shaped by our interactions with others. In the early years of a child's development, when brains are growing at a rate up to one million neurons per minute, interaction with adults based on a dynamic called "serve and return" creates a neural structure that provides the basis for verbal and social development. According to the Harvard University Center for the Developing Child

> "healthy brain architecture depends on a sturdy foundation built by appropriate input from a child's senses and stable responsive relationships with caring adults. If an adult's responses to a child are unreliable, inappropriate, or simply absent, the developing architecture of the brain may be disrupted, and subsequent physical, mental, and emotional health may be impaired. The persistent absence of serve and return interaction acts as a "double whammy" for healthy development: not only does the brain not receive the positive stimulation it needs, but the body's stress response is activated, flooding the developing brain with potentially harmful stress hormones [2]."

"Serve and return" forms the basis for the phenomenon of attachment, the source of emotional security on which all subsequent development is based. Attachment styles are thought to impact "vagal tone," the basis for emotional regulation. The vagus nerve connects all of the body's vital organs and is the principle source of information regarding safety and stress. There is also a likely connection between the nourishing interaction of serve and return and the healthy development of mirror neurons, which provide the capacity for empathy. Facial recognition is hard-wired into an infant brain as the primary evolutionary mechanism for establishing a secure relationship. Attachment establishes the infant's vagal tone, creating resilience or vulnerability in the developing personality. Where the mechanism of attachment is thwarted by inadequate serve and return, neglect, or the absence of mirroring, self-regulation abilities and social skills fail to develop properly. According to the developmental neuroscientist Dr. Allan Schore

> "if we grow up in an environment that does not nurture our burgeoning emotional self, then the development of the emotional brain can be compromised. As a consequence, we might not be able to learn how to regulate our emotions in a healthy fashion, and could too easily be overwhelmed by them. Being emotionally overloaded for extensive periods of time can cause not only long-enduring states of stress, but also chronic dissociation from our true emotions and needs in order to prevent overwhelming emotions from reaching consciousness [3]."

Dissociation is a common symptom of trauma, frequently leading to "perceptual alterations and somatic symptoms" [4]. These consequences can be summarized as "distortion of proprioceptive awareness" [5], resulting in a distorted or lost sense of self.

Self-regulation and co-regulation are also learned in this critical stage of brain development. Stephen Porges, the originator of polyvagal theory, sees the vagus as the mediator of the social engagement system, the source of information for negotiating relationships. Trauma results in a condition of vagal freeze, characterized by emotional shutdown or dissociation. Because the brain develops in the context of human relationships, this freeze state can lead to developmental arrest if untreated.

This thumbnail sketch of developmental neurobiology can inform our programming goals for the built environment. Positive stimulation remains a necessity for health and wellbeing throughout an individual's lifetime. Positive stimulation is best received from others but can also be provided by our environmental context. If the truncated attachment style of the autist coincides with a greater level of sensitivity to environmental cues it seems likely that other developmental deficits, including dissociation, can also respond to enriched environments that reinforce engagement. The opposite dynamic is also a reasonable hypothesis: environments that do not stimulate can cause or aggravate shutdown and dissociation. And, environments that generate excessive and **dystonic** stimulation can cause stress, with similar results.

Our love of life and our need for beauty, as expressed in the great public spaces of human civilization, must form the bases of our design sensibilities going forward. Experiencing spaces for human interaction around our common needs provides a sense of safety that allows us to express our social instincts. Stress is relieved by relaxed social interaction and the experience of natural patterns. Stress is aggravated by navigational disorientation, unfamiliarity and a lack of environmental cues. Resilience is facilitated by security, agency and nourishing relationships. We are nourished by relationships that provide attunement, whereby we feel seen and our inner emotional states are validated. Such relationships, by definition, can only be cultivated in non-stressful contexts, environments that allow our empathic abilities to flourish.

Just as the phenomenon of neuroplasticity illustrates to us how the brain can change throughout the lifespan, so too is the vagus nerve subject to modification with proper stimuli. Music and the practice of mindfulness are common methods for adjusting vagal tone. Stimulation of the vagus nerve has been used as treatment for depression, obsessive-compulsive disorder, panic disorder and post-traumatic stress disorder. There is a strong influence exerted on the immune system by the vagus nerve, suggesting its potential influence in determining personal resilience. As we learn more about the importance of the vagus nerve in modulating stress and facilitating resilience the role of the physical environment in providing stimuli via this superhighway of the central nervous system is likely to come into sharper focus.

Stephen Porges has asserted, as a result of his work with trauma clients, that "cues of safety are the treatment" [6], as these are received directly by the vagus nerve. Psychotherapist Pat Ogden has observed that

> "the felt sense comes to life in the science of the Polyvagal Theory which teaches us the wisdom that we need is in our bodies and nervous systems and is deeper than cognitive explanations or mental assessments of danger and safety. Polyvagal Theory describes the drive for connection and intimacy as a nonconscious biological imperative situating any relationship…in a new realm [7]."

"The wisdom that we need"—for healing, for meaning, for health and wellbeing. This wisdom is in our bodies and nervous systems. Attunement to this wisdom is a precondition for a healthy life. For this we need the ability to self-regulate and the opportunity to co-regulate. In other words, we need each other.

The Future of Design: Rooted in Evolutionary History

Biometric monitoring has enabled us to evaluate the nonconscious biological reactions of our central nervous systems to our environments. With these tools we have learned that our attention is drawn to people and to face-like patterns, as well as to vehicles whose size and movement can invoke predatory animal behavior. We are wired to assess the safety of our surroundings, and the cues for safety or threat are derived from instinctual reactions created by natural selection and embedded in our genes. We rely on the wisdom of our bodies to navigate our world, and require constant reassurance that our behavior is appropriate and our status is safe. Without such reassurance defensive strategies including shutdown and dissociation may distort our perceptions and invalidate our effectiveness. By understanding that emotional reactions to the built environment are informed by a biological need for safety and belonging our responsibility as designers is, to quote Ogden again, "situated in a new realm."

Regardless of our specific experiences in early childhood we all have an ongoing need for self- and co-regulation. Allan Schore considers the transfer of regulation from external (dependence on others) to internal (ability to self-regulate) as the key task of early development [8]. But there is no absolute completion of this task. While we keep it together to handle the stress of our jobs, our relationships, and the vagaries of living, we crave the soothing influence of a loving other, or the supportive connection of friends. It is Schore's observation that a newborn and the primary caregiver are in essence one being, sharing experiences in an undifferentiated manner as if based on the processing of a common central nervous system. This condition develops through "serve and return" until the infant's central nervous system reaches a sufficient developmental threshold to allow for a differentiated identity. This process, which can take two years or longer under optimal circumstances, is analogous to the commissioning process, whereby the systems of a ship or a building are brought online and calibrated. Without this critical empathic interaction between the caregiver and the child the personality cannot develop properly, resulting in a lack of neural resilience and possibly a lifelong personality disorder. Under these circumstances only a successful therapeutic relationship, the psychological equivalent of a retro-commissioning process, can reclaim the individual's agency and integrity.

The nature of the central nervous system is to seek the dynamic equilibrium of a regulated system. If a primary caregiving relationship does not provide the necessary commissioning for a sense of self-worth and agency then an alternative caregiver will be sought, consciously or unconsciously. If an experience of beauty that transports and uplifts is not at hand, a trip to a gallery or show, museum or park, will be sought. If we are lonesome or in need of intimacy, we will seek a partner. Our environmental interventions must respond to the deeply ingrained needs of the human central nervous system if they are to be successful. The payback in increased personal and social health is likely to be greater than any other single policy initiative or health regime.

Our fundamental biological adaptation to our environment is currently understood as the response of genetic potential to experience. The variability of our genetic nature is thought to explain our differing responses to similar events. Underlying this dynamic lies the phenomenon of **epigenesis**, defined as "the study of the mechanisms of temporal and spatial control of gene activity during the development of complex organisms" [9]. Not only do our genes inform our responses to our environment, but our environment can also determine the expression of our genes. The phenomenon of epigenesis provides us with the scientific basis for establishing environmental factors as critical to health and wellbeing. Epigenesis has even been described as the causative factor in trans-generational trauma, demonstrating its potential for lasting negative effects over time. The concomitant lasting effect over time of positive impacts is equally likely.

Gene expression has a time dimension that is generally overlooked in environmental psychology. Human development is marked by specific critical thresholds that are facilitated or thwarted by environmental conditions. The phenomenon of the "rite of passage" in indigenous societies illustrates cultural reinforcement of the transition to adulthood. Religious traditions frequently memorialize developmental passages. Circadian rhythms find expression in all aspects of our genetic code. And yet our built environment provides little context for our biological and spiritual development, the minimal conditions for social and personal health and wellbeing.

Program for Tomorrow

With the prospect of imminent irrevocable damage to environmental systems it is our responsibility as a species to become healers, of ourselves and of the world. This task falls to all, but to none more so than to the design professions. Medicine and psychology can have only a limited impact in this endeavor, but we can learn from these disciplines and others as we take on the challenge of creating a sustainable world. There are a few simple truths that we must keep in mind as we assume this role:

- an ounce of prevention is worth a pound of cure
- the economic value of health and wellbeing exceeds any expense required to achieve these
- our lives and happiness are inextricably intertwined with the quality of our environments
- exploitation is no longer an option, and
- we cannot wait until another time.

Our physical context can provide the opportunity for genetic expression in harmony with our most profound human potential. It can facilitate proprioception, our sixth sense by which we maximize our sense of self as a body in space, reducing stress and overcoming **dissociation**. It can elevate mood, enhancing our immune response. It can bring us together and allow us to share our common aspirations and fears. It can build a sense of agency and purpose by expressing values and demonstrating the beauty of life. And it can provide us with a source of nourishment that builds resilience, health and wellbeing.

Asked to provide a program for tomorrow, we can hardly hope for a more robust set of goals.

References

1. Postel, S. (2021, Mar. 3). *Replenish: Supporting the Virtuous Cycle of Water and Prosperity* [Webinar]. Smart growth Network and Maryland Department of Planning. https://islandpress.org/videos/replenish-supporting-virtuous-cycle-water-and-prosperity
2. Center on the Developing Child. (n.d.). Serve and Return. Harvard University. https://developingchild.harvard.edu/science/key-concepts/serve-and-return/
3. Rass, E. (2018). On the Same Wavelength: How Our Emotional Brain Is Shaped by Human Relationships; Excerpts from an Interview with Allan Schore by Daniel F Sieff. *The Allan Schore Reader.* New York: Routledge.
4. Scaer, R. C. (2001). *The Body Bears the Burden: Trauma, Dissociation and Disease.* New York: Haworth.
5. Ibid.
6. Porges, S. and Dana, D. (2018). *Clinical Applications of the Polyvagal Theory: The Emergence of Polyvagal-Informed Therapies.* New York: W. W. Norton & Company.
7. Ibid. 48.
8. Schore, A. N. (2003). The Effects of Early Relational Trauma on Right Brain Development, Affect Regulation, and Infant Mental Health. *Infant Mental Health Journal.* 11(1–2). 201–269.
9. Holliday, R. (1990). DNA Methylation and Epigenetic Inheritance. *Philosophical Transactions of the Royal Society of London: Series B, Biological Sciences.* 326(1235). 329–338.

ACRONYMS

ADA	(American with Disabilities Act of 1990)
AP	(Accredited Professional)
AIA	(American Institute of Architects)
ANFA	(Academy of Neuroscience for Architecture)
ANS	(autonomic nervous system)
ART	(Attention Restoration Theory)
ASHRAE	(American Society of Heating, Refrigerating and Air-Conditioning Engineers)
ASTM	(American Society for Testing and Materials)
BD+C	(Building Design and Construction)
CDC	(Center for Disease Control)
CNS	(Central Nervous System)
CUA	(Catholic University of America)
DHEA	(Dehydroepiandrosterone)
DNA	(Deoxyribonucleic Acid)
DSM-5	(Diagnostic and Statistical Manual of Mental Disorders, 5th Edition)
DSP	(DeafSpace Project)
EBD	(Evidence Based Design)
EEG	(Electroencephalography)
EDAC	(Evidence Based Design Accreditation and Certification)
EHI	(Environmental Health Index)
EMA	(Environmental Maintenance Assessment)
EMDR	(Eye Movement Desensitization and Reprocessing)
FAIA	(Fellow of the American Institute of Architects)
FEMA	(Federal Emergency Management Agency)
GAS	(General Adaptation Syndrome)
GSR	(Galvanic Skin Response)
HSW	(Health, Safety, Welfare)
HVAC	(Heat, Ventilation, Air Conditioning)
IBC	(International Building Code)

ICC	(International Code Council)
IECC	(International Energy Efficiency Code)
IEP	(Individual Education Plan)
IES	(Illuminating Engineering Society)
IgCC	(International Green Construction Code)
IDEA	(Individuals with Disabilities Education Improvement Act 2004)
HPA	(Hypothalamic-Pituitary-Adrenal)
ICAA	(Institute of Classical Architecture & Art
ICC	(International Code Council)
IECC	(International Energy Conservation Code)
IgCC	(International Green Construction Code)
IWBI	(International WELL Building Institute)
KBTU/SF/YR	(Energy per square foot per year)
KL	(Kuala Lumpur)
LBC	(Living Building Challenge)
LRE	(Least Restrictive Environment)
LEED	(Leadership in Energy and Environmental Design)
MD	(Medical Doctor)
MPH	(Master of Public Health)
NCARB	(National Council of Architectural Registration Boards)
NGO	(Nongovernment Organization)
OECD	(Organization of Economic Cooperation and Development)
PhD	(Doctor of Philosophy)
POE	(Post-Occupancy Evaluation)
RIBA	(Royal Institute of British Architects)
RA	(Registered Architect)
SNS	(Sympathetic Nervous System)
STEAM	(Science, Technology, Engineering, Art (including Architecture, Math)
STEM	(science, Technology, Engineering, Math)
UEP	(Urban and Environmental Policy and Planning)
UNEP	(United Nations Environment Programme)
USGBC	(United States Green Building Council)
VR	(Virtual Reality)
WELL	(WELL Building Standard)
VAS	(Visual Attention Software)
WHO	(World Health Organization)

GLOSSARY

Term	Definition
Activities, Programmed	Those that require a license, sponsor or organizer.
Activities, Semi-programmed	Similar to unprogrammed activities in that they are self-initiated, but they require the availability of some specific facility.
Activities, Unprogrammed	Those that people initiate on their own, as part of their individual use of the space.
Affordance	1. The property of an object that defines its possible uses. 2. A resource or support that the environment offers.
Agency	The capacity of individuals to act independently and to make their own free choices on their own behalf.
Akinetopsia	"A neuropsychological disorder in which a patient cannot perceive motion in their visual field, despite being able to see stationary objects without issue." Zeki, S. "Cerebral Akinetopsia: A Review" *Brain* 114 (2) (1991): 811–824.
Allostasis	"Allostasis allows us to mobilize the appropriate amount of energy and focus for coping well before, during and after a threat or challenge." Stanley, E.A. *Widen the Window*. Penguin Random House. p. 14.
Allostatic Load	"Without adequate recovery after chronic stress and/or trauma, the mind/body system remains activated and doesn't return to its regulated equilibrium. Instead, over time the internal systems involved in allostasis—the brain, the ANS, the immune system, and the endocrine system—become dysregulated. When this happens allostasis stops functioning properly and we begin to build allostatic load. And, as allostatic load accumulates, we experience dysregulation, which manifests as a range of physical, emotional, cognitive, spiritual, or behavioral symptoms." Stanley, E.A. *Widen the Window*. New York: Random House. pp. 14–15.
Amygdalae	The survival brain region involved with neuroception and worry. Part of the brain's limbic system, this is where emotions are given meaning, remembered, and attached to associations.

(*Continued*)

Glossary

Term	Definition
Ancient Brain	For this analysis, both hindbrain and midbrain; the brain stem, thought to have evolved during the Pleistocene period, consisting of medulla, pons, thalamus; both hindbrain and midbrain. The center for our primitive and emotional responses—survival and pleasure—as well as remedial, life sustaining functions.
Anterior Cingulate	The anterior cingulate cortex (ACC) lies in a unique position in the brain, with connections to both the "emotional" limbic system and the "cognitive" prefrontal cortex. It likely plays an important role in affect regulation.
Anterior Insula	"The AIC integrates bottom-up interoceptive signals with top-down predictions to generate a current awareness state while providing descending predictions to visceral systems that provide a point of reference for autonomic reflexes." Xiaosi, G., et al. "Anterior insular cortex and emotional awareness" *Journal of Comparative Neurology.* 521: 15.
Anthroponosis	Pathogens sourced from humans and passed between humans, as well as sourced from humans and passed to non-humans
Attention Restoration Theory (ART)	ART suggests that mental fatigue and concentration can be improved by time spent in or looking at nature. Kaplan, R. & S. 1989, 1995.
Attunement	A kinesthetic and emotional sensing of others knowing their rhythm, affect and experience by metaphorically being in their skin, and going beyond empathy to create a two-person experience of unbroken feeling connectedness by providing a reciprocal affect and/or resonating response. Erskine, R.G. "The Therapeutic Relationship" *Transactional Analysis Journal* 4/1/1998: 132–141.
Belief System	An ideology or set of principles that helps us to interpret our everyday reality.
Biodiversity	The biological variety of natural environments, the destruction of which can offset the balance of Earth's ecosystems.
Biometric Monitoring	Data collection of changes to human traits and body parameters, used to assess users' emotions and behaviors. Elements that might be measured include temperature, heart rate dynamics, skin conductance, visual pathways, brain activity, etc.
Bioregion	An ecologically and geographically defined area that is smaller than a biogeographical realm, but larger than an ecoregion or an ecosystem.
Code, Construction or Building	A set of regulations that guides safety and quality standards for construction projects. Typically local laws, these regulations must be met in order for projects to gain building permission.
Cognition, Embodied	"I am proposing that the operation of embodied cognition is, when it produces emotional nourishment, what we mean by a sense of place…sense of place is our conscious and unconscious emotional reaction to our body-mind's kinesthetic and cognitive experience in, and in relationship to, our immediate surroundings… it is our lived experience in defined urban spaces." Tullis, R. "Sense of Place" in UX + Design 2020
Cognition, Situated	"Much of what and how people think is a function of our living in the kinds of bodies we do. It reveals most, much more than we previously knew, of human thought is neither logical nor linear, but associative and unconscious…what the new paradigm of embodied or situated cognition reveals is that the built environment and its design matters far, far more than anybody, even architects, ever thought that it did." Goldhagen, S.W. *Welcome to Your World.* New York: Harper Collins. pp. xii–xiv.

Cognitive Map	"A representative expression of an individual's knowledge about the spatial and environmental relations of geographic space." *International Encyclopedia of the Social and Behavioral Sciences* 2001.
Commissioning	The process of assuring that all systems and components are designed, installed, tested, operated and maintained according to operational requirements.
Communitas	An unstructured state in which all members of a community are equal allowing them to share a common experience, often through a ritual or rite of passage.
Community Strength Building	Strategies at the building scale that support the strength of community residents and systems.
Consilience	The linking together of principles from different disciplines especially when forming a comprehensive theory.
Discrepancy	As used by Daniel Siegel this term describes a mismatch of expectations with environmental context. Discrepancy will alert the amygdala that there is a potential threat detected.
Dissociation	A disconnection between a person's sensory experience, thoughts, sense of self, or personal history, often manifested as a sense of unreality and loss of connection to time, place and identity.
Dissonance, Cognitive	The mental discomfort that results from holding two conflicting beliefs, values or attitudes.
Distress	The condition of being under physical, emotional or psychological stress.
Dysregulation, emotional	An absence of regulation in emotional responses which can result in inappropriate affect or behavior.
Dystonic	Dissonant affect or stimuli; unpleasant or aversive.
Ecosystem	A biological community of interacting organisms and their physical environment
Emotional Engagement	The state of attentive connection to another or others.
Emotional Nourishment	The experience of deep connection with others and with one's inner self. This entails experiences that bypass the critical defenses and restores a sense of wellbeing and peace to the central nervous system.
Environmental Enrichment	Stimulation of the brain by physical and social surroundings.
Environmental Remediation	The removal of contaminants from soil, groundwater, sediment or surface water.
Environmental Risk Factors	Any environmental factor that creates individual, social or environmental health risks. Such risks may vary according to one's developmental, cognitive and physical disposition, or constitute risks to an entire population.
Epigenesis	The process of genetic expression based on environmental influences.
Equilibrium, Dynamic	A state of healthful balance.
Eustress	Moderate or normal psychological stress interpreted as being beneficial for the experiencer.
Evidence-based Design	The process of designing based on scientific research to achieve maximal outcomes.
Exteroception	Sensitivity to stimuli originating outside of the body.
Eye-tracking	The process of measuring either the point of gaze or the motion of an eye relative to the head.
Fractal Scaling	Mathematical term used to describe irregular geometrical structures whose shape appears to be self-similar regardless of the level of magnification at which it is viewed.
Fractals	Infinitely complex patterns that are self-similar across different scales.
Galvanic Skin Response	Changes in sweat gland activity that are reflective of the intensity of our emotional state, otherwise known as emotional arousal.

(Continued)

Glossary

Term	Definition
Gaze Path	Gaze plots show the location, order and time spent looking at locations on the stimulus.
Gist Extraction	"Our ability to rapidly 'download' only the features of new information that are of use to us in the task at hand." Tullis, R. "Sense of Place" in UX + Design 2020 p. 19.
Heat Island Effect	Due to limited greenspace and a preponderance of buildings, roads, and infrastructure that absorb and re-release heat, urban temperatures are both day and night consistently higher than temperatures in outlying areas.
Hippocampus	A part of the limbic system which plays an important role in the consolidation of information from short-term memory to long-term memory, and in spatial memory that enables navigation.
Informal Urbanism	Acts of urbanization performed independent of formal frameworks or assistance.
Insula	The insula subserves a wide variety of functions in humans ranging from sensory and affective processing to high-level cognition.
Interoception	The conscious awareness of bodily sensations. Plays a major role in regulating and recovering from stress arousal.
Literacy, architectural	A term used to describe an understanding of the traditional (i.e., "classical") components of architectural design.
Medial Orbitofrontal Cortex	Part of the prefrontal cortex that receives projections from the medial dorsal nucleus of the thalamus. Its function is to learn associations between context, locations, events and corresponding adaptive responses. Interaction between multiple memory systems may explain the changing importance of the MOC to different types of memory over time. The MOC likely relies on the hippocampus to support rapid learning and memory consolidation.
Mind-body System	"Our entire human organism; the brain, the nervous system, neurotransmitters, the immune system, the endocrine system, and the body, organs, skeleton, muscles, fascia, skin and fluids." Stanley, E.A. *Training your Brain and Body to Thrive During Stress and Recover from Trauma* 2019. New York: Penguin/Random House.
Mirror Neurons	Thought by some to encode the meaning of actions. May play a role in empathy.
Myelination	A process by which the fatty substance myelin affixes to nerve cells, allowing them to transmit information faster and carry out more complex brain processes.
Narrative	A way of presenting or understanding a situation or series of events that reflect and promote a particular point of view or set of values. See also: "Belief System"
Neuroception	"An unconscious process of rapidly scanning the internal and external environment for opportunities/safety/pleasure and threats/danger/pain. To support neuroception the survival brain has an implicit learning and memory system—fast, automatic, and unconscious, bypassing the thinking brain." Stanley, E.A. *Widen the Window.* New York: Random House. p. 13.
Neuroendocrine	Both neural and endocrine in structure or function. Neuroendocrine cells receive neural input and, as a consequence of this input, release message molecules (hormones) into the blood.
Neurogenesis	The process by which new neurons are formed in the brain.
Neurological Resonance	As used in this text, a deep subjective response to external stimuli.

Neuron	The basic working unit of the brain, a specialized cell designed to transmit information to other nerve cells, muscle or gland cells.
Neuroplasticity	The ability of neural networks in the brain to change through reorganization and growth. "Nervous systems evolved to enable us to adapt to the environment and determine the best course of action in any given situation, based on what has been learned from past experience. This is the case not just for humans, but for all organisms that have a nervous system. That is to say, nervous systems evolved to change, and so neuroplasticity is an intrinsic and fundamental property of all nervous systems." Costandi, M. *Neuroplasticity*. Cambridge, MA: MIT Press 2016.
Neurotrophic Factors	A family of biomolecules that support the growth, survival and differentiation of both developing and mature neurons. In the mature nervous system, they promote neuronal survival, induce synaptic plasticity and modulate the formation of long-term memories.
One Planet Living	A vision for living healthily and happily within the bounds of the Earth's resources. A concept introduced by "Bioregional" in 2002, intends to reduce carbon emissions and consumption by changing peoples' behavior through design.
Orbitofrontal Cortex	The area of the prefrontal cortex that sits just above the orbits (eye sockets). It has extensive connections with sensory areas as well as limbic system structures involved in emotion and memory.
Osmosis	The process of gradual or unconscious assimilation of ideas, knowledge, etc. Also, a process by which molecules of a solvent tend to pass through a semipermeable membrane from a less concentrated solution into a more concentrated one, thus equalizing the concentrations on each side of the membrane.
Passive Survivability	Design principles that support the continuous habitability of buildings during extended power outages or interruptions in heating and cooling systems.
Place	Exterior public spaces that can be experienced as a single entity, taken in by the human senses as a single experience.
Placemaking	The creation of a legible space within the city fabric, one that has the power through its form and use to be memorable and attractive to people, and thus have identity and meaning.
Plasticity	The capacity for change.
Pre-attentive	Unconscious. The senses are constantly collecting information, most of which never reaches consciousness.
Programming	The research and decision-making process that identifies the scope of work to be designed.
Proprioception	The sense of self-movement and body position. The central nervous system integrates proprioception and other sensory systems, such as vision and the vestibular system, to create an overall representation of body position, movement and acceleration.
Prospect	An unimpeded view over a distance for surveillance and planning (terrapinbrightgreen.com).
Refuge	A place for withdrawal from environmental conditions or the main flow of activity, in which the individual is protected from behind and overhead (terrapinbrightgreen.com).
Regeneration	A state of consciousness and being that is able to engage a continuous process of rebirth, of understanding and engagement with the dynamic and evolutionary system of life.

(Continued)

Term	Definition
Regenerative Buildings	Structures designed to improve their surrounding environments by restoring, renewing or revitalizing their own sources of energy and materials.
Regulation	An emotional state of relative equilibrium in which one is able to maintain one's composure.
Resilience	The ability of natural and human systems functioning to withstand disruption and challenges.
Resilient Design	Building codes, sustainable design, passive survivability and community strength building combined in ways that enable designers challenged with environmental stress to provide basic human needs today while preserving social systems for tomorrow.
Resonance Circuits	In neuroscience these are circuits within the mirror neuron system.
Riparian Corridors	A riparian corridor is the vegetation system growing near natural bodies of water. These corridors play many roles in maintaining the local ecosystem. They protect against erosion; preserve water quality by filtering sediment from runoff before flowing into rivers and streams; create flood water storage capacity; provide wildlife habitat; and preserve open space.
Salutogenic	A quality or character of supporting human health.
Satellite Cities	Smaller municipalities that are adjacent to a major city which is the core of a metropolitan area. They have municipal governments distinct from that of the core metropolis and have the potential to be self-supporting.
Sensory Processing Disorder	A condition in which the brain has trouble receiving and responding to information that comes in through the senses.
Service Life	A product's total life in use from the point of sale to the point of discard.
Shutdown	Numbness or detachment; an inability or unwillingness to connect with other people on an emotional level.
Social Design Justice	The practice of design as a means to promote social justice.
Social Vulnerability Index	A Center for Disease Control's metric using 15 U.S. census variables to help officials identify communities that may need support before, during or after disasters.
STEAM	STEAM is an educational discipline that aims to spark an interest in and capacity for science, technology, engineering, the arts (including architecture) and math in children from an early age. These disciplines all involve creative problem solving, collaboration and multiple methods in practice.
Stimming	Short for self-stimulatory behavior. This can be hand-flapping, rocking, spinning or repetition of words and phrases.
Stress	Emotional or physical tension, the body's reaction to a challenge or demand.
Stressors, Mental	This includes any factor that causes emotional stress including death of a loved one, divorce, job loss, chronic illness or debt.
Stressors, Sensory	Information from the six senses can cause stress and overload based on pre-existing conditions or neural deficits. This has been shown to be true for people with autism, ADHD, PTSD, fibromyalgia and multiple sclerosis.
Stressors, Social	Factors that create social stress include anxiety about being accepted, tension in relationships and unequal distribution of responsibilities among colleagues or partners.

Symbolic Interactionism	A view of social behavior that emphasizes linguistic or gestural communication and its subjective understanding, especially the role of language in the formation of the child as a social being.
Systemic Inflammation	The result of release of pro-inflammatory cytokines from immune-related cells and the chronic activation of the innate immune system.
Systems Thinking	An approach to integration that is based on the belief that the component parts of a system will act differently when isolated from the system's environment or other parts of the system.
Thigmotaxis	A change in direction of locomotion in a motile organism or cell which is made in response to a tactile stimulus, often observed as edge-hugging behavior in humans and animals.
Trauma	"An internal response, on a continuum with stress. However not all stress is traumatic. Trauma can occur if, during a stressful experience, we also perceive ourselves to be powerless, helpless or lacking control. Trauma is especially likely to result if aspects of the current threat or challenge contain cues or triggers related to earlier in our lives." Stanley, E.A. *Widen the Window* p. 14. New York: Random House.
Triangulation	Some external stimulus provides a linkage between people.
Universal Design	An approach to design that increases the potential for developing a better quality of life for a wide range of individuals. It is a design process that enables and empowers a diverse population by improving human performance, health and wellness, and social participation. -universaldesign.com
Universal Design, Principles of	(1) Equitable use; (2) Flexibility in Use; (3) Simple and Intuitive Use; (4) Perceptible Information: (5) Tolerance for Error; (6) Low Physical Effort; (7) Size and Space for Approach and Use.— National Disability Authority
Urban Fabric	The physical urban environment (elements, materials, form, scales, density and networks), and its psychological, socio-cultural, ecological, managerial and economic structures.
Urban renewal	A process whereby privately owned properties within a designated renewal area are purchased or taken by eminent domain by a municipal redevelopment authority, razed and then reconveyed to selected developers who devote them to other uses.
Ventilation	The intentional introduction of outdoor air into interior environments, which can improve indoor air quality as well as control temperature and humidity.
Wildlife Wet Market	A marketplace where live wild animals, including those considered exotic, are bought and sold. They pose a high threat for zoonoses and foster inhumane conditions for the creatures traded there.
Zooanthroponosis	The transmission of disease from humans to non-humans.
Zoonoses	A disease transmittable to humans from non-humans.

INDEX

Note: *Italic* page numbers refer to figures and page numbers followed by "n" denote endnotes.

abandoning properties, cost of 166
"ability model" of emotional intelligence 220
Academy of Neuroscience for Architecture (ANFA) 15
ACE *see* adverse childhood experiences (ACE)
acoustics 60, 76, 77
adequate ventilation 151
adrenaline 34, 41, 43, 87
adverse childhood experiences (ACE) 44
The Aesthetic Brain (Chatterjee) 32
affordances for stress reduction 49
agency 47, 215, 230
"The Age of Biology" 140, 147
"The Age of Chemistry and Physics" 140
"The Age of Engineering" 140
age-old adaptation strategy 186
aggregated eye-tracking data: Amsterdam gaze paths 143; Amsterdam heat maps 143; Boston gaze paths 141–142; Boston heat maps 140–141
AIA *see* American Institute of Architects (AIA)
AIA Task Group on Building Regulation 154
air conditioning 85, 180, 182, 183
air handling systems 85
air pollution 88, 92, 195, 207
Alexander, Christopher 111, 112, 118, 137, 222, 224, 232; *The Nature of Order* 223; *A Pattern Language* 226–231; *The Timeless Way of Building* 225
allostasis 40, 43
allostatic load 40, 45, 47, 49
Altenmüller-Lewis, Ulrike 78
Altman, I. 14
American Institute of Architects (AIA) 150–152, 216, 217
Americans with Disabilities Act 56, 58
Americo, Lara 55

Amsterdam, testing technology & streets in 137–139
amygdalae 4
"amygdala hijacking" 42
ancient brain 33
ANS *see* autonomic nervous system (ANS)
anterior cingulate 5
anterior insula 5
Anthes, Emily: *The Great Indoors* 220
anti-racist de-colonizing design resources 46
Antonovsky, Aaron 20
apparent lack of empathy 65
Appleton, Jay 113
"appraisal" 4
Aranda-Mena, Guillermo 219; *Creating Emotionally Intelligent Workspaces* 218
architectural design, evaluating 234, 240–241; behavioral incidents in children's psychiatric facility 239; bias 235; confounding 235; epidemiologic methods 234; legibility of interior space and wayfinding satisfaction 238–239; patient anxiety and agitation 238; recovery from surgery 236; relationship between daylighting and school performance 236–237; statistical methods 235; strength of association 235
architectural elements 118–125
architectural programming process 28, 56, 179; curb cut effect 58–59; implications for programming phase 64; principles in concert 60–64; redefining disability 59–60; universal design 56–58
architectural space 126–131
Architecture and Embodiment (Mallgrave) 36
The Architecture of the City (Rossi) 120
The Architecture of the Roman Empire, Vol. 2, An Urban Appraisal (Donald) 124
Aristotle 131

Index

Arnheim, Rudolph 130
ART *see* Attention Restoration Theory (ART)
ASD *see* Autism Spectrum Disorder (ASD)
ASTM International and the Illuminating Engineering Society (IES) 154
Attention Restoration Theory (ART) 20, 26
attunement 13, 46, 245
autism spectrum 59
Autism Spectrum Disorder (ASD) 65–79
autonomic nervous system (ANS) 34, 35, 46, 137

Barker, R. 14
Bauman, Hansel 59
Baumers, Stijn 68
"beautiful room experiment" 133
Beauty, Neuroscience and Architecture (Ruggles) 21
Beaver, Christopher 69n1, 78
Bechtel, R. B. 10
BedZED ecovillage 168
behavior-setting theory 14
belief systems 3
Berkowitz, L. 13
Berry, Wendell 176
bias 234, 235
Biederman, Irving 36
Biederman Redevelopment Ventures 114
big-brained species 162
de Bildt, Lyske Gais 148
biodiversity 162, 164, 168–169, 202, 205
"bio-hood" familiarity 161
biological wiring 13
biometric monitoring 136, 245
biometrics 29
biophilia 5, 13, 19–22, 26, 87, 155, 242; and human health 25–30; research in 48
biophilic design 20, 26–27
biophilic element effective 47
Biophilic Interior Design Matrix 28–29
biophilic stimuli 26
bioregion: case for programming in 159–162; environmental management is human mandate 162–163; human health is environmental health 163–165; problem of data 170; programming for resilience 167–168; programming for sea-level rise 169–170; restoring habitat, food chain and biodiversity 168–169; risk assessment/goal setting 165–167; social programming 170
bioregional EHI 164
bioregional identity 170
bioregionalism 160, 170
Black Death 150, 151
Bloomer, Kent: *Body, Memory, and Architecture* 131
Body, Memory, and Architecture (Moore and Bloomer) 131
Boston heat maps 140–141
Boston Redevelopment Authority 197
Boston Sensing Streetscape study 137
Boston, testing technology & streets in 137–139
brain and environment 14–15

"bread and circuses" 169
building codes 150, 167

Cambridge Zoning for Resilience Task Force 189
Carmona, M.: *Public Places, Urban Spaces* 132
Carter, Rita: *Mapping the Mind* 36
Catholic University of America (CUA) 94–95
Center for Disease Control (CDC) 44, 194
Center for Health Design's Evidence Based Design Accreditation and Certification (EDAC) 10
Central Artery 197
central nervous system (CNS) 4, 42
Certificate of Occupancy 217
Chatterjee, Anjan: *The Aesthetic Brain* 32
Chicago heat wave 187
child health: and learning 84–85; programming for 85; in schools 85
children's psychiatric facility, behavioral incidents in 239
Chivian, Eric 168
chronic environmental stressor 9
chronic stress 43
Churchill, Winston 110
circadian rhythms 246
circadian system 46
"circumplex model of affect" 13
city attributes, enhancing 207–208
city open space: through extension 200–202; through reassignment 198–200; through renewal 197–198
civic spaces and communitas 130
civil rights legislation 56
climate change 1, 88, 92, 93, 151, 160, 161, 163, 166, 170, 178–181, 182, 188, 190, 191, 195, 200–202, 204, 205, 207, 209, 243
climate-related hazards 187
CNS *see* central nervous system (CNS)
code development process 153
code enforcement community 152
The Code of Hammurabi 150
codes and architecture profession 150; architecture's role in environmental health 151–152; stewardship 152–154; transformative impact 154–155
Cognitive Architecture (Hollander and Sussman) 102
"cognitive mapping" 5
Collage City (Koetter and Rowe) 120, 128
Collins, Paul 67
"Comm Ave" 198
"Commissioning, Operation and Maintenance" 216
commissioning phase 29
common resilience strategies 184
common-sense resilience perspective 192
"communitas spaces" 3–4
community activist groups 174
community and learning 88
community empowerment 97, 99
community engagement 82
community facilities and programs 115

community resilience 186
community strength building 178–179
concert, principles in 60–64
control theory 14
"Cool Points" model 189
coping strategies 44
co-regulation 244, 245
cranial sacral therapy 176
Creating Emotionally Intelligent Workspaces (Finch and Aranda-Mena) 218
creative economic incentives 168
"creative placemaking" 111
cross-disciplinary research project 61
Cullen, Gordon 118; *Townscape* 126
cultural identity 161
curb cut effect 58–59

daily characteristics 114, 115
Davis, Alexander Jackson 200
daylighting and school performance, relationship between 236–237
deaf community 59
DeafSpace Guidelines 59
Deaf-Space Project (DSP) 59
The Death and Life of Great American Cities (Jacobs) 176
Der Stadtebau (Sitte) 127, 128
Design Forecast 2021 9
design programming process *12*
design thinking 100
developmental neurobiology 244
Diagnostic and Statistical Manual of Mental Disorders (DSM-5) 67
Dickenson, J. I.: *Informing Design* 11
directional decision-making 230
disability, redefining 59–60
discrepancy 4, 5
"Disruption, Evolution, and Change" 151, 152, 155, 217
dissociation 244, 245, 247
distress 13, 41
DIY urbanism 230
Dollard, J. 13
Donald, William Mac: *The Architecture of the Roman Empire, Vol. 2, An Urban Appraisal* 124
Doxiadis, C.A. 129
"dream" school approach 70
DSP *see* Deaf-Space Project (DSP)
Dutton, Denis 33
dynamic equilibrium 163
dysregulation 3
dystonic stimulation 244

EBD *see* evidence-based design (EBD)
The Economics of Biophilia 29
"economies of scale" 161
ecosystem 2, 159; development 172; health 164; stability 168
educational environmental stress 76

educational environments 67, 78
educational programmers 84
effective decision-making process 170
effective learning: childhood health and learning 84–85; community and learning 88; Fales School 92–93; key planning and programming elements 81–82; natural environment and learning 87–88; neurological research and learning 82–84; physical safety and learning 85–86; social and emotional safety and learning 86–87; St John New Brunswick Elementary School 91–92; visioning process 88–89; Weymouth Middle School 89–91
effective shading 186
"effortless attention" 26
Einstein, Albert 171
Eisenman, Peter 224–226
electroencephalography (EEG) 26
EMA *see* Environmental Maintenance Assessment (EMA)
EMDR approach 48
emergency lighting 186
emotional arousal 5, 143
emotional engagement 2, 87
emotional health 83
emotional intelligence 220
"emotionally intelligent workspace" 220
emotional nourishment 49
emotional safety 86
emotions 35, 83, 220
empathetic design 75, 78–79
empathetic programming to foster inclusion: Autism Spectrum Disorder (ASD) 65–67; empathetic design 78–79; Empathy Sketchbook 69–74; irony of empathy 69; reading sketchbook 74–78; square peg 67; "torture starts" 65
Empathy Sketchbook 69–74
Employee Benefits Plan 20
"empowerment for health" 97
energy transfer 164
"enriched" environment 220
environmental enrichment 220
environmental health 2, 163–165, 179; architecture's role in 151–152; human health 163–165
Environmental Health Index (EHI) 164
Environmental Load theory 14
Environmental Maintenance Assessment (EMA) 140, 143
environmental management 162–163
environmental psychology 10; bridges *11*; principles 9, 11
environmental racism 45
environmental remediation 206–207
environmental resilience 163
environmental risk factors 40
environmental stressors 39–42
environment-behavior relationship 10
epidemiology 234
epigenesis 246

"Essentials of the Brain" 33
Etcoff, Nancy 21
eustress 41
evidence-based design (EBD) 2, 10, 15, 18, 29, 42, 48, 99, 155, 216, 218; decision-making process 18
evidence-based knowledge 18
evidence-based medicine 10
exteroception 4
extravaganzas 115
extreme heat, climate hazards 180
Eyck, Aldo Van 131
eye movement 48
eye-tracking 26, 142; experiments 133; glasses 137; measures 136–137; technology 4

facades 113
facial recognition 244
Fales School 92–93
familiarity 4
FAR *see* Floor Area Ratio (FAR)
Federal Emergency Management Agency (FEMA) 188
Felitti, V. J. 44
Finch, Edward 219; *Creating Emotionally Intelligent Workspaces* 218
"five second rule" 114
flooding, climate hazards 179
flood management 165
Floor Area Ratio (FAR) 203
Floyd, George 46
fractal patterns 21, 26, 133
Francis, Pope 110
Fromm, Eric 5
frustration-aggression hypothesis 13
Fuller, Buckminster 6
fundamental biological adaptation 246
fundamental evidence-based standards 97

galvanic skin response (GSR) 137, 143–146
Gatje, Robert 128
gaze paths 140–143
Gehl, Jan 109, 112–116, 118, 128, 131, 137, 142
gender minorities 55
gene expression 246
General Adaptation Syndrome (GAS) theory 43
Gensler 9
Geographic Information Systems (GIS) 170
The Geography of Risk Gilbert M. Gaul 167
gestalt theory 14
Gibson, J.J.: *The Senses Considered as Perceptual Systems* 131
Gifford, R. 10, 13
GIS *see* Geographic Information Systems (GIS)
Gladwell, Malcolm: *Talking to Strangers* 18
global urbanization 170
Goldhagen, Sarah Williams: *Welcome To Your World, How the Built Environment Shapes Our Lives* 132
Goleman, Daniel 42
The Great Indoors (Anthes) 220

green design 176
greenhouse gas emissions 151
"Green Score" zoning ordinances 189
GSR *see* galvanic skin response (GSR)

habitat degradation 168
Hamilton, D. K. 10
Harvard Architectural Review (Peterson) 130
Harvard Chan School of Public Health 85
Hatfield, Rudolph C. 33
hazard mitigation plans 180–181
health benefits of biophilia 29
"health-first" designs 9
healthy ecosystem 168
healthy stress 41
heart's nervous system 35
heat island effect 186
Heath, T.: *Public Places, Urban Spaces* 132
"heat maps" 137, 140–143
heat-related deaths 182
Heerwagen, Judith 32
Heidegger, Martin 124, 125
Herzberg, F. I. 219
Heylighen, Ann 68
hierarchical social systems 3
higher-level cognitive functions 83
Hill, Sir Bradford 235
hippocampus 5
historic redlining 44
"holistic health, safety, and welfare" (HSW) 152
Hollander, Justin B.: *Cognitive Architecture* 102
Holly Whyte, William 112, 115
hospital-based projects 10
HPA *see* hypothalamic-pituitary-adrenal (HPA)
human abilities 16
human behavior in public open space 112
"human-centered design" 56
Human Centric Evidence Based Design for WELLbeing 94, 99, 100, *101–103*, 104
human culture 25
human engagement, programming urbanism for 19, 109; activity and use 112–118; form and space 118–131; sense of place 131–133
human-environment relationships 14
human-experience design 9
human factors 1, 109, 111, 115, 118, 120
human functioning 42–44
human habitation 3
human health 177; adaptation strategies 185–186; backup power 186; biophilia and 25–30; building and zoning codes 188–189; capacity building and situational awareness 189–190; community 186–187; environmental health 163–165; heat and 181–182; power of adaptation 178; power of national resilient standards 191; programming for climate 187–188; programming for resilience 179–184, 192; resilient buildings 188; role of resilience in design 178–179
human nervous system 146

Humphreys, Simon 68
hypothalamic-pituitary-adrenal (HPA) 42–43

ICC *see* International Code Council (ICC)
"ideal" educational environments 76
IECC *see* International Energy Efficiency Code (IECC)
IEP *see* Individual Education Plan (IEP)
IgCC *see* International green Construction Code (IgCC)
immunological systems 5
inclusion, empathetic programming to foster: Autism Spectrum Disorder (ASD) 65–67; empathetic design 78–79; Empathy Sketchbook 69–74; irony of empathy 69; reading sketchbook 74–78; square peg 67; "torture starts" 65
"inclusive design" 56
Individual Education Plan (IEP) 66
individual resilience 172
Individuals with Disabilities Education Improvement Act (IDEA) 66, 67
indoor air quality (IAQ) 178
indoor environmental testing 95
indoor spaces 195
informal urbanism 58
Informing Design (Dickenson and Marsden) 11
insula 5
integration theory 13
integrative design 176
interdependence 3–4
interior environments, programming: color 18–19; design for health and wellbeing framework 15–18; design meets science 9–10; design-related hypotheses and theories that inform programming 12–14; environmental psychology and interior design 10–11; evidence-based design (EBD) 10; "health-first" design 19–22; neuroaesthetics and neuroarchitecture 14–15; stages of design 11–12
interior space and wayfinding satisfaction 238–239
internal stressors 42
International Code Council (ICC) 152, 154
International Energy Efficiency Code (IECC) 152
International Family of Codes 154
International green Construction Code (IgCC) 154, 216, 217
International WELL Building Institute (IWBI) 95
interoception 4, 5
intra-species tribalism 164
intuitive design sensibility 47
intuitive emotions 37

Jackson, J. B.: *Sense of Place, Sense of Time* 132
Jacobs, Jane 137; *The Death and Life of Great American Cities* 176
James, William 43
John Montgomery 137
Jonker, Zoë 148

Jung, Carl 25

Kaplan, Stephen 20, 26
Kaplan, Rachel 20, 26
Kellert, Stephen R. 28; *The Biophilia Hypothesis* 26
Khare, Rachna 68, 79n4
King of Babylonia 150
Kinnear, Marijke 68
Koetter, Fred: *Collage City* 120, 128
Kopec, D. A. 10, 13, 15, 19
Kopec, Dak 12
Kopek 19
Krier, Leon 125
K-12 school programming 85

Laudato Si (Pope Francis) 95
Lazarus, R. S. 40
Leadership in Energy and Environmental Design (LEED) rating systems 154, 178
least restrictive environment (LRE) 67
life-enhancing habitats 222; *A Pattern Language* 226–231; searching for quality 223–226; wholeness and centers 231–232
Lila, An Inquiry into Morals (Pirsig) 172
limbic system 33, 34, 83
long-term learning 83
Lotze, Rudolf Hermann 69
LRE *see* least restrictive environment (LRE)
Lynch, Kevin 6, 119
Lyndon, Donlyn 132

Mace, Ronald 56
Mallgrave, Harry Francis: *Architecture and Embodiment* 36
mannerism 120–121
Mapping the Mind (Carter) 36
Marcionne, Francesca 148
Marsden, J. P.: *Informing Design* 11
Mary-Britt 148
Maslow 219
McAllister, Keith 68, 79n2
McHarg, Ian 167
McMullen, Patricia 98
medial orbitofrontal cortex 21
Mehrabian, A. 13, 19
melanopsin pathway 46
mental stressors 68
metric-based approach 2
microclimatic anomalies 182
mid-density fractal patterning 133
"mirror neurons" 5
Mlodinow, Leonard: *Subliminal, How Your Unconscious Mind Rules Your Behavior* 147
mobile eye-tracking 141, 146; glasses 137, 147
modernism 131
Moore, Charles: *Body, Memory, and Architecture* 131
Morris, William 225
Moser, Edvard 148

Mostafa, Magda 68, 79n3

narrative 6
National Flood Insurance Program (NFIP) 188
National Hurricane Center 180
national resilience code 191
national resilient standards, power of 191
natural environment and learning 87–88
natural light 87
natural ventilation 27
The Nature of Order (Alexander) 223
nervous system arousal, tracking 143–146
neural wiring 4
neuroaesthetics 14–15, 21
neurobiology, integrating architecture and 2–6
neuroception 4
neuroendocrine 5
neurological research and learning 82–84
neurological resonance 2
neuroplasticity 16
neuroscience 2, 6, 10, 15, 26, 29, 31, 32, 35, 39, 42, 49, 111, 132, 133, 147, 155, 218, 243
neuroscientific knowledge 14
Nguyen, Nam 148
Nicholson, Nigel 146
9 Foundations of a Healthy Building 85
non-absorptive materials 85
norepinephrine 34
nurturing 83

Obama, Barack 209
occupational environments, insights from 218–221
ocularcentric species 16
Ogden, Pat 245
Olmsted, Frederick Law 200
"One Code: A Program for Building Regulatory Reform" 154
One Planet Living 160, 168, 169
On the Optical Sense of Form (Vischer) 69
orbitofrontal cortex 5
Orians, Gordon 32
outcome-based performance code 153
outdoor spaces 195
Oxford English Dictionary (OED) 69

Palladio, Andrea 31
panathenaic procession 129
parasympathetic nervous system 36, 43
passive survivability 177–179, 186
patient anxiety and agitation 238
A Pattern Language (Alexander) 226–231
patterns: behavior 33; of biophilic design 27; cognitive 2; of consumption 168, 172; design 17; energetic 176; energy 174; environmental 159; floor 16; and *A Pattern Language* 226–231; regional distribution 160; visual 5, 33, 35
performance-based approach 216–218
performance-based codes 150, 153
performance-based design 152, 216

Perkins Eastman 97, 98
personality disorders 3
"person-behavior-situation variables" 14
Peterson, Stephen 131; *Harvard Architectural Review* 130
physical safety and learning 85–86
Piazza della Signoria 110
Pilgrim Circle 122
Pinkert, Steven 33
Pirsig, Robert M.: *Lila, An Inquiry into Morals* 172
Plague of Justinian 150
plasticity 16
Plato 131
pleasure-arousal hypothesis 13
POE *see* post-occupancy evaluation (POE)
political expediency 215
polyvagal system 18
polyvagal theory 244, 245
Porges, Stephen 4, 46, 244, 245
Portland Urban Architecture Research Lab (PUARL) conference 2018 229
positive stimulation 244
post-occupancy evaluation (POE) 216, 217, 240
post-occupancy surveys 95
post-pandemic city 194; enhancing city attributes 207–208; environmental remediation 206–207; pandemic and city life 195–204; threat of zoonoses 205–206
post-traumatic stress disorder 48
pre-design research 12
PreK-12 educational plan 88
pre-pandemic activities 195
Probst, Robert 218
programmed activities 114
programming for health and wellbeing 11–12
programming-planning paradigm 215–216
project-based learning 83–84
"project language" 228
project planning 27–28
proprioception 4
prospect 5, 48, 246
prospect-refuge theory 13, 113
psychotherapy 25
public chess games 113
public open spaces 112, 206, 208
Public Places, Urban Spaces (Carmona, Heath, Taner and Tiesdell) 132
public spaces 112, 200; plan community-building events in 111
Pursuit of Pattern Languages for Societal Change (PURPLSOC) conference 2017 229

"racial battle fatigue" 44
Rebuilding of London Act of 1667 150
refuge 5, 13, 76, 87
regeneration of natural systems 161
regenerative buildings 153
regenerative development and design 171–176
Regenesis Group 173, 174

regional planning 166, 167
regularly scheduled events 115
regulation 3
(dys)regulation 3
"re-inventions" 103, 104
religious traditions 246
resilience 39, 42–44, 161, 167, 172, 173, 177, 188, 245; building and zoning codes that require 188–189; community 186–187; design applications to promote 47–48; in design, role of 178–179; development of 161; ecosystem 164; environmental 163; fundamentals of 46–47; programming for 167–168, 179–184, 192; social 49; strategies 170; sustainability and 160
"Resilience Quotient" model 189
resilient design 177, 179
resilient planning 188
resilient programming 179
resilient strategies 188
Resnik, Denise 59
resonance circuits 5
resource evaluation, categories for 166
Rickard-Brideau, C. 20
riparian corridors 202
risk assessment 167
Robert Wood Johnson Foundation (RWJF) 44
Roger G. Barker and Frank Lloyd Wright 14
Rose Kennedy Greenway 198
Rossi, Aldo: *The Architecture of the City* 120
Rowe, Colin: *Collage City* 120, 128
Ruggles, Don 15, 49; *Beauty, Neuroscience and Architecture* 21
runoff reduction strategies 185
Ruskin, John 225
Russell, J. A. 13

safe drinking water 151
"salience network" 40
Salingaros, Nikos 29, 131
Salutogenesis 20
salutogenic design 10, 20
sanitation 151
satellite cities 197, 202–204
Savory, Alan 176
school construction 88
School of Architecture and Planning 94, 97
school performance, relationship between daylighting and 236–237
school planning process 93
Schore, Allan 244–246
Seabrook, John 218
sea-level rise, programming for 169–170
Second Law of Thermodynamics 172
self-awareness 5
self-regulation 244
Selye, Hans 42, 43
semi-programmed activities 113
Sennett, Richard 195
sense of place 111

Sense of Place, Sense of Time (Jackson) 132
The Senses Considered as Perceptual Systems (Gibson) 131
"Sensing Streetscape" 137
Sensing-Streetscape eye-tracking 148
Sensing-Streetscape studies 143, 148
sensory detection abilities 16
sensory stressors 68
"serious public health threat" 44
"serve and return" 243, 244, 246
"service life" 2
Seven Principles of Universal Design 56
severe storms, climate hazards 180
Siegel, Daniel 4
"Simmel's Mask" 147
Simoneau, Josh 128
Sitte, Camillo 112; *Der Stadtebau* 127, 128
Situated Cognition 111
"sleep hygiene" 47
social and emotional safety and learning 86–87
social and emotional wellbeing 83
social cohesion/connection 46
social equity considerations 191
social grouping environments 77
"social isolation" 187
social learning theory 14
social stressors 68
social systems 5
social vulnerability index 182–184
socio-ecological model 95
"soft fascination" 26
sonic landscapes 60
Soufre, Alan 4
"Space and Anti-Space" 130
Space Syntax 238
spatial orientation 59
special education services 66
Speck, Jeff 116
stewardship 152–154, 207
Stichler, J. F. 10
stimulation theory 14
St John New Brunswick Elementary School 91–92
stress 3, 245; design applications to promote resilience 47–48; environmental stressors 39–42; fundamentals of resilience 46–47; and human functioning 42–44; prevent introduction of 76; reduce amount of 76–77; reduction beyond the individual 49; relieve the built-up 77–78; and systems health 44–46
stress-free environment 37
Stryker, Susan 55
student engagement 89
"subjective sense of meaning" 5
subliminal brain 136; heat maps & gaze paths 140–143; testing technology & streets in Boston and Amsterdam 137–139; tracking nervous system arousal 143–146
Subliminal, How Your Unconscious Mind Rules Your Behavior (Mlodinow) 147

supportive academic environment 82
"surveillance system" 148
Sussman, Anne 16, 109; *Cognitive Architecture* 102
sustainability 2, 27, 29, 82, 85, 88, 92–93, 154, 160, 163, 175, 178, 216, 217
Sweet, Stephen 94
Sympathetic and parasympathetic reactions 35
systemic-level stress conversation 46
systems thinking 1

tactical urbanism 230
Talking to Strangers (Gladwell) 18
Taner, O.: *Public Places, Urban Spaces* 132
tension 4
"tension modulation hypothesis" 4
Terrapin Bright Green 27–29
Tetteroo, Jolanda 148
Tiesdell, S.: *Public Places, Urban Spaces* 132
thigmotaxis 112
"third-party" commissioning 216
3M's Visual Attention Software (VAS) 101
The Timeless Way of Building (Alexander) 225
Titchener, Edward 69
Townscape (Cullen) 126
"toxic stress" 44
traditional classroom 83
triangulation 113
"turbine plaza" 127
type 2 diabetes 44
typology 119–120, 126

Ulrich, Roger 48
unconscious eye movements 137
unconventional housing amenities 208
uni-directional decision-making arrangements 230
unique opportunity for programming: classroom building 98–99; dining commons 98; dormitory 97–98
United Nations Environment Programme (UNEP) 205
universal design 56–58, 60, 61, 87, 95
University Campus 96–97
un-programmed activities 112
urban architectural space 126
urban design strategies 203
urban fabric 121
urbanism for human engagement 19, 109; activity and use 112–118; form and space 118–131; sense of place 131–133

urban planners 6
urban renewal programs 195
urban spaces 109, 110, 118, 120–122, 126–128, 134, 226
U.S. Centers for Disease Control and Prevention 187
USGBC LEED rating systems 2
U.S. Green Building Council (USGBC) 178
U.S. Heat-related illnesses 180

Valdez, P. 19
Vessel, Edward 36
Vina del Mar project 175
Virtual Reality (VR) technology 26, 29
Vischer, Robert: *On the Optical Sense of Form* 69
visioning process 88, 89
visual processing 16, 141
Vitruvius 31
Vogel, Clare 68
volumetric figural space 130
vulnerabilities, assessing 181–189

waste management 151
watershed movement 56
wayfinding 19, 76, 87, 159, 238–239
Welcome To Your World, How the Built Environment Shapes Our Lives (Goldhagen) 132
well-being 20, 99, 219
WELL Building Standard 95–96, 100, 104
WELL Certification on university campus: case study 100–104; Catholic University of America (CUA) 94–95; Human Centric Evidence-Based Design for WELLbeing 99; Unique Opportunity for Programming 97–99; University Campus 96–97; WELL Building Standard 95–96
Weymouth Middle School 89–91
White, Edward T. 118, 126
Whyte, William Holly 112, 116
wildlife sanctuaries 206
wildlife wet market 205
Wilson, Edward O. 5, 13, 87; *The Biophilia Hypothesis* 26
"window of tolerance" 42
workable resilience strategies 169
World Health Organization (WHO) 96, 194
World Wildlife Fund 160
written communication 57

zoonoses 205–206